300

THE TIME IS RIPE

THE 1940 JOURNAL

of

CLIFFORD ODETS

THE TIME IS RIPE

———•———

THE 1940 JOURNAL

of

CLIFFORD ODETS

With an Introduction by
William Gibson

Grove Press
New York

Published by Grove Press
a division of Wheatland Corporation
920 Broadway
New York, N.Y. 10010

Library of Congress Cataloging-in-Publication Data

Odets, Clifford, 1906–1963
The time is ripe: 1940 journal/by Clifford Odets: with an
introduction by William Gibson.—1st ed.
p.   cm.
ISBN 0-8021-1034-7
1. Odets, Clifford. 1906–1963—Diaries.   2. Dramatists,
American—20th century—Diaries.   I. Title.
PS3529.D46Z477   1988
818'.5203—dc 19
[B]   87-35332
CIP

Designed by Irving Perkins Associates
Manufactured in the United States of America
First Edition 1988

10   9   8   7   6   5   4   3   2   1

CONTENTS

PREFACE

Because this journal is first appearing in print so long after it was written, the question of its whereabouts during nearly a half-century has naturally arisen. It's the old story—it was in a trunk, or mostly so.

It seems clear that my father wrote the journal, the only one he kept during his adult life, with some intent to publish it, or decided shortly after its completion that it might be publishable. In April 1941 Bennett Cerf wrote my father responding to his query about publishing it. And in the same month, Fay Wray wrote and suggested that my father hold off publishing it because he might feel differently about what to leave in or take out with more distance from it. In October 1942, Edward Weeks at *Atlantic Monthly* inquired about whether my father or someone else could bring him a copy of the journal—he would come to New York himself, he said, but was in the middle of the Christmas edition of the magazine. About nine months later Weeks seems to have returned the journal with a "Here you are . . ." Finally, in 1944 my father wrote a half-page entitled "My Confessions," which appears to be an introduction to the journal:

> I do not know who you are who read this book, but I care. Certainly I must care if you are under thirty, and I am intimately concerned if you are of college age. For in many ways this is your book, young man and woman, this book that is a small token of the times in which we live.
>
> I also want to say here, you, student, young and keen, that too seldom is the truth of life today printed in a book. I do not see or know one living American writer (and I know many) who has the talent or character (or freedom of schemata) to look at American life and write down truthfully what he sees.
>
> This book is personal, intensely so, but that is its reality, that is its American reality. It is the daily diary, often naïve, sometimes crude, occasionally pompous, prejudiced, mannered, unfair, even conceited and arrogant. Its pages cover almost a full year in the personal life of a "successful" writer living in a very "successful" country. For yourself you will very soon discover the meaning or value of such success.
>
> Finally, I am glad to hand over the book for young people to read. That it may reach the minds and feelings of a few hundred boys and girls is ample reward for the abuse it will cause to be heaped on my head.

So I will dedicate this book to a boy who probably will never read it. He is described on an inside page, the boy who stood beside the railroad tracks as the mighty Santa Fe Chief roared by, alone, musing, waiting and yearning he knew not for what.

When my father died in 1963, he willed to me his "personal effects," which included, by the definition of the state of California, all his papers. This huge amount of material remained in storage—in steamer trunks—in Los Angeles for several years. When Margaret Brenman-Gibson began her biography of my father, we moved the material—a Bekins moving van full of it—to Stockbridge, Massachusetts, for her use.

As Margaret finishes with the material, I have been inventorying it and giving it to the Lincoln Center branch of the New York Public Library. It was in 1984, during such an inventory, that I first read the journal, liked it a lot, and passed it on for comments to Charles Schlessiger, who is literary agent for my father's work.

The original of the journal—or as original a version as appears extant—is a typed manuscript, and that is now in the Lincoln Center archive.

Walt Bode, of Grove Press, did most of the editing on the original. That editing consisted of the removal of some repetitive material, but it was a job which seemed to me to improve impressively the clarity and flow of the work. I then made a handful of editing suggestions, some of which have also been incorporated in the final, published form. So while not absolutely in its original form, the journal, as presented here, is perhaps ninety percent of the original content, and, I think, virtually all of the original intent.

We have chosen not to encumber this intensely personal record with extensive reference notes, a task that would demand much research and might obstruct the continuity of reading it. Some few notes clarify contemporary references that may now be obscure. One appendix briefly identifies those who were close to my father in 1940, and a second provides a short chronology of his life.

Finally, I would like to offer my thanks and appreciation to Paula Harrington and Joyce Leighton, both of whom provided much invaluable help with the early preparation and initial editing of the original manuscript.

Walt Odets
Berkeley, California
January 1988

INTRODUCTORY
FOR THE YOUNG

by
William Gibson

Nobody knows how to act Odets anymore. In recent revivals on television I see actors working to be sincere, restrained, believable; the characters come out dull, and the once-famous dialogue falls heavy on the ear, self-conscious and false. It is, in their mouths.

Odets once said—to Sammy Davis, for whom he was adapting a black musical of *Golden Boy*—"I'm going to write this play in your mouth!" It was how all his best plays were written, for the actors of whom he was one in the Group Theatre, and the rhythm of that idiosyncratic acting style was the rhythm in the typewriter. All the people in Odets have a twist of caricature, like gargoyles; under Clurman's direction those actors—Adler, Bromberg, Carnovsky, Cobb, Garfield, Kazan, Lewis, Meisner—were a tribe of citizens not seen before on the stage, tasteless, slashing, self-mocking, erratic, tender, hostile, comic, hopeful, bitter, all fast hoofers with words tumbling out of them like unsuspected grenades. Not in my theatre-going since have I seen such a fusion of writing and performance, and you that are young shall never see so much.

Too much, says the author of this journal, who aspired to a human norm; "I always feel," he said, "either superhuman or subhuman."

The plays captured the decade, six of them—*Waiting for Lefty, Awake and Sing!, Till the Day I Die, Paradise Lost, Golden Boy, Rocket to the Moon*—in four years, and in 1939 Odets published a volume of them as a "first-period group." It was Beethoven of course at the back of his mind when he so labeled them, and the grim irony is that no second or third period followed. In 1940 *Night Music* failed. "A lovely delicate child, tender and humorous, knocked down by a truck," he writes; "this is murder, to be exact." Months later he notes,

"These goddam critics have dented me badly," and tells Strasberg it has begun "to stop me from writing." A scatter of four more plays came in the next twenty-three years, but lacking the early exuberance of detail; and for the last nine of those years Odets was silent, except for movie scripts. In 1963 he died of stomach cancer in a Hollywood hospital, a "burnt-out genius."

It is that very turning point, the *Night Music* year, that this journal takes us into. A play has failed, the Group is disintegrating, the world of the thirties is being blown apart by Nazi dive bombers; his marriage to a movie star, Luise Rainer, is down the drain. Odets is now thirty-three, with five dazzling years behind him, and more than a celebrity—his face on the cover of *Time* was captioned, "Down with the general fraud"—he is the conscience of a generation, and a serious young artist. In these pages what we overhear is the artist, in more trouble than he knows, talking to himself.

Not entirely, he is inviting us to read over his shoulder. But to whomever, it's all good talk—ten years later Odets afire was the best talker I'd ever heard—and it engrossed me when I first read it in his own typescript, post-mortem, hearing in it his vanished voice. Again now I regret coming to the end of it.

It is of course a unique document in the annals of our theatre. That it takes us on an authentic look-see backstage into the production of a flop on Broadway, and into the Hollywood offices of a studio preparing it as a movie, never made, is fascinating enough; neither end of the show business axis was any less deadly for a writer fifty years ago. But the journal moves outside the confines of theatre. It comprises extremes, the personal gossip of family and the accumulating horrors of the war. The celebrities of the time appear in profusion, unprettified, from the "self-indulgent coquette" Stokowski to the "sordid raccoon" Billy Rose. Odets, the prophet of the left, was not conspiring at midnight with revolutionaries, as good patriots feared; he was making the nightclub rounds with Leonard Lyons and other intellectual lights—an actor whose métier was offensiveness stops him to say, "You're a first-class man, what are you doing with these nitwits?" And he was entertaining a sequence of ladies in bed, some of them famous, each hoping he wanted her for keeps; the poor things first had to listen to Beethoven sonatas, and Odets kept thinking "obscene thoughts" about his discarded Luise.

*   *   *

These matters are the seeming substance of the journal; its real theme is a quest for himself, and a desperate quest it is, by a theatre man with a hemophiliac wound.

It is best read in context, and its context is of a different era. Find any "drama section"—a lost category—of the *New York Times* in 1940 and its front page is nothing but theatre: the Atkinson "Sunday piece," the Hirschfeld cartoon of a current star, the "News of the Rialto," an interview with a director, a stage photograph or two, a hopeful article by the playwright of the week. No television, movies and radio are inside, and pop music gets a mention somewhere in the back. Mass entertainment is not culture. Theatre is. In the twenties O'Neill had single-handedly made the stage a serious place, and the great depression of the thirties saw a flood tide of native art coming of age in every medium, not yet internationalized by the war: Harris and Copland were creating an American music, Benton an American mural painting, Graham an American dance. A dozen established playwrights brought work to Broadway every season. In this context Odets was hailed as "the new O'Neill," and not oddly he took himself seriously as a creative man.

Coming out of an unread family, and himself a high school dropout—Waldo Frank said, "Clifford was illiterate"—Odets was an autodidact; much of this journal is studded with the great names of music, literature, painting, exciting discoveries made on his own, with whom he is here going to school. What is he reading at night?—Stendhal, Hauptmann, Heine, Strindberg. He sees himself as a continuing part of that elitism defined as the best that man has thought. He feeds upon it, the better to carry the conscious burden of his fate as an artist; he feels like a freak in the world of entertainment, and is. And he is obsessed by the problem of "form."

The word is here on every third page. "Form is driving me crazy." Half of the time what he means by it is technical, that shaping of a dramatic action whereby its opposites are brought into fruitful interplay and resolution. All playwrights have an instinct for this, it's what distinguishes them from novelists. But the other times he means the shaping of his own life, where resolution eludes him.

Its opposites are tearing him apart. In the definitive biography of Odets up to this year,* those opposites are examined in painstaking detail; what is remarkable is how much of them Odets is consciously elucidating in this journal. It is in fact its raison d'être. "Know thyself"

*Margaret Brenman-Gibson, *Clifford Odets: American Playwright* (New York: Atheneum, 1981).

is written in invisible ink across every page, entry after entry grapples with the contrary demands in him, the consumer is eating up the producer; it will be a war to the death. And the death is already in these pages. "A Great Monster behind me, I often feel its breath on my neck." Halfway through this year he tells "the true ending of the story of Aladdin"—success is the jinni who kills. Hope-filled as it is, this journal is a record of a doom in the making.

"When I mention the word American, it is myself I mean." The indictment of life in America was always his subject, and it may occur to others than me that what Odets failed to get said in his plays he perversely made his life itself say, most eloquently.

THE TIME IS RIPE
THE 1940 JOURNAL
of
CLIFFORD ODETS

Saturday, January 13, 1940

Rob Bernstein here. I am a gentleman of property and need an accountant and tax expert, which Rob is. A matter of ethics. The government claims I owe them more than I paid. They send an agent and the agent can be bought off. A nice delicate question of "Shall I live as I think or shall I live as the Romans do?" Everywhere there is graft and corruption—a man of principle is so rare—only he who is afraid of apprehension or who has money enough, he does not graft. I even read in a magazine that [Mexican President Lazaro] Cardenas has stored away money in this country, but I don't believe it.

My Aunt Esther here, my mother's sister. A big peasant woman growing old, gross, healthy in impulses, although she has many assorted pains and aches. To the lower-middle-class pains and illnesses are prime indulgences, necessary, an element of the constant battle for self-respect and not to be merged in the working class. Yes, their vaunted nervousness, rheumatic pains, and heart diseases are what make them special, important and set off from the mere working class. Illness is a compensation with them, giving them importance in the eyes of themselves and their neighbors. Illness is a luxury and he who can afford luxuries is someone special and alive and THRIVING!

When my aunt left, after giving her a check for her son's family and taking over the tax payment on her house—she has such a peasant cunning, is so inquisitive; she looked in all the closets and drawers here, laughing all the while and commenting on her own curiosity as she threw in household hints and suggestions—I told her with a real wave of self-pity that I could use a little help and happiness myself. I indulge myself this way with a wry smile and a nonsensical inner chuckle.

Two weeks ago I met a nice sweet little girl of the age of twenty-one, Bette Grayson.* She is fresh from California, a young actress. She is living here with a crushed sour girl, her sister,** who is that way

*Née Bette Lipper, later Bette Odets, mother of Walt and Nora.

**Née Janet Lipper, later Janet Sachs.

because she's been freshly divorced. She has a two-and-a-half-year-old girl who's been sick for a week. I was very touched to hear of this unhappy young mother with a sick child. They didn't need any help when I offered it. Now the child is at Mount Sinai Hospital, dying of uremia. I am as engaged in the whole thing as if the child were mine. That's my nature and one can't go against his own nature, I suppose, but I am depressed that I am depressed. Am dressing and washing to go up now and meet Bette outside the hospital.

I notice that the unhappier and lonelier I am, the more I want to mix into other people's lives and be as generous to them as possible. I am not sure that the impulse is an unselfish one, but I won't worry about that.

Fay Wray hasn't written to me for over a week. She needs a man near her, not far away, a man of whom she can be more certain than she is to me, even though she yearns for me. Yes, she will make a real compromise if she can find a good man to be husband to her and father to her little girl. She used to write with such an edge of urgency. Now she is calm, quiet, writes seldom: she has found some man.

About Luise [Rainer]? I haven't seen her for over a month. It is good for me to keep out of her orbit, although nothing more can happen between us.

F. [Frances] Farmer? Unhappy, stiff, rude and uncontrollable girl, but with a real purity. Billy Rose spoke to me about her the other night—he had heard we had some "connection." He tried to make her look more feminine, use her beauty, but she stared him to scorn and as good as told him to mind his business. She is playing in the Hemingway show [*The Fifth Column*] which he is backing.

In relation to the second note, that of lower-middle-class ills—is it one hundred percent true? No. Is it seventy-five percent true? Yes. The sense of self-aggrandizement which accompanies, the relish with which stories of diseases are told to one another, all are sufficient proof of the truth of what I say. Ailments are medals which they pin on themselves.

———————•———————

Sunday, January 14, 1940

I am thinking of the Delacroix journals, listening to Chopin scherzi. They were friends—D. appreciated Chopin very much.

A full springish rain all day. The little Sperling baby died late last night. Bette came over here but I took her home. Bette is like Cleo in *Rocket [to the Moon]* and the Sparks girl in Lawson's *Pure in Heart*. Bette is coming over here now. I told her she is my girl and it does not make her unhappy.

F. Farmer is refusing to play in the Guild show. Billy Rose called— what can I do? She says she is sick, mentally unable to continue. Billy is furious—illness, he says, is pneumonia, etc. Rode up to the theatre T. to see what Harold [Clurman] could do about it, but he says he told the Guild people that she is really near a nervous breakdown. So will call Billy and tell him.

Often, in the middle of the winter, there are these deceptive springish nights when it rains and the air is soft all over and the feeling is April or May. They are like a woman before she pounces on some innocent world of yours—then follows the bleak winter! We'll have it icy again, and soon.

Before dinnertime Hanns Eisler and Gadget [Elia Kazan] came down here and we ran over, on the organ downstairs, the song Hanns has written for Gadget to improvise in the first act of *Night Music*. Hanns is really very talented, as each of his songs shows. I suppose an act of mine seems as mysterious to him as one of his songs does to me. Only I don't think he envies a playwright as much as I admire a good composer. A little song like this is a real help to the play even though it doesn't really need music. We are going to use my organ; I'm renting it out to the Group . . . I shall make some money!

Bette came down after spending the entire day with her sister and aunt. They didn't bury the baby today—the mother was too knocked out—but tomorrow it will take place. Bette says her sister drinks when she is unhappy. We are raising a whole generation of girl and boy drinkers who drink hard and full and so dull the whole gleaming (sinister gleaming, often) surface of life. It is a weak generation: it can't stand pain, nor can it accept certain bitter facts of life. I find it in myself, too, often approaching a hard fact obliquely or trying to avoid it completely.

Anyway, Harry Gurdus, who is working on my phonograph set, came in and Bette and I left and drove uptown. If Harry hadn't walked in we'd have gone to bed with sherry wine in us and love around us . . . she is a very beautiful young girl, soft, giving, emotional, but seeming to have been deeply hurt by someone or something; and that has closed her up although she is easily aroused by kindness. For her, truly, the motto *sine sole silio.*

Look at these beautiful fat round oranges on the desk here—the best and fanciest California fruit which it is almost impossible to buy in California. Fragrant fruit, passive and globulated, fat and satisfied, satisfied to be a fruit.

We (Bette) had a hasty late dinner in the Armenian Restaurant and ran around the corner to see a Marx Brothers picture (poor) and Leslie Howard and Ingrid Bergman, a new Swedish actress, in *Intermezzo.* The picture tries to be scrupulously honest—a triangle story—but is dishonest in every detail. But it doesn't try to do too much and so seems better than it is, like Howard himself.

I shall eat one of these beautiful oranges and read a story by Hans Andersen. Gurdus is behind me, working on the phonograph. If I talk to him he won't work.

I was thinking, for the modern murder love play, the couple must go to out-of-the-way movies and restaurants like the one I took Bette to tonight. Illicit love lives in the submerged half-lit world of depressing jointlike places, everything on the sneak and faintly ribbed with terror.

Confidence is repose.

———————•———————

Monday, January 15, 1940

Sometimes, in times of stress, I feel I am bleeding from the eyes. Stress? What is stress? The daily newspaper is like a club to beat you on the head. The war, the death, the rising dangers, the announcements today that perhaps America should have enough arms for a million men, a group of seventeen Fascists broken up by the Federal men yesterday as they were about to complete some plan of violence. I bleed right out of my goddam forehead. And that forgets the pressures of the theatre, a play now in rehearsal, business of the theatre, a sheaf of contracts on the desk right now, and casting the leading girl in the play, and hurried dinners, and trying to get to bed early so one can be up for the rehearsals tomorrow.

A picture called *Goodbye Mr. Chips*. Saw it tonight with Gadget, a very successful picture. In fact the critics here (critics?) awarded Mr. [Robert] Donat (doughnut?) an award for giving the best performance of the year in this picture. And what does it show? A good man, a kind man, a man of "heart," an English lower school master who does his duty and "plays the game." We are asked to sympathize with and admire this foolish man who doesn't know why anything happens to him, who doesn't understand his part in cheerfully preparing young Englishmen for the blood bath of war. Mr. James Hilton, who wrote the story, writes always from a core or center of self-pity. True, an audience can easily give its collective and personal self up to this sort of thing—it is a portrayal of a "safe" world, a world of "eternal" and standard values, days on days of comfortable items—warm tea, security, really essential irresponsibility, blindness—do ye but your duty and lo it shall come to pass! What shall come to pass? War and death for what Mr. Chips calls, on his deathbed, my thousands of children. In England there will be no new impulses in the theatre, in art, or life until one man gets up on the stage and asks, says, shouts, "Play the game? But for what? Tell me for what, you rascals, you slick-pants rogues! Carry the ball, carry on? Why? For whom?!" They need a new hero there and he must break down every existent form before their death is replaced with life.

When I came home, near midnight, Sid Benson was standing down at the front door . . . lonely and frustrated. I invited him up here and managed to relax myself by listening to a Mozart piano sonata. Sid said nothing and I said nothing. There is nothing to say to him. He is a real son of the proletarian wilderness, now hankering for the comforts and soft spots of the middle class. Herman [Odets's secretary] told him two days ago, at my request, that he'd have to leave the apartment downstairs. He is disconsolate, tacitly, but I can't accept responsibility for him.

Yes, Bach the king. I can hear the kingly tone. Played some Bach preludes and fugues. Bach I can always admire. I have recognition of Bach, but it is impossible for a person of my temperament to love him.

Sid sitting here made me realize that I use friends for two purposes, either to relax me or to increase my tension. A friend is unbearable to me when there is a need for tension and he relaxes me. But he is utterly impossible when I need relaxation and he tenses me. These two twin needs completely determine, I think, what people I reach out for in any given time.

I have not the slightest capacity for happiness. Woe to my wife! Good night.

———————•———————

Tuesday, January 16, 1940

This journal will be almost worthless if you try to write something clever in it every time you make a daily entry.

Looking back on the day at three o'clock in the morning:

The rehearsal was off today. We are having leading girl trouble again. [Eleanor] Lynn is out because she is absolutely wrong for the part and will dislocate it, she being way off type. Waif is wrong and she is a waif. Harold is talking to K. [Katherine] Locke, foolish girl, while he waits for word from the coast concerning M. [Margaret] Sullavan, who wants to do the part but must get permission from MGM.

Arranged to borrow five thousand dollars from Murray's bank in order to give it to the Group so they can start paying out expenses. Am going to get Bette Grayson a small part or understudy in the show; I want her to come up to Boston with us, mainly want her to be with me. It seems to me that she has acting talent.

Morris Carnovsky walked in here at three in the afternoon. I think he came here to suggest that Phoebe [Brand] be given a chance to read the part. But we played some music and then went for a long auto ride in the cold air, far up the Hudson, up into Westchester. We talked generally and he expressed a general bewilderment about life—muddled, he said. It is not muddle—it is just fear and lack of daring and courage, in my opinion. How middle-class life can hedge one in with restrictions!

Al Lewin* sent a genuinely tender note. I had mentioned in a

* A producer at MGM (where he worked on *The Good Earth*, which starred Luise Rainer) and Paramount, Lewin had recently formed his own production company with David Loew, and they were to produce the movie of *Night Music*.

previous letter about Luise and my marital troubles. Al is a sweet, hurt, soft man with a good supervising talent, nothing original or creative in any large sense, but he is much above the average movie man in all ways.

Finally called Bette in the early evening. She couldn't come here because she had to stay home to dinner with her sad sister. Called for her in the car and went over to Bill's [Kozlenko] house. From there went to see the new Garbo picture [*Ninotchka*], a satire on the Soviet Union. I can't agree that it is a vicious picture—it is foolish, of course, but it humanizes things which Americans think monstrous.

Bill annoys me—he can be very callow, very arrogant, very unfeeling, very dull. All of which he was tonight. Sometimes I am sorry for Lee, his wife. She is a better all-around person. Bill picked up in early youth an idea that he was an artist and critic. Of course he is neither, but it will be years before he finds it out. In the meantime everyone around him must suffer.

Took Bette home and kept wishing she could stay here with me, but her family ties are just enough to send her home on this clear cold winter's night. Her energy is low and her hands are always cold, but she is a sweet young girl and I miss her very much when she isn't around or I don't see her.

Also, Fay Wray sent one of her special delivery airmail letters. She liked the play very much and her letter was written out of loneliness and need for a base. It is easy to be swept away by a woman of such true womanliness, particularly when she tells you that she adores you and needs you and admires you. Fay is very clever with a man—the man is everything to her and she keeps showing you that she sincerely means it. She must have been born with that real quality; nothing in her life shows that she got it from intimates. A woman like that touches me. All women are beginning to touch me, get into me. For the first time in my life, I really feel the difference between a man and a woman. What a confession to make as late as thirty-three.

———•———

Wednesday, January 17, 1940

When I got out of bed near noon there was a small snow going, a gentle, delicate flurry, even tender, little snow. Faint of heart, it lasted an hour and stopped.

Nothing, nothing done, except to give away some money and receive a few letters for more. No leading girl for the play yet, although they are looking. Called off the rehearsal today, but there will be one tonight. In the meantime Harold suggested I look at Sylvia Sidney for the part. The Locke girl is out. Sylvia happened to call, telling me she had a ticket for me for Luther's [Adler] opening—he's up in Boston now with the Rice show [*Two on an Island*]—so invited myself to dinner there for tonight.

Billy Rose called, cozened me a bit, wanting the friendship of eminent intellectuals. He is still hot about F. Farmer leaving his show. In fact they have engaged Locke, whom he thinks all wrong for the part. I should worry, I should care.

Sluggish, overweight, but better than to be nervous and flying around. Being overweight anchors me down, is good for the nerves.

Went to Sylvia's house for dinner. Her mother there, a dry, shrewd woman, a typical mother of a famous daughter—they run to types, all right. Luther is up in Boston. The household is very comfortable, warm, a real home, very middle class. If Luther isn't careful he will revert to type and Sylvia with him. Sylvia has found a solid form for life and Luther needs form—he will easily drop into this thing and it will quite finish off his progress as an actor, although he doesn't dream of this. But of course there are many good things about this sort of domestic stability. Their baby is fine, weighs twelve pounds, and looks very much like Luther—big blue eyes and a big mouth and real gravity, like a little mummy, but the features well formed. He'll be around looking for a job in a play before long.

Then left and went to rehearsal. A strange blond girl was reading, the type, the American "schoolmarm," as Gadget called her, but young. Bette was there, sitting in the back, looking interested and shy, listening to the play. She is much more shy than she seems, from being uncertain of herself.

After the rehearsal we went over to Sardi's where we were to meet Jane Wyatt, a girl who has been acting ingenue leads around for about six years and is quite well known in the theatre. They were afraid she was a little too much society girl, but when we took her up to the office for the reading of a few scenes, she was quite the type and Harold says he will be able to work well with her. So Jane looks like the girl unless Sullavan gets in under the wire by tomorrow morning.

This Wyatt girl stirred something in me. For she is the type of girl I used to go for when I was a young man. I didn't realize why, but I understand myself better today. That was my *Sturm und Drang* period; I was mixed up, swirling, whirling, confused, handling a big bundle of emotion and impulse. In a girl, as in the rest of my life and reaching out, I was looking for form, clarity—unconsciously, of course. So I always went for these Nordic girls, clean, wholesome, stabilized, competent on a limited scale, although then I didn't realize or see the serious limitations of the type. The type is very well represented by K. [Katharine] Hepburn and such.

Men, this is sure and simple, turn to the sort of women they need, those who complement and fill a lack. In my first contacts with Luise Rainer I knew instinctively that I was making a great mistake. At least I felt it. But at the point of marriage I knew and was certain a mistake was being made. Now I regret nothing of my experience with Luise— some of it was splendid and extraordinary—but she was never right for me, I never for her. We both were looking for a staunch rock out of a turbulent sea—neither Luise nor I, if I may say so, are sturdy pillars, although I find myself changing in more interesting ways than one.

My interest now, I think (how can I ever be sure of something while it is happening—I'm an after-the-fact boy!), is a young girl to whom *I* can give form and shape. This, I think, is why I am so attracted by Bette. Much of love for me is in giving. Unfortunately, I am not one of the receivers in life. I receive badly, restlessly, shamefully. How much easier it is to give than to receive. It is strange to me that people are not aware of that fact.

Bette is a darling girl and both Harold and Gadget remarked tonight on how sweet and gentle she is. She was very self-conscious in Sardi's tonight. I held her hand to give her a little reassurance. The thought of her lifts me out of this room a little.

———•———

Thursday, January 18, 1940

It's past five in the morning of Friday. Just drove Bette home, the cab scuttling warmly along the snow-covered streets. It started to snow while Bette and I fell asleep in bed after coming back home from seeing Verdi's *Otello* at the Metropolitan. Bette is a good girl, a dear girl: we are good for each other.

In the early afternoon went to the rehearsal of *Night Music*, and things seem settled now that we have a girl [Jane Wyatt] for the lead. The small parts are being very well handled by players like Lou Polan, Phil Brown, Pearlie Adler, Harry Cooke, etc., etc. The whole shape of the play is already there, for the script is an easy-playing one—it almost mounts itself. What actors need, from what I can see, are a few more playwrights like Odets and directors like Clurman!

The opera at night, a usual performance. Panizza conducted very well, but what was on the stage, except for a moment here and there, was dead. Martinelli sang the title role; he's old, his voice and dynamo gone, but there is sweetness in his work, good craft on an operatic level, and an amazing ease and relaxation. You'd think he was alone, in his own bathroom, to watch him. Rethberg sang the unlucky wife, foolish as an actress or stage personality, but she had her moments and her voice is good. Evidently her simple German soul was touched by the prayer scene in the last act, for she performed it with real sweetness and dignity. Brownlee as Iago was below comment!

And then Bette and I came back here, and here I am after all those hours. She is a rosebud girl. Good night, Rosebud.

———————•———————

Saturday, January 20, 1940

Yesterday most of the day was taken up with attending rehearsals. Drank a few eggnogs at Sardi's—all the young actors hang out there now, if they can afford it—and then drove Bette to her house and came home and went to bed as soon as possible, for I was dog-tired. Had a dream that the brain was taken out of my head and I didn't feel badly at all, only a faint whirring but silent headache and general emptiness. Incidentally, the doctor on this extraordinary case was my father. What can that mean?

So today up at noon and a good sleep behind me for the first time in weeks. Gurdus came and worked on the phono, putting in a new and powerful transformer. Up at rehearsals found Harold standing the first scene on its feet. He is still indecisive and shaking about actual physical staging, but as splendid as ever about explaining the character's psychology to the actor. He has the patience of a devil (not a saint), for his patience is somehow involved with what he wants, something which comes from the ego. He is the supreme type of a man who has made a virtue and strength from every weakness. He is reaching out. This can only mean that Stella [Adler] has made clear to him that she will not permit any relation between them.

Took Bette to the rehearsal. I mean *away* from the rehearsal. I am thinking much about the sextette play, the one about the six or seven homeless men. Every time a blast of winter air creeps under my coat I think of those homeless men in my mind. Bette and I came down here and listened to some music—she is a very relaxing girl—in fact she is sitting behind me now, three o'clock in the morning, as I type these words. She listens very givingly to music; it excites her deeply. We drank some champagne and went to bed for a few hours, then we went over to Second Avenue and ate assorted Jewish dishes at Ratner's, all of the food being new and extremely pleasant to her. After that we rode around the dour dark waterfront streets of the East River; I showed her Brooklyn across the river, pointed out the bridges and interesting spots. Then we did the same thing with the Hudson River, riding up the ramp and turning back under the Washington Bridge.

It is very cold out and now we are here, smoking quietly and reading the Sunday papers. The tower clock says 3:15; the city is quiet and asleep.

It seems Luise has called here several times in the past week, but I didn't call back for I don't want to speak to her or see her. I go deader and deader on her each day, but it is a protective thing, out of an ego scorned. How amazing to me was my reaction when she told me about her Englishman when she returned to New York from London a couple of months ago.

Well, boy you are no Amiel* —this is plain to see!

* Henri Frédéric Amiel, nineteenth-century philosopher who gained lasting fame for his *Journal intime*, in which he recorded his intellectual struggle for values against the skepticism of his age.

Every other week a little bell goes off in my mind and it says, "Stendhal." I bought several two-volume editions of *The Charterhouse of Parma* to give away as gifts. Surely he is one of the half-dozen best novelists of all time, aside from being a rare and unusual man. Most artists are not rare men as men, they are idiots.

———•———

Sunday, January 21, 1940

Always I am very thankful that I am an artist, that I write about life, that I reach people with what I write. Any other existence would be intolerable to me. For myself a life is useless unless there is a "what for" not connected with the self and self-interests. I would be a very sick and unhappy man if I were not a writer. Nothing else can satisfy this hunger to be useful, to be used for a common good.

I am growing uneasy—a new play is coming on. For me, this creative uneasiness excuses everything. Otherwise my inability to follow up assumed personal responsibilities would be another strong item to make my life unhappier than it is. Everything-for-the-work is practically the only way I can feel and think—notice that I put the word feel before think. Right now, these days and weeks, I am very clear in my relationships with the theatre, friends and intimates, almost the world. And that clarity of relationship is the prime necessity for doing good work.

Loneliness—the business of living alone—seems to have one of two results for a man. Either it makes him excessively romantic; or it makes him sour and bitter. Sometimes, however, there is a curious blending of both, a tart personality emerging, a sort of eccentric. In fact, all three results add up to an eccentric.

John Barbirolli conducting the Schubert Seventh this afternoon, on the radio. An English musician or conductor!—the very words are contradictory! Although there are some good words to say for [Sir Thomas] Beecham, who seems to have lifted himself into the top ranks of conductors by sheer will. He plays everything with great muscularity, forcing the music. Particularly true is this of his Mozart. He has discovered the "demon" in Mozart and will have the demon out even if he breaks the orchestra apart! But he really has his points,

Beecham. But Barbirolli? We went over on the same ship when we went to London with *Golden Boy*. (Or was it the return trip, on the *Champlain*?) He scowled and strode darkly through the passageways of the ship, romantic and glamorous, or trying to be. It's easy to hear, in his conducting, that he is quite a mild fellow, so mild that I keep looking to see what is holding up the music from behind. The symphony board here, in the case of Toscanini—since they claimed that people came to see and hear only T.—erred on the side of distinction. Then they got Barb., whose personality would not overshadow the aggregate personality of the orchestra . . . and they erred on the side of *extinction*!

Well, have had a shower, and Bette and I are going to walk uptown, it now being close to six in the evening.

I dream and dream, empty vacant bits and shards of dreams. Then I wake up and turn over to sleep some more. I understand a general worry in myself, but what is troubling me particularly is difficult to discover. Of course some of it has to do with the present play in rehearsal. Much deeper and fuller than I ever admit to myself consciously is the fear of running the gauntlet—for opening a play in New York City is really the equivalent of running the gauntlet. That is what I don't want to face, that is one of the things that disturbs me deeply. I even find it militates against sitting down to the typewriter and starting a new play.

Harold has the whole first act up on its feet by now. I sat through the whole rehearsal, watching, listening, minding my business, and thinking that I could do an excellent job of direction myself. My ensemble would be much more dynamic than Harold's, more brusque, more impatient, more dash and verve, but not as excellent psychologically. Also, I admired Miss Jane Wyatt as I watched her. She is very handsome and youngish, slim, pert, to the point (too much to the point), competent, very Catholic—the other day she blushed at a line I suggested, one using the name Christ. She is very womanly in a small neat way and is probably a good mother to her child. A maniac like myself should have a wife like that.

I sat in the dark ugly theatre as the rehearsal went on, alongside the watchful, almost somnolent Bette—her face is so soft that sometimes she seems sleepy, and her childish quality adds to this impression. Bud is doing very interesting work in a small part. Bud is very middle class: he starts working on a part with fresh and original impulses. But soon he gets worried, for the outcome won't be sure and he is not certain. So he falls back into a conventionalization of what he started to do. In this way he applies a middle-class dictum to his acting: "will it work?" or "will it come off?" Like the middle class, he mistrusts an impulse which leaves the result in doubt. Mistrust of self is what leads the middle class to so many foolish patterns of behavior, when one thinks about it.

The terror of my childhood was that either or both of my parents or my sisters might die. Many nights I stayed awake as child and boy, fearful that my parents had been killed in an auto wreck, etc. These thoughts really terrorized my youth. And that terror is one of the reasons that now I am so chary of forming permanent relationships of an intimate or personal nature. I can't face the possibilities of serious illnesses or death to others close to me; for myself I am not much mindful. This is really one of the things which makes it so difficult for me to give myself over to others.

Sent Bette home after the rehearsal and Harold and I went over to Roth's Grill and cut the first two acts. I laughed when I said to Harold for a third time, "That little girl, Bette," or "Bette, you know." That is my way of disavowing relationship, so I laughed to Harold and stopped it immediately. Admit nothing, secrets, the spine of middle-class life!

A letter from Fay Wray when I arrive home here. Read the morning papers. Again a column printed something about Luise's Englishman. She ought to get a divorce, I thought, as a ripple ran up and down my ego. It's four in the morning and I'm going to bed now. Good night.

Today I read a fine quote from the Talmud, in the *American Guardian*, as follows: "In the distance, as I was walking, I saw what looked like a beast. When I got closer I saw it was a man. But when I got still closer I saw it was my brother."

———•———

Tuesday, January 23, 1940

The period of courtship, in any matter, gets to be a shorter and shorter affair with me. This is because I am getting shorter and shorter on self-delusion. Let us get to the heart of the matter, I feel, and let us get there quickly and put things on a working basis. I am anxious for results and impatient, unfortunately, with the steps which lead up to the results. This is growth from one point of view; from another it is sheer backsliding.

Yesterday they gave Browder* four years in jail for a minor offense which usually would go by unmentioned. Obviously the Roosevelt government has decided to put up Browder's head on a pike, to satisfy the clamor of reactionaries who think Fascists and Communists paddle the same canoe. Browder is out on bail and spoke last night at a Lenin memorial meeting in the Garden. I think it was mistake of taste, a real error to say, as he did, that Roosevelt is interested in war and munitions because a son of his married a Du Pont girl. They will probably find some other silly misdemeanor with which to convict another Communist leader or two and then call it quits.

Communism needs to be Americanized before it will have any effect in America. My personal feeling about social change is this. I have one opinion as a private citizen. But in the world of the theatre, in relation to my plays and audiences for them, leftism as understood by the Communists is impossible. Any excessive partisanship in a play defeats the very purpose of the play itself. To be socially useful in the theatre, one can not be more left than, for instance, LaGuardia. Unless one is writing pamphlets or agitational cartoons, only clear but broad generalizations are possible. But one must make sure to write from a firm core even though, in my opinion, an attempt to reach as broad an audience as possible should always be taken into consideration. I thought once that it would be enough to play in a small cellar, but I soon saw that those who would come to the cellar were not the ones in need of what I could say. Personally I am of the opinion that Steinbeck and myself are the two young American writers who see clearly what must be done and are doing it, each in our own way.

Hanns Eisler and I went to the opening of the new Rice play in which Luther is playing an important part. A weak play, dull, less than platitudinous, unworthy of a critical estimate. Which does not mean that the critics did not treat it very gingerly this morning, with much deference and respect. Forgive me, but I get a real sense of power when I go to the Broadway theatre. Alone, by myself, I am mostly apt to think what a small talent I have. But when I look around at these boys I can only think that I am a giant. What shallow, false, untrue fabrication! [William] Saroyan, by the way, was referred to the other day by some Hollywood wit as "the only permanent flash in the pan I ever met." Hanns said about the Rice play, "If I would attend such a thing in Europe, spit me in my face."

* Earl Browder, leader of the U.S. Communist Party and its nominee for president in 1936 and 1940. He was arrested in 1940 for irregular use of his passport.

There is nothing more ridiculous, in my opinion, than the average American intellectual; and nothing more useless under the sun. They are forever rushing into print in the liberal weeklies with what?—half-baked ideas, weekly settlements of the deepest problems facing mankind. Quick solutions! "American" and "intellectual" seldom go together. There is something so pathetic and palpitant about the type, so *serioso*, a tuft of hair sticking out of a boy's face: Mr. [Malcolm] Cowley, John Chamberlain, etc., etc., etc.

Another note from Fay. She doesn't know what to write, for she can't write what is really on her mind, that she needs me and wants me and oh will I give her some sign or answer. So she writes brief critical estimates of things and people she sees; they are very slight but they keep us connected, she feels, and she needs connections.

Saw Marc Blitzstein at the opening. One of the things which explains a peculiarity about Marc which I've always felt is this: he always wants to come right side up, wants to always be on top, and that makes a certain coldness in him. But, as I said to Hanns after Marc moved away, "Even the most masculine man sometimes lets the woman get on top." Filthy!

The rehearsals dull and one responds dully. I have the usual mid-rehearsal feeling. Restless, impatient, off-focus, anxious inwardly, timid about stepping on the toes of the director or actors, *boldly unobtrusive*.

Went to dinner with Bette, Harold, and Gadget. Met Aaron Copland there—he's back from the coast where he did the music for [Lewis] Milestone's picture, *Of Mice and Men*. They all went back to the rehearsal, but I went on to a revival of *Juno & the Paycock*. The production was a quick one, but the play stood up for all of that, although the performances, mostly Irish, were better than the average American performance. The play is really talented, but [Sean] O'Casey is old news by now. But he'd better get down to writing a good play soon or he will really be old news. In a small way I have been influenced in my own playwriting by O'Casey, but it is mostly because we must be similar men: he lives physically, not with the noodle.

———•———

Wednesday, January 24, 1940

Up sleepily at noon to meet Mrs. Watson for luncheon and met her and was met! The exclamation point is explained only if you know Mrs. Watson!! Sometime later I'll write her down as a social type, but now I'm too tired. Anyway, I left her past four in the afternoon and went over to the rehearsal with my pockets full of vitamin pills to give to Gadget, my sister Florence, and Bette. Bette I spirited away and brought down here. All I wanted to do was to play some light music. We went through Chaliapin's recorded singing. And then Bette and I went through each other and it was lovely, it was very lovely and soothing and resting: deep warm connection and good friendship.

Took Bette home past midnight with an armful of records for her sister and her to play. Then rode nicely up along the Hudson River and in the shadow of the Washington Bridge turned the car around and drove home in the cold air. Leo Kapps, the elevator and desk boy, had a few drinks here at my invitation. Every so often I invite him in for a drink. He chatters away, a footloose American boy, very respectful of success and education. Now he has a girl and wants to get married. He met her when she lived next door to him. She said he was a bum and all he ever brought up to his room were whores. Oh, he says, I suppose I am not good enough to go out with you. You certainly are not, says she. Then she lost her job and he lent her the five dollars for her room for three weeks; also he bought her some food. Well, says Leo, that made her change her mind about me. She seen the kind of feller I really was. And do you know, he says, she paid me back every nickel, but I didn't let her pay me back for the food—I wouldn't do that. But another way she knew he was a bum was through the fact, as she said, you don't even have no pictures up in your room. Well, said Leo, what do I want with pictures up in my room—am I a girl?

My way of demanding attention seems to be by withdrawing attention.

We have the Plymouth Theatre for *Night Music*. Another worry settled at last.

I dare not face my own possessiveness. This comes from the prime split in my personality which is the split between a good heart (excuse me!!) and a strong ego, as strong as Havana tobacco. These two represent in me my mother and father, although I am making a simple out of a complex at the moment. When I satisfy the ego, the result, dictated by the heart, is remorse. But when the good heart leads me by the nose there is general outrage under my scalp. It is really a constant battle inside me, for I am always afraid, ashamed—what you will—of letting the ego expand overtly. Until an amalgam is made, or until one wins over the other, all sorts of nonsensical items will continue to embitter and outrage me. Luise was always outraging me in this way: she outraged me on the two fronts of the personality, took advantage from both sides, so to speak.

———————•———————

Thursday, January 25, 1940

Up at noon, after a surprisingly sound but short sleep, to meet Richard Lockridge, the drama critic for the *Sun*. And so met and ate and he a timorous man, as all the others are, writing, as he said, detective novels, and stirring or exciting nothing in me, leaving me as cold as the day itself. We came back to the house here and I played a few records for him, showing off the phonograph, and then he went away, murmuring polite nothings at the elevator door, and it is probable that we will never meet again. On his side, I didn't seem to make much of an impression on him. He is a nice, honest, and stubborn man, an American from Missouri, reminding me of [Robert] Ardrey, the playwright.

In the late afternoon I decided to ride up to the Bronx and see the Jeidels. Which I did. Only Mrs. J. was home, peering at the evening papers, and living somehow. Edgar came in from a movie, a true eccentric, still with his wry flashes of attempted humor. They invited me to stay there for supper, but it distressed me; took Edgar to eat at a restaurant and then drove away.

Instead of going to the rehearsal, went over to Kozlenkos'. Bill wasn't there, but Lee opened the door, surprised, embarrassed at greeting me alone, she dressed warmly in a robe under which her nightgown showed. She was visibly disturbed that we were together alone, but we talked, mostly about Bill, and she calmed down. Bill, Bill, what to do with that boy! We talked about him for two hours. Lee realizes him very objectively, saying that she is turning more to the

baby since Bill can only be half-contacted. She is a good wife, fortunately, for him. Another pair would long ago have been separated.

What is sad about Bill is this. Most of his life has been spent in hiding
his crippled leg. But a thing like that obviously cannot be hidden. If
only he could have said to himself, "Christ, they can see it—it can't be
hidden, no matter what I do," his history might be different. To hide
this crippled foot he has managed to hide or submerge three-quarters of
his humanity and real traits. He has made an "intellectual" of himself,
swallowed pages of books and aphorisms to quote, completely
SHIFTED THE DEFECT FROM FOOT TO FEATHERED
PLUME, so to speak, desperately hoping, as Byron must have done,
that if he spoke big words fast enough no one would notice the leg. Bill
is a baby who has not uncovered himself to himself, nor yet discovered
himself; he will not live with the facts of himself or the facts of life,
married life and fatherhood included. He has transferred a mere crippled foot right into his insides and made for himself a crippled life—
much, much worse. How can this boy be helped? It remains to be seen.

Before I left, Lee and I spoke of Luise. It made me think that Luise
plays a series of roles in life, steadily, completely, with wonderful
actor's faith. It goes this way: Luise Rainer is making a sacrifice . . . she
is now considering the role of motherhood. See Luise Rainer being
kind and pitiful to a group of poor refugees. She considers the great
artists of Florence. She tames the American savage male—she will do
her best. Now she mourns for the welfare and health of her parents.
She considers doing a noble act. Now Luise gives herself up to the
man, passive, open, his slave unending. And she comforts from her
deep well of compassion. Yes, Luise sees herself move by in a continuous series of film shots, doing, watching, saying to herself everything
she speaks to you. She befriends Katz, she rejects Katz, she is gay,
brave, alive; but now tired, defeated, and she will sleep. Yes, she is all
things to all men—she is Luise, lonely, afraid, but going on with fever,
forever, alone, alone.

Saturday, January 27, 1940

Dear Fay, I'm trying to keep a journal and what you are getting is a carbon copy of today's entry. Please take it as a letter?

Yesterday? I don't know what happened yesterday. Those are the bad days in life, when nothing happens, when nothing fresh is conceived by the mind—a sort of invalid day when the three nurses of lunch, dinner, and supper reach out with comforting hands and the patient merely rolls over from stupor to deeper sleep. A winter day, a rehearsal day, a routine day, an empty day. Yesterday?—I don't remember, dearie.

But Gurdus was working on the phonograph when I got home in the morning hours. It is beginning to sound like something on an ideal level: the highs are brilliant, almost piercing; the low end drops down below a hundred cycles, but I like it that way—the level is very good otherwise, the whole set powerful and ample.

Yesterday is coming back now. Luise and I share the same lawyer, Arthur Krim. He came to the theatre yesterday to talk over some movie contracts. Suddenly I noticed that I was trying covertly to convince him of my ability to discuss Luise impartially, reasonably, and coolly. By asking him about her in a certain casual manner I was trying to disavow a real thread of feeling which still connects me with her. She has gone down to Washington, he told me, to play St. Joan for a week for the benefit of the Red Cross. For God's sake! As for Luise, I reject her on all counts with the surface superficial elements of my personality, reject her with crudeness and masculine nonsense; but the deeper part of myself, the part or core which is young growing artist, that part is deeply grateful to her for now and all time. Hanns Eisler was very charming when I mentioned Luise to him the other day. (Hanns is the only person with whom I ever speak on the subject of Luise—probably because he is a European.) He said when you look back in years on a former wife (his present is his third, named Louise, by the way) it will only be with humor, with kindness, with wondering how you can help her. Hanns is talking with a thought of the idealizing effect of time and distance, but also he is talking, despite his first-rateness, with some of the cynicism European men have in relation to their women, but it is from leaving out many important facts. But if

European women are satisfied—and they seem much happier than American women—it's none of my business!

Havana tobacco increasingly becomes an item of pleasure and comfort in my life. It doesn't take long to tell a good cigar from a poor one. To this day I retain an element of shame about indulging myself in a "rich man's" pleasures. For years after my first bath of success I sneaked around, ashamed of having money and spending it. Perhaps overgenerosity (of which I can justifiably be accused) is a way of salving the conscience: you beat your wife—you buy her flowers! Anyway, I like to smoke a fine cigar and will continue to do so!

Today's rehearsals showed the play slowly taking shape. The girl is going to be very good; there is something very admirable in her own character which comes out whenever she relaxes on the stage. Gadget, too, will be very winning. Given a few such performers in every play, it would be possible to seduce the audience to any point of view, matricide included. Morris [Carnovsky], curious fellow, is opening up a very interesting character in Rosenberger: heavy, bullish, slow, deliberate, frowning, operating from the good heart of a very realistic police functionary. What he shows here is something different from anything he's ever done on the stage before. Whatever he is doing now in his personal life (a transition period for him) will determine what he finally becomes as an artist. Important years for him.

Important years for me, too, if I may say so. You may say so, Mr. Odets, but don't delude yourself by the writing and thinking of lazy words like these. All right, admit it. I can't *think* anything into being. It all has to be lived and experienced again and again. I am the boy who has to be hit on the head ten times, not once, to realize that he is being punished. I progress by absorption, osmosis, what you will, some sort of slow, painful, and disagreeable process which, by now, I am content to permit functioning without dabbling too much into the whys and wherefors. I creep and crawl by instinct alone—ugly thing—and move in fits and starts which some people euphemistically call inspiration. I am almost like the young maiden who suddenly bursts into tears, and when you ask her what it is, she answers, "I don't know—perhaps I am unhappy!" If he, the novelist, was Madame Bovary, I am half Cleo Singer, even up to this day of thirty-three years and six months. I am Steve Takis and the file of boys and men behind him. And I am in love with any abstract statement which abstracts my painful experience for me, whether stated by myself or another, often Harold Clurman, who is always doing that when he discusses, interprets, or directs a play of mine. Also, that is the only way I explain and interpret myself to myself—by writing a play. Perhaps this constant uncovering of the self is one of the prime impulses in the creative mechanism, it and the constant effort to relate the self to persons, things—a woman—outside of the self. All of the characters in my plays have the common activity of "a search for reality." Well, it's my activity before it's theirs. And before it was mine it was the activity of almost any serious artist who ever lived, from the breakdown of feudalism till today. When you say an artist died still looking for his form, as, for instance, Beethoven and Cézanne did, you mean he died still looking for his reality. A man named Turner wrote a book on Beethoven and was very smart—he called the book "Beethoven—the search for reality." Woe to the artist who is able someday to look at his life and say, "Yes, this is it. Here I rest, I've found it." From that day on the poor man is no longer an artist. For a long time he may delude his public by resting on the oars of a craft or technique, but finally lack of fresh impulses, lack of vital concern, lack of inner disharmony will dry up his work. "Harmony of connection" is another way of expressing the phrase "search for reality" . . . the harmony of the inner and outer realities. Are these mystical-sounding items? Not at all! Unless having to move off a hot radiator on which one is sitting, for example, is mystical! What is truth? Truth is whatever you can live by in utter harmony. Is utter harmony possible? No. Is truth possible? No. Resolved? Are you finished now? No. Why no? Some impulse, inner and unrelated to logic of any school or place, drives you on: the search for reality!

Six in the morning of Sunday now. My mouth is sore and puckered from smoking cigarettes. It's still dark outside; the steam heat's coming up. The lights of Jersey flicker to the left, uptown to the front, uptown and the tower clock. Quiet city, powerful beautiful city, good night.

———•———

Sunday, January 28, 1940

Listening in to radio sketches, one after another, almost convinces one that either America lacks a good heart or it is desperately in need of a good heart. Most of the characterization in these sketches consists of players acting out gentle voices, mellow, fatherly and motherly people—all dominantly of the good heart, proving that life is worth living, that, goldarn it, people are okay through and through, and that people will always come through in a pinch! By heck, by gosh, gee! The men who write these sketches—I met one this past summer in Maine—insist that they are very superior to this material; it is what the people in the sticks want, they insist, but the writers, I notice, are in no way above their audiences except that they are sophisticated in the sense of reading *The New Yorker* every week. A European must laugh at that sort of sophistication, but here it passes for the real thing.

I read today that [United Mine Workers president] John Lewis said Roosevelt had many words, talents, and abilities, but that he is essentially superficial. That struck me immediately as being correct, although I hadn't thought of it before. Brilliant, but superficial, like an actor of the John Barrymore sort—style, swing, background, ease and facility, but superficial. And yet how the American people, myself included, yearn towards this man, as to a comforting father who will take over the responsibilities and leadership. By virtue of its youth the American character is always yearning for a hero, someone to look up to and admire, a person to lead and express by his very being all the yearning of the boyish heart.

Walter Jeidel arrived here with his cab as I was getting out of bed this afternoon. He wanted to take me up to the Bronx for a duck dinner, but I had him drive me up to the theatre and left him with a bottle of wine to add to his family's dinner. He's thirty-five, an old withered man long before his time, a horrible example of what can happen to an unguided and wrongly educated man in our democracy. He might have been trained into a useful good manhood, might have been educated in some simple manual work—a carpenter, for instance—and take joy and dignity from the mastery of a simple craft. And yet Walter votes, has opinions and rights along with the schoolteacher. There will be no democracy as long as that democracy does not take the responsibility of educating and training its citizens into genuine self-reliant manhood and most complete amplitude of all individual talents. Walter's brother, Edgar, is not much better; but he is much more intelligent. His personal pain, if he ever thinks about it, must be immense: a man of thirty-four, he lies in his room downstairs, separated from the others who sleep upstairs, rolling his own cigarettes on a little gadget, reading detective stories, washing dishes, painting the rooms, clipping nickels and dimes from his mother, dreaming of white fat women, growing older and stouter and losing his hair, day by day adding more of the vinegar of prejudice to his "opinions," making wry jokes from a general warping of the self; and finally a kind of eccentric, unrelated to any living thing.

Yesterday sent fifty dollars to Louis Veda—he wants to come to New York and try his luck here again. Boys, boys—they know less about themselves than I do! Which is no sign of my insights or brilliance, but a sure mark of their lack of insight!

Harold was drilling the actors when I got there, again and again running through the first and second acts. The latter is still quite crude, but both acts are complete in outline and will soon spring to life. I'm not satisfied with the overexpressiveness of most of the small characters; the actors are on a holiday, feeling, as they do, in a friendly relaxing atmosphere. Harold is very overindulgent as a director— whatever idea he gets while directing he permits himself to use—he hasn't yet learned to cut as a director. Nor has he yet learned how to physically stage a scene. Often I writhe as I sit there and watch him fumble with a scene which I could straighten out in two minutes. But it's his job, so I control my impulses instead of correcting his efforts. He, on his part, is quite aware of his deficiencies in this department, so it's a nervous time for him if I happen to be sitting in the theatre when he is staging a scene. I've already made a mental note of the various things which need changing and restaging in the first two acts. Harold breathes a sigh of relief, I'm sure, whenever he sees I'm not there, for my silence is more critical, apparently, than my voice. From time to time, as now, I get a desire to direct one of my own plays myself. It is really the ego which is demanding this satisfaction, nothing else; for the truth is that Harold can direct seventy-five percent of a play better than I can. However, if the Group Theatre setup breaks down —there is a good chance of it happening and, frankly, I'm not dismayed at the prospect—I don't think I'll furnish plays to Harold as an individual. He thinks I will, but I think not, although I'd not be adverse to a producing partnership with him, both of us to share executive command. Don't let me forget profits too. I have an urge for profits too.

Can a new Group Theatre be made, using the materials and background of the old one? It will positively have to be done if the theatre is to survive. Unfortunately, the changing and increasing needs of Harold, one man, have brought the Group to its present state. The state is this: if they did not have my script, there would be no Group Theatre. This is the exact realism of the situation, not what Harold says—that there is a sphere of influence spread out among the actors, a need on their part which will keep them united under a Group roof.

MORE ABOUT THIS IN DUE TIME, for the due time will soon enough approach: in many of the people the thin varnish of idealism is going and a clash of wills and ego and material needs will soon assert itself. Myself, by virtue of the strength of my position, I'll be on the outside of the clash, ready to do something for a Group Theatre which interests me, not for a group of "sincere," half-baked, immature people.

Monday, January 29, 1940

Suddenly getting old, feeling old, looking old, all my friends and contemporaries, and myself. The boyish look is going from their faces, going from mine. Care and responsibilities, constant nervous tension, these leave their marks. Overindulgence in food, not walking down the street, lounging in the house, drinking, all leave their marks. Truly the lyric flight is over and the wedding into life has become firm and lasting.

And the young brides are no longer young, the Phoebes, the Lee Kozlenkos, the actresses who started ardent and eager with the Group ten years ago. Consolation: ten years from now it will really be horrible!

I see more deeply into, understand better a person at a first meeting. After a few meetings I lose my original fresh sense of the person and begin to take him on his own terms, at his own evaluation. This comes partly from a certain naïveness, partly from simple laziness. I never explore a man unless he is genuinely unique or unless he forces me to do so. A woman I have "instinctive" reactions to—I understand and know them from a core of desire, from how they touch my sympathy and my sex.

An American girl who has been left money by a hard-working father marries quickly, in a row, four Italian or European "aristocrats." What does that mean?

Bette came down here with me last night, after the rehearsal. We listened to two Beethoven sonatas, drank two small bottles of champagne, and went to bed. She woke up at twelve, had to go to rehearsal. Since I was up I drank my morning coffee and ordered some new phonograph records, chiefly Verdi's *Falstaff*. The records all arrived in the late afternoon. Played them, puttered around, and went over to Bill's past ten in the evening. He has a bad cold. Rode Lee down the Jericho Turnpike, got her home safely, and sat up till the early morning looking over the Bible, trying to find a quote for the girl to read in the play.

It seems to me, without much thought, that the works of our best writers, painters, and musicians today are of interesting quality only when they are modest in intention. Their big works are pretentious, incomplete, failures. Blessed is the artist who is aware of his own limitations—his shall be the kingdom of heaven!

Tuesday, January 30, 1940

For the play, for the girl, found the Biblical quote—from Ecclesiastes: "Remember now thy Creator in the days of thy youth . . ." It is going to be a beautiful production; I'll eat the script if I'm wrong. They went up to Hanns Eisler's house to hear the music early this evening, but I had to be at the lawyer's office, arranging details of the movie deal, so didn't hear the music. Chiefly I want to hear Steve's clarinet solo at the end of act 2—even the simple thought of it stirs me deeply. If I could write music, if I could play music . . . what yearning and loneliness to put in that moment, a thing that words words words can never do, unless it were written by some great lyric poet, a Heine, a Shelley, and they would miss the particular thing which is the loneliness of the modern man. Sometimes there is a flash of what I mean in Stravinsky's music, in Debussy, in some of the younger French modern composers. What I mean is tense, nervous, homeless, seeking, lyric, thrown back on the self, boyish, tight, being emotional without exposure, ceaselessly turning turning, the pivot steady, even a little giddy, the modern masculine self dappled with feminine shadow—the modern man: the Picasso blue-period man. (The pivot *un*steady, I mean.)

My instinct to make Steve Takis a pierrot, a clown type, "the rejected democrat," was good, deeper than I thought while writing. From here, from Steve, it is possible to branch off, past Charlie Chaplin, into many interesting characters, all of them functioning and being propelled from a core of rejection.

Jane Wyatt interests me. I told Harold there were two things I didn't like about her: one, she is married; two, she is not divorced.

Harold and I left the rehearsal at past eleven tonight. Went to Sardi's and cut more out of the first two acts. After it closed went to another restaurant and cut some lines out of the third act. Now I'm home and going to bed in a few minutes. Played some of Debussy's opera *Pelléas and Mélisande*. Beautiful.

Bette looking lonely at the rehearsals. My sister Florence too. Gadget very tired and so dull in his acting impulses. Jane a steady delight to my eyes. Morris C. shaping out one of the best performances he will ever have given.

Good night.

———————•———————

Wednesday, January 31, 1940

What a delicate exquisite instrument is the throat of E. Schumann, the soprano. "Don't hurt me," it seems to say, soft, womanly, beautifully controlled, perfectly modulated, lyric in the finest sense of the word, warm and living, sensitively aware of its limitations, sensible, flexible—exquisite, in a word—a very hummingbird or butterfly of a voice. And yet it is far from the highest type of art, finally summing to the decorative rather than to the truly interpretive or creative. For every song she sings is reduced to the same (and I am not forgetting the supreme intelligence in the handling of the voice and the song) level of singing the notes, never the meaning of the notes or the words they accompany. Always the emotion is general, never particular, never a unique experience different from that of any other given song. In short, there is a technical experience which the listener gets, never an emotional one, except generally. In the end it is always a kind of exalted slumber music, soft, delicate, far away from the realities of the words, from the pain of true experience. There is exquisite good taste, not food for a steady diet.

It's four in the morning of Thursday. I've had a pint of champagne and am going to bed. I looked over the file of the actress play and saw in it some notes I'd written but never sent to Luise. (If only Luise had some of Schumann's craft!) What I want to do is to start on a new play, but these rehearsals emotionally tie my hands, even though it's not necessary for me to be at them. Anxiety, but curiously not with the conscious mind at all. There is just a background inner drive which keeps me uneasy, anxious, unable to do anything but move painfully to the rehearsals. Altogether there is never any satisfaction in this period of production. I am like some dumb beast, trying to be patient and calm, but always tense and uneasy, even though I trust Harold with the direction almost completely.

Picked up Bette at the rehearsal and drove over to Hanns Eisler's house to hear, for the first time, the music he has written for the play. He played it on the piano, but I can't hear it that way, although it came more alive for me when he explained the orchestration. He had some German refugee friends there and, as Bette remarked, they are like people from another world. They always are; but Germans are so capable, so able to take care of themselves—they fall on their feet, like cats, all the time—they know how to get along—they are so goddam industrious! Much more than Americans are supposed to be. Germans, I must confess, I don't like as a people, although there are some exceptions like Hanns and a few others.

On my desk now are the following files, one of which will be the next play, but I can't make up my mind: the sextette play, the suicide play, the actress play, the war veterans, an antiwar play. But which one to do I don't know. The whole problem is beyond me.

What explains the form of a girl like Jane Wyatt? How it moves me, stirs and excites me. Is it the social register background or is it the Catholicism? Yes, my cold piteous friends, form is a lovely thing in life, desirable and necessary. What a sad thing it is going to be for me if I never find a form. It will mean an unhappy life if there is never in work or personal living some place to stop and rest. Young man without a form! It is exactly this lack which will both make you and break you, young man. No choice, so take it as it comes: you are what you are and the rest be deeply damned!

Was it? Did it, Fay? Were you here once? Truly? In this very room? In that very room? No, I don't believe it. You were here and we were together? No, I can't believe it. I'm tired and tight, Fay. Not with neurotic sparkle, Fay—just tight, just tired, not unhappy. But were you really here? Did I kiss you? You me? Did we do the male and female act together? Fay, I don't believe it!

———————•———————

Thursday, February 1, 1940

Notice, the beginning of another month!

In the Moussorgsky songs, if you do not have the emotion you do not have the song, not even the shadow of the song. Chekhov could hope to find and did find actors to play his plays; where can the talent of M. find singers to sing his songs? For the point of each of M.'s songs is not in the notes, not in the words, but between them, a sort of suggested emotional line without which the song simply does not exist. Here is where the conventional songsinger is shown up for what he is, a tracer on glass, a sharper or duller instrument at his use, but not more. The trouble with the damn singers, unless they are fat and fifty, is that they do not give themselves a chance. They don't listen to the songs, they are not open to the music and what it emotionally suggests. Leaving aside the emotional significance, they can't even play with humor, with charm, deftness, alertness. Their backsides should be kicked till they ache!

Perhaps I am the only one—if anyone else thinks about the nature of my talent—who realizes how closely my talent is related to that of the songwriters, those writers in small forms, mostly more perfect than my own work. We start together from a core of lyric. Each of my plays, certainly the many-scened ones, I could call a song cycle on a given theme. However, my work lacks the perfection and clarity of any of the better lieder writers, certainly the purity. But they are European, I American, and a certain crudeness, loudness, vulgarity, overspilling, lack of form is natural to our character and its youth. But I can learn from men like Brahms and Hugo Wolf. Of course the content of their time and place is so different from ours today and here: resignation is not one of the distinct colors in our American spectrum—we die, when we do, with a trumpet of a Bronx cheer on our lips. And the romantic surge of a Schumann song, unfortunately sometimes, is another color we lack.

A letter from Fay Wray this morning. Had dinner with B. Cerf, my publisher.* A foolish fellow, when the naked truth must be told. A big booby boy who is personally offended and tells you he is unappreciated when you tell him you want more advertising for your plays.

———————•———————

* Bennett Cerf, Co-founder of Random House, had enticed Odets away from the publishing house of Covici-Friede in 1935 and published *Six Plays* in 1939.

Friday, February 2, 1940

Rehearsal, of course. But took notes tonight, at least a dozen pages of them. The rehearsal was poor, the people low and tired. Later went over to Sardi's with Harold and found he agreed with most of the notes, most of which had to do with more clearly defining scenes through readings and restaging of small things. There is a way of sharpening and italicizing a scene so that even dull writing is made interesting. Harold never does know how to do that, so I usually have to come in at this stage of rehearsal and tell him where things should build, not be dropped, graded up or down, etc., etc. He, by the way, has a real itch to direct other Broadway plays, Behrman, Anderson, etc. I feel sure he wants to direct for the Playwrights' Theatre [Playwrights' Company], but think he will run into some very perplexing problems when he begins to direct in leading parts actors who have not been trained by the Group; he won't have much point of contact with them and his points of reference will necessarily be limited, just as in the case of Lee Strasberg directing *On the Outside*. The Group frame of reference has its own terminology, often as technical and bewildering as steam turbines would be to a poet.

Into Sardi's walked my old friend Harvey Screbnick, now called Scribner. He had to take a girl home but agreed to meet me down here at two in the morning. Which he did. We drank, listened to music, and discussed music and the theatre. He was both too tired and tight for the conversation to have much movement or point; and I am not the fiery zealot he knew ten years ago. But he seems to me as fine a fellow as he ever was, and I was glad for meeting him again.

Form, form, form! I am thinking a great deal about form these days. How the form of one's life makes the form of one's artwork, big or small. How some search for life-forms, how some have them thrust upon them, etc., etc. . . . all very interesting and more about it at some later time. Form, form, form, what a fascinating problem. Not that writing about it here will settle anything. But I begin to understand myself and my drives better by trying to find a personal and working form for them.

Saturday, February 3, 1940

Went up to the theatre at six to take Bette and her sister to dinner. The sister, Janet, was nothing like what I thought she'd be. She's the kind of girl who sits around in bars, quite crushed but trying to be what is nicely called "a regular fellow," damned American nonsense. Bette seems to think her sister is quite a person. Well, maybe she's right and I'm all wrong.

A slow rehearsal again. I begin to see that Harold thinks it is supposed to go larghetto throughout, but I insist on every other scene being played scherzo if possible. The play has to come off as a party or it is going to be depressing in part to an audience. A certain gayness and on-the-toes quality is absolutely indispensable to the final production. I'll watch carefully in Boston. Tonight I had to bawl out Ruth Nelson, who has deliberately been coming to her scenes late. She is possibly disgruntled about the part or the salary and is taking it out on the director by being sullen and inimical to any direction or suggestions made to her. I simply lost my patience and lost control of my temper for the first time in months.

The drive to get to the essence of the thing is essentially a poetic drive. But it can do horrible things to the personal life.

———•———

Sunday, February 4, 1940

On this day we drove up to Boston by car, in the Cadillac. We—Hanns Eisler, Bette, and I—started out at noon and in seven hours we were there, having passed through the states of New York, Connecticut, and Massachusetts, all beautiful and wintery states in February. A ride of this sort is always relaxing, absorbing, and abstracting—very good for nervous people. The last two hours we rode in night-darkness and the glare of headlights made me think once that the eyeballs were going to drop out of my head; but the eyes are still intact.

We are at the Bellevue Hotel, where I wrote *Waiting for L.* [*Lefty*].

Bette and I came to my room and read the papers; I took a hot bath and we went to bed and it was a beautiful bedding but tiring, to tell the truth, on top of a tiring previous twenty-four hours.

———•———

Monday, February 5, 1940

The main thing is that the company arrived here in the early afternoon—we are opening here this Thursday night. The scenery was being set up all these past two days. In the afternoon we gave a party for the critics and drama editors of the Boston papers. Not one living face did I see among them, although we were very nice to them—a very squeamish job made worse by posing for a lot of photos. They have so much vanity, these provincial newspaper people! So much ego and pride to hurt by a thoughtless gesture! One of them is interviewing me tomorrow morning with the orange juice.

By the time I got to the rehearsal in the evening, Hanns was already working with his musicians down in the cellar. That is what made my heart go banging—the music! not the new scenery. What an excellent little workman Hanns is! How he whipped those fellows into shape, turned them, taught them, flattered and pushed them—got exactly the results he wanted. Tomorrow the music will be ready to hear—tonight his organist was missing.

I don't know what I think of the scenery. Some of it is loaded with details, exactly as some of the small-part actors are overloading the delicate line of the play with overexpressiveness in their unimportant roles. But more tomorrow when I can see better.

Harold C. and I never face each other when I have to criticize some of his work, as tonight. I am unhappy about some of the scenes, but it is next to impossible to talk to him about them. I did say a few words of what I meant. Tomorrow I'm taking a line rehearsal while he attends the technical run-through. He suggests I make the changes I suggest while the actors are reading. Which I'll do. But what is needed is certain restagings. This time I'll see it through and it will be the first time since I've been a playwright. To see something which is obviously wrong and to permit it to pass for fear of hurting a friend's feelings . . . what soft stupidity! And yet all my life I have been unable to say, in troubled times, what is on my mind without first getting angry and then letting the anger act like gunpowder behind bullets. Yet that is the very thing which helped and started me as a playwright.

———————•———————

Tuesday, February 6, 1940

One of the last places where a man of talent, sensitivity, and imagination makes a compromise is in his woman. When this compromise is at last made, he is then settled down for life, unless, as infrequently happens, a recrudescence occurs. Marriage, said Voltaire (?), is the only adventure open to the coward. He meant it in this sense; in any other sense he is all wrong—it is foolish bachelor talk.

Usually the man of talent and imagination finds the most difficult thing in life is the one of necessary adjustment to other people and their ideas. Adjustment, however, is the very essence of a successful or creative marriage. The talented man then finds it necessary—if he wants to be happily married—to tamper with his own personality which is his chief working source (and that includes his wife's tampering!); or he must make a compromise by marrying below himself, in a good sense, where the shallow level of contact makes only a shallow level of adjustment necessary. There are exceptions to this, but they are few and far between, very few and very far. . . .

Today another hard rehearsing day. Anything else which happens must cluster itself around the rehearsal period. But I was interviewed by a columnist and let off a few good ideas, particularly about my objections to the word "escape" when it is used in connection with moving pictures. I say a man doesn't go to a film to escape, but rather to extend and project his personality. All human impulses are positive, never negative—extension of personal potentialities is almost an instinctive drive in humans. But this is merely mechanical. More about it some other time.

Another way to say the "search for reality" is to say "the desire for completion." The closing of the gap, and the gap (poor word) is life.

Why are American men, myself included, so ashamed of baldness and growing stout? You tell a man he is losing his hair, or he is putting on weight, and he goes to considerable lengths to deny it. What is the shame in it? What fear is expressed? This reminds me that I find in many ways I am a very average American male, not different. That doesn't frighten me, for it means that I understand that type and he, after all, is one of the chief weapons in my arsenal of types and characters. Often I find that I understand both sides of an argument, the conservative and the radical, for I am both of them. My boyhood and youth give me a good sense of all the reactionary's aversions.

What a lazy journal this is! I never write in an item that I don't think to myself, how much deeper my knowledge is than I am writing it on the paper. Simple animal laziness, or too tired, or a book to read, etc. When this laziness creeps into the writing of a scene—and it happens—that's the dangerous time!

When I was thirteen and lived in the Bronx it was profoundly my opinion that a certain man living in our house was a criminal of a very dangerous order—he was a well-known Socialist!

I'm getting quite a belly. How do I excuse it? It anchors, I say, my nerves down!

———————•———————

Friday, February 9, 1940

Do you know, I'm beginning to think you are a very ordinary fellow. You are vain, dishonest, morally lax; you are proud, you are lazy, and self-indulgent. You do not extend yourself sufficiently in any direction, you seldom "intend" your thinking and activity. You are constantly excusing yourself for all these patent deficiencies by saying this sort of jellyfish existence is a prime requisite of the creative personality. Is that true? Aren't you really sinking deeper every week into the feather bed of a successful career? Right now, friend, you are excusing yourself by saying, "Here again is this old foolish American cry for competence and result every minute!" These are the whispered thoughts which will ruin you. The amused expression on your face right this minute denotes a certain lack of seriousness which is beginning, like an odor of dead flowers, to suffuse your entire personality. Read this again in a week; in another week, again. Don't be afraid of harassing yourself, of nagging yourself. The wife is dying out of you and only the self-indulgent husband will soon be left. You are sitting on the floor of the deserted room, like Captain Boyle in the last scene of *Juno & the Paycock*.

Hanns's music keeps ringing in my ears. Last night at dinner Harold said the same thing. The music is sharp, incisive, small, and complete, with a gemlike quality. It keeps ringing in my ears over and above the inflection of the actors' readings.

I've missed several days in this diary, jumped over the opening which was followed by mixed but favorable notices. Provincial notices, which means: afraid of New York opinion after them, timid, captious in a petty way, written out of heartfelt inferiority, a provincial inferiority—never honest reactions but rather what one is SUPPOSED TO write! For instance, a woman critic who told me three dirty stories at the critics' party objected to the hero of the play for his brusque, brash, and generally immoral behavior.

On Saturday night the play fell into place for the first time and the performance was almost ready for a New York opening—a good all-round performance with everything jelled into place. The whole effort now is to make the play a success, a pitiful effort. Even we forget about the charm of the play, its delicacy and poignancy. . . . Everything drives towards success. The American theatre, excuse me, is vile and a stench hangs over it. Here is one young man who would weep at its death! A dog's life, believe me, veritably a dog's life! And what of the play form? Very easy—in the end it will never be a satisfactory form, never very subtle, never possible of fulfillment for an artist as is painting or music. And here it is complicated by a thousand business details, necessarily, hopelessly, disgustingly!!

———•———

Monday, February 12, 1940

Hanns is going back to New York tomorrow. A real talent, a real heart, a glittering particularity in a world of mostly glittering generality. I bought drinks for a large group of our people wishing him a good farewell. Bette I told to go to her room to sleep and here am I writing these words, quite full of Scotch, quite depressed. The performance tonight was very poor because the actors were trying to act out about thirty cuts which we gave them this afternoon. I am lonely, depressed, a nice girl like Bette solves or resolves nothing in my intensely personal life. I need a woman who can take me out of myself to be more myself, a woman with form, a woman with clarity . . . I need, I need, I NEED! So you see I am a very greedy fellow, really unhappy, really unfounded. I used to enjoy these rockets of yearning in my head—now they only make me weary and more and more passive; they throw me in on myself more and more, they cut me off from the normal life around me. It is possible to yearn with such depth and strength that finally you are cut off from the very things you yearn for.

I am a dastard! Several times I found myself talking to Jane Wyatt about Jews, trying to show her how objective and impersonal I was about the problems of Jews; really trying to disavow being a Jew, if the truth must be told. I yearn for acceptance like a youth of eighteen, and in a curiously twisted way (although she doesn't know it) I reach out to her for her form and clarity, even though I know it is young and quite incomplete.

Yesterday I enjoyed a quiet hour's walk down Beacon Street in the wind. The houses along the street are old, with real quality. I bought some oranges and ate three of them at night. The room is suffused with the aroma of fruit, pleasant. Go to sleep, Stevie, tomorrow's another day. Tomorrow I'll write something here about self-indulgence. Good night.

Tuesday, February 13, 1940

It is getting to be "another day" here. Harold sort of pecked at the lack of rehearsal discipline at the rehearsal he called for today. The show was very slow and unconcentrated last night. By now, of course, the whole thing bores me almost beyond endurance; so I left the rehearsal and walked up the avenue and bought some shirts and some toilet water and French soap for some of the people. Then there was a late dinner and the evening performance which I watched with a hypnotic glare born out of absolute boredom. Some of the Theatre Guild people were over to see our show which they seemed to like. Tomorrow and Thursday there will be exchange matinees—their company sees our show and we see theirs.

After the show, while Harold, Gadget, and I sat over drinks at the

Ritz bar, I kept thinking about my real need for a certain kind of woman, one who would be able to control me and help give this blasted life of mine some kind of form. I feel sure she is hiding in an Eskimo igloo! This way, alone, half of my life is wasted, without definition and clarity. How a good woman could help me; for I seem unable to help myself.

The other day I was realizing what happened to me as a child in school and that the same thing must happen today to children. The school system and the teachers bred in me such a respect for authority that it amounted in the end to a sort of systematic terrorization. Most of the time in school I was also numbed by fear that my ability to think and see what they put in front of me was close to nil. I distinctly remember my fear of competition too—if I had to work rapidly and competitively it was all over with me before I started. Actually those early school years taught me to immediately reject what was not immediately simple or soluble for me. The fear of failure and concomitant disgrace, censure, and punishment actually made a sort of half-wit of me. I think with difficulty although my logical sense is fine and my feelings and intuition are first-rate. It is only in the last few years that I am able to follow a difficult thought out to its resolution.

"Open for me, open, darling—open the door!" That, if you please, is the cry of youth, the cry of the poet, my personal cry. When you stop crying that, you are getting old.

ABOUT SELF-INDULGENCE: when you look for accommodation from everyone and everything, when you demand comfort and affirmation from all contacts, then you are what is called self-indulgent. That has its value and its place, but it is ruinous as a steady diet, for it develops nothing of genuine importance in the personality. It is as if one lived in a cushioned cell with never a new book to read; it is never meeting people in their amazing variety. Development comes from directly dealing with what irks and troubles one; self-indulgence forbids such direct dealing.

Jane Wyatt sits around at rehearsals, her skirt slightly lifted. I yearn to see her legs. Finally, after weeks, her skirt lifts high enough for me to see them. I quickly turn my head away, I can't look.

There is a favorite expression in our country: be yourself. Which means exactly the opposite of what it says. It means be like me and my friend, not like yourself. Conform, it means!

The mysterious K—the magic C!

Wyatt comes from the American aristocracy. In herself she shows some of its best qualities, but her relatives who visited her after the opening, they show some of its worst. Their faces are handsome, blank, and brutal. They remind one of the Italian aristocracy as painted by the great Italian painters. The face of Doris Duke, often seen in the newsprint, is a good example. There is little or no nuance in the face; it shows a lack of inner life and experience, a lack of values of the spirit. The men and women behind these faces will brook little or no opposition, accept no "incomplete" values, entertain no complexity of emotion or situation. Finally, they are not really open to life, but only to that which is grasped immediately, to all that already conquered, already certain. The wages of their sins are in what they are: they are deeply punished for their easeful wealth and position!

Father Coughlin* said on the radio, last Sunday, that only two choices are open to the world today—Christ or Marx. *Selah!*

I used to worry about this question: "Is this my best play to date?" Now I say, "This is another play."

More and more I grow to have deep respect for good workmanship. It is almost impossible to accept sincerity and sensitivity in its place, particularly when they are generalized under the heading of "art" or "artiness."

Self-indulgence may come, too, from an ardent (but secret) desire to bring a divided personality together. In other words, you have nagged and despised yourself, refused to accept yourself for so many years— now accept, do not refuse any impulse.

Luise Rainer was one of the several persons in my life who prepared me for life. She is alive in me in many ways, some excellent. Our brief time together was necessary for both of us.

I am crying out for form (and a person to give it) in a confused wilderness of many feelings and contradictions. This problem in myself, a minor artist, makes me understand the same problem in a major artist, Beethoven. This is true of his personal life and his work: every time he found a form for his content he simultaneously found that his content had progressed in depth and a new form was necessary—a very Tantalus of life! He, however, had the hardheadedness to see it through to the very bitter end—he obviously died looking for a new form—and he died having pushed music to a level which before had never been attained nor has yet been equalled. Great unhappy man!

————•————

* Father Charles Edward Coughlin, Catholic priest whose extremely popular radio broadcasts had given him political influence. In the late thirties, Coughlin became an outspoken supporter of Fascism. In 1942, the Church silenced him.

Wednesday, February 14, 1940

The music of Beethoven is much in my reckoning. If I am reading a book and want to lay it down, I mark off the page by Beethoven opus numbers—page eighteen, for instance, "stopped at the Lobkowitz Quartets."

The *Fifth Column* people came over to see our matinee today. I could see they liked the show—Franchot, Miss Locke, Lee Cobb—but they fiddled and faddled around, as usual, when they came backstage to see our people. Lee Strasberg was there, reserved, as usual. The bearer of a terrible uneasy calm which will crack his arteries prematurely. He gave snatches of criticism to Gadget, but he has so little courage to directly front something that everything he says comes out in mysterious bits and fragments which add up to making no sense whatsoever. A peculiar character, more and more withdrawn into himself each year. He knows more about actors and their working problems than any man in this country, but he is something like a great pianist who dries up before a concert audience. At present, from the Theatre Guild he is taking orders meekly enough, keeping his mouth shut and minding his own business. In the Broadway theatre he is a fish out of water; for one who knows his talent he is a moving figure. But he has made all his problems for himself, including his break with the Group.

Stuffing one's stomach is a way of putting one's self in whack with the world, an easy way of doing it, an animal way.

The big item today is a sixty-mile gale which brought in a snowstorm such as I haven't seen since boyhood. When it stopped there was a fall of thirteen inches on the streets and walking was next to impossible. Harold and I went to see the Guild show which was doing good business while ours was not. We went back to see their actors and I fiddle-faddled there as much as they did in our theatre. Terry Helburn asked me, springless lady, to come over to her hotel and suggest any ideas for changes that I had. So we all trudged through the snow to the Ritz Hotel and for two hours I told her and cohorts what I thought. The show is weak, although good material is abundantly implicit throughout. There is a hard core of improbability in an artificially introduced love story, which no amount of rewriting will dissolve. My first impulse was to be helpful, but gradually I sat back and let them scratch their own egotistic furs which satisfied them well enough.

Full of Scotch and soda, traveled home through the snow with Harold and Kermit Bloomgarden, who came up by delayed train to see our show and thought it was better than when he saw it last. We had some drinks in my room and they went to bed. Read a few essays by Max Lerner,* particularly on Veblen, and turned over to sleep. There is a good full-length play in Veblen, but it will be fifty years before it can be successful in America. It could be successful in Russia today.

I cut my wrist trying to help push a car stalled in the snow. It aches dully.

———————•———————

Thursday, February 15, 1940

A week from tonight we open the play in New York. Frankly, considering all the conditions of the theatre, it will be a little anticlimatic.

Bette is so open and giving that it is a little awesome. Unfortunately for her and myself, I am not in an awesome mood these days. Nor these nights, if the truth must be told, although we are very happy to be together in these cold friendless nights with blue snow on the streets from corner to corner.

Our people went over to see the Guild show and none of them was impressed beyond my own personal impression. We all agree that the play deals with a worthy theme.

At night I looked over some ideas for the actress play, for I am thinking about possibly writing it next. I find it's not as simple as it seemed two years ago. Now I more deeply understand the people— the simple scorn I felt before would have made the writing of the characters easier; now I know too much about them for my own good. I told Harold in the afternoon that I wanted him to know that Stella Adler is not right for the actress part. He, as usual, was noncommittal, as he always is when he is not able to handle actual material from which to start reacting. He is the best reactor I know, but with no actual material as a base he is hopeless and lost. His talent is deeply analytic,

* Max Lerner, the editor of *The Nation* and later a nationally syndicated columnist and editor of *The Portable Veblen*.

never synthetic, as I more and more find out from day to day. In a curious way he is only half a man, a kind of centaur, a sort of Rodin man half out of the block of marble; but the man half is amazingly alive and real, sensitive, struggling in some mysterious ark fashion which I only half understand. He usually says, "That's how I am," and delivers abstracts on self-acceptance and lets everything else ride by. In a strange way he suffers more humiliations than any man I know, and this is not exaggeration! More about this tomorrow.

I want to work out a solid tight story line in the actress play, what is nicely called a plot play. In the beginning I had a first-class dramatic instinct which took care of all my technical problems, but since then I have developed a good deal of conscious theatre craft and I mean in this play to use it and the other to the tops of their bents.

Myself I cannot give easily to another person, thing, or situation. I learn and accept with great difficulty and slowness. This comes from (or makes in me) a very unyielding quality. The unyielding business is my misfortune as a person. But it will be in the end my salvation as an artist.

———————•———————

Saturday, February 17, 1940

Two more performances in Boston today and the show is finished with its tryout run. This hasn't been a pleasant experience, for several reasons. One is that we haven't profited from the tryout period, and the other reasons all stem from Harold's character. He has a deep lack of capacity for work. He falls into certain doldrums, certain Sargassos of the senses. Twice he sat at afternoon rehearsals and permitted the company to rattle through their lines. Later, when I asked him why he hadn't used each rehearsal for some particular purpose (work on characterizations, etc.), he stammered out some feeble apology, flushed into silence, and that was the end of that. There are periodic times in Harold's life when he falls into a sort of profound bafflement; they are bad for the people he is working with, myself included, for they drag all of the work down to the level of these subnormal phases of his life. In the end, now at least, I will have to say this about him: he is no organizer, one-half director, great critic when and if one of his clear phases meets material before it. His inability to establish discipline, for rehearsals and other purposes, is shocking. With some exaggeration of fact, the merest member of the company is able to gain more personal respect from his fellow actors than is the director of the play! This has one good effect—it relaxes the players so that their most creative feelings and ideas are permitted free play. But as you watch, week after week, you discover that the actor needs a firm hand to guide and tie up his ideas into proper forms and finished performances. This last half Harold is unable to control or direct up to practically eighty percent. He has been able, in other words, to set a whole microcosm spinning, but is unable, after that, to control any of its actions. I think he is extremely fortunate to have Group actors with whom to work; other actors would show up this fatal flaw in him almost as soon as he started with them. This flaw or split in Harold's personality seems to me explainable by the quality of his genius or talent, although genius is close to the proper word. That quality is best explained by the phrase "the Russian temperament" as it was used in the old sense when talking of Dostoyevsky characters. They are men of moods, not of action; they are deeply intuitive, "irrational," and their experience comes slow and whole; nothing in life, not life itself, is utilitarian in any sense of the word; they bathe in their impressions, they stammer, are incoherent nine-tenths of the time, and yet their inner climate is one of intense spirituality and truthfulness; they are mostly completely the opposite of the average American male—inefficient, inept, clumsy, never impatient of results, never "complete," trusting an inner "instinct," lacking clarity, general instead of concrete . . . in short, the Russian soul!!! See any of the writings of D. or Gogol, even Turgenev, although he was perhaps as much French as he was Russian.

All this about Harold is troubling me, although I don't take it as seriously as it sounds on the page. First, I share myself some of these "faults" I find in him; and second, he is nevertheless enormously gifted as a stage director. But what troubles me is his kind of philosophical detachment about his faults, i.e., "that is how one is and that is how one goes." That won't build up a theatre technique, nor will it mine the talent up to fourteen karat quality. Nor will it help one acquire a theatrical form, a desideratum not exactly to be despised!

But Boston was an unpleasant experience this time for other reasons too. One was the quality of the reviews and reviewers. Not to mince words, they were stupid, not much more intelligent than the audi-

ences who attended the play and laughed only at the most obvious
lines, seldom appreciating the quality of the script or production. They
are all of them corrupted by the movies and cheap magazines, and I
hold a magazine like *The New Yorker* just as cheap as those of the true
confessions type—one has more "tone," that's all. Seemingly the most
intelligent of the Boston reviewers, an Elliot Norton, wrote a two-
column interview with me, but it turned out to be all about my
"changing political beliefs" and scarcely a word about my plays and
their various qualities. This gentleman admired me as "an intense
serious person whom it was a pleasure to meet"; and kept breathing
through his piece one long sigh of relief that I was not really a Communist at all—meaning, apparently, that I was not considering blowing up
any dams or bridges at the moment. And that is called dramatic
criticism in America! That is why, by the way, when a play of mine gets
fine notices, it nevertheless does about one-quarter the business of the
average potboiler. By now the theatre audiences have an idea that I
write political tracts—and who can blame them? Would you pay good
money to hear the average political tract?

And Boston seemed very shabby this year too. Poor and run-down,
needing a good coat of paint all over, needing new snap and some sort
of gayness.

But there is a good word, at least, to be said for Worcester. In their
Evening Gazette a man named George Foxhall wrote a review of *Night
Music* which half-repayed me for the Boston feeling. His kind of simple
good clean enthusiasm, his evident honesty, his "uncorrupted behavior," was a joy to read. He sent the review to Morris, who sent it on to
me. "This," said I, "is why I write plays!" And it was and it is, and may
there be more Foxhalls in life!

A humiliating life, this one of writing in and for the theatre. Immediate critical reactions from everyone in sight. One lady said to
Harold, "I find this play very lovely and moving. But tell me, Mr.
Clurman, is it really great?" And this is not to mention the thousands
of pieces of advice heaped on one by what I used to think were
well-intentioned friends and acquaintances. No, they are not well-
intentioned at all! For I perceive, perhaps at this very late date (I learn
so slowly, slowly, drip, drip!), that their advice and suggestions are
impelled by their vanity and egos; the insistence with which they
demand that you listen to and take their advice is proof enough of what
I say.

There is a real technique for trying out a play out of town, I now
learn. Take little or no advice, except from a chosen few. Do not read or

heed the reviews of the play, good or bad. Keep away from too many performances so that your view of the show is always as fresh as possible; and remember your original intentions in the parts and whole of the play and performances. (Bring up a trusted friend who has not seen the show before.)

Franchot Tone, learning that we met in a certain bad restaurant most nights after the show, walked in there last night. He was ill-at-ease, tense, and obviously very lonely or he wouldn't have joined us. All of us tried to put him at his ease, but he is poor table company. He wanted to go out whoring and drinking at a speakeasy (liquor after 1:00 A.M.), but was unable to find a companion. Franchot, with all his fame, money, and position, is still afraid of rejection and repudiation. He is blustery and pushing, anxious and uneasy, just like Steve Takis, but slightly more adult; in short, he is an Ernest Hemingway hero, and that is saying the whole thing.

H. [Harold] Freedman, my agent, came up for the final performance tonight. Heavens, to pay a man ten percent of your earnings to bore you! What a life!

———————•———————

Sunday, February 18, 1940

The entire company left for New York by train at ten this morning. I went by car—the Cadillac has never once left the garage for all the two weeks we've been here. Boston streets were slushy with soft snow, but the highways were in fine shape and we reached New York in seven hours, Bette Grayson with me. I was very tired, for at the very last hour last night an idea for a new play came to me and I wrote it out on the typewriter. A little play, but amusing and sad—"bad girl," like Lily in *Night Music*, wants to marry and settle down. I laid out two acts in twice an hour. That is the nature of my talent—bing! and there is a play. It's always a cinch for me to write a scene when I know the types and their feelings; this girl, Mae or Julia I'd call her, arouses me all over. Anyway, the notes are in the inside pocket of my jacket. I'd go right ahead but for the fact that I'd like to be sure of having ready a big play for next season, one of bigger feeling and intention is what I mean. We'll see, Charley, we'll see.

The house looked the same and I was very happy and relieved to get back. Major disappointment was the phonograph apparatus—Gurdus had not yet completed it.

A sweet note from Fay Wray here, plus a big stack of other mail, chiefly requests for one thing or another. Richard Wright's new novel, autobiographical, and may it be good—I want to help him all I can.

Gadget, I discover, is not quite ready to play leading parts. His technique is on a very simple level, but what gets him by with any audience is his winning personality. In *N.M.* his characterization is very incomplete and more or less mechanical. In most places it is as if he walked out of his dressing room in his street clothes and shoes, Elia Kazan, not Steve Takis. He lacks variety of approach, variety of voice, although his perceptions are good; he has flashes of genuine charm too. A certain uncouthness hits me, too, a sort of boisterous quality; real shyness he does not give, although he simulates it mechanically. In the middle of the rehearsal period he did have some of the pierrot quality that Harold was working for, but now it's all gone—the play suffers for it.

In a certain way what I am complaining of in Gadget is form—he lacks form, form, form! It's on my mind all the time these days.

I have a great capacity for admiration, and little or nothing in the way of object on which to lavish it. This is what makes a person excessively romantic in certain moments. It is a cruel thing to carry unsatisfied. Admiration, I am sorry to say, is the only channel through which I can give myself in any full way; and I would rather admire than be admired any day in the week!

———•———

Tuesday, February 20, 1940

The production again—work and thought about *Night Music* and the acting of it and the restaging of certain bits and changing a line here or there. The whole day clusters around it and so does the whole night. A poorish preview tonight, but the preview audiences are no indication of what a show is worth in terms of audience appeal.

Alvah Bessie sat with me at the performance tonight. He enjoyed the play, even though the performance was very low because the actors were tense and nervous. Brought Bessie down here after the show. We played German lieder, drank a quart and a pint of champagne. He wanted to talk—he is nervous, unhappy, unconnected. But I was very tired and didn't listen too much. He is very frightened about the war; says he dreams of it every night and that it is doubly terrible to him because of his recent experience in Spain. He constantly deplored the fact that someone hadn't written a good play on Spain; he hoped I would do it.

———————•———————

Wednesday, February 21, 1940

Final preview tonight. An intelligent audience, for a wonder! Given by a progressive school and its friends. They liked the play very much. Seems that the show starts slowly—the first acts mounts very slowly for an audience and makes them, fortunately, look forward to a better second act. Our second act satisfies them, for it builds up from where the first one left off. The third act is satisfactory. If the show goes as well tomorrow night as it did tonight, we are in for a run.

I'm tired, very tired, but I feel a strong impulse to work on that new small play, *She Wants to Marry!*, as I'm calling it in my mind. But I'm very tired.

Met Sid Kingsley and wife, Len Lyons and wife, in Sardi's after the show tonight. Mrs. K., Madge Evans, looks a nice girl, something like Fay but not as bright or quick inside, not as clever. Saw Bill Saroyan there too. He is very cordial and very restless under his youthful face. His mind, as he talks to you, is always tinkling like a tinkle-boy, but not with what he happens to be saying to you at the moment.

I need a good wife.

———————•———————

Thursday, February 22, 1940

This is the time for opening the play. Harold gave the cast a brief line run-through, but I stayed at home, sleeping, resting, lounging it out against my slowly constricting nerves. Restless, finally, I jumped into the roadster and rode out to Sunnyside to take Bill and Lee to dinner. I chattered away, quite calm, really, to that peculiar point of indifference which comes from having done all that one can do in a situation. We rode into New York and had dinner across the street from the theatre, at Sardi's. A lot of the people who are going across to the show were eating dinner there—it was like running the gauntlet. Stella Adler was there with a party, smoke-eyed and neurotic—usually when you are dying she is more dramatic about the event than you are! Finally I pushed my way through a lot of well-wishing people and went over to the theatre. The cast was in fine shape, quietly making up in their own rooms; no noise, no excitement backstage, things routine and orderly.

The audience was no better or worse than the usual opening night crowd. If anything they were an edge more respectful. Harold I had met outside the theatre for a moment—he was white and tired and was going to see a musical comedy, true to his habit of never attending an opening. I, on the other hand, get a kind of perverse spiteful pleasure from attending an opening. I saw none of the critics but shook hands with several friends.

The performance of the play was tip-top—the cast had never been better. The play suffered from what had always been wrong with it because of a certain lack in the direction—a lack of clear outlining of situations, a lack of building up scenes, a certain missing in places of dramatic intensity. But none of these things was enough to do vital harm to a beautiful show, smooth, powerful and yet tender, fresh, moving, and touching, with real quality in all the parts. But I could see during the first act that the audience was taking it more seriously than it deserved; and I knew that the old thing was here again—the critics had come expecting a *King Lear*, not a small delicate play. It all made me very tired, but at the end I thought to myself that it didn't matter, for the show was more or less what I intended; it was lovely and fresh, no matter what the critics said. And I knew, too, that if another and unknown writer's name had been on the script, there would have been critical raves the next day.

People surged backstage after the curtain—they all seemed to have had a good time. There were the usual foolish remarks from many of them—"Enjoyable, but I don't know why," etc., etc. Also a good deal of insincere gushing from a lot of people who would like nothing better than to stick a knife in your ribs, God knows why!

I invited some people down to the house for a drink. Along came the Eislers, Kozlenkos, Bette, Julie [John] Garfield, Boris Aronson, old Harry Carey and his wife, Morris and Phoebe later, Harold, Aaron Copland and Victor [Kraft], Bobby Lewis and his Mexican woman, etc., etc. We drank champagne, Scotch when the wine ran out, talked, smoked, filthied up the house, listened to some music. Then they went and I dropped into bed, dog-tired, unhappy, drunk, knowing what the reviews would be like in the morning. In and out I slept, in and out of a fever—all of modern twentieth-century life in one day and a night.

Friday, February 23, 1940

The biggest shock I have experienced since the auto crash in Mexico a year ago was the reviews of the play today. Perhaps it was the serious lack of sleep which kept me so calm and quiet. I wanted to send the *Times* man a wire telling him I thought his notice stupid and insulting, but I gave up that idea after a while. Equally distressing to me was the attitude at the office, an ugly passivity. They are quite inured there to the humdrum commercial aspect of doing a play this way—close if the notices are bad.

My feelings were and are very simple. I felt as if a lovely delicate child, tender and humorous, had been knocked down by a truck and lay dying. For this show has all the freshness of a child. It was Boris A. who called the turn. He said, "This show is very moving to me, a real artwork, but I don't think they will get its quality—it is not commercial."

In the morning I cashed fifteen thousand dollars worth of the baby bonds I hold. I thought to spend it on advertising, to keep the show open, etc., but by the time I finished at the office in the afternoon it was easy to see the foolishness of that; the show costs almost ten thousand a week to run.

So, friend, this is the American theatre, before, now, and in the future. This is where you live and this is what it is—this is the nature of the beast. Here is how the work and delight and pain of many months ends up in one single night. This is murder, to be exact, the murder of loveliness, of talent, of aspiration, of sincerity, the brutal imperception and indifference to one of the few projects which promise to keep the theatre alive. And it is murder in the first degree—with forethought (perhaps not malice, perhaps!), not second or third degree. Something will have to be done about these "critics," these lean dry men who know little or nothing about the theatre despite their praise of the actors and production. How can it happen that this small handful of men can do such murderous mischief in a few hours? How can it be that we must all depend on them for our progress and growth, they who maybe drank a cocktail too much, quarreled with a wife, had indigestion or a painful toe before they came to see the play—they who are not critics, who are insensitive, who understand only the most literal realism, they who should be dealing in children's ABC blocks? How can the audience be reached directly, without the middleman intervention of these fools?

I think now to write very inexpensive plays in the future, few actors, one set; perhaps hire a cheap theatre and play there. Good or bad, these "critics" must never be quoted, they must not opportunistically be used. A way must be found to beat them if people like myself are to stay in the theatre with any health and love. Only bitterness results this way, with no will or impulse for fresh work. The values must be sorted out and I must see my way clearly ahead, for I mean to work in the American theatre for many years to come.

I have such a strong feeling—a lovely child was murdered yesterday. Its life will drag on for another week or ten days, but the child is already stilled. A few friends will remember, that's all.

————————•————————

Sunday, March 3, 1940

More than a week has passed since I last wrote in this journal. I have no heart to sum up the week—it has been one of blind fury for me, with a hard tautness of nerves. I am still smarting from this strange so-called critical drubbing which I took at the hands of the reviewers. Everything they wrote was beside the point. We answered them a little, I in an article in the Saturday *World-Telegram*, Harold in an article in today's *Times*, an article which I'm using for the published version of the play.

The pain of the past week has been a double one for me. On one side are the reviews and the really irresponsible men who wrote them; and on the other side is my profound dissatisfaction with Harold's direction of the play and the general condition of the Group at present. Harold must lessen the gap between his first-rate critical perceptions and production intentions with a play of mine, and what he finally produces on the stage. There is something positively weird and ununderstandable about his inability to work into a production the brilliant ideas with which he starts rehearsals. For instance, he starts with an idea that Steve Takis is a Pierrot and must be played that way. It finally ends up with Gadget Kazan getting brilliant notices for a clumsy, brutal, clodhopperish performance of the part. In truth Gadget is giving a good performance in this play. But wherever he is "good" the play is bad, for he is not playing the characterization but himself, and that is not Steve Takis. The rest of the production is the same way, heavy and sonorous; the actors, with a few exceptions, are torturing to death a few delicate deft lines. The only ones who are playing in the style of the script are Sandy [Sanford] Meisner and Jane Wyatt. The rest are so "profound" that they are boring.

Al Lewin flew in with his entourage to see the play. He was dissatisfied, as above, with the production, but he expressed delight that the script was exactly what he thought it. Al and I had a few talks about the movie and I begin to see headaches ahead. Al, despite a certain gentleness and sensitivity, is just as much a Hollywood man as a Mayer or a Zanuck.

No, I have no patience to write anything here. I am restless and squirming all over. Last Sunday Bette and I went out to Luther and Sylvia's farm. Sylvia saw the show and inveighed against the production for two hours. I couldn't agree with her because of the spirit from which she talks—she is against the Group and all that it stands for, and she is turning Luther against himself as a young growing artist by showing him how foolish he is to remain in the Group without sufficient financial gain, etc., etc. It is not difficult to turn Luther against his best self, for he is only half an artist, inclined to be weak-willed, always looking for support and a steel wrist to guide him. He wants money and obvious respectability; he wants "advancement" and a high place in the theatre, but he does not want to work hard as an artist, but would rather look for comfort and accommodation on all sides. Sylvia gives Luther comfort and accommodation—things which he particularly must eschew—and simultaneously she gives him death in small doses. She is not at all a bad girl, but her daring and youth are spent and she is on her first real spree of nest-building—even nest-building can assume the characteristics of a spree! Luther falls in with all her plans because she makes her plans seem his plans. In the meantime Sylvia's mother is cannily and bitterly watching everything from the sidelines. She is shrewd and acquisitive but puts a look of contemptuous placidity on her face. She tries to appear to be saying, "It is all for the best—everything will work out fine," but in reality she is saying to herself, "Fools who understand nothing about life! To me they don't listen, me who knows through experience." But the truth is that she is an ignorant woman who knows only how to squeeze a dollar until it screams. From time to time she will almost furtively tell you how much she has done for her daughter's life, and she will let you know that even now Sylvia takes her into her confidence, that Sylvia does nothing without consulting her. Her whole implication is that but for her, her daughter would be nothing, on the rocks, long ago gone to the dogs of ruin.

And into this nest has fallen Luther. The most living thing out on their farm was a litter of eight puppies born to their two Airedales. I'm thinking of taking one if and when I decide I can take care of a dog. Some friend must throw up a few danger flares in front of Luther. I want to do it, but don't know how. During this coming week, due to the dissatisfaction of the actors and myself about the Group, we are going to have a meeting or two. We must all come to a decision about what we want the Group Theatre to be. Luther will be at these meetings and I want most carefully to watch and sound him. On the basis of that I will know what to say to him. Right now he is so busy justifying his new life that every little situation offers him an opportunity to sound off. The errors of Harold's direction, for instance, are proving to him that his new course of life is the right one. Sylvia, of course, is right with him. One morning they will both wake up dead; at least he will, for there is too much talent there for him not to realize its demise at some future date.

Don't ask me to write here clearly about myself and the failure of *Night Music*. I am much too confused. In the meantime I took over last week's losses, between three and four thousand. For this coming week we have taken ads which announce the closing. Losses will be another three or four, I imagine.

In the midst of all this I began rereading Stendhal, *The Charterhouse of Parma*. I learn much from him and am entertained greatly. He offers, by the way, an absolutely indispensable picture of his times for an understanding of Beethoven. B. has a great deal in common with Stendhal heroes; so have I, so has many a modern middle-class youth a hundred years later. Class lines are very well drawn in Stendhal too. The issues which agitated the surface of that life are all written out and explained by S. [Stendhal]. Haydn, for instance, wore a powdered wig and Beethoven did not. That seems a small trifle, but read S. and you find that wearing one's own hair unpowdered was the sure sign of the radical of the day, etc., etc.

At the moment, because of this production catastrophe, I have no direction, only confusion. My one desire is to get out and away from this painful treading of water. Also, I am torn between my friendship for Harold and loyalty to my own development as a writer. Harold no longer helps me, rather hinders me. And no friendship can help me excuse the lamentable bungling of my last two scripts under his hands. You must learn to speak the most important things in your mind, not the unimportant but easy and comfortable ones. You have a despised weakness this way—change it, fix it, make it better!!!

But this horrible experience has not been all dead loss and waste. No, I learned a few indelible (!) items from this production. One is to never never trust an American audience to understand a character whose psychology is in any way involved. Absolutely indispensable to *Night Music* was what is nicely enough called in Hollywood "a rooting interest." This had to be aroused on Steve's behalf in the audience by very clearly stating to them at the opening, "This boy is the hero, I want you to know that he is a nice boy; like him, laugh at him, don't take him too seriously." Without this greased slide into the play an average audience in this country (not Europe) is able to relax and sit back and enjoy the play. An American audience wants everything clearly explained and labeled before a scene starts. Otherwise they will not hear a line of the scene and they will complain that the play is confused and unclear. Nor, once you have shown them the type, must a character indulge in "unpredictable" behavior. That was the trouble for them with *Rocket to the Moon*. I showed them familiar types but their end behavior was not familiar at all. For this reason they said the first half of the play was brilliant, but the second half was confused. The second half was not confused at all, but it contained MY conception of the behavior and meaning of the familiar types. It was the conception which they could not follow, would not or could not take. Ibsen had this same trouble. In fact, I seem to remember that this is what Shaw's essay on Ibsen is about. I must reread it. But right now I know that Ibsen overcame this problem in a rich craft way. *A Doll's House* and others will bear rereading and study. I can remember that the way he leads up to Nora's final act makes you accept the final act, unconventional as it was at the time. That is what I must learn to do. Even at that, my audience will not accept the unconventional point of view, for they understand, with that intuitive sense that all audiences have, that what I am saying is really opposed to them and their interests as respectable citizens of society. The freezing of a wealthy benefit audience at a first performance of *Paradise Lost* I can never forget! Yes, great craft cunning is necessary and you are not working enough on it.

Now one beautiful thing this past week was a boyhood sense of the seasons of the year which suddenly came upon me. It gave me a deep feeling to sense the winter going and spring rains coming. It is March now and wind and rain is here and the rightness of it makes me feel very good, just as it did when I was a boy. I would be missing a good deal to give up the imminent spring by going south or to California now.

Last night we went to hear some ballad singers at a benefit given for the Sharecroppers Union. Leadbelly sang—what a man!—and a new young fellow named Woody [Guthrie] made a fine impression. It was an evening very well spent. Will Geer was the emcee, with Aunty Molly Jackson helping. She is a severely limited old woman, despite her background, and I would not trust her too far.

It has been raining for two days. Warm March rain, warm in feeling but cold in fact as wires and poles are coated with ice. Warm to me, for it is the beginning of spring and I hope a useful healthy spring! There is so much work to be done, so much work oh work work and use of the self in earnest sincere useful work!

———•———

Tuesday, March 5, 1940

Yesterday and today, as during the past week, find me with a very tired body and a confused mind. The nerves are stretched out of shape and length and all I can do is sit back quietly while the nerves slowly relax back to order and silence. All sorts of contradictory impulses take charge of me . . . and I let them charge themselves to death, mostly in the silence of this house, although I did do the round of nightclubs with Len Lyons last night and went to bed at dawn.

But one feeling is very clear in my mind: I must have it out with Harold Clurman about the future course of the Group Theatre; and about his directorial relationship to my own plays. This I started to do tonight, when we met at Barbetta's for dinner. After a few false starts, I was able to express myself quite clearly. What I was looking for, I said, was a Group Theatre setup in which *we* made the circumstances as much as possible.

It seemed to me, I said, that some few circumstances, such as excessive union wages and strictures (a very curious evil, but resulting from the whole social system, not merely from the unions), we could not remake. But other than those few, I went on, I expected and intended to force the New York Theatre to adapt itself to us rather than to continue adapting ourselves to it. This is to be done by real planning and foresight, by hard work, by constant thought and practice. It is no longer, I said, my intention to buck Broadway in terms of *its* values and standards.

Harold answered all this with a flow of energy which seemed to me to come from relief on his part. Apparently, it seemed to me, he thought I was going to talk about our personal relationship, which, by the way, I did not do this night. He agreed with what I said but adjured realism, adding that help from the left was no better than help from the right. Since I had not brought up the question of lefts or rights, I didn't listen to that part of his conversation but went ahead insistently on my own line. To this he brought up the question of a certain lack of line in some of our people. I assured him that in my opinion insincerity and lack of line were almost exclusively the property of Luther Adler and no other single member of the Group I could think of, excepting possibly Lee Cobb; also, I pointed out to him signs of real growth in people like Morris Carnovsky—they are now ready to assume mature responsibility for their individual actions within the Group whole.

That was where we left the discussion and went to a new documentary film made by Pare Lorentz. A worthy picture, cleanly and efficiently done, is the best I can say for it. Met Dolly Haas, German actress, and was introduced by Harold who had met her out on the coast. I kept looking at her face because she is so much the same type as Luise, but so much the same that they could be twin sisters. Type, type!—the most gifted people run to types. Although Miss Dolly seemed to me to have less flare and talent than Luise. But it was a peculiar feeling standing there, for there was such a spontaneous feeling of intimacy—things known, felt, and done together—created in me. She is the wife of John Brahm, a German stage director now working in Hollywood of whom Harold speaks so highly. Anyway, this moment of meeting this strange girl made a warm, aromatic impression on me.

Luise I think of from time to time, but never with real necessity, never with a long-term need, so to speak. It is late at night, alone here, that I think of her. Or I am in bed and I think of her, or occasionally I will have a snatch of a dream about her; or think to myself of what she looks like, her shoulders, her breasts, her legs, or the rapid manner in which she walks. And so this train draws away and only the faint high sounds are left in the night and you are standing there in the dark. What a girl, what a girl! Will she ever develop her talent? Her true genius?

Last night I was determined to start immediately on the sextette play, the one about the group of homeless men. It needs a rage and there is no reason why I can't start it on my present feeling. So I think it will be the next play. And I won't mince words in it either. It won't be what I'd call Apollonian either!

For me to go to "plot plays" is a retreat, and I must never forget it!

A young Harvard student has written a thesis on me and I am both happy and sad to say that it is the most consistently critical article ever written about me, meaning my plays. From coast to coast there is no really considered theatre criticism in the whole country. There is hardly even a literary critic worthy of the name. Edmund Wilson? Perhaps. Waldo Frank? But he is busy trying to write novels.

The admirable unhappy Beethoven must have been a very tough man to have done what he did in his art, a very very tough man. If poor Schubert had had some of his toughness, what a miracle might the world have seen! Schnabel playing the Waldstein on records makes me think of Beethoven.

Met Sandy Meisner and Lehman Engel at Sardi's after the show tonight. They are both up to the ears with plans for a small opera company. To produce good old and new long and short operas, particularly whatever modern works they can get. Sandy envisioned it originally as a sort of studio of the Group; now he is thinking of it independently, making of it a way of escaping from the humility of the theatre and his personal problem, which is that of being a talented young man but of a continental type seldom used in American plays in any leading capacity. He used to be very intense and personal about this problem, often blamed it on the Group and Harold; but now he understands it more impersonally, for he has situated himself better in his understanding of the entire theatre and he has much more confidence in his talent. Fact: he made a great personal success in *Night Music*. Fact: he was really the one actor who caught the acting style in which the entire script should have been done and, curiously, was in each role most significant of all.

Wednesday, March 6, 1940

The neurotic tangle is just what I like in a woman—it gives color and verve and bite to the character. It gives swiftness, dart and recoil, tension, nerves, and heat. I like all that, but can't take it steadily, week in and week out, not even for a few days at a time. And that is what was lovely and sad about Luise. Of course, other things too, my own serious faults (from whose viewpoint, liar?); but these are the things I am thinking at the moment. Those things are good to have in a mistress, but not in a woman who is going to be a longtime wife and mother of children. And yet Luise was that rare woman who might have been all of them rolled into one. That rare poet's woman, that *rara avis*! But you have to be grown up for that, and secondly, that marriage is a career in itself: I am having all I can do with trying to handle the one career of playwright.

The Group Theatre tangle is not going to be controlled or fixed with fine phrases. It is going to need plenty of hard work, clarity, and discipline and control to make a real Group Theatre on top of what now exists. The actors called a meeting tonight. Their minds are amorphous, without shape or point. Their feeling is good and so are their hearts, but there is not a headpiece in the bunch. However, they are all determined that their "ideal" of the Group be worked into practice and life. How that is to be done is more than I can see at the moment. I go with them fifty-fifty, half with Harold, half with them; but all their talk of Group democracy seems to me to be so much rationalization of their vanity. Democracy in any shape or form will not give them any more artistic discipline and work on the self than they have at present; they will be just as lazy and uncritical of self as ever. I told them again what I feel, but exactly: "If you are not strong enough to stand alone, you are not strong enough to stand together." The four-hour meeting, completely pointless since what was accomplished could have been done in fifteen minutes, resulted in Bud, Morris, Jim Proctor, and myself being delegated to draw up a plan of what an ideal Group Theatre should be. We are meeting *in camera* Friday night.

I wrote the first six pages of the sextette play up until nine o'clock when Sid Benson came around. I don't think the pages are good, but it's a start. I am not much good on ideas before work, but working ahead on the typewriter brings out ideas as I go along. I'm going to stay with this and see what happens.

At the meeting I sat alongside Eleanor Lynn and thought how nice it would be to sleep with her tonight. But I was really ashamed to broach the subject.

This is an empty life, this sort of drifting living. Clarity comes to me only in hot hard flashes. I shoot ahead like a bat out of hell in those moments. But the living on both sides of the flashes is rather low and coarse, floating around, sensitive in the feeling tone but not much so in the thinking. Idiot!

———•———

Thursday, March 7, 1940

The problem of my writing, as I was discussing it with Sid Benson late tonight in Lindy's Restaurant, is one divided into three main parts. First, there is the problem of keeping in the plays a content full and progressive, radical to the extent that it reevaluates ordinary daily life around us, giving fresh insight and interpretation to familiar types, both personal and social. Next there is the problem of finding a form for this material, a form which does not exclude the richness of the material, but is as inclusive as the material itself. Finally, there is the problem of adjusting that form so that it is acceptable to a typical American audience—that is, a completely enjoyable and understand-able play from start to finish.

This is not an easy load to carry; and unfortunately no other play-wright in the English language is working in a similar field at the present time. I do not know one playwright who is even aware of the problems mentioned above or can talk of them in the simple terms outlined above. The only help I can see is in the earnest perusal of progressive writers of other days, Turgenev, Ibsen, Hauptmann, and others. I am going to look at some Americans too, Frank Norris and any others I can think of. Even old Upton Sinclair might be a useful man to study. I think, too, it might be wise to examine the old "well-made" plays, those of Pinero and Jones. Material doesn't bother me—I am teeming with ideas, characters, and hot language—but form is driving me crazy and its lack is preventing me from working, although it shouldn't. I should hit hard right through the middle!—but these goddam critics have dented me badly. But from now on I am going to hit just as I have to do, *sans* caution, with both fists. Yes, the trick is to worry after the fact of writing a play, not before, not before, not before!!!

Now I am going to work on the sextette play—Group meetings have been spoiling my working evenings—and from there (my present inclination) I'd like to go to a reworking of *The Silent Partner*. What a sweet season that would be for me next year. Then I am turning over in my mind the following rather quixotic idea: write plays under three names and so produce them, bewildering critics and enemies, for I begin to think that I have enemies around the city. Under another name than Odets a play of mine would have a better chance of enthusiastic acceptance, and the simple fact of the hocus-pocus of double or triple identity would give me a certain zest and sparkle. More about this as and when it occurs to me.

Harold called a meeting of all the Group people and the others who in one way or another have connection with the Group. He spoke in generalities—the Group and its idea would go on, etc., etc. It sounded to me as if he were generating impulse and enthusiasm chiefly in himself. Most of the people were unimpressed—he no longer has the power to make the ears prick up because the people do not believe in his ability to perform any of the ideas or work he outlines. He says we will buy and do five or six plays next year, but even that—if he could do it—would not solve any of the problems which the Group faces in the months to come.

———————•———————

Friday, March 8, 1940

I want to put this on record so that I never forget it. If I do not, in the future, trust my own instinct in the theatre, then I deserve to be hacked to pieces as is now being done to me with *Night Music*, its notices, and the fact that it is closing tomorrow night. All during the last two years I have been refusing the pleading voice of this instinct of mine, with the result that I have lost boldness and courage in relation to my plays and the presentation of them. Partly this has been Harold Clurman's fault, partly mine and the circumstances which surrounded me during the past years. From now on, TRUST YOUR OWN INSTINCTS IN THE THEATRE!

Morris, Bud, and Jim Proctor met down here with me after the show tonight. We began to examine the Group problem and not much in the way of planning was arrived at. But one thing was clear to me—we must limit our planning to what can be done, two scripts planned ahead, a low price for top seats, and an organized audience. The rest, I insist, will fall into place. The boys, on the other hand, were all for planning six productions ahead, a studio for acting training and experimental productions, revivals of new and old plays, etc., etc. Anyway, we will meet again and see what can be worked out.

I met George S. Kaufman at our theatre tonight, watching the play.

"Fancy meeting you here," he said in a sort of shy painful way. Ed Wynn was there too, enjoying the show, as he told me later. Len Lyons and wife too. Vincent Sheehan too, but he seemed a little drunk and foolish to me. Very sweet is Harold's brother, the doctor. He wags his head with great indignation, says he wishes he had a million dollars to keep the play open, and adds, "Don't you worry about this, forget it, don't worry!"

———————•———————

Saturday, March 9, 1940

When you go to bed with a plan for sleeping eight full hours and keep waking up every half hour, then you know you are an unhappy man, no matter what you try to think or do with your conscious mind. Snatches of dreams and each time waking up and looking at the clock; then note with weary amazement that only an hour has passed since you last twisted around to look at the clock.

Figaro on the radio in the afternoon, which is something in my present enraged troubled life.

What shall I say tonight? "This too shall pass"? It was impossible for me to stay at the theatre tonight, even though I planned to see the whole performance. I went to the parking lot instead, after the first act, and took comfort from the solid mechanism of my car, for which I have great respect. If you are living in this capitalist system you might as well have comfort from the respect for its best products!

I came home and put on the NBC Symphony program; for the last half-hour I've been listening to Tch.'s [Tchaikovsky] Fifth; good sounding in the ear. I am so irate that not even his emotional intensity can match mine with a few brandies behind it. Everything is in my head at the moment, Canada, Mexico, California, France, England—I am thinking of some place to go and write two or three plays; I am thinking of peppering the place with plays, all of them under different names. I am outraged, enraged, boiling with wrath, but not depressed. They make me fight, happily, fortunately. So everything is good and as it should be! But at what a monstrous cost!

What I am grateful about is that I am so alive in every part of me. The failure of this play may turn out to have been one of the most useful things that ever happened to me. I am very much alive all over and that is something! There is one thing to do. Leave town, go west or east or north or south, young man. Come back in a few weeks with a new play! Glory be!

I read that they are singing a new song in Europe this week—people sing it on the streets and it goes this way: "Wind, wind, take me away with you!"

B. came down here after the show. She drank a pint of champagne and I continued with brandy and soda and finally we arrived in the bed and bedded down good and warm. Later I woke up, sleep impossible, so prowled the other room from five till past nine, reading, drinking hot tea and milk, and feeling as enraged as before, albeit very weary.

———————•———————

Sunday, March 10, 1940

A simple day. B. slept me out, hour for hour, till five in the afternoon. All I could think of was the work ahead and she saw my feelings. So it was easy to call out the car and drive her home. A windy dusky day and evening. Stopped off at Barney Greengrass, the Sturgeon King, where I bought some wares for B., Morris C., and myself. Left B. at her doorstep and rode gaily downtown. Stopped in at Morris's, gave him his cheese, bread, and smoked butterfishes, talked a little, chiefly about a character for him in the sextette play. Phoebe came in, said that Marc Blitzstein had been furious because so few Group people showed up at his performance of his new work, *No for an Answer!*

And now, at ten in the evening, I'm here at the desk, clearing up the sextette notes. Think I'll leave town in a day or two to work, work which is better than women and better than wine!

———————•———————

Monday, March 11, 1940

You sit here like this in the still house, dawn already up at the windows, and you think that any sort of marriage is better than this solitude; and then you marry and you think any sort of solitude is better than this marriage. Where are you any way you take it?

Late this afternoon I was thinking about Fay Wray in California. Her divorced husband [John Monk Saunders], a character out of Hemingway, but much more real since he did what H. characters threaten to do, hung himself in a Florida bungalow. I wanted to telephone Fay, but I was so dead inside that nothing responded. Instead I wrote her a brief note. Later in the evening I thought about marrying her. Tasted and sensed her all around me, thought of what a home with her would be like. Her child is lovely and we would have the child together and maybe make a good life together for ourselves. She is mature, adult, a real woman, womanly in a lovely way, very loyal, beautiful. Then what am I waiting for, particularly since she will have me if I ask her? Well, I am waiting for guarantees, like any American boob with pragmatic eyes. Will it work? Will we be happy? And I am waiting, foolishly, after all these years, for the hot rich shambles of love which will never come except in my head! What I want is a woman to whom it is possible to say the Song of Solomon and mean it! Or is that what I used to want? Can you be truthful with yourself? Then say it this way: you are looking for a woman who will permit you to combine the best features of both married and single life without the woman being unhappy about it. What you want you will not give up for. You want it hot and cold, north and south. And yet and yet . . . someday you'll wake up and you will be dead, very dead. . . .

Assorted many notes on the sextette play. Intend to shortly leave town to begin actual work on it. Want, too, to have a long talk with Harold Clurman before I leave. I have not forgotten my discontents with him, and now is the time to talk about them, for they begin to well outweigh the contents.

Late at night found time and inclination to drive over to Bill's. We ate some sandwiches at his house. Lee woke up for a few moments—she went back to schoolteaching today. Later we talked of Ibsen and I was reminded of my old idea of adapting *The Wild Duck* into an anti-Nazi play. So hopped in the car and rode home and reread it. It is a possibility, but honestly I was not overstirred by the thought of the adaptation. The play is very good, of course, but the whole feeling is dated and what were once startling characters come over now almost as types, dry and spare. Of course that is one fault with most of Ibsen—his technical and constructive ingenuity finally mechanizes the inner life and spirit of the characters who begin to function for the twists and turns of the plot instead of for themselves and their psychological progression. The didactic tone, too, of the plays is annoying from time to time.

———————•———————

Tuesday, March 12, 1940

Wait, wait, be patient! Be patient, my heart! Wait with work, wait with love, wait with life! Wait, wait, stupid heart! But there is one thing to say and I am sure of it—it is not the business of an artist, particularly a young artist, to be patient and reasonable! And one of the worst mistakes of my young life has been the attempt to foist on my naturally restless and impulsive nature a regime of patience and "rational" behavior! So, if you please, you are twice an ass! (Taming you, they are all busy taming you! Tame the wild beast, the primitive, the savage! And Luise started it and she started it well!)

Luise called today from Washington where she seems to have made a fine hit in a week's showing of Shaw's *St. Joan*. She didn't say what she wanted and I didn't have the heart to talk to her. I am not in love with her, but I am not indifferent to her either—let it stand that I am unsettled with her.

Finished a rereading of Hauptmann's *Flight of Gabriel Schilling* this evening, a play which would certainly be incomprehensible to most American men. We don't act that way with a woman; either we shoot her or we drink ourselves insensible. Yet I'm not sure that our solution is not better than Schilling's. A play like that, I think, would seem to an intelligent American audience like something extremely personal to the writer; but the truth is that the experience in Europe must have been typical. I like the device of the older artist and his young mistress standing on the side through the action of the play and then, when marriage and intercourse between men and women have proven so impossible and disastrous, the side characters deciding to marry. It makes a very successful final curtain, forward-looking and optimistic, as life itself is upward-moving.

I am trying to wear myself out and can't help it. Every time I feel any sort of tension in me, immediately I do something to smash it to bits. The result is that I am tired all the time. At midnight I went over to Second Avenue for some food. Then I rode uptown and then downtown, along the waterfront, looking for a site for the sextette play. An old steam shovel and a truck trailer seemed to me interesting if one of them is placed against a ramp alongside the river, nighttime Brooklyn, and the Edison Power Plant across the river.

Earlier in the day I called Harold and found he was sick in bed with the grippe. His tone was very listless and a little embarrassed. Evidently he knows or has heard how dissatisfied I am with the show. I suggested that he reread *The Wild Duck*, for the Group could make a great impression with it. He said he wants to talk to me before I leave town, which I told him is my intention.

———————•———————

Wednesday, March 13, 1940

I am thinking now about the tone of the Group and what it has been for the last two years or so. There is one word—flabby! There is an adjective to be added—VERY flabby! The only improvement I can see creatively in any of the people is some in Gadget, some in Bobby Lewis, and a little in myself. It is curious how the personality of the director sets the tone of the entire group of people. Harold is not at all in the blame totally for this, but his conduct has been deplorable in more instances than I can remember. We have all had our Hollywood at home, right here. Lack of form, personal and artistic, lack of intention, sluggishness of the bowel, brain, and heart have been general throughout the organization. Lack of respect for each other, creative or personal, is the rule and not the exception. And of all this I have partaken of myself. The manifestations are on all sides. In a curious psychological way the people seem to be trying, by this sickness, to revenge themselves on each other, themselves and the director. This is plain to see in the rehearsal discipline and the tone in which each addresses the other. The correction of this ailment is in personal discipline for each man or woman in the Group who calls himself artist or democrat. They keep blaming Harold for this general blight, blaming it on lack of "democracy" (whatever that means). They have gone in for subtle but nevertheless genuine moral and spiritual sabotage. But already it seems to me that Harold, in a moral sense at least, has not realized at all his responsibility towards the simple souls who essentially are the Group Theatre. When they hurt him, he lashed out against them; and when they were open and receptive he filled them with half-digested abstractions, a kind of pap he manufactured out of a greedy necessity to be creative and alive. When a man cannot be a husband at home, let it be noted, he will become a husband elsewhere, in his office or on his stage.

There is another thing about Harold. He seldom plans ahead. A situation, an object or person, or a problem right before him starts reactions in him; his own reactions begin to excite him and add more fuel to the fire. Soon he is blazing and is apt to be very talented while blazing. Then it is all over and he is very exhilarated for a short period of time. After that comes another long period of hibernation. Well, he is a Russian soul in the true sense of the phrase, chaotic, erotic, and profound!

At two in the morning I rode uptown to eat at Lindy's. Met Billy Rose and his fair bride there and went across with them to their new house on Beekman Place. It is a fine sturdy house but their taste in fixtures is exactly that of the usual newly rich. Billy says he wants to live "exquisitely!" It is as exquisite as a Hollywood combination bar and restaurant.

———————•———————

Thursday, March 14, 1940

Why do I torture myself this way and bring myself to the very edge of nervous derangement? Is it because of Luise, and in some way you are trying to punish yourself or her or both of you? Do you fear to go out in the world and demand and take what you want?

Here are two possible explanations. Many times, when I wanted to hit Luise in the heat of an argument, I hit myself instead, pulled my own hair, banged my fists against the walls. This is self-infliction when you want to inflict pain or punishment on the other. One other possibility or explanation presents itself. You have certain impulses which are considered low and criminal, even by yourself. Instead of opening these impulses to public gaze you share them only with yourself. Notice that for a time you were unable to face them yourself and in the midst of these sprees you almost acted as if they were not happening. Then came a phase of belligerent acceptance, the feeling of "what about it—that's what I want to do!" When you started typing this page it was with a kind of casual air: "All right, I'll write it down, but it won't mean anything!" Now you are being rasped by your conscience. What is conscience in this case? Simply a voice from an inner source, a voice which tries to preserve in you that which is best in you. This voice is, of course, speaking with social conditioning; by which is meant moral training, etc., etc. But there is a real side to the voice. You are a talented man and every time you weaken your inner or outer, spiritual or physical life, you are weakening your talent which is still a young and developing one. Ofttimes you mention to yourself—sometimes with satisfaction, it seems—that you are in danger of falling in the swamp of your greedy senses. Well, this is it, idiot! What you have in your hands is the development or casting off of a fine second-rate talent which can be very useful and important in this world of no first-rate talents, a world where writers of good heart and goodwill are needed as never before in history. Will this writing help you, Mr. Odets? Read it again in a week, in a month.

Manny Eisenberg died today. He had a pilot take him over New York's bay in a plane. He attempts to jump out; the pilot fights him down; Manny hits him with a wrench; in the meantime the plane is rapidly approaching the water. In the end the dazed pilot creeps out of the wreck and Manny has drowned. Recently, after many neurotic hysterical years, he returned from a half-year in Mexico. He told everyone he was in fine shape, raring to go. But it was only an illusory hope before the darkest day of his life. Rest in peace, poor man.

This morning there was a review of *Night Music* in *The New Republic* by Stark Young. Now is the winter of his discontent, not mine. Mr. Young is so isolated from modern and American life that, although he vividly (critically, he thought) described the average American male in his description of Steve Takis, he complains the hero of the play is a figment of my imagination, my common and low imagination, I should add. Doubtless he sees himself as the typical American male, he whose every impulse is from a past generation and even century. And yet he is a perceptive writer, sensitive albeit involved, and twisting his curious sentence structures around his own neck until it hurts, not him but the reader. Here and there in his articles one is able to find a line not of criticism but of sensitive REACTION.

Bill Kozlenko came over for dinner and we went to the Café Royale. Anyway, on an impulse, talking about Barbirolli as a visiting faker in a class with Gogol's *Inspector General*, an idea for a farce about theatre critics came to me and I jotted it down on the tablecloth. It would be an amusing satire, but I can't promise to write it: the enjoyment of that sort of work is in conceiving the idea, not more or longer.

Then I came back to the house here to meet with Morris, Phoebe, and Bud. We are acting as a sort of committee to draft out on paper a plan for a Group setup which will work better than the Group has been working in the past few years. We did get some work done, but all through the four hours I was being surprised at the inability of the three of them to keep to a straight line. If they learn, instead, to intend [*sic*] their minds they will be better actors for it. It is no longer useful or wise to apologize for that sort of mental form, saying they are artists. It is exactly the artist who must develop form in every part of his life. Even in the work of a genius like Schubert such a lack is not always to be forgiven.

Good night. No, good morning—it is past eight in the morning of Friday.

———————•———————

Friday, March 15, 1940

Water goes to its own level, an old saying. But I did not realize till tonight how Stendhal, Delacroix, and Heine cluster in my mind as one atmosphere, one feeling, one central source of a rapport which I feel with their time. Tonight, talking, I suddenly realized with warmth and thrill that I have three great friends in the world! And from this realization, tired as I happened to be, I was comforted.

In the sextette play, the character of Sam Roberts must be left alone on the stage after a horrible scene, warming himself at the fire. He seems to be feeling the strength of the night, testing and tasting its quality. Then he must say with quiet New England dryness, "I want to

say something to you . . . God. We have our eyes on you . . . that's all."
Curtain.

Some of the essential difference between the youth of five years ago
and the young man I am now is this: I want to deeply listen—before I
wanted to tell. Now I want to listen. Not to the easy amiability of fools.
But to the simple and true ones, to the fine masters in the arts, to the
surflike sound of the rough and real masses of my countrymen. Oh,
how I want to listen.

The apathy of poor people, the apathy of the injured, the insulated,
and the damned, the apathy of the rejected, of myself, the periodic
apathy of a talent like Harold Clurman . . . all of that is a covering or
unconsciously acquired callous to mask or dim pain.

How sadly amusing it is to find in yourself that two sides fight here
and neither wins. There is the side that yearns for a worldly and
voluptuous life, and a side which tells you to sit at your desk. And
between both of those whirling busy worlds you lie, apathetic, almost
prostrated. Three long years of that!

Saturday, March 16, 1940

My sleeping and wakeful hours are confused and I don't know one
from the other. I get up at five in the afternoon and find myself at a loss,
not knowing what to do or where to go. The only things which seem
certain are several books I am reading. The newspapers are positively
distasteful to me. At seven tonight I was alone and lonely. I called E. L.
on the phone. She was home alone, distracted, nervous, unhappy, for
personal and for career reasons. She came over and soon went to bed
and it was very nice. It was very lovely and sensible, the whole
evening. She is a good child, very gifted from her nerves up. She went
home and I had drunk too much sherry. I sent over for some food, ate,
and got in bed and read an essay by Stefan Zweig on Stendhal, not
good, journalistic. His essay on Casanova, which I read the night
before, gave me several good ideas, particularly for a play about a
modern sort of Casanova to be played by a fellow like Franchot Tone. It
is not the great lover element which interests me at all; the element of

adventurer, swindler, fake prince among American aristocracy, etc. is where the play lies.

A good idea might be to sleep in two shifts, four hours now and four hours then, with eight wakeful hours between each sleep.

I have a good title for a play—*Perpetual Motion*.

Sunday, March 17, 1940

It is early evening. I am so depressed I could jump out the window. All these Group people are so rude and discourteous, so flabby and apathetic. That can be excused only in great artists, not in very minor ones. Again and again these people, Harold Clurman very much included, disappoint me and let me down. I make great sacrifices for them, assume responsibilities way beyond my capacities, go out of my way to be kind and thoughtful with them. And I get for those things exactly what I have always received—blank, blank, blank! They are all so slothful, so busy with themselves on their minds—one would think it was an extraordinary colony of bee geniuses we have here. Would there be happiness in some other sort of theatre? No, not much more, but at least I would never be open to this sort of pain.

Half of my languid fever of the past few weeks, I discover, comes from the repression of my feelings about the bungling of *Night Music*. Why the hell should I repress what I have to say, what I wanted to say, and will continue to want to say? All this gets me is a mouthful of dust and a thunder sheet for a heart. I sit here, believe it or not, like a juicy melon and they all keep coming at me with a spoon or a fork or both! I am enraged by all sides, the critics and theatre conditions below, the Group personalities above. Now is the time for all good Odets to come to the aid of his Clifford!

The average American is afraid to know himself. It is a disagreeable sensation, looking in the mirror and seeing a baboon!

The pillows are so heavy, so heavy!

The bad reviews of *Night Music* threw me back on myself, but that was good, that is very good, that is as it should always be! But the self *independent*, resolute! Let there be light, an inner light, a personal light, a light which touches unconscious negative plates of the plays to come with exactly the correct intensity. Keep away from those sensitive negative plates all light from the outside, but all! Later there will always be time to respond to the outside beams.

———————•———————

Monday, March 18, 1940

Two hours of sleep and a dream out of which I must struggle like the very devil. A curious light is glowing in the room. I put on white glasses and it is green. I put on green glasses and it is white. This seems very peculiar to me. I think I had better get out of the room quickly, for I feel something horrible is going to happen. I make for the door and suddenly I am thrown to the floor and pinioned there. I struggle, simultaneously saying to myself, "This is a dream—take it easy—just coast out of it." And then I wake up and can't return to sleep. Four hours, two hours, I don't sleep more.

I am pretty bad inside, but a sure sign of growth is that I understand these periods now when they happen. I am learning to think, that is why, a very painful process it seems. I am a romantic, enthusiastic, and moral idealist, like any young Stendhal hero. The so-called practical and realistic world has impinged itself upon my consciousness. The nature of the beast comes clearer to me each week, and one must actively take arms against it or be corrupted into a twisting cynical rascal of a diplomat. What a shock to march up a hill, banner in hand, and suddenly look down on that Hollywood in the valley! The first impact can stun you for life!

Anyway, a conscious choice in all these matters lies before me. [Danish drama scholar Georg] Brandes says that some of what shocks Hamlet into inactivity is this very discovery of deceit and treachery in the world. I believe that is true. Every day I discover myself and my problems more. The days are almost over when I was pushed into one thing after another without knowing what was happening. The focus widens out, but then, of course, it is not so intense. Van Gogh with a wider focus is out of the question. And this, by the way, was one-half of his problem too. Also Nijinsky's. This is the personal half of their problem; the social half is another thing. In each of their lives there is a beautiful play. Why not make one of the characters in the sextette play such a man who, once he understands what the world demands, drops it and becomes a tramp.

Stendhal, growing into the world, kept asking: "Is this all?" How well I understand that question! "Is this all?" Those in the high and responsible places in his day were no better at close range than the same people today.

I could be a better and broader man if I were not known, if I could wear a mask or change my name.

Wednesday, March 20, 1940

Yesterday I decided to break out of New York no matter what my state of mind was and is. The night before I had dinner with Harold Clurman and told him, in part at least, what I thought of his production.

Anyway, I sat in the big car and rode to Philadelphia to my Aunt Esther's house. My Uncle Rossman's plight moves me very much. He has been having an occasional seizure which has all the earmarks of epilepsy. As we sat in the kitchen talking he had right before my eyes an attack of another sort, perhaps related to the other. There was a temporary aphasia with an almost complete speech block. My aunt took this whole thing very lightly; my uncle tried to talk in answer to the questions or remarks made—it was as if he had awakened out of sleep and was not quite awake or aware of what was going on around him. In a few minutes he was quite normal, albeit brooding. My aunt complained to me that he refused to take medicine or pills or the doctor's advice. He astringently shut her up, although she is not one to easily be shut up. When I remonstrated rather mildly about his attitude he said he knew more about his own condition than any doctor. What he needed, he said, was steady work, the old ability to earn a few dollars and keep his self-respect, not doctors and not medicine. He tries, he said, not to think about these things, but the very sight of me sitting there in the kitchen had started him thinking of his hopeless condition despite his best and otherwise intentions. Then, too, he is worried and ashamed for his son, Ben, who is, as he said, a beautiful boy, raised and born in this country, and now he is working on the streets. I thought he meant streetcleaning, but it turns out that he is digging ditches for fourteen dollars a week. My old-man uncle is a real soul, a real heart, a poet in the old and rare sense. He sat there singing old Jewish dirges to himself. He is not taken too seriously around the house—my aunt and cousin laugh and poke fun at him. But he rocks himself into a silent sharp peering edge from which he emerges occasionally to make some caustic remark about the state of the world and what he would do to Hitler if the both of them sat down at a table. In a modern world of autos and highways there is something outlandish about this man who has not been five miles away from his home in thirty years. He is a simple peasant of very modest tastes and appetites; whatever is modern he eschews with scornful dispatch. Today I made him drive over with me to see my sister Genevieve in Camden. It was the first time he had been across the Camden Bridge since it was built, about fifteen years ago. He has an idea of opening a fruit stand in a butcher shop. The main thing he has learned by now, he said, was to keep down the expenses. He needed the sum of one hundred dollars to start this business. I gave him the money in new bills and he gave it to my aunt to keep till he begins next week. But he won't make a go of it. My aunt said he trusts everyone, once gave a woman forty dollars' worth of fruit and vegetables over a period of weeks, then let her settle for a dollar eighty-five. Now that same woman, my aunt says, has just gone to Florida for a vacation! They jibe and jeer at each other, my aunt and uncle, but it is all done with an edge of good feeling.

My aunt and uncle proudly escorted me out to the car when I left. All their neighbors seem to know who I am and are very curious about my appearance and personal property. Sons of the grocery man across the way examined the auto for almost an hour last night. Last night my uncle could not rest when the garage sent over a man to pick up the car—he was sure the man was a thief and would never bring the car back.

I rode through the streets in this Philadelphia, in our America. What a sad place, what an impoverished city. Rabbit warrens are more cheerful and admit more light. Whenever people talk to me of the incomparable advantages of America, I think of all these broken middle-class lives which I know so well. I think of the fright and the dark rooms in which all these people move. But here we talk of our material advantages over those who live in other countries, never saying that the European, no matter how poor, has a whole inner life built around the facts of his poverty and its acceptance. Here there is only shame and regret, resignation, bitterness, frustration, and an all-abiding sense of inadequacy and anxiety. Here they keep muttering to themselves, "Hopeless, hopeless," and are degraded. In Europe they say, "This is what it is," and they work within the form of poverty and manage to make good rich happy lives for themselves. To meet a happy person in America is to usually meet a person of little or no power, of limited imagination, sensitivity, or perception. From this generalization I exclude certain types of master craftsmen, those who have mastered their work no matter how humble, who have established mastership over materials, things, wood, machines, whatever it may be.

At my sister's house in Camden I came across a photo of Luise in a low-cut evening gown. It moved me very much, depressed me, moved me.

I had my uncle take me around the corner and show me, on George Street, the house in which I was born thirty-three years ago. The house, which reminded me of the sort of place in which Betsy Ross made the first American flag, that house looked down at me and I looked up at it—a draw: neither of us was impressed!

Thursday, March 21, 1940

I forgot to say that last night I decided to stay over here another day for a mammoth concert given for the benefit of China. [Leopold] Stokowski, [Eugene] Ormandy, and a half-dozen eminent soloists are appearing and playing. And I did not mention that yesterday, because of the leap year, was the first day of spring and a worthy day indeed.

Talking about normal hours: I've been up since nine and it is now almost three in the afternoon, but I am almost ready for sleep. I can't adjust myself to these daytime hours.

For a long time a certain quiet air, calm and restful, has appealed to me in connection with Philadelphia. I have been half thinking about the possibility of getting a small apartment here, a hideaway in which to retreat for thinking and working. I walked around for an hour this morning looking at places, almost tempted to stop here instead of moving south in the car. I think I'll let the idea go this time, but it will bear serious thought in the future.

The living, as I say, is not restless here, and it is inexpensive; I might even be able to keep a place here as well as in New York. This idea interests me.

———————•———————

Friday, March 22, 1940

An interesting twenty-four hours, interesting in the head, which I suppose is the way I find life most interesting always. Perhaps cutting off all my hair has sharpened my wits during the last few days, for consistently I find myself enjoying what is going on in my head. Or, to be serious, it might be that the failure of *Night Music* has thrown me back to myself for the perusal and consideration of myself. The failure, by the way, is all to the good; I've known it for the past two weeks. Now for steady work on a new play and I shall find myself a "happy" man before I know it!

My Uncle Rossman, speaking of his troubles the other day, said: "Don't you know, my dear sonny, that everything combines together?" I neglected to mention yesterday that my aunt and uncle sit in their front room every night and listen to radio programs for several hours without once turning the machine off. Best of all he likes the news broadcasts, he said. Every time he hears of more people being killed in Europe he begins to talk to himself as he rocks himself to and fro like a mourner in a synagogue. Mr. Goodman, the star boarder in their house, very particular about his eggs and tea in the morning, is a shirtcutter by trade. A writer looks at your face, a cobbler at your shoes. Naturally Goodman looks at your shirts. As I shook his hand in greeting he said, "Three-and-a-half dollars."

What with all the discussion of Stokowski because of the concert for China, in Philadelphia last night I decided to meet him. In the late afternoon I sent him a note by messenger and in a half hour he had called me on the telephone. He was very cordial, asked how I was, what I was doing, how I was feeling—and it was impossible to get a word of answer back to him. I told him I was going to the concert and he suggested that I meet him backstage at the end. Then I went to the Leofs for dinner and they were all very nervous there because they have done most of the arranging of the concert. Maddie had a ticket for me, but it seemed that several of the boxholders had heard I was coming and wanted me to sit in their boxes. I finally wound up in Mrs. Ormandy's box, much against my will. Mrs. O. was not interested in Mr. O.—I kept wondering why she had invited me. Politics probably.

There was an intermission in which Mrs. O. and I went into the lobby for a cigarette. Again there was this curious lack of interest in me, but like a good hostess she quickly turned the conversation into something on which I am supposed to be an expert, acting. Stokowski then played Debussy, *Afternoon of a Faun*, and I suppose he played it better than any living man can play that sort of music, not excepting Koussevitzky. Then Ormandy conducted the "Love and Death" music from *Tristan*. (I yield to no one my dislike of Wagner, even *Tristan*!) Then came Feuermann in the Bloch Mess [Mass], which he played valiantly. But the performance of the evening belonged to Szigeti, truly a great violinist. He gave the Chausson "Poème" great distinction, like you might cut something out of a silver alloy, always firm, neat to the edge of sharpness, ease, mobility, and great sense throughout. For my money the best violinist living. He has what Heifetz pretends to have, true elegance and simplicity masking thousands of hours of hard work. I am talking of that Vermeer simplicity which makes white a living color. Furthermore, I never did before see a man whose instrument seemed so much a physical projection of his own body: the violin stuck out of his chin as if it were a continuation of the jawbone, a sort of extraordinary horn taken for granted, just as a unicorn's horn seems to belong to its head.

Then Stokowski backstage where there are some very unusual scenic effects. All of the musicians, for instance, undress, change clothes, chat, and pack their instruments there. The bass fiddles are apparently not taken home by the players, but encased and left flat on the floor where they look like so many coffins or mummy cases.

Stokowski. I wanted very much to like and admire him, but my sense of him from his conducting was the correct feeling. He conducted me to an empty dressing room while he flirted with some middle-aged woman and gave her his phone number. Of course he is a coquette, but manly, in a continental way. Blond or gray, I could not tell what color his hair was; but it is sparse and carefully brushed around to make it look like more. The face is self-indulgent; not exactly weak, but not exactly strong either. He makes an attempt at proving to you that he is personally very interested in you (as later with three different doormen), but of course there is no real connection with you. The whole thing is a form, the trick of which he learned many years ago. All of it bores him very much; even his democratic intermingling with the orchestra men, which I saw later, is a form which bores him, although he plays at it in a way which might seem convincing to an imperceptive person.

What he made of me I can't say, except that he was not very anxious to know anything about me. But he was anxious to impress upon me his own feelings about anything I might mention. I said something about the failure of my last play and he filled my ears with a talk on how necessary failure is to the artist. Then he excoriated people in general, when I mentioned the word form, for not acting as they really felt. "People might want to be happy at a funeral," he said, "because there is wine in the blood that morning. But they put on a mournful face instead because it is the form, the thing to do, etc., etc." Then I used the expression "second-rate artist" and he quickly caught me up. I explained that Mozart and Beethoven were first-rate in the sense that I was using the phrase. But no, said he, he was beginning to have a different sense of Beethoven. The last period of Beethoven he thought dry and intellectual, but of course Mozart was a different question, although he would not like to be quoted on this because then people would say, "Oh Beethoven up there and this little man (meaning himself) down there!"

———————•———————

Sunday, March 24, 1940

Continued in Chapel Hill, North Carolina

By this time Stokowski was getting bored with sitting in the dressing room, and I was less uneasy. Let us, he suggested, go to a party they are giving for some of the orchestra people. At the Metropolitan Club, a typical small-town "art club," he introduced me to several women, again typical. It struck me that not one person there could or would contradict a thing Stokowski might do or say. So bored, so bored that man was; and yet he made nice remarks about the food, about the gathering, about the people, and under all of it was an edge of contempt, of strained playfulness which might at any moment come out as an explosion.

I was introduced to the Philadelphia consul of the Chinese government. He was typical, too-small smiling, anxious to please. With me he
was quite impressed and kept bringing people over for introductions
all evening. There was a pestiferous lady under forty who had years
before taken a shine to me at some party in New York: amazement,
amazement that I remembered her and her name! If, to tell the truth, I
had not been so busy watching the people I'd have been more bored
than Stokowski. By this time I had introduced myself rather timidly to
Szigeti, saying that I was a writer and not a musician, but it was not
necessary for he knew all about me. This surprised and pleased me.
We were walking towards the coatroom—Stokowski had asked me to
come with him to some musician's house for a drink—"real Siberians,"
he kept assuring me, as if it had some special meaning. Szigeti's mind
was somewhere else as we went for our coats. Finally I realized that he
had been trying to get a private word into Stokowski's ear all night. I
discreetly left the coatroom, waiting outside, while poor Szigeti tried
to arrange some further concert business. It struck me as rather
pathetic that so fine an artist had to be kissing the hand of Stokowski in
a coatroom, but that is just what he was doing.

On the street I found myself with Stokowski and a cellist from his
orchestra, a man whom I immediately disliked for the way he "put
himself out" for the older man, promising him all sorts of exotic wines
and liquors at his home, promising him everything up to his wife in
bed and maybe that. An ambitious narrow face which could be very
haughty with people below him, and I didn't like it. At his house—a
penthouse at the Drake—were Feuermann and his wife and Heifetz
and his wife, this the cellist who used to be with the Kolisch Quartet. I
reminded him that we had met before—Luise Rainer's husband, I told
him. Ah, ah, oh, oh, with his sour jealous wife joining in.

I am sitting next to Stokowski, but not in an hour does one of the
others in the room look at me. It is all Stokowski, hanging on his lips for
the next work, quickly turning the talk to wherever he wants to take it.
This town? Beautiful town. That town in Poland? Ah yes, wonderful
city. Oh yes, certainly, cer-tain-ly! His sister in Russia? She would love
you! By now Stokowski is making all sorts of underhand lewd remarks
to the women: "A zipper on your dress?" Oho! Hee-haw, ha-ha! He
wants a woman to sleep with, but no one pretends that they understand his meaning. He even rings me into the circle, saying that Odets
is not an innocent man by any means. The host plies him with drinks,
try this, open that bottle, the other one. . . . Finally Feuermann is the
only one with courage enough to say they must go. Two of the women

are falling asleep on the couch. Stokowski wants apple strudel but there is no apple strudel. But next time, next time! But by a stroke of genius, who should have apple strudel but this young man, down in my car, a present from my aunt. I give him the strudel, he gives me his phone number, we say we will meet again in New York, etc., etc., and Heifetz takes Stokowski home in his car. I hurry up to my room and relieve my distended bladder. So ends an evening with a great conductor.

His views about music are exactly what one hears when he conducts. Music, he says, consists of big blocks or chunks of sound contrasted with each other. He is antimeaning or significance in art. When I said to him that his conducting of any piece meant something, that it meant himself which I could clearly discern in whatever he played, he answered, "Yes, the personality expresses itself."

When he spoke at the beginning of the evening about the necessity of failure for the artist, I had the distinct impression that he was talking about himself. For he is very self-conscious, if not self-derogatory. "Art," he said, "is like a high mountain which one keeps climbing with never the top in view. An artist reaches a plateau and thinks it is the top. He rests there and stays there for the remainder of his life, but it is not the top at all."

A bored unhappy man with a quality of great yearning about him, which can be heard in any piece of music he plays. And yet there must have been something very idealistic about him in his youth. His personal character has much in common with those of the composers he plays best, Wagner and Tchaikovsky.

A final word about Stokowski. He proves to me a point which at last is clarified in my own mind. A form which does not fit one's content is intolerable to the creative personality, whether in work or in daily life. You cannot live in old forms, or work in them, when your life has brought you ahead to a new point. Try better to keep a child in last year's coat. It is simply an intolerable contradiction which must be resolved consciously in order to bring the life and/or work up to a higher level of creativity. Otherwise the spirit dies a death and sterility is the only outcome. Beethoven is the only man or artist I can think of at the moment who never once faltered in this difficult task: he was a fanatic! He hacked and chopped, twisted and tortured, but he did not EXCLUDE a drop of his experience from his work; in each phase of his life he found the right form for an increasingly higher and deeper experience. That is Beethoven's final lesson, if an artist may teach a lesson. Life is a series of rebirths, year after year more difficult, never to be refused, but always to be worked with, coped with, understood, used and used by, never going back, but always moving ahead and higher. Which is what Beethoven did. Easy words to write, these! Why is Brahms an inferior artist, all other things equal? Because his last period is given over to "resignation" and acceptance. He did not have that same passion of the HEART which was Beethoven's. That is why any last Brahms work is child's play compared to any last Beethoven work.

Beethoven's work, it must be said, represents the deepest expression of man's faith in life which has ever been written by a man. No artist before or since expressed so deeply the will to live and accept every fact of life, to be both figuratively and literally crucified for his belief that the way to conquer life is to live without ever once relenting or letting up in that living. It was Beethoven who understood the passion of Christ, not Bach, for he lived it and experienced it while Bach heard about it in a sort of secondhand way. What some writer once said is true: Bach sacrificed the Church, Beethoven sacrificed himself. His last quartets, a record of his sacrifice (or crucifixion), are more moving to the modern man than any page in the Bible.

Stopped over at a melancholy inn called the Princess Anne at Fredricksburg, Virginia. I run across this interesting item in the papers, ad for a new movie: "THAT FIRST KISS! It's a sizzler—it's a scorcher—it's a whizz! It makes her leave her slaphappy home, give her pigtails a permanent, and jump off the dock—all in twelve delirious hours!"

This is this past Friday evening I am talking about. Other spiritual items in the news are that his brother has erected a fourteen-foot statue of Huey Long on the lawn of the capital. Then there is the story of the woman who lifted the American press to seventh heaven. She announced she was expectant of quintuplets. Immediately a fund was created for her, she was given free and wonderful prenatal care. The world has been beating a path to her doorway for several days—her husband and herself have already been photographed in every position but the marital one. Yesterday the bubble burst: only one baby is to be born, according to the latest X-rays. The woman has been dropped like a hot plate loaded with veneral diseases. What interests me about this case is the possibility of a satiric play on American life. Into the files with it!

I was told of a case in Philadelphia. A girl in her early teens was awarded a framed print for honor work in school. The child refused to accept it but burst into tears when the picture was finally forced on her. The teacher was quite indignant and impatient with the girl. It was finally revealed that the girl is living in one room with three families sharing it by putting up sheets as walls. The girl lived in the section which has only sheets for walls and there was no place to hang the picture.

It seems to me that this sort of violence, so raw and primitive, could happen only in America: a man in Colorado wanted to kill himself. He stood on a box of dynamite and lit the fuse. There was only a partial explosion so the man crawled over to another box, his left leg almost blown off but still dangling, and began to light another fuse but was stopped by friends.

Driving in the car for long stretches makes me think a geat deal about American life, particularly since it is expressed so vividly in signs and billboards along the road. I was thinking that when I was a boy the whole promise of American life was contained for me in Christmas cards which showed a warm little house snuggled in a snow scene by night; often little boys or girls were walking up the path of the door and carrying bundles of good things. This represented protection, a home and hearth, goodness and comfort, all things which become increasingly more difficult to attain.

One of the most exciting experiences of my boyhood was the time when we followed a young couple out to a field across the railroad tracks. We followed them cautiously, several of us, at a distance. Suddenly the pair disappeared in the field. Twenty years later I still remember the sound of the girl's voice when we finally discovered the pair had stretched out in a small pit. She was saying in a low piteous voice, "Max, stop, Max, please stop, stop it, Max". She stopped with the voice, but he continued with what he was doing. We crept away, awed, scornful, and, I understand now, delighted. We were twelve or thirteen at the time. We knew the girl—Minnie by name—and ever after she was referred to on our block as "Minnie the whore." What in the world did that girl of nineteen or twenty think when, walking down the street, her hair neat with braided coils, a little boy would dart out of an alley or cellar door and hiss, "Hey, Minnie the whore" and then run for all he was worth!

My friend Ernie Mills (née Milstein) took to a retching sickness down in the cellar of the Longwood Apartments when we first informed him of the amazing story of how babies were born. This sick feeling of his was transferred to me whenever I saw a big birthmark on my back. I used to shudder at the sight of it and finally decided that the way out of my dilemma was to never look at my back in the mirror while standing up in the bathtub. Psychologically this is interesting, for despite the fact that this mole is very large, for ten or fifteen years I forgot it was there until a girl called my attention to it.

I was very fortunate in that I grew up with a bunch of boys. I pity the child who is raised alone; it would have ruined me!

Leaving Philadelphia, arriving at Washington, I found myself very depressed while in transit. Around Washington I circled twice in the car, trying to decide where to go. I made my way to Route 1 and went ahead into Virginia. Virginia made me think of Fay Wray and her husband. I thought to myself that when I ride along alone this way it is not difficult for me to understand what makes a man do that. Then I saw a sign which read "103 miles to Endless Caverns." Good God, I thought, just what I need in life—more endless caverns! This made me laugh and I felt better by the time I reached Fredricksburg and took a room at the Princess Anne Inn.

By the way, it is necessary to smile when at this age, after so many hotels, I am still nervous when I sign the hotel register. The way you right yourself in such a situation is usually that you harshen your voice, become very peremptory with the clerk and badger him as much as possible. Or you can make exorbitant and silly requests. Like more drinking glasses in the room, or a better room—much bluster on the telephone. I don't do all this, but most American men do in such a situation. On top of this you let the bellboy know that you are used to excellent service and you tip him well. With such a silly man, if the woman loves him, it is necessary to be very tolerant.

Meeting a living face around this country, a man or woman with a real inner life, is so rare that you can remember the ones you have met over a week: some weeks there are no such meetings. Fellow country-men, let there be light!

If you want to know something about American men and their impoverished insides, read a copy of *Esquire* magazine—pitiful and paltry!

Saturday morning started the drive to Chapel Hill, North Carolina. Good roads and easy driving. The car is powerful and easy to handle. I am always impressed by the fact that even if one is going seventy or eighty miles an hour the mind is able to keep relaxed and thoughtful.

In a restaurant I find myself requesting "a large coffee" of a waiter. Why is that? Because I want him to know that I know there is such a thing as a SMALL coffee! Shades of my young manhood!

Notice the nervous rejection of the self, or experience, by refusing to listen to criticism whether it be given by yourself or another. That nervous fitful rejection is a very American habit, almost an American reflex, one might say. It might be interesting to list those things which have come by now to be truly national reflexes.

Chapel Hill reminded me of California when I finally arrived here at five in the afternoon. Stopped off at Abernathy's bookshop. Came to the Carolina Inn and am paying six dollars a day for two rooms in a small town in Carolina! Wonder of wonders, there is a real Viennese café here, run by refugees. Civilizing influences in the wilderness.

Form, form, I go crazy when I hear some of these goofs say I have no form! Debussy had no form? Certainly not—he had none of Beethoven's form! And some of Beethoven's last piano sonatas had no form. Yes, none of Mozart's form. These idiots do not realize that there is no such thing as abstract form! Form is, like style, an intensely personal thing. The truth is that my plays have much more form and shape and pattern than thousands of well-made American plays which are simply a scaffolding holding up nothing. I am a talented individual, seeing and handling material in an individual and creative way. And these so-called critics do not understand that when they ask for a ready-made form from me they are simultaneously asking for the death of my talent. Well, everything is your own fault—you read what those stupid men write!

Monday, March 25, 1940

A final word on form which thought occurred to me last night. Form is that vehicle by which the content is most fully communicated to the listener or reader. (This is a sinful simplification of the matter and yet it is really a complete definition if one first defines "content.")

Today I went to see the two rooms of a Viennese refugee lady living here. The two rooms were really a home in the sense that a European seems to be able to make a home out of straw and boxes. This lady is a writer who has published a dozen little books. It amazed me, cold and tired and painful as I was, to see how this woman of almost sixty had made an enjoyable life for herself. When, as I often do in this journal, I mention the word American, it is myself I mean most of the time.

Well, Americans, for the most part, have no talent of the sort this lady has. How I envy the homemaking instinct, and how I need it in someone around me. Shaving, looking at myself in the mirror, I was thinking if it would not be advisable to quickly get married and settle down in a home—that battle and need would be out of my way and I could concentrate on my work with a fresher heart and a clearer eye. In some ways—or so it seems to me now—it doesn't matter who one marries. So long as she is good, clear, loyal, and intelligent. I say this but I would never be able to do anything like it.

When, as it happened late last night, a sudden rush of desire for Luise comes over me—a wish, a yearning that she might be in the same room with me, dressed, undressed, awake, asleep—a rationalization presents itself to me in this manner: "Poor Luise," I think, "how lonely she must be—how she must need me."

A Southern type of gentleman: "When I hear a man say Negro instead of nigger, I know a radical is standing before my eyes!"

Americans have no patience with the facts of digestion. I mean this literally and figuratively. A mental concept, news, a new experience, all of these are no different from food, but few Americans will chew them over and rest while the digestion is taking place.

For a long time I have known as well as any man living what the real meaning is of Dr. Jekyll and Mr. Hyde. They are Caliban and Ariel, those twins in every man's heart. Only in the sensitive and self-aware is this DUPLICITY of self ever realized and understood.

No, I am not saying that one has to be destroyed or banished for the sake of the other. To any living or creative personality both are not only good but necessary. But what must be done is to balance this duplicity within the nature. The devil and the angel in one nature must each be subordinated to the interest of the nature itself, to the continued good health and functioning of the self. It is in this sense that there is no good and no evil—there can only be balance and a clear and strong mind to always be holding the balance with the grip of steel. Surrender nothing, give up nothing, make no inner compromise, but hold tight!

There is some connection between what is written above and an idea, very slight in outline, which came to me tonight for a full-length play. A man develops some writing talent in prison. (For what reason he is in prison I do not know at the moment.) His talent expresses itself in several works which are produced or published outside the prison. For the reason of his unusual talent he is released from prison under parole. (All this is revealed in the first scene.) Outside the prison walls he receives fame, success, money, life. He receives all of the shocks an idealistic nature is heir to. And the end? He yearns again for his cell! And he commits some crime which will again return him to the cell.

Not to have known the world, as I did not know it in my youth, was tantamount to living in a cell. Five years after the fact of becoming a well-known and successful artist, that the world and its people are a constant shock and sickening disappointment to me. Nothing I have met in the way of situation or personality has lived up to the ideals and morals of my boyhood and youth. It is this very thing which is so anguishing about life, and so corrupting and fatiguing to the self. And yet I understand what makes the world and its people this way. These are not the days of Melville or Stendhal. There is Marx and an open but difficult road to socialism, in my personal world the only thing which keeps me working as a creative dramatist. This world must be changed! And there is today a way to change it! No matter what the detractors of Russia say, it is the new Russia which will lead the world in the road of change. I believe, as I believed five years ago, in the destiny of men and women, the high and flowering destiny, and if I did not believe in it I would not want to live as a good man—then would you see a Caliban! (This, dear Clifford, you must read again. This, dear boy, you must bind on your head and your heart as a sign!) If only I could always keep before my eyes this small but fine role I have to play in the modern world. In my beginnings as a writer I had it, but the years have turned and twisted me and I am not half as clear as I was before. The purpose of this journal is exactly that, a self-clarification, a constant call to the arms of the self. I tell you, heart and mouth, awake and sing in the thought of your use to mankind, to life and its constant progress!

Life was mysterious and impressive to Beethoven, and like a true artist, he was gratified when it showed its face to him. The caprice of fortune he understood very well, the uncertainties of life were always with him. This is clearly in all of his music. What is the romantic temperament? It is amazed, impressed, delighted, and enraged by the caprice of life. It is impulsive, swaggering, remonstrating, scolding, pleading, straining, sulking, appealing, denouncing the unfairness of life. It is the romantic who cries out that he is out of harmony with life—by which he means that life is not in harmony with his vision of it, the way he saw it as a youth with moral and idealistic hunger to mix his hands in it and live it fully and deeply. The classic art is to accept life, the romantic to reject it as it is and attempt to make it over as he wants it to be. The classic accepts the forms and conventions of life around it.

The romantic breaks them down, rejects, and rebels against them—they do not fit him—they were made for the dead and let the dead clutch them in the graves! Yes, with the romantic it is all self-discovery and self-exploration. The injustice and coldness of life is constantly throwing him back on himself, and it is from this center of the expanding demanding growing ego that the romantic functions. The romantic's nature inwardly is one of chaos; this is because there are no accepted or standard values for him—he will not and does not accept a code made by others. Everything must be tested and measured by his own experience—anything else is rejected. It is typical that Beethoven scorned the teachings of Haydn and only when much older was able to return to those lesson books and say that he should have paid attention in his youth to the lessons. But to have paid attention would have implied not a Beethoven but a Haydn! The roar of pain which comes from the romantic is real pain, albeit often a pain self-made. Beethoven roars, Chopin complains, Brahms is resigned and sad. But in each case their pain comes from this real meeting: their ideal vision of life met the reality of life, and they are left with this utterance, "What, is that all it is? Is this all? Nothing else? Down with it!" True, there is something vastly self-destructive in the essential nature of the romantic, but when he is a good artist he builds a form to gird him in, to prevent the scattering of his life—his art teaches him a way of life and he lives it! Simply that he insisted till the moment he died that his ideal vision of life, of the conduct of men and their interrelationships, was the correct and most valid way to live—his world was better, and he was willing to fight and die for this belief: he did!

The romantic of the Stendhal type is rare. He understands what has happened to him and his aspirations—HE DOES NOT ASPIRE IN HIS WORK—and this detached sense of what has happened later forms the basis of his work, writing, in this case. But this is possible only when the man waits for a good ripe age before setting to work. Stendhal, if we chose, we could call "a romantic iconoclast," the romantic turned ironist, psychologist who looks underneath to reveal with contempt the pitifully paltry forms of life and convention around him.

———•———

Tuesday, March 26, 1940

Go away to some place where you are not known. Then the gratification of vanity does not enter into your life.

What does one ask? To be happy? No! But to be *reasonably* happy—? Is that not possible?

It was wrong for me to stop at Chapel Hill. The first item on this page explains why. The sextette play is still dead under my hands. I don't seem to be able to write it because I don't want to, probably. The content of the play is no longer exactly my content—the men are all introverted and will force a style like that of *Paradise Lost* which for long has not been my style of writing. I am no longer like that myself and it is very difficult for me to write characters now who contain themselves and suddenly explode out into a series of dramatic and lyric ramifications. With me it is simple: what I am I can write. It is for this reason that I was able to say about *Night Music* that Steve Takis would be the last character of that sort I would write for some time to come.

Paul Green was here for dinner last night. He brought with him Phillips Russell and two undistinguished men, one of them named Couch, the publisher of the university press here. Mr. Couch is that sort of reactionary who pretends to be only half a reactionary—at a certain point in the conversation he will indicate that he has been joking and nothing he has said is to be taken seriously. Paul, as always, is mild and diffuse, a poet, a man with a good heart and a set of morally idealistic values. He has not done much to develop himself as a playwright and it is easy to see why, for he has a line of tender feeling, but not a line of working it out into actual work.

Russell interested me more this time than when I met him last. He is a mild-mannered liberal who teaches literary writing here. When I think of the years of boredom that must have been his lot, when I consider the thousands of mediocre young men and women who must have passed through his hands, I can only shudder and not find any blame in my heart for the sorry old man he has become. But, it must be said, a proper technique of life must have in it those elements which will keep the personality living and fighting for wakeful life. This is one of the reasons that life in its best sense will always be more of an art than art itself, needing greater technique and objectivity; for after all there is always the artwork outside of the artist and that becomes a way of measuring and locating the self and its movement. The creative life does not have that measure, unless it is the younger men and women that one has helped, etc., etc.

A letter came from Harold Clurman today. He says he must go out to Hollywood to earn some money over the summer. That his debts are very pressing and troublesome. He says that "we ideologists" do not include the necessity of living and expenses in our ideologies. But he does not say that ideologies have a curious way of shifting and adapting themselves to the money problem—that danger, that possibility of death he does not mention.

A long time ago I noted in Sean O'Casey a certain problem. He wrote a vivid "parochial" drama at first, proletarian life in Ireland. Naturally he was not content to keep repeating these genre pictures and wanted to move out into the wider world where he would have the opportunity of showing other types and the lives they lead. This shift from one life to another must be watched very carefully, for it is possible that in transit the whole talent may fall off the moving van. This happened, in my opinion, in the case of both O'Casey and Eugene O'Neill. And if I am not careful it will happen to me too. I don't want to continue writing about Jewish life exclusively if I can help it, but great care must be observed while I move to other fields. It is so easy for the reality of the work to go, so easy to find one sweet morning that you have been handling dead life and straw characters instead of the real and impulsive life which was indigenous to your own nature and feeling content. Some writers, Maxwell Anderson, for instance, make the same mistake when they go from "realistic" drama to "poetic" drama. They quickly become dissatisfied with naturalism, find it easy and elemental; they yearn for higher forms of expression, poetic conceptions, nobility of line and purpose—and soon their work is abstract, recondite, high-sounding and dead as an empty bottle. These problems, with all of their ramifications, are now your problems, and you had better tread warily.

An actor like Paul Muni, his background and understanding, his rhythm, his speech inflections and turns, his emotion and its color, all are intensely Jewish. For this reason he, aware of his differences from the average American actor, is tense and uneasy in "straight" roles. His problem is this: how can he keep his true and vivid creative impulse, necessarily Jewish, and yet present to the average American audience a character which is not considered "exotic" and special by them. And that in a certain way is exactly my problem.

I discover something more about pain. I was in Boston when we put *Rocket* into rehearsal. I was unhappy because of Luise, unhappy because of the play and the hurry-up work attendant upon putting it into production. I was lonely, confused, wrathful, repressed, nervous, tense, and unhappy. To none of these things did I give much surface expression. One morning I was combing my hair in front of the mirror. Suddenly I almost fell to the floor with a pain in my back so intense that I would have sworn on the witness stand that a stranger had crept up behind me and buried an axe in my back. The pain was treated by massage and X-rays and examinations by an eminent specialist. He told me to keep my arm in a sling so that there would be no weight on the muscles of the back. And it was in this fashion that I attended the first rehearsals of the play. Now while all this was happening I had the unflagging sense that the pain lacked sincerity and truth, for there can be a truth to pain too. I mean that I was unable to convince my mind that the pain had genuine physical or organic sources. All this while, of course, the pain was truly agonizing, so much so that I groaned every time I turned in the bed. But, I noticed, it was very comforting for me to surrender to the pain—I lay back in it like the softest and most pleasurable of beds—which was what aroused my suspicions. Back in New York I was plied with friendly concern and electric heating pads, not to neglect mention of a high stiff collar which was supposed to make my backbone straighten itself out. I made use of all these devices and ministrations, but inwardly smiled a grim smile to myself and that was the end of it; the pain dwindled away and in a week was gone.

Now, today, I wake up unhappily, fresh from a dream which I shall tell about later in this entry. I have a shower and am brushing my teeth at the mirror. Suddenly that pain, THAT EXACT SAME PAIN, stabs me in the back. I stand still, cautiously lifting the arm—yes, it is that same pain, full and capacious. But this time I resolve to refuse to pay homage to this demanding prince! I quickly propose to myself to talk it out of existence by saying the following to myself: "You are having this pain because you are unhappy and want with some real part of yourself to lay back. You are looking for an excuse which will permit you not to work and yet permit you to retain your self-respect and even the respect of others who might say you don't work enough. Cut this out. Stop it; the truth is that you want to rest and do your work."

Sure enough, the pain begins to drain out of my back. I go into the bedroom and begin to dress, but suddenly I notice that I am dressing with great eagerness. What is the eagerness expressive of? I ask myself. Then I understand that I want to get out quickly and go out and meet some people. Those at the bookshop, for example. Why? I want to tell them about my pain. My vanity wants attention and sympathy. As soon as I understand this I manage to get rid of it (or most of it!). But as I am finishing dressing I sense about myself a certain smugness which makes me understand another thing: what the self proposes to do is to keep the pain but not mention it to anyone. In that way the personality will have the satisfaction of saying, "You see, I have this terrible pain but don't mention it to a soul—I am suffering in silence!" When I have uncovered this third subterfuge the pain is still with me but no longer as intense. All this time I am shaking my head and snorting out a sort of amused tolerance about myself, for after all it is not every day that a sensible man talks in scolding dialogues with his aching back.

An hour later I end up at the bookshop. While I have outwitted the pain it nevertheless demands that I mention it to Abernathy. This I refuse to do, but the weather happens to be damp and chilly and the Pain (I will personify it with a capital *P*) demands that I realize that the weather is not helping matters. But I stubbornly refuse to mention the Pain all day, although from time to time I find myself turning as if with a stiff neck. Is this because I hope someone will notice my awkward movements and ask the reason for them? Probably. Only at night do I mention this struggle to a man, explaining it as written here. In two minutes, incredibly, every trace of the pain vanishes, although a trace of it has remained up until this writing.

The personality seems to use pain as a retreat, as an aggrandizement of the self, as an evasion of responsibility, as a saver of the face, as an appeal for sympathy and/or attention, as a builder-up of self-respect, etc., etc. Inner disorder or confusion (to merely generalize) seems to force itself out in a focal point, pain of the back in this case.

I continue to foster in myself the illusion of frugality or at least economy as opposed to wastefulness. A man wants to borrow fifty dollars, for instance, I tell him I'll give him forty-five and that's all he gets! I find myself buying dinner for five at ten dollars; an hour later I will go up to my room and grow angry because I am charged five cents for washing socks instead of four. This is now a joke, but at a time it was very serious and still ramifies through my personality. How, if not, does one explain the fact that I have rented two rooms here when one would do just as well? For show or swank? Not at all. I am merely trying to beat down in myself this middle-class fear, engendered by a middle-class home, of wastefulness which is associated in all middle-class minds with sin. Enough of nonsense!

I cannot understand why, since his name has been mentioned here, I have never communicated with or met Sean O'Casey. Surely we should have a great deal in common and could get to be warm friends and helpful to each other. Reading about the opening of a new play of his at the Unity Theatre in London made me think of this. The Sunday *New York Times* headed the cabled review, "O'Casey Turns Red." If at all possible we will meet as soon as possible.

This journal has its dangers too. It can easily give you the illusion of creative activity and rich inner life, becoming a substitute for working thoughts and ideas into activity. But worry about this some other time, you damn fool!

Tonight I went over the notes of the murder play. Probably this is the play I will soon turn to, a modern love story using some of the facts of the Judd Gray-Ruth Snyder murder case. But I could never permit my hero and heroine to be overwhelmed by the petty fears and spiritual disorders of middle-class American life as happened with Gray and Snyder. There is something deeper and more noble in the human race than the hatred and babbling which were the lot of Snyder and Gray at the end of their ropes.

———•———

Wednesday, March 27, 1940

The last few hours of sleep are never sound with me and this morning was no exception.

After awakening from a curious dream, it was impossible to get back to sleep again. First I must preface this story with a dream I had four nights ago. I found myself, in the dream, walking along the edge of a pool with Mr. and Mrs. Roosevelt. Without fuss, quietly, the three of us dropped into the pool with all of our clothes on, seemingly with a complete calm faith in the fact that one always drops into a pool with all the clothes on. Mrs. Roosevelt and myself stepped out of the pool, still dressed and dry as before and did not seem surprised at that either. Mr. Roosevelt stayed in the pool, but looked up at me with only his head above water with a mischievous glance, saying, "Oh, you Bolshie you." I was about to take offense at this remark when I turned and saw that Mrs. Roosevelt was both calm and friendly. This made me merely smile back at Roosevelt. A moment later the three of us were lying side by side, flat on the stomachs, while many people were passing by us exactly as if we were lying on a boardwalk and sunning ourselves. Then Mrs. Roosevelt or myself suggested that we go to another place. We found ourselves at the door of a big office building, tenantless and locked. She had the only key which opened the building, and we walked upstairs where we finally stopped on a kind of outer staircase landing. Now it was night. Suddenly there appeared before us Miss Katharine Hepburn and that was not surprising—our greetings were friendly and calm, calmness seeming to dominate the entire dream. By now I was looking out at the sky and saw the most brilliant Milky Way, cluster on cluster of powerful stars. This seemed to astound me and I turned and spoke of the beauty to my companions. At this point I woke up.

The dream this morning was again about Katharine Hepburn. I had left another woman with whom I'd had sexual intercourse. I am tired and going home and I meet Hepburn. Immediately I want to sleep with her despite weariness and everything else. We are in some place, can't remember where; she is responding to my wooing when she remembers that she must make a matinee at the theatre. We hurry to her theatre and once in her dressing room it is the evening performance for which she must make up. She begins to undress and does not seem to mind my presence. Then I see that she is eating, not preparing for her performance although it is only fifteen minutes to the curtain. I tell her I will go home now since she must play the play. I ask her if she will come to my house and carefully repeat the address several times. She says she will come there after the show, a rendezvous, but I don't believe her and keep begging her to come. She says she will, I wake up. (The dressing room, by the way, had become a small kitchen.)

This dream had great reality for me and depressed me for several hours later. Why? Probably because it increased my sense of loneliness, of not having a desirable woman, of being unrooted. But during the day and evening I had the distinct feeling of the dream being true and it made me smile inwardly and feel rather good.

A lovely spring day. Walked around the town a bit. Genuine spring fever, the sort of day that makes you drink milk. It is as warm and mild as May would be in New York. A student here, a nice boy named Katz, came to see me in the afternoon. The last time I was here we had what they call a "bull session" and he asked if we could repeat such a session tonight. I agreed, for there is no telling when a random remark or one's spoken sense of some element of life may make a mark in a young man and inspire or influence him. To inspire or influence a boy is part of one's work in this dead world. Katz then mentioned a girl who lived here and reminded him of Cleo Singer in *Rocket*. Not only that, he said, but she was given a copy of *Rocket* and read it six times. This impressed me about a girl of eighteen and I asked to meet her. We rode out to her poor house and she came to the door at which Katz knocked while I sat in the car. The girl almost fell over backwards when Katz said I was sitting out in the car. She joined us and we rode away.

Her name is Ouida Campbell. How did you get that name? I asked. She said, "Father just dreamed it up. Momma didn't like for me to be called by that name 'cause maybe he got it from some woman he knew. But he insisted and I was called Ouida." Truly a Cleo Singer, a type no matter where you meet her, here with a broad Southern accent. When she left the room for a minute I asked Katz where he had met her. He said that a friend told him, "Take her out. She is a sure lay if you give her a few beers." He said he went to her house and took her riding with that idea in mind. I was a little shocked at this talk, for with a girl who touches and moves me as this type does I am always already half in love. But Katz went on to say that she began to talk and he just listened and it was fine because he had never met a girl like this one before. Which raised my estimation of Katz, for I saw he was touched by Ouida exactly as I was.

We talked some more. Ouida was a little uncomfortable because she wasn't dressed, as she said, for going out. Her father had recently left home again, she said, for the second time. It seemed to be his habit to just disappear and return months later. He had another woman in Raleigh. Her mother was always forgiving the father, but this time she herself would step in and shoot him if he returned. (I believe Ouida would.) They were poor. Her mother's family, strong Baptists, kept watching her conduct, her mother being very strict with her. In fact she had to call the mother and plead to be permitted to stay out for dinner. She was very nervous but with a real fluid inner life inside her rather ungainly and not quite developed body; but her face had real freshness, determination, and beauty. Her intelligence was obvious in a remark like this: "You don't know what to do [talking about the opinions of students], don't know what to believe. Who are you to believe? If you say one thing you are a reactionary. If you say something else, why then you're a radical. But if you don't say anything and just stand inthe middle, why then you're nothin' but a nothin'."

I was struck by this girl, aside from the fact that she is one of my most interesting and least understood characters come to life. Down at dinner I kept wishing Katz were not there; then Ouida might have spoken more with that rueful stubborn mouth of hers. I had given her a small book of my six plays—she clung to it as a precious thing. I was sorry when we returned to my room and the other boys and girls came for the "bull session." Ouida said or asked nothing, leaving that to the others who seemed to me to be the cream of the campus. Ouida had to be home by ten and since I could not leave the gang alone one of the other boys was glad to drive her home in my car.

Naturally the students put me up on a pedestal, treating me and adjusting to me with great respect. I naturally fell onto the throne they had set for me. An activity of "to reign" set itself functioning within me, and I saw that with such an activity I could talk without vanity, simply, but with the same wit and intelligence and character insight with which I write plays. In fact I would not at all be surprised to find that this is one of the activities with which I sit down to write.

In the afternoon, I forgot, called M. P. [Marion Post] at her office in Washington. She was working out in the field, not there. I was thinking about that last time in Long Island when we had been swimming and came back to my room and how I peeled off her wet swimming suit and together we had the finest before-dinner appetizer imaginable. But, as I say, today she was not to be had.

———•———

Friday, March 29, 1940
to
Sunday, April 7, 1940

Since I have not been doing my duty by this journal, I will attempt to make one large entry to cover nine days of interesting events and thoughts.

THURSDAY: drove out to Paul Green's house where I remarked again to myself the good normal life he leads. He has a good wife and four fine children. I spoke to them for a while and wished they were mine and the house mine and the roots mine and the whole settlement mine! Then we drove back into town, he to go to a rehearsal of his old play,

The Field God. But we stopped in for some supper and talked for a long time. He is very pure, almost artless, and wished that a group of poets/ artists might get together and form a vast art center. The Group Theatre, he admitted, was a good start, but it was too particularized, too local. Too much of one color, not representative enough of America. Paul, I am afraid, goes right to the general, forgetting the particular. He is the only man I know who has real connection with the men of Jefferson's time. And indeed he is forever quoting Jefferson as if he lived down the street. He is a true poet, with all of the virtues and faults of the poetic nature.

I called Bill Kozlenko in New York when I reached my room later in the evening; invited him down here. The next day he sent the wire, saying he would arrive Sunday by train.

The delayed spring is here at last and the soft balmy air is everything that a spring in the South should be. It makes a fine relaxed feeling in a fellow like myself. I must say that such periods of relaxation, as now, are very rare with me. For some reason, one of mistrust, I do not permit them. Foolishly, relaxation—a state of not doing—seems to me sinful, a sort of creative death. Relaxation is not an American habit or reflex. In a certain sense there is no holiday in American life. But to relax is to refresh and to renew, as important for an artist as work itself.

Stendhal's *Charterhouse* is very disappointing in its ending.

An essential difference between the artist and the private citizen, aside from the privacy matter, is this: velocity of growth and completion, with the sad fact thrown in that the genuine artist is never done with growth and dies incomplete; and this is why the genuine artist can seldom live a normal life, for there is no normal life out of velocity! In the end the artist is a weary and constant traveler through life but often a deep and noble one.

The scars and bruises on a man's body! Did you ever look at them? Ever think of the time and place from where they came? I have them all over, legs, fingers, chin, wrist, and each of them is a place and a time, some of them terrible, all unhappy long-off times since idealized by time and the even unhappier present.

It is an old story, but new to me, that there is a deep tragedy in the life of Woodrow Wilson, a first-class play. Perhaps it should be called *The New Freedom,* after his policy and practical effort to make democracy work. In a short time now we may see history repeating itself (this time as "a farce," as Marx puts it) when F.D.R. begins to meddle with America's position in relation to the present quiet war in Europe.

Quixotic American presidents scorn socialism; that is why they are quixotic!

A Wilson play might open with this statement, made by Wilson perhaps: "Gentlemen, the war is over!" This same play might end when the broken Wilson appears on the balcony of his house on Armistice Day in 1924 and says it was cowardly of America to reject the League of Nations. He is by this time a dying man and is dead shortly afterwards.

The artist is always "emerging," always "becoming," to use Waldo Frank's words. "The artist, like an advancing army, should stick close to his source of supplies" is another remark of Waldo's that I find in his young book, *Salvos*.

FRIDAY: a letter came today from [Louis] Nizer, the lawyer. Luise is ready to get the divorce and Nizer, since he is my lawyer too, wrote a typical lawyer's letter, polite, studiously warm, detached, patently attempting to be fair, judicial in tone, the language a little stilted and old-fashioned, expressing simple things in a complicated roundabout manner—a lawyer's letter, as I say. I answered and told him to go ahead; and later was glad that I did not feel badly about it, although I suspect that my haste in answering was to show them that I did not feel badly about it. Luise wants me to pay the expenses for a Mexican divorce, half of them, which is fair from the fair. If you ever use a character like Van Gogh or Nijinsky, put opposite him a man who thinks and talks like the lawyer in this letter. It will show perfectly the sort of deceit in the world which mystifies and drives mad the idealist who knows only honest and straightforward means of communication.

Later in the afternoon the Katz boy came over again. He said he wanted to talk to me about Ouida. He is half in love with her, being touched by her, but doesn't realize it or won't admit it.

He said he was afraid that she would go to the dogs and he didn't know what to do about it, how to help her. I tried to explain her character to him by analyzing for him the character of Cleo in *Rocket*. Both these girls, I told him, are the hope of American life, the most typical hope. To begin with, this type always starts with a good heart and sound instincts, by which I mean an intuitive rightness about what is good and progressive in the life around them. Like Beethoven, Nijinsky, Van Gogh, myself (!). They find themselves in a world which has no use for their values. They are almost immediately in opposition to their environment. They are almost never intellectuals in the strong sense of the word, but they fight or become stubborn and more determined in their convictions and feelings when they and their aspirations are blocked. (Obviously I am describing, again, the moral idealist!) How do they solve their environmental contradictions? Girls like Cleo and Ouida, being girls, give in easier than the men. You will find many whores like these girls, naïve, of profound feeling, honest; or they get stuck in an impoverished life (as Ouida probably will) and raise a brood to whom, frequently, they give some touch of themselves. Another type along these lines becomes a class-conscious radical, does Communist Party work. Another type becomes a Dillinger and lets his rage out through the medium of the gun; and of course this implies the artist type who does not get out of balance and lets his combined RAGE AND LOVE out through the medium of art. And still another type tries "to beat the game" and is beaten by it—Joe Bonaparte in *Golden Boy*. Beanie Barker and Rosamond Pinchot are other similar types to think about: their solutions are very unhappy ones, suicide, drink, perversion—half-artists on the fringe of a world that still rejects them, this time in the art world of the theatre. I MUST KEEP ON WITH THESE YOUNG TYPES, for they, I discover only now, are the stuff of my art—they are all myself and I understand them, their problems, their impulses, pulls, contradictions, their aspirational lines, their timidities followed by violent activities which often wrench them out of the context of normal life.

Not even when I was writing these characters—in at least four of my plays!—did I realize what they meant and how they stem out of my own character! You can see how useful it has been for me to meet Ouida Campbell!

This is a very important page to me, for it explains the very dynamo of my own personality to me. It explains the impulse behind all of the writing I do. It makes me very happy to have written this page.

After this talk with Katz I found myself so enthusiastic that I proposed we ask Ouida to dinner again, which was done, this time we eating in my room since I had noticed how uneasy she had been in the dining room of the inn before. (I was very pleased with my thoughtfulness in this respect.) I talked like a blue streak all night. The only thing Ouida wanted to say she said several times: "How can you possibly see anything interesting in me?" I explained to her how a little genuine life (not that I called her little) was more interesting than a whole litter of pompous famous impersonalities called personalities.

SATURDAY: I thought of the phrase F major, wondering if you could say that a couple in bed were in F major. Well, it is spring and I am feeling good. Today the printed books of *Night Music* arrived, a handsome blue job.

I wanted to write in this journal but was restless and scuffled around the room. Finally I decided to invite Ouida to dinner, this time alone. Why alone? For two reasons—I wanted to talk to her alone, and I had a sexual idea about her which I knew I could never even broach, no less carry out. I drove to her house and talked to her two brothers, one sixteen and Jimmy three, while Ouida dressed belatedly since she was fresh from working at her grandfather's post office all day. Ouida and her family were having the naïve enjoyment of having a "famous man" come visit their house, although the mother refused to come in and meet me because her hair wasn't done up right, as she put it. Finally we drove back to the hotel and at dinner she told me all about her life, of how she felt about her runaway father, despairing since the responsibility for the entire family now rested on her to the extent of curtailing her education and making her go out and work. She spoke, for an eighteen-year-old girl, with uncommon good sense and I told her so, trying to show her how to trust her own inner promptings since they are so unerring. By this time it was impossible for me to think of sleeping with this girl, but that I did not tell her. On top of this she told me that she had been lame up to the age of fifteen when an operation lengthened one leg. This just floored me so that even the unkind sexual side of my nature melted into the rest of me and I was altogether as mild as a pussycat.

SUNDAY: Bill arrived here, we ate a big breakfast, came to the rooms, and I had to nap, being so tired. Bill seems to have several dominant tones. One is a sort of reserved admiration, next is a sort of general sympathy which is never quite geared in with one, and the third is a sort of exasperating bumptiousness. Wrongly, I gave him the journal of this trip to read. Then he was immediately an expert on everything in it, understanding all of the problems with a great display of words which quite readily revealed to me that he did not even begin to understand the problems. (Bill is nothing if not critical.) I wondered as I watched him if he had any sense that he was being watched and listened to as critically as I watch and listen to myself. How to start talking to him about these problems of his young curiously warped life is more than I know. There is no doubt that he will end up badly if he is not helped now. He offers opinions a thousand a week and I have yet to hear him utter one original opinion of any depth.

Bill and I decided to drive to Black Mountain College tomorrow.

MONDAY: when a fellow like Bill tries to take in and make his own certain experiences that are not organic to his own nature it can only come from the fact that his own nature is bare of experiences. His ready and glib understanding of whatever one starts to tell him, his assurances of understanding, all tend to give me the impression that he is frightened to death, for the truth is that he cannot think consecutively from one to two. He is like a warped mirror that throws back an image distorted and nervously stretched beyond recognition. Then why do I like him? Let me be as honest as possible. Perhaps it is because I can use him as a sounding board. A wiser man, Waldo Frank or Harold Clurman, for instance, a man with a more adult ego (since Bill's ego is a boy's vanity, really), would not be content to be a mere sounding board.

In the car I explained to Bill what makes up the creative personality. The talk was that the artist has in him many elements. Some, if they were isolated, would be bad, some good. But all of these must be held in a firm balance by the artist. None of these elements must be mechanically excluded from the artist's life. No, everything must be included. The man of genius walks, talks, sleeps, eats, loves, and works with a load of dynamite in him. If he carries this load carefully—in balance—its power for good work and use is enormous—it can land-scape a whole mountainside. Abuse—out of balance —is suicide and a bitter grave. It is in this sense that the artist, if he makes a proper amalgam, is beyond good and evil, for everything in him is for creation and life. For example, let us say that Dostoyevsky had impulses of rape in his heart. An American man would try to cast out this true inner life and experience. But see how a great artist held this part of himself within his recognition and acceptance of what he was. Its creative uses were enormous. It gave him work, tone, feeling, anguish, a wealth of feeling. Finally, it was just such "weaknesses" which gave Dos-toyevsky's novels their religious ecstatic fervor. In other words, as few Americans know, inner contradictions are not solved by throwing out half of the personality, but by keeping both sides tearing and pulling, often torturing the self, until an AMALGAM ON A HIGH LEVEL OF LIFE AND EXPERIENCE IS ACHIEVED! For the artist there is not "bad." He must throw out nothing, exclude nothing, but always hold in balance. When he has made this balance he has made and found his form.

The fine summerlike day went right with us up into the Blue Ridge Mountains which become the famed Smokies on the other side of Asheville. At last we reached the college, which is set up on the side of a mountain, a setup like Mann's Magic Mountain. There we met the director, Robert Wunsch, whose last name I could not remember for two days—kept calling him Watch, Mauch, Munch, till I was sick of it myself.

Black Mountain College is a progressive school in the best American sense of that phrase. Robert Wunsch is a small clean alert man, a liberal with a reactionary Southern upbringing from which he broke away. (He told us that an uncle of his still has a cigar box full of mementos of various Negro lynchings—fingers, burnt patches of skin, etc., etc.) We asked him if we might stay here for a day or so and he said glad to have you, so we went to our room and washed up. There are seventy students there and they knew soon enough of their distinguished visitors—I made that plural, for Bill travels everywhere under the title of "Editor of *The One-Act Play* magazine," a title which I give him as soon as I introduce him anywhere since it makes him feel good and important.

Next we went to dinner and immediately I smelled "exclusion," using this word in the sense of the creative problem written about on the page before. By this time Bill was using the words inclusion and exclusion as freely as if it had taken him years of hard creative work to discover them. (By the way, the two words happen to be the property of Harold Clurman, who got them from Waldo or André Gide, I think.) The boys and girls were good to look at, but they gave me a sense of restricted living, or not raising enough hell for young people, of something goody-goody and YMCAish. Here and there I did see a petulant or twisted mouth or a frown between the eyes, but the odor of exclusion persisted. Lack of upheaval in young people is like a painted ship upon a painted sea. Wunsch and I had a long talk about progressive education. I said that I thought that no education could be so valuable as the one that taught him or her who he was, where he lived, and helped situate him in the world. We went up to bed, chilly, tired, and a little hungry. I no longer have that warm glow of having talked well and having made important points, for now all points are important to me and nothing is high or low but all is interesting whether said by you or said by myself. What I was thinking was that I am homeless wherever I go, always lonely, and that all these students and the long rows of doors with their names on them, all of these meant that they were at home here and I was not.

TUESDAY: they eat breakfast here at eight o'clock. But we got up at ten and went out to the little typical American village of Black Mountain for our bad coffee. The typical American village is clustered around a main street that is usually the main highway too. It contains two drugstores, four gas stations, and a post office, third or second class, depending on the amount of stamps they sell. None of these things has any personal quality, character, charm, or dignity. The people are slow and rather indifferent to any real values of life: the radio has corrupted them even more, for it is no longer necessary to bother making opinions when the radio hands them out already designed and cut to fit any topic of importance. The people are all polite, but it is courtesy which comes out of vacuity, so it is meaningless. All of the old homey virtues about which people used to talk, all of these are gone. No one bothers to read books or think seriously about serious problems. Many people are on relief and the WPA continues to build small projects or fix roads. The food in all of these places is beneath contempt, and, as I pointed out to Bill, this means that these people do not handle or bother to understand the character of the food they have in their hands. Just get it cooked—out of its raw state—is all they understand, and for the life of me I cannot understand why they don't just eat the food raw; in that way, at least, it would retain its original character and flavor. Now if these people do not know or understand what secrets lie hidden in lamb, veal, pork, and beef, in fine fresh vegetables and eggs, then they surely cannot know what secrets and characteristics reside in the people around them, their husbands and wives, all relatives and friends. American life is a sad life, a purblind sterile life. The turnip has no blood and the people have no souls.

I had a sexual dream about Stella Adler. She wanted me to sleep with her, but I resisted all her blandishments, but only up to the point of not going in her—everything else I did, inclusive of chewing on her breasts. Two reasons held me back from consummating this quaint little party—one was my loyalty to Harold and the other was my fear of being ridiculed by a woman who had had so very many lovers, some perhaps great experts and extraordinarily equipped, as I am not equipped.

Only now do I dare admit to myself the constant disappointment of meeting the world since first I became a writer of repute. This constant disappointment slowed me down, blunted my impulses, took my appetite and zest away: I didn't want to work. Only now, I think, I will be ready. I am the only one who realizes how emotional, idealistic, and hopeful my nature is.

In the evening I read *Night Music* to most of the school. At first I wanted to read *Rocket* because I happen to have been thinking so much about Cleo and what she represents; but I thought the boys and girls here would like better and understand better the latest play. The reading of the play, by the way, went very well; no one could understand why the play had failed. Nor could I. It was and is a real crime on the part of the reviewers.

WEDNESDAY: by the way, Carlos Merida, the Mexican painter, is here. I met him in Mexico last year. In fact it was at a party at his house that I drank almost a whole bottle of brandy and went out and cracked up the Pontiac. Merida is a delicate man, deaf (with the sweet smile of the deaf), spidery, and poetic in a sort of broken Mexican way—which is exactly what his "abstractions" look like, many of them being exhibited here now.

We decided to ride in to Asheville, Bill and I, and did so, a short drive of sixteen miles. Went over to a credit jewelry store where my Bronx boyhood friend, Ralph "Red" Roth, is working. Bought a wristwatch for myself (for a change!); got it wholesale. Ralph was glad to see us but we couldn't stay long. He is a strange fellow and seems settled here forever. Like a cheap movie symbol, my watch broke (the old one), the only useful gift Luise ever gave me, just when she started readying herself for the divorce.

We drove back to the college in the late afternoon. I went to watch Wunsch direct a rehearsal of scenes from *Ah Wilderness!* Ah stink!— play and work on it. I could not say much about the work I saw and said so.

Several times I had been asked to give a talk on creative writing. I said I could not shape my material into the form of a talk but would accept questions and proceed from them. Well, there was a large turnout, including Fielding Burke, the novelist. Before I knew it I was ranging along like the first movement of Beethoven's *Eroica*, meeting all comers and all questions. I felt more alive and useful than I'd felt in weeks. Through the medium of my projected quartette play, I was able to explain the creative approach of writing as opposed to the merely mechanical. The students asked intelligent questions and that helped. For myself the most useful part of the talk was a kind of quick and rough "anatomy of success" which I made in answer to a question. It was an effort to explain what happens to the talented young writer in this country, showing how he went from maladjustment (which started him writing to begin with) to a deeper and more horrible maladjustment which was beyond repair. Quick and noisy success, uncritical acclaim, personal bewilderment which becomes resentment when the first success is not followed by an even larger one; the seeking and finding of awards and regards; LACK OF REPOSE; money problems; drinking for stability; and tonic effects; Hollywood in one guise or another; looking for immediate results in every phase of the life and art . . . all of these and more made up this part of the talk.

THURSDAY: we decided to leave after lunch. The whole school seemed unhappy about it. The boys and girls, including a few of the faculty, waved goodbye from the porch. It was touching for a moment.

FRIDAY: if the man of talent is in opposition to the values around him— all artists of today are men of opposition, says Malraux—it stands to reason that he must be out of the context of "normal" life. Considering this, the simple human desire to be loved and accepted must necessarily clash with the artist's work. I mention all of this because in the past few years the yearning for acceptance (even by fools!) has done something to my work. Here and there an element of truth has been lost: the truth of how one sees the world. Watch out for this "mellowing" process, hang a red lamp on the dead branch of the dead tree of acceptance!

The University of North Carolina has been having a drama festival this week. Theatrical groups from all over the South have been attending. Probably for the reason that I am a radical I was not formally invited to attend any of their sessions. But this morning they called me—would I appear and talk at their Playwrights' Luncheon? Finally I accepted the invitation. Bill and I sat at the speakers' table with such profound theatre theoreticians as Barrett Clark and daughter, Professor Koch, Archibald Henderson, famous as Shaw's biographer and one of the six men who understand Einstein's theory of relativity, and Paul Green. These straining hounds of hell were mastered by DuBose Heyward. Rightfully in one sense, wrongly in another, Hallie Flanagan, who had been sitting at my side, disappeared before the luncheon began. She said later that she had not wanted to speak and that she was so indignant with the several hundred scrubbed faces before her—since they had most of them done nothing in the way of trying to save the Federal Theatre when it badly needed friends—that she had retired to her room. She did not say that she was very tired and still crushed by the death of her husband three weeks before.

Anyway, I gave a brief effective talk on the fact that all of us were beginners in a country of beginners and beginnings. We must not create from hearsay, I went on to say with booming confidence, which came, I am almost ashamed to add, from a feeling of contempt for these people before me. Why contempt? Because most of them were so self-important, interested in "theatricals," gleaming with ignorance—the more you polish brass the more you show it to be brass—interested in me because I am famous, "a personality." There was something wrong: I had flattered the prejudices of the meeting in a subtle way. And why was that? Because I wanted them to like me! Which is the behavior of a rat in two shoes!

Next we went out to Paul's house where he was serving drinks and a buffet supper. Many interesting persons were there—Hallie Flanagan again, Norris Houghton, Zora Hurston, who is famous for a fund of Negro stories, and Mr. Philip Stevens, who gives out ten million Rockefeller dollars a year for the "humanities," whatever that means. Here it means money given to theatre groups. Hallie, Houghton, and myself had an interesting talk on the possibility of decentralizing the American theatre so that New York would send back to their native cities many of the workless but talented theatre workers; at home they would start Group Theatres, each remaining in its place, forgetting New York forever. (I have been thinking about this idea and mean to consider it later on in the journal.)

At night we all went to see a production of Paul's play, *The Field God*. Before the curtain went up he gave a charming poet's talk on how he came to write the play and what it meant. He got the idea from the Book of Job, he said, but he improved on the work of the unknown fellow who wrote Job. It was true—in terms of thesis and humanistic approach to life he had improved the story. But, as usual with Paul, the thesis had not been dramatized and the play was poorly constructed, containing, however, two very powerful scenes. Paul, if it is not too late, ought to work with another expert craftsman of a playwright for several years. After that he could put collaboration behind him and stand on his own feet as a theatre man. Unhappily, I have an idea this will never happen. Now he is frittering away his time and talent on pageants dealing with historical events in the South.

At the show we met Ouida and Katz and took them in for coffee after the play. Then drove them home, then drove ourselves back to our adjoining rooms, Bill and I. We had determined to leave early for New York in the morning, but it was difficult for me to get to bed. We talked for a brace of hours and turned up two interesting points. One concerned how American schools teach children how NOT to think; and how difficult it is in later years to force yourself to think on a straight line. I was able to show how my father had done the same thing with my sister Genevieve, scolding her for being lame and not attempting to walk straight, etc., etc.*

The other point concerned the small American businessman like my father. This type is always going in and out of some small business, frantically running around to raise a few thousand dollars. Then he opens a loft shop and hires four or six workers. He is going to make a profit on their work, but often he does not get as much out of the business as they do. New York is full of such small unhappy despairing men. Finally they take on the quality of gamblers and racketeers. They borrow money from friends and relatives, from loan corporations. In the year ten they are repaying money they borrowed in the year one. But they never go hungry and they often manage to send a son or two to college. They are not bad men, but this is the only way they know to live, as small entrepreneurs who try not to be in conflict with monopoly capital. They live on a set of illusions that they are not of the working class, above that class. They do not save, for they are so used to being broke that when money comes in they spend it just as fast, so often living in luxurious suites or apartments. Life is a series of pre-dated checks for them, of slipping in and out of traffic as long as the gasoline holds out. A very interesting type of which my father partakes unwittingly, although he is not exactly the type.

The night clerk at the hotel gives me my key and says, "Good night, Mr. Odets." An attractive girl turns, interested by the name; I think, "Oh lady, come up with me, up to my room, oh lady. Come up and stay with me and let's do it!" The girl, as it happens, does not know that I have noticed that she has noticed me. But side by side we step into the elevator, lady and gentleman, pale, restricted, each deliberately plunged into the inscrutable self. I get out at the second floor, she at the third. As I open my door I think of the electric currents running wild within the most restricted forms.

SATURDAY: and now the long drive north, the weather favorable, the car performing with beautiful response. Five hundred and fifty miles in twelve hours, much of it going at a speed of seventy and eighty miles an hour. It is not the speed which fascinates me now, but the steady driving pushing ahead. For this fine peice of automotive machinery I have nothing but admiration. It makes me sense a character, his trust

* Genevieve had polio as a child, leaving her with a limp.

and love of people shot, turning to the perfection of machinery, a motor, an engine, with love and constant admiration.

My eyes are very tired—smoking weakens them, I think, smoking excessively as I do. I notice too that when I am very tired I get extremely lonely. Even a friend sitting next to me does not help that feeling.

As the car sped through New Jersey we were able to hear Tosc. on the radio, playing an all-Tchaikovsky program. It is not that he plays this music badly. Abstractly, he plays it very well, with elegance, with almost brutal energy which is even more powerful since he holds it in so well. Yet the romantic generalization has gone out of it, the love of the part above the whole, the swelling emotional insistence, the rhythm of the slavic Russian, the crouch which leaps out despairingly into a blatant flare of metallic sound. What has happened here? For what we are getting is a truly noble failure. It merely shows that the genuine artist, Tosc. in this case, can proceed only from his own center. He cannot demean himself by being another man. (Ormandy, for instance, can demean himself—he can play ANY music!) A performed piece of music is as much a critique of Tosc. as his reading of it is. Where he shares the composer's feeling and view of life, there he is great. Otherwise, mostly with the romantics, we will have a noble failure.

Now arriving at home. The house is dirty, bed unmade, as unhomelike as possible. I vent my rage against the walls, muttering and talking to myself. If Herman had been here I'd have blown him up! Mail, magazines stacked up. A letter from Fay which I was glad to read. I was feeing so despairingly alone that I'd have proposed marriage to her had she been here. In the newspaper I saw a picture of a nude statue, the body of which looked like Luise's. I cut it out, cut off the offending unfamiliar head, and kept it here on the desk till the early morning. Also there was a letter from my father who wrote an extraordinary line which he half meant, which the whole country means. Said he, "Business is bad, but I am keeping smiling till the sun begins to shine again. I'll go along till I meet a fellow who's even smaller than me. I'll knock him down and take it away from him!" Well, what more is left to be said? Dog eat dog!

About Tosc. above. An American would call that a limitation in him. Of course it is exactly his greatness.

MONDAY: how comfortable is the rightness of anything. I am thinking of the April rain all day and into the night, the warm spring rain. If one could always know, in life, that this rain of today is the flower of tomorrow! At night a yellow fog came down on the city, so thick that the tower clock on Fourteenth Street was completely blotted out of sight. I was warm in my house, secure, active in mind. Bought some new records, several pieces by Berlioz and some songs of Darius Milhaud. In this journal I wrote several pages of this past week. Sid Benson was over for an hour in the late afternoon. Otherwise I enjoyed my splendid and pregnant, if you please, isolation. Let there be rest.

———————•———————

Monday, April 8, 1940

In the music of Berlioz you will find something petulant, like a man with a toothache. I write this because I am thinking of the *Roman Carnival* overture which I played this afternoon. There is something historical about this piece, some strange and new outburst—the "peeve" has come into art, the sense of personal rejection, the man unwanted and unheeded. What a strange sad man Berlioz must have been. Aaron Copland says the music of Berlioz is strange too, in the sense that one never knows where it is going or what the artist's intention is (if I am reporting correctly) but I don't understand what Aaron means: the music is followable enough to me. One might almost say that the nerves and hysteria of the modern man have come into the art with Berlioz too.

The older I get the more miserly I am getting with my time. Truly the days and nights are too short for all the thoughts that come, for all the excellent books and music there are to read and listen to. I find increasing pleasure in staying at home, hugging myself to myself and what interests me. Now if only I had a wondrous beauteous woman who stayed in the closet and stepped in and out as wanted and not wanted! How brutal this is to a woman, and yet it is true to your nature, fight it as you will till the end of your days. Women in other men's windows are most exciting to me—that is because they represent pure desire in me with no need of responsibility towards them.

People are always saying to you that you have gained weight or lost weight—it is a foolish point of contact between two persons when neither knows what to say to the other on meeting anew. I mention this point because I notice how different I look and feel with a haircut. With a great deal of hair I look and feel sensuous, artistic in the grand style, flatulent, sybaritic. But with my hair clipped short I look and feel alert, police dogish, intent and fresh, even military.

The American wants the personality which IS, not that which is BECOMING. That is why the American is anti-facts of life, as Harold Clurman puts it. After all, my countrymen, is there any life which is not BECOMING? What do you want, boys? The perfection of death? Forsooth, a wondrous perfection!

As all other certainties break down, says Gide, the certainty of self remains. So this is the end of individualism: the modern man has his nervous distraught self with his supersensitivity and his feminine sensibilities. See any page of James Joyce.

Gide (I am reading his book on Montaigne) quotes Sainte-Beuve quoting the younger Pliny: "I have lost the witness of my life. I feel I may henceforth live more carelessly." What a fine saying, what a splendid remark!

Success can be a lightning rod. So can a wife—Luise.

My appetites veer like those of a pregnant woman. Some days I am off on a spree of eating fish three times a day. Or it might be boiled ham, sliced and fat. Now I am on canned pineapple, have been all day, thinking of buying a case of it tomorrow. I never doubt that some lack in my system, some special need is sending me to these foods to supply the lack.

———•———

Tuesday, April 9, 1940

Up late and, already in a splenetic mood, annoyed by Mr. Herman. He brings to my attention that I am expected to pay the lawyer's expenses in connection with his work on *Night Music*. When I point out to Mr. Herman that I am only one member of that corporation, he begins to argue with me, pretending to be discussing the affair out of a sense of fairness to all sides concerned. It is a usual form with him, for mostly his "sense of fairness" is just plain disagreement for its own sake, out of his pride. Impossible to contradict him on anything, including subjects about which he knows absolutely nothing, playwriting, for instance. In the meantime it is possible for anyone to have his ear—he will present anyone's case or plea to me, exactly as if the other person were his employer. This enrages me, but I keep my mouth shut.

Wondering how she was feeling, I called Helen Deutsch, who came down here for dinner. We sat around and talked for two hours and I realized that there is nothing in the world I want from her. She is extraordinarily self-centered, much more than is usual in a girl of her age, chiefly, it seems, because she has an idea that people for years have been trying to tear her away from herself and her values. Her self-consciousness is less painful than it used to be, but her watchful rhythm is still one of quick thrust and retreat. She said herself, "There are two sorts of men in my life: the ones I can lord it over, and those who try to beat down my wings." Which is putting very well a certain thing in her character. She always tries to make a sort of doll of me, sitting me here or there, patting me on the cheek, next a little kiss, then a little joke, jumping up, sitting down, generalizing a little bit about art or poetry, assuring you that she understands you and what you are saying, flattering you very consciously. . . . Master, master, to master is all she wants. Which is not to say that she has a bad heart. Besides, she is capable of extreme shrewdness at times; but she lacks the courage to be shrewd, for she is afraid that you will see she is being shrewd and won't like her for it. She talks very warmly, sentimentally almost, about her father and two brothers. This is because they represent family to her, a spot of security. She always has two or three men she is thinking of marrying—she will mention their names and qualifications and a moment later assure you the idea of marriage is of course ridiculous. At one time I was deeply graven on this preferred list; not so today. She has real audacity, her sarcasm or irony intentional, so quickly does she withdraw it. Her self-confidence, to which she is afraid to give full sway, is enormous; it comes from her true enough sense that most of the people around her are incompetent and not half so clever as she. She is a woman divided, easily explained. There is in her the strong, rather talented impulse and with it the fear of the impulse: impulse and refusal.

Harry Gurdus came in to work on the phonograph and Helen and I went to supper at Ratner's on Second Avenue. By this time I was getting a little tired, for it is wearying to watch a bird which flutters and flutters and will scarcely stand a moment on one branch. But we enjoyed the supper. She wanted me to ride to the country with her— stay there for a few days. Well, if I wouldn't do that, would I ride up to Fiftieth Street and meet some friends. I said no. She said of course it was silly—she didn't want to see the friends herself. She drove away. I got my car out of the garage and went over to Bill's house. Bill was out but Lee was there and we talked for an hour, about Bill, before he returned.

Bill is going along under the assumption that he is a playwright. His wife said she is letting him work out his destiny while she continues to work at school, for that at least adds up to a certainty of interesting work and a weekly salary. She is a good girl. As for Bill, I wish him well but don't think anything will come out of his venture into the theatre except a certain easing of the vanity; but later it will be really bad, for he will intelligently see his last self-illusion punctured. I can see only failure ahead for this young man, my friend, in any direction he moves.

Today there is Marx. Looking at some early writings of Waldo Frank and Van Wyck Brooks makes me think of this. Twenty-five years ago they were beginning to examine the American scene, in turn despairing and optimistic. Today there is Marx and a party which has been arousing in American intellectuals (workers less, I think) a new sense of how a living world can be made. Despised and scorned on all sides, this party has yet had deep and extraordinary influence on every aspect of cultural life in this country. It has even been the dynamo for organizations and new patterns of thought many times removed from its radical core. It has given writers like myself a reason and a way of life. Of course this party has had behind it the enormous prestige of Russia and the profound philosophical system of Marx, Engels, and Lenin, a load they have not always carried with ease and distinction. And yet, because of it, new inroads have been made into American life, paths that will not be given back to the wilderness. The reactionaries are trying to fight life with death: it is a trick which will never work in America in my opinion. In the meantime live with lust and pleasure—there is at last a way of life in which one faces and works within life instead of evading it, instead of being devoured by dead sterile forms, perversions, sybaritic living in the senses, and assorted mysticisms.

Mozart, in his best work, has the profound sadness of a man trying to break out of a form not his own personally: which is to say a man trying to break out of prison. Child and man of his age, he was above it by being underground in it. On the other hand, the personal tragedy of Beethoven, the man, is that HE DID BREAK THROUGH THE FORM! (In Mozart's case it is like the Negro who walks around, personal life in him, contained in a social form which he did not make and from which he can never escape!)

In certain periods where the forms of art are breaking down (because of social breakdowns and changes) it is a bondage, a sign of servility, to work within those forms when one's content is in advance of the times. It was between these two worlds that Mozart was beginning to be caught by the time he had reached the age of independent manhood. Against him was ranged the entire world of common usage of the artist, represented by his employers and his very own father, a perfect servant and minor diplomat. The overlords did not want to know or hear what he was feeling and sensing; they wanted only the shell of his genius, never the substance. Here, in the simple and natural protection of his genius, is where Mozart began a subtle change in his life. He pretended a servility (as Haydn did not have to pretend) by retaining the old decaying forms. And this is how he went underground—he moved around in these forms freely, saying exactly what he wanted to say, loading them with a rare precise vehemence (which Beethoven was later to bring up into daylight!), often expressing all sorts of censorable materials behind opera masks.

He is a man of great elegance in his art, not all of it natural to his nature. His technical equipment is excellent and enviable. His playing contains a contained feeling of which he is somewhat afraid; and he possesses, when you think of it, little quality of the spirit. His name is Heifetz, and you know all of this when you hear him fiddle Mozart.

———————•———————

Wednesday, April 10, 1940

Books, books—the house is stacked with new books. So many books astound me. It is impossible to look at them with mute admiration, hoping that the day will come when there is time enough to read most of them. I buy them because they are bargains in catalogues, because I need some of the materials for future plays, etc., etc. This is not a poor man's pleasure.

Without knowing why, I have had a curious impulse to starve myself the past few days. That is exaggeration—I want to eat only fruit, almost as if it were just too much trouble to eat lots of food and have to sit around while it is digesting.

I have been feeling very good, full of spirit and vitality. What I need, as I told Sid, is a harem of choice beauties. I told him it was very painful to start an affair with a good sensitive girl; you could not be free with her, for a protracted relationship would give her a semblance of continuity and permanence which you did not intend to fulfill. Then there is the pain, for her, of the break-off. Try doing this five times and you will see that you don't care to face a sixth. This is the case with Gr. B. [Bette Grayson]. You want to be rid of her—that is your honest feeling. You are completely irresponsible with girls and women. And yet you have urgent need of them. And yet you fear to damage them and wound them in their pride and well-being. So you are always sitting around at your desk alone, not wanting to start something you know you won't finish. Then go, dear friend, and consider the knot hole!

We sorted out all of the books I have in the closet here. I called Lee Strasberg on the phone—he did not have some of them. So Sid and I went over late in the evening and gave him the books and spent a few minutes there—they were going out, Lee and Paula. He says he wants to talk to me about something—"I am in a didactic mood for a change, for once," he said. I think it is something about the Group and our last production, so I'll go over and chat with him soon. He is still the most talented theatre director in the English-speaking theatre and it is my opinion that the only place in the country for him is within the walls of the Group Theatre. By all means the contradictions of his and Harold Clurman's natures should be resolved into what must necessarily be a higher level of synthesis for the Group.

Have heard for a long time of a nightclub around here called Café Society, and not having gone there because it embarrasses me to walk into such a place alone, I asked Sid to go there with me. He knew everyone there—it is a place frequented by radicals and friends. Who should be there as press agent but our old friend, Ivan Black. Ivan was glad to see us—he knows no high or low, all is equal in his experience and sense of life, so he was able to bring to mind a score of little experiences we had had together ten years ago: how I had acted out all of *Volpone* from the bandstand in Central Park, what we said to Isadora Duncan's brother one afternoon in the Metropolitan Museum, etc., etc., none of which I remembered. Ivan smiled and told me I had a remembering Boswell in him. Sid and I drank steadily and by this time the floor show was on. Chief among the show people was Hazel Scott, apparently a well-known Negro singer of popular songs. What with her lively eyes and real dusky beauty (not to mention the liquefaction of her breasts), her shy sort of independence, her talent for singing and playing the piano, her fresh youth, it was plain that any man in his normal senses would beat any other man on the head for her. Scotched, spring-fevered, this seemed a quite normal attitude to me. Ivan talked on and on and we drank more and stayed for the second show. Hazel sat with us after that, plus Mr. Dugan, the movie critic of the *New Masses*, the gent who wrote that the movie of *Golden Boy* was better than the play! Hazel had a pair of drinks and I walked out with her, ahead of the others. I drove her home in a cab. I told her that it was very difficult not to put my hands on her, but why do it—she was so lovely, so much herself, etc., etc. But I meant it. When we got into her little den in, as she put it, "a house of four women—my grandmother, my mother, me, and the female dog, a doberman pinscher," I found in her a sweet-natured normal girl of nineteen, tractable, pliable, a sort of concubine type. So we kissed and kissed and listened to a radio playing faintly. Then she played two Beethoven overtures on records and we kissed again. Now I saw it was daylight outside. I kept asking myself why I was here and what did I want here and why didn't I go home to bed. Which is what I did. She seemed to like me and I promised to come soon to the club again. When I got home it was past six; I washed Hazel's lipstick off my face and dropped my dead body into the bed. Thinking about Hazel now, I am sorry I was half drunk— that made it impossible for me to talk to her and get to know her. I scarcely have a sense of what her quality is like. I'll go to the club again; maybe I'll sleep with her.

Thursday, April 11, 1940

By today Ivan had two foolish items in the papers about the fact that I had been to that nightclub. Now everyone will know I am in town, a fact I have been trying to hide since I returned from Chapel Hill. Why hide it? There is a real yearning for privacy, a desire to lose the identity.

My main concern today was that of getting in touch with Gr. B. I thought she should know I am in town and that we should sleep together. Both were easily and well done: soft, warm, young, ardent though repressed. Then out of bed to eat some supper out of the icebox and to hear some music. Then turning to dress so that I might drive her uptown to her home; but then falling in bed again. Then it begins raining as we leave the house, tender springish rain. And a cool drive back to my door. Then sitting and reading in Casanova for an hour. Only recently did I purchase his life, which is a fine picture of his times. You cannot get too excited about his sexual adventures—they are so numerous and he is unable to convey his excitement as he is not a professional writer. But there is enough there to make you grit your teeth. I gritted my teeth and went to bed happily wearied.

Friday, April 12, 1940

Perhaps the main activity of the romantic, often idealist, is that of giving, that of offering himself up, of throwing himself at the world. The trouble begins when the world coldly refuses him. Nothing daunted, again the leap, again the throwing of the self. Again repulsed, again and again! Finally you have a tired, embittered, and frustrated man, or one of resignation, or one who has learned to modulate his behavior and values to those of the world. In Beethoven we have the glorious exception to all the rules: He never stopped the fierce activity of throwing himself at the world, of *demanding* attention for his values above all others, of *insisting* on the validity of what he was above all current social values. This persistence created, finally, one of the greatest bodies of art the world has ever seen, but it cost the man dearly—it cost him his life, his home, his friends, all ordinary comforts and amenities. It crippled him almost beyond recognition. But even on his deathbed he suddenly started up and threw himself at the world with a clenched fist.

Back copies came today of a French art magazine called *Verve*. It is loaded with unusual plates, most of them fine replicas of world master-pieces ranging from twelfth-century work up to the most modern. All these pictures delight me—Bonnard, Matisse, Persian prints, books of hours—all of them get me exactly in the pants, to tell the truth. (And I don't forget Renoir!) Of course if you look at Rembrandt's series of self-portraits, you get something else.

As a matter of fact, before going to bed near dawn, I went over some

van Gogh prints and thought about certain drives and incidents of his
life. I am going to write a play about him in the next three or four years.
Many of the notes in this journal appertain to his life and, it seems to
me, I will be able to write that play better than any playwright living.

Sid Benson came over in the late afternoon, bringing me certain
materials which I had asked for having to do with Woodrow Wilson and
his inner and outer death. I am gathering materials for a possible play
on his life and its meaning.

We played some music, discussed the beautiful *Verve* prints, then
went to dinner on Second Avenue at the Rumanian restaurant. And,
believe it or not, a real snowstorm greeted us as we left the table. The
thermometer dropped to twenty-six and spring had hidden itself in
fireplaces. We returned to the house, dropped in for a moment on
Morris and Phoebe, who said they'd drop in later after a meeting of a
study group at their house. I'm trying to tell her of the unusual
coziness of staying at home during the past few days, of listening to
music, of feeling "at home"—so rare a feeling with me. Here it was
again. Morris and Phoebe came up at four in the morning, she looking
very well. They stayed for an hour. I noticed a curious quality which is
creeping over Morris—a sort of inner irony which comes to a man who
is disappointed in life and is not doing what he wants to do. This is
bound to grow stronger in him in the years to come. Then they went
home, Sid left, I thought about van Gogh, then turned to sleep.

———— • ————

Saturday, April 13, 1940

It seemed a nice idea to me to have a large dinner party. Which was
why I began to call friends in the late afternoon, Sandy, Hanns, Morris,
Bill K., inviting them all to dinner with their wives or girls, not to
forget Boris Aronson. But we ended up at a roast baby lamb dinner
with only Bill and Lee, Boris, Bette, and myself. Good enough. An
excellent dinner and good spirits, all of which made me think that it
would be a fine idea to have such parties at least once or twice a week. I
am all for the spirits from the belly and the appetites, instead of the
vinegary nervous spirit of the modern intellectual. What we lack today

is gusto, normal and rich appetites. Let there be more suppers and more bottles of wine, say I!

We came back to the house and listened to Tosc. playing an all-Debussy program on the radio. By this time Hanns Eisler had joined us, his wife sick at home. Debussy, I could not help noticing, has been so desecrated and pilfered by the movies that he seems to have lost some of his originality and quality. This led Boris to say that the intensity and drama of modern life and its wars made it almost impossible for an artist to create work interesting and stimulating to a modern audience. In the meantime Hanns, energetic, restless, ego-itching, was hopping all over the room like a billiard ball, unable to sit, constantly breaking in—rude, apparently very nervous. Several times Bill's face flushed and his mouth set—he does not like to be refused, even though he may be uttering the most arrant nonsense, as is mostly the case. Hanns has no patience with nonsense.

Boris spoke of many art problems—he is always the artist, always the bohemian, but in the best and true sense of the word. This art talk led to a certain appraisal of the movies. I turned up what seemed to me to be an interesting notion, namely that a movie story is interested not in building up life—a development of a love story is over at its introduction (that moment when the male star looks at the female star), but in breaking down life. More about this when I have thought more about it.

It is curious, incidentally, to notice how Bill wilts and tires when he is crossed or contradicted—soon he says he is tired and has to go home and does. All these hungry egos! Hanns' ego, too, is a very greedy one, constantly demanding attention and satisfaction—he is usually quite unhappy and nervous when another person becomes more assertive than he. A strange gifted unusual little man of great quality—one does not mind his ego at all.

An evening like this is fine, a rare event in American life. We must make more of them. Such is my intention once I settle myself in an apartment that feels more like home.

At home, Bette with me, time to be asleep, I saw in myself one of my worst faults. In an hour it is possible for me to think about five different play ideas—Wilson, van Gogh—I think in fragments and scraps. Nothing gets itself done that way, unless one counts the final sense of urgency as something done. I am a man of patches and shreds, almost unable, except at the point of actual work, to concentrate myself on one idea or subject for even a whole day or night.

Sunday, April 14, 1940

The morning was gray and we slept till way past noon. Sun came in and out, but so did suggestions of snow. Sylvia Sidney called me last night, asking that I come out to the farm. Sleep or not, farm or not—at two in the afternoon Bette and I drank some coffee, washed our faces, and set off for the New Jersey farm in the car.

Luther and Sylvia are still working on their house, making life more and more comfortable. Luther's show closed last night; this week they are bringing the baby out there. They have a house, a farm, themselves, a baby, four dogs, and a comfortable bank account. If you asked me what else they have, it would be difficult to answer. As a friend, I would like to see that they had more. Luther is very uneasy about the Group; he wants to leave, but there is some small spot in him that wants to stay. I think he will stay if the Group becomes a working functioning organization, something it has not been for years, despite a string of excellent productions.

We spent a comfortable ten hours there—I read a few of Shaw's old dramatic criticisms—and drove back to New York. It was one-thirty in the morning. Bette I dropped off at her house. Then, at my house, I spent a half hour with Morris and Phoebe, listening to some Chopin nocturnes. Then I went to bed, thinking that it had been a comfortable but a dull day and night. What do you want? Fireworks all the time? Yes, that is exactly what I want.

———•———

Monday, April 15, 1940

Started to work tonight on the murder play. Wrote half of the first scene. The day, otherwise, was dull and I am falling back into the old slothfulness. This apartment, this small round of activities, no schedule, everything hit or miss, seeing only those few persons who chance to walk across your path—this is a dangerous existence. I am anxious to move out of this place; think everything will be different when I am living elsewhere. This is no home for me. Despite the fact that I am not bothered by multitudes I nevertheless feel that here I am living along the side of a busy road, as if in a gas station.

What really annoys me about my life is that the day and night do not cluster themselves around my work. Instead there is a lazy line of following where my sensations take me, and it is around my senses that all the hours cluster. A horse cropping grass in a field seems to have more sense about its life than I do.

I plan to take in a lot of shows, to spend three or four days on end at the movies. But nothing happens. I make these notes. I am unable: one, to make a plan; two, to follow it out. About such inabilities there is something diseased.

Then what will you do? I don't know! You need order and discipline in your life. This Oblomovism will sap all of your talent and vigor. You are living like a bullfrog on a lily pad! WHAT IS THE FEAR which is doing this to you?

Yes, it is some sort of fear! But forget the idea of fear for the moment. Put it this way—make a simple of a complex. You must begin to lead a normal and healthy life—in waking and sleeping hours, in recreation and exercise. Will you do it? I don't know. Then make yourself know. Start out with the most concrete small thing. A walk in the park, let us say. After this, an hour of concentration on some simple working problem, etc., etc.

What you are doing is indulging in childish rebellion, against the forms of middle-class life which were thrust upon you as a boy and young man, against all the compulsions and responsibilities you did not want to assume, against your shame when you did not want to keep them and then broke them. This rebellion has been going on for years now. Is it not time for you to begin to build a life with intention and purpose in it? Is your position in the theatre no incentive to you? (No!) Do you not have sufficient respect for your own talent which is the best theatre talent in the country? (Yes!)

Now begin to work, begin to give yourself simple commands that you will then carry out. Start with the simple reality of a pencil and a piece of paper if necessary!

———————•———————

Tuesday, April 16, 1940

The spring is creeping up on us. To me it is always a pleasant necessary experience and I found myself surprisingly unhappy to twice have missed the coming of the spring while in California in recent years.

Otherwise a wretched useless day for me. I lie supine in the middle of my little world here of books and music and food and permit my senses to crawl over me like the tenants of a hill full of ants. Gulliver tied down in a warm scented world while over him swarm a hundred miniature imperfections of the self.

I made an appointment to have dinner at Lee Strasberg's house tomorrow night—we will talk about the Group Theatre and its problems: one, a leadership of more than one so that continuity of life can be guaranteed under any circumstances; two, on the artistic front, set up so that creative progress and development are guaranteed to all Group members and apprentices; three, extreme efficiency in the business organization so that Group members can be guaranteed a reasonable financial return for their work.

Alongside of the most genuine idealism there are the most ignoble and selfish elements imaginable, great self-indulgence and even cynicism. It is the fight for a creative balance which is staring me in the face. I am not unhappy about it, for I think I will fight a good and exhilarating fight.

To put it simply, the artist's problem is this: to superimpose order upon chaos, his own chaos. Each man must make his own order. It doesn't matter where he is, in what city, with or without a wife—any starting point is as good as another. Of course he is surrounded by traps and pitfalls—indeed, most of them are in himself! On top of that, what orderliness is he to aspire to? That of the phrase? Of the paragraph? The scene? The three-act play? The ten-scene play? Well, for that he must trust his own nature and the quality of his talent—he must trust what he is, what he represents to the world around him. Oh artist! you must let yourself be f——! And yet you must retain a balance more exquisite than that of a tightrope walker. Artist, you are a divine oyster—your shell you must keep open—you must permit the ocean to wash through you, laving, wrenching, giving, taking—and then you must know when to close your shell and begin building the pearl by patient accretion! In turn passive and active, your rhythm is essentially "female"! So it must be!

Wrote seven more pages of the murder play. Interesting, the way the hero is coming to life—my present sense of usefulness!

———————•———————

Wednesday, April 17, 1940

Two short dreams, one pleasant. A cordial and warm meeting with Mrs. Roosevelt. She was very charming, very friendly, and very sad. Then I dreamed myself into a broadcast of a Ford hour. I walked into the broadcast studio after the program had begun. I was warned to be very cautious as I treaded my way up a sort of tower staircase—the broadcast was taking place in a high, well-furnished attic. Here Mr. and Mrs. Henry Ford were holding court—they actually were like a king and queen at a small court. People seemed to be swooning with considerate servility. I had difficulty finding a seat and changed my seat, always on the floor, several times. I did not hear any music but everyone seemed attentive, as if to music. I was sitting on the floor next to Ford's chair. He left and I followed, going with him to a field where he selected several small pieces of lumber. All this time he was talking dryly, looking narrowly at me. He asked my name and I told him. He said that I had come far in the world for a young man, but that he didn't agree with the stuff I believed in. I tried to explain my position as a radical, but he refused to listen. I thought to myself that I had never seen so bigoted a face and planned to tell this to people when I could later mention the meeting. Next I was with Mrs. Ford. The same thing occurred. She had a harsh, strong, and discordant personality, extremely unfriendly. I had followed her out into a courtyard on some errand. She refused to listen to anything I said and ran on ahead, rapidly, waving an arm at me. My feeling throughout the dream was I CANNOT GET IN! I was trying to get in and could not get in. I had two emotions, fear and hatred of them—a third was comtempt for the people of the court. This dream—its masks of personalities—comes from reading last night about Ford's police and strike-breaking activities. The article mentioned that it was impossible to get into the plant unless you knew Mrs. Ford. What is interesting is how the personality takes names and persons met during the day and proceeds, in the dream, to arrange them in relation to one's inner life and problems, from one's point of view. The dreaming personality is a true artist—its selectivity is absolutely unerring!

In the early evening went to Lee Strasberg's house for dinner. Paula's mother was there, preparing the dinner, and I understood a great deal about Paula from seeing her mother's weak face. For the first time in ten years the tensions are down between Lee and myself—we were both able to relax. He spoke of what he called "the blight of Ibsen," saying that Ibsen had taught most writers after him how to think undramatically. He illustrated this by an example. A man who has been used to living in luxury finds he is broke and unable to face life—he goes home and puts a bullet in his head. That, Lee said, any fair theatre person can lay out into a play. But it is not essentially a dramatic view of life. Chekhov is dramatic, he said, for this is how he treats related material: a man earns a million rubles and goes home and lies down on them and puts a bullet in his head.

He also said that he thought it would be better for my playwriting if I put several ideas in combination instead of hammering one idea into a full-length play. It is his sense that the modern dramatists spin out for three acts something which can be expressed in one act, in a short play. There he is certainly correct. I think this comes from two reasons— first, that the modern artist is essentially a worker in small forms, quick, nervous, one lyric shot, with plenty of social causes to explain this; secondly, the American sees his material mechanically, pragmatically, machine made and moved, instead of starting from a creative psychological and biological core. (Who will ever understand this!) I know exactly what I mean, but don't feel like digging at the moment.

Then we talked about the Group Theatre, both of us agreeing that it was not necessary to talk about what had been wrong in the past. Objectively, he said, the Group was the only place where it would be possible for a theatre worker to function in the theatre. He was cautious and for obvious enough reasons could make no final statement about coming back—after all I could not be very particular in my talk. But I made my feelings clear, expressed all of my dissatisfactions.

He mentioned several interesting production plans he had, one of Chekhov's *Three Sisters* seeming very interesting to me. He was able to outline in particular the bedroom scene during the fire, styling it in outline and feeling from an Oriental print on his wall. He saw Chekhov, he said, not as an oil painting, but easily, in terms of pastels and watercolors.

I came home and wrote (badly, because tired and spent) several more pages of the first scene of the murder play.

———————•———————

Thursday, April 18, 1940

I am beginning to see the dawns again and getting up at two in the afternoon. Today there was a letter from W. Fa. [Fay Wray] I was glad to have it. Her letters always give me a good sense of her womanliness—she is not run-of-the-mill. And yet she does not seem to know what to write to me. Her letters give me the feeling that she thinks she should answer; they are rather hurried, mostly in reaction to a line or two I have sent her. I wonder what is really going on in and around her. She asks if I am coming to the coast.

Heavenly Express opening tonight; I sent a pair of wires. Looked at a book on the history of the theatre up to myself by John Gassner. It seems, like all of his things, almost the thing but not quite.

At seven-thirty Gr. B. came down, looking fresh and very young, dewy as if fresh from a bath and patting her hair into place around her forehead. We chatted, drank some sherry, and went to bed for several happy and tender hours. We ate lovely preserved fruit, figs and pears, cream cheese and crackers, boiled ham—an excellent supper. Then we dressed and went to a movie, taking along Sid Benson, who was haunting the lobby downstairs when we got there. Then we drove Baby home and on the way downtown we stopped at Lindy's for a bite.

Billy Rose called us over. He was sitting at a table with Small, an agent, Stella Adler, and Stretsin, Broadway man and businessman. Stella seemed tired, a little hoarse, dressed flamboyantly, unrelated, very feminine. She said she had met Luise yesterday and she was looking well. Stella knows much about the feminine heart, so she was able to say of Luise, "She was very friendly with a bunch of refugee Viennese whom she didn't like, but very unfriendly with me whom she does like." Meaning that a type like Luise (and Stella) could not be easy and friendly with a person whom she admires and really likes if that other person offers competition; better to stay with people you don't care for—your ego is safe.

Stella and Stretsin left. Billy, answering a joke, offered to back my next two plays sight unseen. If not for the Group I think I would have concluded the deal right then and there. In the joke I had offered him two plays, one a success, one doubtful. The truth is that the joke masked a great discontent which he seemed to sniff out in his dandy little way.

A comic who works for one of Billy's shows came in and sat down next to Small, who is his agent. The comic had a friend with him. It was amazing to see the scale of values, which ran something like this. Billy Rose is at the top. Small acts as stooge for him. The comic acted as stooge for Small; and the comic had his stooge in his friend, who sat mutely at the other end of the table drinking Dutch beer. When the comic leaves Lindy's he certainly has some smaller potato who acts as his stooge. Finally it gets down to the man who knows the man who knows the man who knows the friend of the comic who knows Small who knows Billy Rose. Reflected glory indeed—a whole list of rascals whose lives are lighted from that excellent sun above!

———————•———————

Friday, April 19, 1940

Rain, rain, April rain, indecisive, but rain. And for me sloth and more sloth, getting up at four in the afternoon today. I made my "morning" coffee, smoked my blackest-tasting cigarettes, looked over my news-papers and a weekly magazine—this time reading unfavorable reviews of [Gottfried] Bein's *Heavenly Express*, which I shall see tonight. Some art books arrived from Goldsmith's; I considered them apathet-ically—what have I to do with French stained-glass windows when all is said and done? (What an uncomfortable chilling time to live in those days must have been!) I remember a dream, a long dream in which, despite the aid of two cars, I could not get started on a long journey. A friend is with me in a small car in which we are to travel up a side road until we reach a main highway where my car is waiting. When we reach the juncture we are unable to proceed for various reasons. Finally, disgusted, I begin to watch a girl playing with wild animals, rabbits, martens, and foxes, as I remember. Amazingly the two mar-tens are suspended in midair, as if held by invisible wires. The girl is small, attractive, dark, with spaces between her teeth, which gives her a very charming smile. I wake up, not interested in the dream, not interested in sleeping or waking either. After my coffee, in walks the census taker. It takes him only two minutes to get the necessary information. Census taking means a good living for thousands of boys like that—four cents for each name, for each person in the family, and twelve cents for the apartment in which the person or family lives.

There is such a thing, too, as sensory repose. If you come to it it's because you have been seeking it, perhaps unconsciously. In this respect your life is interesting, if not exemplary.

Stella Adler said last night that she has a theme for a play—this. An American woman making her way in the world in these times can pass through certain casual love experiences without being touched or spoiled by them. It is in the nature of her present ascendency. But the American man cannot do this—every time he dabbles casually in love he is scarred, unmanned, desexed. I think this is true of the pale intellectual. The neurotic nervous involved man. But I am not at all certain it is true of the man who is able to have, take, and give without worry, completely and joyfully. Harold, she said, agreed with her thesis. If this is so I am not certain that Harold is not agreeing with some inner "deficiency" which she has womanlike marked off in him. (Does Stella mean she is making her way untouched?)

At night Bette and I went to see *Heavenly Express*. As usual the critics were profoundly at fault, as profoundly as our civilization cripples all mankind. The production is creative in all of its parts and is obviously the best show in town, despite its many faults, particularly in the lack of duality of stylization and a constant submersion of the story line. (It would be a friendly act to write Bobby Lewis, the director, about this.) The impending failure of this play so depressed and saddened me that I was almost speechless when I went backstage and saw some of the cast. (Jane Wyatt and mother, Louis Nizer and wife, Alvah Bessie and girl, Herbie Ratner and friend—all were at the show.) The cast was having a meeting on stage, the usual sort of meeting. The night after you open a play with creative merit, a play and production in which the threatre as a whole is making advancement, you call a meeting and tell the actors that the only way you can continue running is if everyone will take a cut. The stagehands never take the cut—they have a strong union and are not interested in art or spirit—but the actors usually take the cut and play piddles along for another two or three weeks. This was the sort of meeting that was taking place when we went backstage. We chatted with Mrs. Harry Carey for a moment (she must have been a very beautiful woman; her spirit is still admirable) and then went down to Julie [John] Garfield's room. Al Bein was there, a lost boy as always, but with a world of sweetness, looking guilty, as if the bad notices were his fault. Kermit [Bloomgarden] was looking depressed and harassed in the role of entrepreneur. Julie was gauche and well-meaning; his performance was not the best in the world, but it had his energy and zest and a certain directorial intention throughout. On an impulse I said I would furnish half of the needed five thousand dollars if Julie would furnish the other half. Such an idea had never entered Julie's mind, but what could he do in the face of my dramatic proposal? He accepted and I fear we are now both out twenty-five hundred dollars, money I cannot afford at all to give away. But for me this is a necessity of the spirit—my inner happiness depends on it.

I saw Art Smith (who was quite good in the show) and Aline Mac-Mahon for a moment, telling her of the possibility of doing *The Wild Duck* next season. Then a group of us went up to Lindy's for something to eat. We drove Bette home, still raining, Herbie Ratner and I; then I drove him home to Brooklyn. He spoke sweetly, always an unusual boy from another planet, so remote is he from the realities of life. I asked him if he needed some money (Rockefeller Odets, Inc.!) but he said he had sold his piano. I asked him how much he had received for it, but he did not know—which is typical of him. I was so saddened by the evening that, lost in the rainy night, I drove around Brooklyn for an hour before I stopped to ask my way to one of the bridges to Manhattan.

How far behind all the other arts is the theatre in this country! How childish! It will be many years before they accept any but the most literal realism! I mention this because it is typical. Mr. Richard Watts, Jr. said of *Heavenly Express*, "I know this is just the sort of thing I should like, but I didn't like it!"

Anyway, I crawled into bed along about five in the morning and enjoyed fifty pages of the excellent book by Meier-Graefe on van Gogh. It is a pure and honest book, surprisingly so for a modern German; useful.

I wondered why it gave an extra edge to an affair to get in bed with a wristwatch on, the girl wearing, for instance, a necklace. Simple—because these triffles emphasize the nakedness!

Saturday, April 20, 1940

Herman woke me an hour later than I asked him to call me; I bawled him out gently—an auspicious beginning to another rainy day. Not that I mind these spring torrents, feeling part of them, as I do. There is a high wind and there is rain. In Europe the war continues with our newspapers sensationalizing every small item to such an extent that the wisest thing to do is to read the weekly news magazine. In my own life there was another dream dealing with a fruitless trip. First there was a fragment of a dream in which a town in which my family lived was being bombed. I wanted to help the others but first found it absolutely necessary to run up to my room, very dishevelled it was, to get my hat, hoping in this way to keep bomb fragments out of my head. Next I found myself beside my father in an automobile which he was driving while he was looking through a large book—four novels in one. I claimed there were only three novels in the book, but he showed me where the title of a fourth was painted on the front cover; it was painted in white, two words which I cannot remember. In the back of the car sat my mother, my Aunt Esther, and my sister Florence. We were on our way to visit an English movie studio. We passed several English children, precocious and very mannered—Florence blamed their upbringing on Eva LeGallienne. Then we arrived at the studio, but they would not let us enter without special permission. A guard pointed out a fat man to us, saying we would be able to get in if he signed the pass. My father was all for going to this man, then wanted me to approach him, but I refused because I was shy; fruitless visit— end of dream!

The thing which interests me is the difference of experience level of two persons involved in one situation or affair. I seem, for instance, to be a man of the world, quote unquote. That is not true, but it is true that young love is old news to me. Here is a girl of twenty-one who is in love with me. Our arms are around each other. The difference of experience is that of day and night . . . what she is thinking, feeling, what I am thinking, feeling. These are two touching worlds, dualities, together and yet miles apart. This is the curious paragraph—it means something—I don't know quite.

The question of fantasy in the theatre. First, how is the script to be written if one approaches the problem consciously? Bein did not quite succeed in his new play. Is there something to learn from his incomplete attempt? Fantasy is first, I think, a style which comes from the way the author feels and sees his material. (French painting after Delacroix seems all fantasy to me.) Yet you cannot leave the problem here, saying that Bein wrote a fantasy because he is "fantastic," although this is certainly half true. Let us find another name for fantasy: heightened realism! Can we then say that the base or start must be realism? I think so. Then what next? The matter of the heightening or "enchantment." (As a technique I do not understand this, although I do it in most of my plays.) I think the way this is done is by dropping out the unimportant realistic details—what you leave will suggest or imply what you have dropped out. It is as if one said the alphabet, "A C G L M N S T V Y Z ," thus implying a continuity instead of literally giving it. In this way the artist gets right to the heart of the matter, as he sees it, hoping that you will share his way of seeing it.

Now I see something else. I realize that fantasy implies *selection out of realism*, a personal rearrangement of materials within a widely understood frame of reference, for purposes of comment by the author. (The question right here is : Am I talking about fantasy or stylization? Or are they one and the same? No, not all stylization is fantasy, unless one would call El Greco's stylization fantasy.) I feel here that the widely understood type, i. e., the villain, the hero, etc., is necessary to successful fantasy. So is the symbol, those which are as widely accepted as the silver dollar or the Christian cross. (Think of Charlie Chaplin in this respect.)

This is getting me nowhere. I am tired and will go to bed and look at this again when I get out of bed. But I mean to look again at *Peer Gynt*. I seem to remember there is a successfully worked out fantasy. The reason this is important to me is because I have sensed in my work a sort of cowardice, a holding onto realistic details in my plays when they are not necessary. For this reason hardly a playgoer is aware that my plays are intensely and personally stylized. (Bobby Lewis stylizes by externalizing the character's inner activity— a bewildered harassed clerk whirls, twists and writhes across the stage instead of merely walking across. Lee Strasberg says that Bobby's styling is too personal for the theatre.)

———•———

Sunday, April 21, 1940

I did not mention that yesterday the cast of *Heavenly Express* sent me a wire of thanks for my help. Nor that I met Stark Young at that show, he very well groomed and very embarrassed, chattering so rapidly in my ear that I could not understand a word of what he said.

Yesterday's main item I left unwritten. In the early evening I called L. E. who promised to call here at nine o'clock. She is going to California soon, says, "I want to be famous and make a lot of money and have everything I want." The theatre has wounded her pride, indeed her basic right to exist and progress. The studio, she said, was very enthused about her test. All this gave her a great air of excitement and unusual confidence, to such an extent that she was perfectly relaxed and extremely candid with me. This air of feverish candor I found very charming, also exciting. But a certain quality of ignorance on her part, ignorance of how Hollywood can destroy—this saddened me. Her general excitement was so intense, however, that it easily communicated itself to me and I undressed her right on the divan and carried her into the bedroom where we sported for three or four hours with the warmest pleasure and lack of reticence. Then we drove up to the Washington Bridge and back in the cool rain, ate a little supper on Second Avenue, and said goodnight at her door. She was never so lovely, so much of her own quality, so full of emotion and excitement, and so vulnerable, it seemed to me.

I had intended to work all weekend on the murder play, but this young lady shot my best of intentions to hell. So goes the creative tension so necessary to good work. But I did find one valuable item for the actress play while with her. It occurred to me, while talking about related subjects, that the writer in that play is THE MORAL IDEALIST AS SUCCESSFUL WRITER while Senior is an extension of the same character or type—the same grown cynic. This immediately gives the entire fat file of that play a focus which it did not have before.

I remark here an old but curious fact about myself. Whatever a person is, that thing he or she brings out in me, but so completely that I am a character from it. A reticent person makes me reticent, a hurly-burly extroverted person makes the same of me when I am with him, etc., etc. I seem to be all things to all men. I hustle and curse with the cabdriver, am modulated and delicate with the professor. This is not something I think out, but it happens that way always.

How many millions of men would say, if a new war came here, "I have nothing to fight for? You have something to fight for? *You* do the fighting then!" Millions of them, every man and youth degraded, impoverished, desexed, all of them should make that answer.

AGAIN ABOUT FANTASY: where the details are improbable and yet the whole sums to probability, of feeling and significance.

Sid Benson walked in here late this afternoon, looking forlorn and crestless. We ate some supper at the Balkan and went to see Disney's *Pinocchio*. This is a picture which delights millions of people, and yet it is only mildly entertaining, its fantasy (!) extremely conventional and unimaginative, but perhaps fanciful and theatrical as compared to the average movie with its deadpan faces and lack of spirit. People are obviously hungry for color and theatricality, also for goodness of the heart and a sense that all's right with the world, all of which is given to them by Disney films. Too, the characters always overcome extraordinary obstacles—gravity, explosions, high winds and storms—all freaks of fortune it gives the audiences a certain sense of omnipotence to see these characters come out right side up.

"Buying on credit" means that the moneyman permits you to buy articles which you would necessarily have to pass by. For this favor he charges you interest, thereby adding profit to profit, insult to injury. In this period it is the only way the moneyman is able to keep this profit system going. Without a continuation of production his money is useless to him since it cannot make a profit for him. That would be the end of what we so proudly hail as the capitalist system. Today, it seems, "buying on credit" is the keystone of the capitalist system. Anything may be bought on credit now—from homes to cemetery plots, not neglecting all of the things in between like autos, clothes, jewelry, thousands of gadgets which combine to make life more vapid and insipid. A man writes, in the *American Guardian*, which I read from time to time, not to envy Mr. and Mrs. when they step out of their car. He says they usually have a ten percent equity in their home, a twenty percent equity in their car, and perhaps thirty percent equity in the clothes on their backs.

Monday, April 22, 1940

I keep carefully out of the way of my secretary. For he has so little taste, so little sensitivity to my wants and inner needs, that at any moment I am liable to flare out against him, to his utter confusion and astonishment. Not only is he not helpful, but he is a positive hindrance to me most of the time—his physical presence, moving in and out of my few rooms, galls me beyond the use of words. He has learned a few things which by now are incorporated into a dead routine. I tell him once that I want some files retyped. From that day on, weeks ago, all of his attention is on the files and everything else is gone to hell. I have been carefully avoiding meeting him as a person, even though I see him every day but Sunday, often for hours at a time. Once I meet him as a person there will be fireworks in the house. I have learned from him how to control my temper; and what I am resenting at present, Tolstoy aside, is having to modulate my personality to his, so talentless, so mediocre, so unstimulating. What I will do soon, if I do not go to California in the meantime to write the movie script of *Night Music*, is to have him come down here only three or four times a week. To have to strain the world, which comes in through the telephone, letters, and new books, though his personality is becoming very irksome to me!

At night I met Lee Strasberg and Paula at the Windslow Theatre where he was giving an acting lesson, a weekly affair, to boys and girls from the cast of *Pins and Needles*. We drove up to the home of his parents in the East Bronx, going there for the supper which opens the Passover holidays. It was a real orthodox "seder," the entire family attending.

Lee's parents are very old and whatever personal quality they once had is sunk in the generality of a tired old age. The mother had to lie down twice during the evening, the father once. The old man conducted the ceremony almost mechanically; the children laughed and gossiped during the readings. That sort of religion and ritual has not long to live—one or two more generations and it will all be over.

The food was excellent Jewish food and we ate without stopping for almost two hours. We left at past eleven o'clock and drove downtown, everyone, I think, glad to get away from the supper and a certain oppressive air it had. Lee was silent going down, although we had a very animated conversation going up, about style and fantasy and

Heavenly Express. I want to hear everything he has to say on this subject, for I don't know anyone who has more knowledge about it. I noticed, by the way, a new thing in Lee during our last two meetings. He is very anxious to get his meanings across; and he singles out for censure a play or performance which does not do this, putting this fault almost above all other ones. This, I feel, is because of something he has lacked in his own personality.

I notice that Luise is almost dead in me. It is as if she never existed, as if we never loved and fought, never almost slaughtered each other. When I looked at a photograph of us together it seemed to me that she was almost a stranger—everything is forgotten, the delights and the aches alike. This is how the personality insists upon forgetting what is painful or incomprehensible to it. She, by the way, has delayed the divorce she intended to get immediately. She telephoned, told Herman she is going out to make a picture. "Girl, girl!" I say. And she says, "Boy, boy!" And that is where it started and that is where it ended!

———————•———————

Tuesday, April 23, 1940

I asked myself if this growing discontent with myself is not my usual way of winding myself up to a tense taut state before beginning work. The only trouble is that each year it takes longer to wind one's self up to the hot working point.

I have an idea, too, that the only way I will get ahead is by burning all my bridges behind me; by making clear to all where I stand on all of the burning issues of the day; by being next to penniless; by giving up possessions and ownership of a library, a luxurious apartment, and all of the responsibilities there. For me, in other words, it is necessary to travel light. This requires great courage—I don't think I have it. Think of that: burn all the bridges behind you!

The first novel I have ever read by E. M. Forster I finished in bed early this morning. *A Passage to India.* This is what I call a civilized useful book, the talent small but genuine to the last drop. I've never read a book which made me understand the colonial mind and colonial inferiority as this one does. You can understand Negroes from it, the

Philippines, Hawaii, Mexico, the people of Cuba. Mr. Forster is a discovery for me; I'll get some of his other books.

Beethoven's most basic drive was to change the face of the world. This activity he shared with Napoleon. But Beethoven, enormously gifted, could not do that. Only today the artist can do that. I give you Lenin as artist.

Regret, resignation, retrospect—the young Beethoven had none of these. That was why he was well on in years before he had any slow movement content. Most of his early slow movements are an "attitude," a romantic generalization. This holds true far up into his work, about to the Seventh Symphony. He was not the complete man at an early age that Mozart was. Such forceful fierce forward drive as Beethoven had did not gather much moss or mold—he hit out rather than permitted himself to be hit; and slow movements come from being hit! The so-called third period of his life is another story. He has told this story deeply and well in his last quartets, in the Ninth, and in the last piano sonatas.

Breeding, brains, and beauty—another trio of *Bs*—seem to be the English upper-class ideal of a perfect woman. I learned this tonight when, with Bette and Boris Aronson, I went to see *Rebecca* at Radio City. It is a sensationally successful movie, but it is just a well-tailored piece of hokum directed by the English [Alfred] Hitchcock. I have yet to see an American movie which was not "canned" and I exclude no picture made in this country.

I see there are two worlds to conquer, an outer and an inner. An old remark to be sure, but for the first time really in my experience. The man who does not conquer both is a half-man till the day he dies. Then, of course, he is complete, but it took death to complete him.

Bette came back here with me. We played two Beethoven sonatas, then went to bed. I had had several brandies. When we were almost asleep I had to get out of bed, falling and almost breaking my back. For my mind was swarming with ideas, maggot-infested ideas for short stories, for beginnings of novels. I was talking the most bizarre streaks of dialogue. This is how I used to write, I thought to myself, in the rocket's red glare, no cautions, no worries about form! You have to write novels now, stories and more stories, not plays, I kept thinking. Form considerations in the writing of a novel would not stop you; it is stopping you in playwriting, etc., etc. So it was at this point that I got out of bed and sat down at the typewriter. Two pages of a queer short story came out. Then I folded the pages in half, put them on the dresser, and crawled wearily into bed and fell asleep.

Wednesday, April 24, 1940

At noon I decided to terminate an uneasy morning in bed. Bette had slipped away to an appointment, leaving a note. I prepared and ate a large breakfast, a very unusual item in my life. (The black mouse has been in my cheese again!)

Then I turned for a look at those two pages of short story. Not good—interesting, but not good. But I remarked to myself with satisfaction that just before writing [*Waiting for*] *Lefty* I wrote several such sketches in the Boston hotel room. I remember that period very clearly—everything turned to words in my mind. I couldn't stop writing, stories, monologues, letters, dialogues, questions, answers, statements and restatements, all kept shooting through my head. Am I ready for another period like that? Let it come! I wrote another page or two of this short story and put it in the files.

Boris Aronson came for dinner. I could not tell him much about the murder play that was why I made this appointment. We had an idea that it might prove interesting for a scenic designer and a playwright to work together on a play from the beginning of the writing onward. In talking to him about the play I was able to clarify many of my feelings about it, realizing, for instance, that the first scene should not be serious.

Old Mrs. Adler came into the restaurant and stopped off at the table. She was very expressively indignant about *Night Music*, saying that it had been very badly directed and acted even worse by the leading man. I did not find myself in disagreement, and for a moment had that feeling of heartsickness which had characterized my own feeling about the failure of the production.

Boris said, putting this in my own words, that where the outer tension is greater than the inner tension it is difficult for an artist to create. I saw he was trying to warn me not to fully develop my characters in my writing all at once, but to save their development for the body of the play. He said that artists let their violence out all the time, in this thing and that: but Americans, he said, never let it out, saved it up and then there was a fearful explosion and often murder.

Thursday, April 25, 1940

I made a half of a real start on the murder play, beginning to rewrite the first scene. This time there is something there, a half flare, the four characters of the first scene half living, heads out of the pelvis. Previously I had begun the scene very seriously; everyone plunged into his troubles. Now I did the correct thing—they do not want to talk about their troubles; instead they banter, try to be gay, DENY their troubles. Oh, cunning fellow!

Sid walked in here at midnight, I sitting in pajamas, typing the scene. Sit down, I say—read, pick your nose, eat fruit, drink soda water—I'm working. Which he does. When I am beginning to be satisfied with the scene, I stop, as usual, a stupid rhythm of work. So I turned to Sid, who is always ready to chatter. Chatter this, chatter that: he told me he had seen John O'Hara at Hazel Scott's nightclub, that he was taking Hazel out tomorrow night if he found the money with which to take her out. (Later I gave him the money.) Then I suggested I dress and we go to the nightclub. After that I sat around, convinced that I should stay at my work. I complained. Says Sid, "You work hard."

So I dressed and we walked over to the Café Society Club, all the way over talking about how dull American nightclubs are, places where bored people go to idle away the time, not like the Club Wakaki in Mexico City, not like the cafés in Paris, where you go to spend some leisure time. We have no civilization here and any nightclub here will prove the point. They all have dance bands blazing away: speech and thought are impossible.

We saw Hazel there. She is a charming child. She was glad to see us but had to go uptown, with a fellow, to hear another singer opening on Fifty-second Street. We ate some well-cooked *arroz con pollo*, drank a beer, sipped a Scotch. Then we drove along the Hudson, talking about poetic impulse and how difficult it is to be a poet on steaks that cost two dollars and fifty cents. Surfeit! I put Sid off at his door and came home and wrote a few more pages of the first scene. I considered my fingers, my toes, I considered my navel. I looked in between the covers of some books.

Stylization, my friends, is essentialization. Of course!

I had fresh flowers in the house today. Yellow tulips, hard and green, ice cold till the warm room opened them up; and white stock. Flowers are good for my heart; they fascinate me the way they did when I was a boy.

The other day Sandy told me about an interesting scene he had given one of his students as an acting problem. A man suspects his wife is going insane. He loves her dearly. The problem is to question her and find out the truth. But he wants to find out that it is not true. Sandy says a young actor in his class did this scene remarkably well. The more he questioned her the more he fell in love with her and did not want to discover the truth. This can make a fine scene in a play.

The year is hurrying into summer. Now by four A.M. the first signs of dawn appear over the eastern side of the city. In another few days they will put daylight saving time into effect and dawn will have been harnessed—lo, an hour late! I see many of these dawns; they come interestingly into my room. The pallid pink sun glides across my desk, hits a mirror to my left, and is reflected to a hall in back of me where my records are stacked. I used to have a head of Beethoven in that hall and it was a real stroke of poetic justice that every clear morning the first light of the sun illuminated the bronze head. The light of the first sunrays is like the warm flush on peaches.

I can tell you nothing of importance today. Bette came down at seven in the evening. We went to a movie. They are beginning to interest me for technical reasons, plot moves, reversals, turns, solutions. A movie with an intelligent theme never succeeds in working out its story. They begin often with character conflict, but they become frightened before they are half through the story. Result, device after device is dragged in, melo [melodramatic] situations and surprises are introduced and the story ends heroically on an issue or two which had nothing to do with what the picture began to say. The cinema people are unable to solve any human dilemma by psychological development or truth. A husband and wife, for instance, meet under difficult circumstances and marry from them. Now comes the problem of marriage adjustment. Things look dark—they make no headway in their mating efforts. But lo and behold!—suddenly the husband is on trial for his life for MURDER! The wife lovingly sticks to him through thick and thin. And so they have made the marriage adjustment and their lives are solved. In a pig's eye!

Every studio has its own style in writing. A Warner Brothers picture always has an interesting linear quality about it, but is always dead in its parts. The picture I saw last night, *Dr. Ehrlich's Magic Bullet*. In some ways it is such an ordinary picture that one is apt to overlook the remarkable assembly and compression of the machinery, for it is a piece of machinery, dead all over, inhuman, but machinelike in its precision and use of parts. Characters never have any doubts which pull them two ways—they are one thing, one color, good or bad, moving only in one direction, on one dimension. In a word, they are not dialectic—they are without those contradictions which are in themselves the source of the deepest human drama.

But I must not forget the superb old German actor, [Albert] Basserman, who played Koch, the great German scientist, in this picture. He had only several small scenes in the picture, but he immediately made every American or English actor in the cast look like a boy. How he did this I am unable to say, perhaps with great repose, a WHOLE grasp of the character, really talking to the other characters instead of acting talking. He was well aware of the meaning of every situation in which he found himself and it was to that meaning that he gave himself, never to something abstract, never to, for instance, nobility in general. In a word, he acted, he was active, he understood, he dealt with!

———◆———

Saturday, April 27, 1940

What world-shaking events occurred in my life today, the life of a minor artist who is only half an artist, half a man, half a human, all creature? The rare jewel in the setting of the day and night was to tell one girl that I would not meet her because I was going to stay home and work. Then I called another girl who came here, fresh and dewy; I undresssed her rapidly enough and over a period of several hours unfreshened her completely. Myself too. This is not absolutely the truth, for the girl, leaning back in the car that I was driving out to Bill Kozlenko's house—a roast chicken and other good things to eat beside us in a big bag—said, "I am so sensitized all over." That is what "loving" had done for her. Me it makes sullen, bored, stupid, a little nervously alert. What is needed, I am sorry to say, is to really love and be loved, not this mere mechanism of erection, death and rebirth, and another death, and then a solemn washing up in the bathroom while the girl smokes a cigarette and looks at the ceiling.

———◆———

Sunday, April 28, 1940

Having to be up early, having promised to go out to Sylvia's and Luther's farm, I did not go to sleep at all. Instead I read, fussed around, and finally greeted Gurdus and Bette, who were going out with me. Gurdus to make a decent phonograph and radio apparatus for them. We arrived there soon enough. The morning was lovely and sweet, the first day of spring; but I was too tired to enjoy it. Luther and Sylvia were still fussing around with their house and grounds.

We sat in the sun for a time, chatted, smoked, ate lunch, looked at a newspaper, and finally I went upstairs for two hours of solid sleeping. By eleven at night we were ready to drive home. Bette I sent home in a cab and up to the house I dashed, ready for sleep. Did I go to bed? Certainly not. It was four in the morning before I turned out the light.

Treading water is fun for a fish, not a human being!

———•———

Monday, April 29, 1940

A sad dream awakened me after four hours of sleep. I woke up and clearly and distinctly announced to the cool darkened bedroom, "My life is a useless one," thereby, I suppose, placing myself in the ranks of characters out of Russian literature, although American literature is enough to worry about!

The dream, the sad dream. I had heard that Luise had a baby son. I went to see the baby; there were several others with me. We sat down at a long table. The boy, about three, was brought to the table and sat on the other side of a man who was acting as a sort of majordomo of the household. Luise, it seems, had put out a story that the boy was the son of her Englishman friend. But when I looked at the boy I saw immediately that he was my son. His eyes and hair were very dark but they were my hair and eyes. I wondered how I could claim him. Then Luise came in. She sat down, acted very cordial and social, but she was very angry at the majordomo for having showed the child. Luther

Adler was on the other side of me. He raised his eyebrows and pursed his lips, meaning "that is your son." But Luise offered no information—she had made up a story and was sticking to it—the child was all hers.

I could not sleep again after this dream awakened me. I tossed and turned, fretted and fumed. Now I am up, typing this page. A certain determination impelled me out of bed: make hours, make working plans—what are you doing in bed! It must be repeated here again—the artist is the husband and wife in one body!

Thursday, May 2, 1940

There are good reasons why I haven't made an entry in this journal for at least several days. The main reason is that suddenly, bang!—out of the blue I have begun to work on a Wilson play. It will be either very good or very bad, but I am riding with it right to the bitter end. For two days and nights, sleeping by day, I haven't left the house and have remained in my pajamas, reading and writing notes for scenes and characters.

My main impulse for the play is the growing sentiment for war in this country. Some sections of so-called liberals are making calls for U.S. intervention in the European war in the name of the old crusade for democracy. Robert Sherwood, the fine espouser of popular causes, has just opened a play in which the Lunts are acting, a theatre piece call to arms. The Wilson play will do the opposite if I am any sort of writer at all; it will show that our present president is treading the dangerous path already bloodied up by Wilson and company. What I personally think of Wilson himself is not clear to me yet—I do not have a grasp of him yet. Of course this puts the murder play to one side, just when I was beginning to get astride in it. It can wait on a siding till the express goes through!

My living habits are very bad, but my mind is clear and alert, albeit larded over with laziness. However, I find I function from a certain new center of authority and that is nothing to sneeze about, although from time to time you should warn yourself that it is very dangerous to be authoritative about a handful of dust!

Tuesday night, after dinner at his house, Lee Strasberg and I went to see the revival of *Liliom* in which are playing Gadget, [Burgess] Meredith, and a new Swedish actress, Ingrid Bergman. The production is quite poor and the famous classic, now seen through more experienced eyes, is not all it's cracked up to be. I would not trade *Night Music* for it, although Lee Strasberg disagreed with me. But it is a very talented script. The direction was bad and pointless. Gadget says that the director, Benno Schneider, takes all of his impulses from the theatre, not from life.

We went backstage after the show and I saw Gadget for the first time in weeks. I was not in a friendly or communicative mood and did not attempt to hide it. He understood and said nothing.

From Sardi's, where we went next, we went to Lindy's. There I left Lee and proceeded with Len Lyons and a lawyer friend to the Stork Club. Next the Monte Carlo and finally Club 18. A lot of brandy and soda passed the barrier of your writer's lips. At the Monte Carlo Len introduced us to a nice girl who is named Mary Anita Loos. I will look her up—she is nice and she sat there with a very giving quality. After this I went home and began to paw over Wilson items and it was here that I decided to work ahead on the Wilson play.

———————•———————

Friday, May 3, 1940

My hours are clustered around the research work necessary on the Wilson play. My present plan is to first get a general outline of the period and Wilson's work, then to narrow down to particular events and personalities. Many of the books are written in what is now an almost incomprehensible spirit of partisanship, for or against, angry and bitter. It is almost impossible to get a clear or understanding picture of Wilson from the memoirs of his friends. In the meantime, too, I have managed to get some phonograph records of men like Harding, Colby, Senator Lodge, and a few others. These tell me more than I can read in ten books. Records of Wilson and others will be coming along soon.

I realize in myself the taking of a very subtle form of revenge on Luise. First, she gave me a watch a long time ago. It was strange to me that this watch I dropped so often (I who break nothing) that finally it was necessary to buy a new watch. Now I see that I really wanted to smash the watch. The new strapwatch, next. I insisted upon wearing it whenever I went to bed with a girl. It gave me acute pleasure, a thing I could not understand, once mentioned that perhaps it emphasized the nakedness. Yesterday I realized what it is. When Luise returned from England last she told me about an Englishman with whom she has been living. She knew it was over between us and she then decided that she would marry this man if it could be arranged. Then for three nights, a last flare-up, during which we were more in love with each other than ever before—since we were both free and not in conflict with each other, irresponsible, we slept with each other. All during this time she wore a thin band of gold around her wrist, a present from the Englishman whose name, by the way, I never asked, although she showed me pictures of him. This gold bracelet I resented, although it gave me a curious perverse pleasure, even intensifying the "affair." She did not remove the bracelet by day or night. And now this wearing of my strapwatch in bed is the subtle revenge of my humiliation, as much as it was a humiliation.

Early this morning I had a dream that I walked into a room where Fay Wray's husband was staying with his small daughter whom he had kidnapped from Fay. I spoke to him quietly, as a friend. Suddenly Fay burst into the room to get her child back. She grabbed the child and told her husband that I was not only her friend but that we loved each other. Then he ran out of the room, to get a gun, I thought. I followed him out into the street, afraid, but he refused to say what he was going to do. Then I woke up. The child, the child, that is what the dream was mostly about, the child, a child!

I am very tired, tired from the heart and in the heart. G. B. [Bette Grayson] came down here in the late evening and we went to bed. I was inwardly against doing this, but something forced me to it. This is sex of the nerves, bad, tiring, useless, immoral—there is no balm in it. Then we had a late supper from the icebox and sat reading for another hour. She went to bed and I continued with reading Dodd's book on Wilson, making dozens of notes, some useful.

Also, a lot of congressional records for 1917 are here. It is a thrilling experience to read the speech of Norris against war. La Follette's speech did not impress me as much, coming, it seemed to me, from some sort of demogogic impurity.

An image of the modern man which some day I will write into a scene is this: he stands before the mirror, talking to himself, sneering.

Then he pulls out a gun and shoots at the hated image in the mirror—
the glass smashes all around his feet and he thinks he has done something or made a point!

———————•———————

Saturday, May 4, 1940

Lee Kozlenko called. She wanted to talk to me about Bill, which she
did. The same old trouble. Rightfully she asks that her husband be a
man in relation to her; instead she has a boy, willful, stubborn, and
adolescent. What is she to do? She doesn't know, needs advice, wants a
friend to talk to him. What advice could I give her, how could I answer
her nervous tremulous voice? Only by promising to think about the
problem and saying I would meet with her early this week. It is going
to be a difficult future life for both of them—his life ruined by his idea
that he is artist and intellect and his desire to exploit both of these
nonexistent qualities as a wage earner, and her unfulfilled hunger for a
husband and man, a father to her child. Until now she has been making
a living for both of them. This has tenderized him beyond touching. It
is a pitiful situation with him, at the slightest word, jumping behind
his boyish ego and from there hurling hot words at her and the world.
Or else he curls up and goes to sleep, unable to keep awake in the
brilliant light of his own incompetence shown to him. Only from a
clean recognition of his own limitations can any progress come, but by
now self-recognition is almost impossible for him. For by now he is
even snobbish about his learning and his "high ideals."

In the later afternoon Waldo Frank called. We made a late dinner
appointment. He arrived and we sat around and drank sherry. It is
almost necessary to treat him as one treats a feminine woman, with kid
gloves, circling around him cautiously. His ego is very demanding, his
personality alert to any possible slight in the form of lack of appreciation of his work and his generally unrealized importance as a writer. I
was able to be much easier with him than usual, even though he
makes, in a curious way, sensitivity his business. I think that is why he
seems to me to experience very little in life—at the moment of the
experience he is busy being "sensitive" to it, seeking to explain what is

happening as it is happening. I think this may be the reason that he always asks me to tell him what happened in this fight, that love scene, the other realization. He is the only man I know who opens me up in the way a woman does. Making me extend myself and divide myself into a series of small cascades of gracious and gallant efforts. (My adjustment to him makes for an interesting character.) He is burning, it seems to me, for general recognition, for he is after all the best social critic in America today; and much of what he says and does comes out of a painful sense of being unrecognized. But, despite his ego demands, there is something essentially honest about him and it is best to approach him honestly and wholly.

As we rode over Second Avenue I proposed an auto trip to California to him. He said he would like that, saying it would be a fine experience, meaning that it would be fine for me as he would explain the country to me as we rode through it. (Am I being cruel?) He is something, I suppose, like a sea anemone, opening and closing, swaying with each movement of the current, pulsing and living with outstretched tendrils. (But this "business of sensitivity" makes me uneasy.)

We ate and drank wine at the noisy Rumanian restaurant, the owner coming over and pestering us away from our conversation several times. Waldo was telling me about a young girl he had recently met— he thinks he is in love with her and that she is possibly rejecting him. He said he wanted my advice about this affair, but it seemed to me that he wanted to show me that he was still consorting with young girls and was very sensitive to the slightest implication of human life. Life, life, he seems so hungry for life and experiences, almost as if he were a young girl with a whole life ahead of him. He seems too conscious that he is getting older, several times during the night *assuring* me that he is fifty years old, even though he feels very young. But for all of this, make no mistake, he is still very much a man, nobody's fool, a real artist.

By this time I was telling him of my needs for a woman, of Fay Wray and some others, starting from the time in 1929 when I went on the road with the Theatre Guild shows and there we met Sylvia Field, Louis Veda, and Sandy Meisner for the first time. He showed me some letters from this young girl who is so interesting to him. But by this time a violent headache (tired and too much wine) was upon me; I found myself leaning back, in a cold sweat, feeling that I would keel over or throw up any minute. Anyway, it was after one in the morning and time to leave; I left.

And the New York [Drama] Critics' [Circle] Award of the year went to Bill Saroyan for his *The Time of Your Life*. A not undeserving award.

By the way, a letter came three days ago from Theodore Dreiser from California, answering a note I sent him asking how he was feeling. He wants to know if I am interested in dramatizing *Sister Carrie*, which he has just sold to RKO. Waldo, too, I forgot to say, gave me a play of his to read. Harold has already read this play and rejected it for production.

———————•———————

Sunday, May 5, 1940

Thousands of people thought as I did today, that it was the long-last first beautiful day of spring. On arising at eleven in the morning, I called Bill and Lee and suggested a ride through the countryside. They happily agreed to the plan and so we were off in the afternoon. Their baby happy and bewildered by all the strange sights. It becomes increasingly difficult to find any country. Everywhere there are smooth roads and intensive traffic. We got off the beaten track though and landed out near Long Island Sound, at Freeport. It was so summery that we quickly decided to have dinner at a place right on the water. We ate leisurely and happily. When the evening began to come we started for home, this time, sadly enough, listening to all manner of disturbing news on the radio. England has been given a staggering blow in the belly by the Nazis. The House of Commons is being "common" and questioning the leadership of Munich and after.

How interesting it was to see all the people standing around at the water's edge there. What everyone was doing was snatching at the real spring, standing in the warm sun, happy to be living, filled with simple but mysterious urges—it was like a French painting, perhaps by Seurat.

Luther Adler called. There had been a benefit for China earlier and many of the participants were at the Stork Club. Would I come up there? Yes. We sat around, talked to Walter Winchell, drank brandy and soda, ate wonderful food and were not permitted to pay the bill because we were with Sylvia Sidney and Molly Picon, good show-pieces for the club. Winchell is a great bore and the vanity of all vanities, but it occurred to us that he might begin to start rapping the poll tax of the southern states. On the way out he seemed interested when I brought the subject up.

Luther sat there opposite Sylvia, bored, restless, a boy in all parts. He roams in his affections, twice got up, once brought Tamara,* his old flame (ours?), to the table. Sylvia said, with a laugh, that the best way to keep a husband was to make him feel that the door was always open. She said, too, to my suprise—since I did not give her credit for that much self-knowledge—that she has grown more cautious and careful, not being the girl she used to be. I did not say to her that that is why she has ceased to be an interesting actress. With a good man in her past life there is a girl who might have become an extraordinary person and artist. But now the wine has been drained off, the lees are left.

Monday, May 6, 1940

The house if full of Wilson books; a dozen more came in today. I am reading slowly, slowly getting for myself a sense of what Wilson must have been like, personally, as a man, although I will never know what he said and did in the privacy of his bedroom.

My sister Florence walked in for an hour late in the afternoon, looking well, seeming to slowly be growing up into womanhood. For some reason I don't want to feel related to my family.

I already note that there is little in Wilson that I can admire or love—he is not "my man"—but on top of this I am stirred by him because of the men who opposed him—I am against that whole caboodle! Hence Wilson takes on an emotional life for me. We shall see what we shall see!

In the later evening I went down to Morris's house to meet with Max, Phoebe, Bud, and Sandy, the committee which is to bring a plan of action to the larger body of the Group. I was dismayed, disappointed, and angered to find the same old sick and timorous fixation on a "constitution and democracy." A constitution, they insisted, was a

---

* Tamara Drasin, Russian-born actress, singer, and dancer, had in 1933 broken off a relationship with Adler in favor of Odets. With equal suddenness a few months later, she announced to Odets that she was marrying someone else.

plan of action in itself. All of the practical workings of the theatre they had neglected to chart. After an angry outburst I could only sit there silently, hoping that they had grown enough in the last year to finally understand that the yearnings of their egos will not make a working theatre.

All of this is not to say that I am not on the side of the actors in this fight to clarify what is the Group Theatre and how it must function in order to exist. Harold had different ideas from them, but I am not in agreement with him at all. It is my distinct impression, which I shall soon tell him, that he has been trying to fit the Group Theatre into his life which is mostly composed of other elements that are mostly against the healthy life of a theatre. Then, too, I shall have to tell him that it is not necessary for him to put all words and theories of life aside, seeing in his own case that he is caught in the grip of a classic device: distraught woman kills good man. Many interesting fumes may arise from the cellar where such fermentation is going on, but shrewd and sensitive analysis will not change the nature of the happening. Harold is a crippled, half-broken man, only half struggling against an early death as a young artist. The sort of life he has been living with Miss Adler either kills or makes a man. Him it will kill because he is an introvert, never a man of action. I would not say this if he were a writer or painter, the artist who needs only himself for creation. But his creative activity is a collective one which needs a group of people to bring it to fruition. This is no problem; it is as simple as written here.

———•———

Tuesday, May 7, 1940

A dead day. There was a sparse diet of Wilson, some more books coming in. There are now about forty books on or concerning Wilson on the table in the hall, and more to come. Who will read them all?— the very number of them dismays me, makes me uneasy.

Jack Bernstein and his accountant came down here to explain to me the workings of the Chelsea Pontiac [automobile dealership] of which I have been a third partner for three years with no money coming in from it. When they were all finished I was able to see inefficiency, not dishonesty. I'd like to get my five thousand dollars out of this, the only reason for having gone into it being my old friendship with the Bernstein family. Let there not be such generosity and there will not be such troubles.

The one interesting thing of the day was a letter from Wr. F. [Fay Wray]. This letter moved and touched me, for she spoke of her loneliness, reaching out to me from between the lines, not daring to ask me directly what I think of her. She is like one of those mysterious dried ferns which will come to life the moment you touch it with water. How can I give her false hopes? I composed two letters to her and then destroyed them because I could not manage the correct tone with which to assuage her heart and yet not bring to life something I cannot later handle. And yet I thought of her with yearning all the night.

To be so tired and to have done nothing all day and night!

———•———

Wednesday, May 8, 1940

My life seems in escrow for a better day. Spring is truly here, each day bland and easeful. Two interesting letters came today, one from my father, the other from Harold Clurman. I answered my father almost immediately, writing to him with unusual concentration and care. He is very gloomy and depressed because he is unable to make a living. This he blames on the fact that he is an old man (fifty-five), saying that they don't want old men. He is selling a sort of neon-light gadget, says he could sell a lot of them but for the fact the manufacturer can't get the necessary materials from Europe because of the war. He asked me to pay for his insurance. That type of man cannot earn a sandwich, but he is careful about keeping his insurance paid up. I sent him a check for five hundred dollars and told him that I would give him a modest weekly allowance if he stopped worrying. His letter was full of the usual foolish philosophy, "The good Lord sees . . . life is short . . . what is it all worth? . . ." etc., etc.

Harold's letter concerned a quiet restful depression. He is unable to get a job out in Hollywood and he needs money. He still believes in the theatre, he says, is a little sad at the foolishness of the Group actors, has bought an option on a dramatization of a novel, is seeing Frances Farmer because she is one of the few persons out there sympathetic to his view of life . . . she is really a lovely girl, he says . . . he is living at the house of John Brahm . . . will I write . . . and he still loves Stella and me. He asks if I am working on a play, a rumor which he heard and hopes to be true.

Well, what can you answer to a letter like that? I will give him back depression for depression, hope for hope.

Later Sylvia Sidney called and I went up to their house for dinner. The baby is six months old, looks very masculine and vital, looking like the Adler family. Also present were the hopeless depressing trio of Sylvia's mother, foxlike, Luther's sister Nunya, and Carrie Slaski with her peculiar inverted ego. With such unstimulating people I find myself the worst of dullards, the most superficial and callow of young men. Later Stella Adler breezed in with a younger girl and another grubby man from the company. Stella seemed very self-conscious, chattered without stop, but looking very handsome and magnetic. Then Stella's old mother walked in. Immediately the other daughter, Nunya, walked into another room as she is not on speaking terms with her mother. Luther followed her to placate her and remonstrate against such conduct. Stella and party made a fuss about the baby who was up for a feeding; then they left while the mother stayed on, saying piteously that no, she did not want a drink—"The doctor has told me that I must not drink. I am taking two medicines. I carry in my purse two medicines." A half hour later she left and then Luther and Nunya came out of the other room. A huge bottle of champagne, a gift from the Stork Club owner, had been opened and everyone was drinking steadily from it. I stopped—it was giving me a headache, or increasingly deepening the headache all these maniacs had been giving me for an hour. Finally I was alone with Sylvia and Luther. They wanted to ride out to their farm then and there, but I pleaded unfinished business on my desk, said goodnight, and walked out into the soft night. It was beginning to rain, big soft spattering drops.

But I didn't go home. Instead I drove to the Stork Club and asked there for Len Lyons. He wasn't there and I was too shy to go in alone, so I walked around for a half hour. I was very depressed, particularly because I was so shy that I could not walk into a nightclub alone. This made me think of the many times Luise and I had gone together to such places, each time being an agony for me. When finally I returned to the club Lyons was there and I found myself very tense and nervous. He had with him what he called "a New Dealer party," Leon Henderson, Judge [Ferdinand] Pecora, and a pair of bankers plus Jimmy Cannon, who kept intruding his personality, insisting that he was

unhappy, insisting on attention until you wanted to sock him in the
nose. Pecora is a man of good heart, a specialist who does not seem too
intelligent about anything else. The same with Henderson, whom I
had not met before. A man, it seems, may become famous in one
certain line and yet have absolutely no inner life worth talking about.

We left, leaving the New Dealers there, on the way out meeting
John O'Hara, who looks very dissipated, even sick, like something
which needs scraping. We shook hands warmly and sincerely and I said
I would telephone him. Cannon and Lyons took me to the Monte Carlo
where I was glad to go because I wanted to take another look at the
Loos girl. Everyone in both clubs was busy talking about a big party
which had taken place the night before—all the bright young people of
the town had been there. Roosevelt's sons, Hearst's sons, Brisbane's
son, Warburgs, columnists, entertainers, all for Harriman's newly married daughter. I want a few parties like that behind me before I write
the Larry and Barry play.

After that drove around in the rain with Cannon, Lyons since gone
home. He wants to be a playwright. What can one say to that? I talked
casually for an hour while driving to ease off my nervous restlessness,
then went home to bed at six in the rainy morning.

———————•———————

Thursday, May 9, 1940

Now is the time to write a tale and call it *The Jaundiced Eye!*

There is a certain nervous state in which it is impossible to approach
a woman sexually. Then shut off the telephone, my friend.

There are two main contradictions in my nature which are going to
drive me on the rocks. (Then I will change the title of the tale, calling it
On the Rocks.) To deal with one of them, at least mentioning it: I can
conceive only that life is for some great and noble purpose. On all sides
I meet fools and charlatans, or rogues, or painted egos, or doctrinaires.
In order to merely survive one must become "wordly," must grow
political (despite the apolitical nature of one's self). How destructive it
is to play out this farce every time one puts a foot out on the street!
How deadening!

Some natures are different, but for me it is necessary for my soul's good to tell a fool he is a fool, to tell a rogue what he is. There is not a living man or woman who knows what I really think of them. I could burn their ears off if for five minutes I dropped this false face behind which I move and think and feel.

So inwardly there is this strong sense of life and the use to which it is to be put. But outwardly, because of wanting to be loved, I suppose, there are the hundred petty compromises of daily life which finally serve to muddy every honest inward impulse. My thoughts and brain cells are rented out by fools because they happen to be close to me, close in space. This is how other people use your life, no matter what purpose you set it to!

Life is much easier if you are a private citizen. Then people do not go out of their way to claim your attention and approbation. False extension of the self is seldom necessary, which is one of the reasons I yearn for anonymity.

Germany has invaded Holland and Belgium. It is three in the morning but the radio stations are going full blast with more bulletins and more and more. America wants its pound of news, but I am sure everyone in England is fast asleep. By tomorrow evening all of our newspapers will know all the inside stories and meanings of this latest war move!

———————•———————

Friday, May 10, 1940

I did not mention that Bette came down here last night, looking young and fresh, elated at the probability of swinging a summer stock company job. She gets along remarkably well, with real self-confidence, for a child who is practically familyless and without backing. We went uptown and saw [Lewis] Milestone's job of *Of Mice & Men*. I was not disappointed, perhaps because I expected so little. At least it was adult entertainment. Milly's masculine energy showed in every frame, but not much more. He is uninventive, a kind of honest carpenter according to his lights.

I awoke out of an erotic dream in which Sylvia Sidney was my partner, Luther asleep beside us in the bed no less! Then there was another dream about roller coasting down the interior of a sewer, laid out like steps down which I bounced. Three times I made this ride, each time landing in the drugstore downstairs. Finally I decided to call it quits and woke up. It was after this that I returned to sleep and had the other more pleasant dream.

Being curious about the handwriting of Woodrow Wilson, I called Mrs. Eastman on the phone and had her come down here. She is a curious woman, too clever and not clever enough. She had many interesting points to make about the writing, didn't know whose it was. She said the main contradiction of his nature was his extreme idealism combined with a very thin skin and an inability to face discord or vulgarity. Also that he had, whoever he was, a very painful necessity of preserving "face," Oriental in its strength. She did not say so, but she gave me enough bits and fragments to make me see that Wilson had a progressive nature built up on a reactionary base. If he lost face, she said, it was very possible he would break down or do something violent, even killing himself.

———•———

Saturday, May 11, 1940

The half-yearly report came from Random House which publishes my plays. I found I earned six hundred and sixty-four dollars for the half year. There was a time when I could have lived on that, would have bartered away my birthright for that much money every six months. What pleased me very much was to find that the ninety-five-cent copy of *Six Plays* sold more than six thousand copies in the first three months.

Bette, Bill and Lee Kozlenko, and I had dinner at "68". A dinner like that five times a week and I'd never write another line. Then we looked for a movie to go to, driving around in more spring rain, but finally drove them home to Sunnyside. Bette and I came back here and read and then went to bed to get up tomorrow at a reasonable time in order to go out to Luther's farm.

———•———

Sunday, May 12, 1940

The sun warm, the air cool out of the sun, a fine spring day. Many cars on the road: it took two hours to get to Luther's farm. Best of all was the little dog who is always glad to see me; she is my little lover—curls up on my lap wherever I sit—it is getting to be quite a scandal down there. That, of course, is the little dachshund dog who always reminds me of Luise. Does that sound like a joke? Well, when I watched this dog in frolic with two other dogs I was easily and clearly reminded of certain "pliant" hours at Nichols, Conn. Definitely.

Luther is falling asleep more each week, the enchanted prince. The fairy tale is a lie. In true life no one comes to wake you up. In America all men, artists particularly, wait for the magic circumstances; it seldom comes, but when it does everyone catches fish as fast as the nets can be hauled in.

Seeing the burgeoning spring, much delayed, in all the trees made me think that all Oriental art has the quality of budding. Curious but palpably true.

I went into the washroom there and glancing at the mirror saw my sister Genevieve's placid animal face staring at me.

I had with me the Millis book, *Road to War*, very interesting. Read it during the afternoon and evening.

Bette was sitting opposite me, reading *The Gentleman from San Francisco*, Bunin. Then she said she had finished it. She left the room, went upstairs. Suddenly I remembered that she and her mother had been crossing the ocean when she was a child. Her mother had died on shipboard, like the man in the story. She went upstairs to cry, I think. I didn't follow her, but I made cheerful sounds when she returned. I don't put myself out to her too much, careful, always careful. Live with someone and don't live with them. Why? Don't want to make an attachment, don't want to make it so close that they will begin to imagine it into the future. A favorite trick of mine, a stupid trick. I seldom acknowledge what I have—don't want the entanglement of ownership or responsibility. That is the way of an idiot or a fanatic. I'll settle for fanatic. *Pissant!*

At three in the morning we all arrived home. First Bette at her door, then Luther at his, finally I to my door and quickly to bed.

———•———

Monday, May 13, 1940

Because you want to "get on" with people you are beginning to lose
your true sense of them. You are a very naïve man in many ways and
your opinion of people is often apt to be based on their own opinions of
themselves. Take Phoebe Brand for instance. She is stupid, doc-
trinaire, pudgy, soft, inhibited, and sentimental, with all the conditioning of her petty middle-class background stuck to her skin like bits
of shell on a chick who is looking at the world for the first time. And this
child talks in the name of a balanced mind, in the name of justice, in
the name of Marxist values! And you, worse fool, you listen seriously!
Most of the Group people are that way—mindless! And they have not
the excuse of youth, of charm, or wit, or beauty. I can no longer move
among them in the name of sensitivity or art or sincerity of intention;
now I know them with cynicism. The other night Mr. Gorelik flew into
a rage because I would not credit him with being a first-rate business
manager. I wanted to shout at him that I only tolerated him because he
had a narrow talent as a scenic artist, that if I had to take him as a
business manager I would right then and there jump out the window
after shooting him and everyone else in the room; I kept my mouth
shut instead. This afternoon Miss Brand backed away from me as if
from a reptile because I refused her request to speak at a strikers'
benefit. If I think of myself as a minor artist how can I think of them as
artists too? I will settle for proficient disciplined workmen; let artists
fall where they may! And not even that among them, excepting two or
three. I will even settle among them for clarity and outline of simple
forms, but that too is lacking. I think I will take the Jane Wyatts of life
and let the Phoebe Brands, sensitivity and all, plot their revolutions in
a cellar without me, boys!

Answering a letter which came a few days ago from Marion Post in
Tennessee. She is lonely, working in strange places. I was sorry to have
missed her when down South last month. I like her. At least she can set
up a tripod and take pictures without puking her ego up. She is a quiet
workman. I asked her to write whenever she had the need, meaning I
would answer.

And a hurried note came from Fay Wray. She was out with Harold
Clurman and she was glad to hear someone who knew what to talk
about; it reminded her of me. This makes me think that from time to

time I want to open a note to Harold this way: "Dear Harold, you know I love you and you know I hate you, and between the two it is not always easy to see you or write to you."

A man who begins to be an artist soon discovers that he is "a man imprisoned in his task," to use a phrase by Wilson. One wants to say to that, "Lucky unhappy man." For me to have discovered this fact about myself has made much for unhappiness. Half of me went on strike, half of me stayed at the desk, in the cell. This is why I am half an artist, if such a thing is possible. But free, on the street, or in the cell, I have not enjoyed myself. I yearn for a wholeness of work, but refuse to give the whole self to it. Of course the only freedom for me is through disciplined work and I know it; and the cell is in me to begin with, not outside of me. I was beginning to gain that sense of power that an artist feels by subduing his materials, the power he gains over the whole world—the real freedom, in other words. But that was last year, perhaps the year before. Now I have a sense of sitting in a cell with all the obscenities of life in my lap. I am a masturbating prisoner among the slops of life. Man, man, you are only thirty-four! Yet everything slides. . . . There is a masculine ending and a feminine ending in music, but this is a neuter ending. The man who wrote *Oblomov* doesn't know as much about his character as I do.

Wilson!

The above explains why I am beginning to be so enraged at people without form, slothful, undisciplined. Caliban at the mirror! What, by the way, happened to Caliban when he married? Did he marry?

———•———

Tuesday, May 14, 1940

At the corner of Fifty-seventh Street and Fifth Avenue, my radio tells me, the temperature is now sixty-six degrees. I thought you might like to know.

What will I do about this feeling of rejection, of not being wanted or needed? Come, you are no longer a boy, you are a "famous" man, your books are published, you have a reputation. And yet what do you pick out of your success, of company, of any intercourse or situation?— always the element of rejection which must be present in any normal function. Even the simple belly rejects food at some time, the body rejects heat, sometimes, cold. There are seasons for all things. What do you want, loafer? Enthusiasm streaming from all eyes at all times? All right, you were a child and your mother did not want you, your father refused you; but that is thirty years ago!

All the above is not true as it is written. There is an element of truth in it, but it is much more subtle. Part of the subtlety rests in the distinction between the words rejection and repudiation. From this, starting in early childhood, has come an inability or lack of desire to assume responsibilities. It works something like this: I won't start or continue something because you may throw me out, meaning reject or repudiate. In fact, it goes, I will throw you out before you throw me out! Finally, from this the self falls back to the self. It is the only certainty: live alone and like it!

That is not exactly peculiar to me; it is a modern disease, well discussed in a woman psychologist's book, *The Neurotic Personality of the Times*, by Karen Horney.

I answered Harold Clurman's note briefly but attached to my note the journal for the last four days, by carbon copy. I wonder what he will think of it. Gadget is out there now, too, having called yesterday to say he was planning to go out for a few weeks' work in a new Cagney film.

In the evening, on the restless impulse, joined Lyons at the Stork Club. John O'Hara was there, tight, insisting that I had no idea how fond of me he was. To prove it he called to mind bits of experiences we had had together in California two years ago; he was playfully offended that I did not remember them. Talking to him made me think that we might be ideal collaborators on the Larry and Barry play. He knows that rotten night life better than I will ever know it. And he looks as if he is waiting for some earnest force (myself?) to generate him into writing activity.

Julie Garfield walked in, having in tow M. [Miguel] Covarubias and party. The laddie is going back to the coast soon: he enjoys this "high life." I begin to think there is not much there to ruin, excepting good intentions, those famous paving stones which in our time have in them too much sand and not enough cement.

Lyons and I prowled around for the balance of the evening, later meeting Winchell in the street. Winchell stopped on a cool corner while he spoke broadly and grandly of his money, of the problems concerning it, how he is worried about another run on the banks. I wondered, as I listened, how a human being could have so little sense of other human beings: he is a vortex of vanity. When we broke up he said, "Goodnight Cliffie," easily, casually, as if dismissing a waiter at the table. This irked me, I must admit, but I began to think about him and the closed-in life, stale, not a fresh perception in a month, that he lives.

———————•———————

Wednesday, May 15, 1940

Yesterday there was a note from Nizer, Luise's lawyer from California, where she is, who had sent some fresh papers; for she is going ahead with the divorce. Nizer wanted to meet with me to explain the papers. I said to hell with it—assure me that they are all right to sign and I will do so. By today this is no longer necessary, for Herman showed me some news items that state the divorce was granted yesterday. I don't even know what they mean, although I read her excuses to the judge, the same judge who married us! You have to give reasons, so the reasons she gave consisted of the facts that I insisted that one career in a family was enough, and some nights I didn't come home. I am sorry to suspect that Luise is trying to give the movie people the impression that she was so troublesome with them because of me. Godspeed if it will help her. The announcement in the paper meant nothing. Legally we are now both free. But the same emotions carry on: there is no difference or cutoff of feeling at all. This is a pool I seldom stir up, the pool of my feeling about her and our marriage. It will come out though, somewhere, sometime, in some writing, for or against some woman or women. The feeling of my love and life with Luise is quietly growing into some mysterious fluid, as grape juice becomes wine in the dark where it is stored. Let it age, Clifford.

Had a long talk on the telephone with Lee Strasberg, making a dinner appointment for the end of the week. Then went up to the offices of the League of American Writers where there was to be a discussion of an antiwar resolution which Henry Hart had drawn up. I had not met most of the people who were there, Folsom, I. Schneider, Myra Page, but Grafton and L. [Lillian] Hellman I knew. Most of the discussion did not interest me, although it helped clarify some of my feelings about the war and a course in relation to it. But the entire evening I was trying to orientate myself in relation to the people, a

curious lot, most of them Communists. The latter were for the resolution, the others more hesitant and wavering since it came out for
complete denunciation of help for the allies. They decided to meet
again next week, in the meantime appointing a new committee to
draw up a new declaration. [Albert] Maltz and [George] Sklar were
there too.

This Henry Hart, as I noticed before, is a curious duck. It occurred
to me that he might be an interesting possibility for executive director
for the Group.

At almost midnight I picked up Bette at her house. Then we drove
down to Lindy's for supper where we met Jack Adler. He told me many
stories in his most amusing and dramatic manner. He should be written down—he is in a class by himself. After we had driven Bette home
he accompanied me down here and told some stories about the women
he had slept with in London. It seems he was the ball of the belle
when he was there with *Golden Boy*. I am able to understand a man
like Casanova from him. He is shrewd, carefully sycophantic, discreetly so, for he could not possibly open himself to such a charge.

Jack, before he left, mentioned *Night Music* and certain incom-
prehensibilities in its production. This made me tell him that I am not
yet over the failure of that play, a truth. Part of this present slump in
my life comes from that failure; another part of it comes from Luise,
although I retain no *conscious* love or desire for her.

Good night.

———————•———————

Thursday, May 16, 1940

The question tonight in my own mind is which way will the Soviet
Union move. She is now standing back and away from the warring
nations, really acting impartially, despite what seems to be an agreement with Germany. For many years she worked for collective
security; the "democracies" refused, for cunning reasons. Then, in
self-protection, the S.U. made a nonaggression pact with Germany.
Then Germany began her war and her assaults have today and tonight
forced collective security on the rest of the world, excepting the S.U.,
for it is plain to see that even the United States is rapidly giving up its

isolationist point of view and will soon be helping the "allies" with materials and loans.

Now the S.U. is outside the circle of collective security. But is this for the duration of the war? Personally I think not. There are two possible moves for her, not more, and I cannot say which will be taken. She can stand on one side and let the "democracies" fight Germany to exhaustion which will be mutual, knowing that revolution will then break out all over Europe. This will constitute the first step in many years towards world revolution, for the S.U. will help it by funds and agitation. Or she can step in now, forgetting her promise to Germany. In this way Germany will be facing the combined forces of France, England, all of the Americas (short perhaps on manpower), and the Soviet Union, plus, perhaps, the Balkans and those countries already overrun by Hitler. In this way the S.U. will forever be free of the German menace. (Italy will be with the victors, I think.) If the S.U. is interested in national development before international development, I think she will soon join the "allies." For this some excuse is necessary. What will it be? I am waiting to see.

This will have an interesting result in this country. The Communist Party will change its line again.

No, in conclusion, I do not see how the S.U. can tolerate an expanded Third Reich under Hitler. She must fight Hitler and help those who are fighting him.

Apathy in easy times, softness, but resourcefulness under stress. That is the law of life that is bothering you, my friend.

———————•———————

Friday, May 17, 1940

There are so many books here, new purchases, that I have had to move several hundred downstairs to the office. I buy on sight some book which will be useful to me some day in the writing of a play; the subject must strike me right. More and more I find myself measuring men for what they were and how they used their qualities. American memoirs are very boyish, raw, uncooked, no matter what the age of the writer. Straightforwardness is the rule, but it is that very quality which eludes depth. And yet honesty, yes, honesty, wanting to do the right thing, wanting to be a good man, moral, being straight—a sort of Boy Scout code. In all the books written on Wilson I do not find one profound passage, not one. Take the best of these writers on Wilson—Lincoln Steffens, in his *Autobiography*. Does one get more than good nature, willingness to work, gladness for mobility, moralistic zeal, a sort of joy from functioning, much energy, kindness, a grave sort of courtliness? Steffens does give a few perceptions, but they are few and far between, and, at the time of writing, he was a man older than my father.

I am very sick from smoking tobacco but don't seem to be able to stop.

In the early evening I picked up Lee Strasberg and Paula. Lee is very much interested in my Wilson project. From time to time I turned the discussion to Wilson, but desisted because I found that we both were talking on a subject in which, as far as I was concerned, all the facts are not yet in.

One of the distinguishing marks of the American, unless he be businessman, is that of not giving an intention to the mind and its thinking.

Going back, the most interesting item Lee and I discussed was how the modern intellectual or student has become separated from the man of action. This is something which troubles me very much. More about it another time.

———•———

Saturday, May 18, 1940

In the early evening Bette came here and we sat in the deepening twilight, listening to war news, drinking ourselves drowsy with sherry wine. The German war machine is driving through the famed Maginot Line, on to Paris.

No one, Marxist or not, is going to tell me that France and England are as bad in this fight as Hitler's Germany. I am not sure at all about America's future role in this war. Things are moving so rapidly that the opinion of today is worse than useless tomorrow.

This is what made marriage with Luise impossible: the constant self-consciousness which she aroused in me, accidental at first, later conscious and "spiteful," from the center of her own instability—she found my weakness and whenever she was balked she exploited it for all she was worth—and not, dear Luise, really knowing she was doing it. If you have to tell a wife not to make you self-conscious, the marriage is over; the man is not a man and the woman is no longer free to be a woman.

Off color and off flavor, there are two types of men. The first is the man who makes women of all other men; the second is the man who makes other men adjust to him as if he were a woman. Perhaps the first is the modern man of action, the businessman, etc.; the second type is surely the modern artist. Waldo Frank immediately comes to mind. So does Jed Harris. And C.O., pal?

When there is a stronger need of it, you will define for yourself your relationship to the Group Theatre in all of its aspects.

———————•———————

Sunday, May 19, 1940

A glance-off, kiss-off relationship such as your present one with G.B. is even more degrading to yourself than to her, if you take into consideration the conscious elements involved. You are exploiting the most superficial elements of that girl, giving her contact but not connection; it is deadening, as all such relationships must be for all involved in them. Such relationships—those but a fraction lived—are among the most dangerous experiences permitted in life. They kill off all the delicate tender shoots and buds of inner life, leaving instead a garden of weeds and worms. Every time you refuse to live a relationship with another person to its most potential depth, you are committing a sin against yourself and the other involved. A sin against the talent of the human race and its spirit. This, believe me, is not too drastic a statement—it is one of the rock-bottom vices that infests American life from top to bottom. It is shown in our literature, our magazines and newspapers, in our radio, theatre, and movies. Our people live next to each other, never IN each other; and that is what you must do with a relationship. LIVE IN IT, not beside it. For your business is with life, not with death, with sensitivity (no matter how you chafe with it), not callousness and indifference. Rather live alone than keep yourself shut to the person with whom you spend time. Leave the scene, make your

EXIT, whenever you find you are not alive AT AND AGAINST AND WITH the person with whom you are spending time. This is a deep fault in you. Again there is a fear at the bottom of it. The fault is that you wait for the other person to bring you to life, and that is why, like so many other men, you move from woman to woman, for the very "firstness" of a new woman makes life without effort. Well, what it must be is that each person you meet (worthy ones) must be for you like a woman seduced. He or she must be wooed out of himself into the common light which streams between you; in that light you will meet each other, mingle together, and clasp each other into a warmer richer more productive atmosphere. Eschew once and for all relationships which are not humanly productive, but first make an effort to make them so or do not begin them, for they are the sleeping pills of life; and in this modern life there are enough other things which make one want to sleep! This is one of the most important items you have ever written in this journal: don't forget it, friend!

It would help if you saw all people actively, as if there were something you wanted to do with each—win over, anatomize, bring out, seduce, radicalize, enthuse, etc. Make man or woman extend himself and you will find yourself doing the same. Project your life upwards from the passive cocoon to the life of the prowling moth, feelers extended, tongue for tasting. Leave the table when you cannot take more, and digest at your leisure.

———•———

Monday, May 20, 1940

Late in the afternoon we drove back from the country where we stayed over at Luther's and Sylvia's farm. I looked through several books while there, even finishing the short novel by Gide, *The Immoralist*.

It is an oversensitive story, special for that reason, the meaning not quite certain to me although I can make several guesses, one of which is certain to be right. Exposure to such special sensitivity cannot be harmful if it is occasional. Perhaps yesterday's journal entry might not have been made if I'd not read this tale.

A letter came today from L.J. [Louis J. Odets, Clifford's father]. The usual moralizing, except that it was once used against me, a sort of attack to prod me into activity, that of finding a job. Now my father uses it to defend his own position, not making a living. The letters are so typical that they are not revealing or interesting.

A letter, too, from Ouida Campbell in North Carolina. Quite sensibly she points out that since I asked her to write, since she did, since I engaged her interest, I now have a definite responsibility, which means answering her letters. The girl is a little warrior; I must answer her. Can I tell her that I am hanging on the ropes, that I am crying help because I'm drowning, that there is "no witness of my life" to help me?

No witness: "henceforth I feel I shall live my life more carelessly." Once the Group Theatre stood as my witness. Six and eight years ago my sense of Beethoven stood as a witness. Find a witness today, for it is an important thing in your life.

Hanging over me is a small swirling cloud which is my memory of the sexual life Luise and I lived. This cloud is composed of images, senses, secret pleasures once shared. Only some woman of equal "intensity" will be able to dispel this cloud for me; it cannot be done alone and there will be no rest for me until it is done.

I am going through the printed reports of the Nye Commission on what brought us into the last war. Read over some of the J. P. Morgan testimony: incredible!

And a fog is down on the city, all over, penetrating and damp. Tomorrow it will rain, all for the sake of the summer to come.

Tuesday, May 21, 1940

Socialism will come to the world in some fresh cool quiet dawn of the future because the words in the phrase "peace and plenty" are contradicting words. Enough men will know this deeply enough to rise up soon and begin the making of the new world. This is my belief; I live for it.

The day is still; a haze is over the city. It hardly is necessary to turn on the lights before eight o'clock daylight time. It is something to sit here twenty-two floors above the city, in the gathering twilight, a string orchestra on the radio, and a fragrant Havana cigar in the mouth.

There is loneliness and there is discrimination. But they are both loneliness. Not that I live by this distinction or by any other one I write in this journal. *I do not live by distinctions, even though my mind often makes them.* It is a fault. Is it?

Now more war news on the radio. Here is a voice coming from Paris. Next is apt to be followed by direct telephone message from London and Berlin. The distressing magic of the twentieth century! France and England are losing every move so far. Germany has driven its way clean through to the channel coast. Also holding Amiens and a direct road on to Paris. France is naturally in a panic: premiers and commanding generals are being changed.

An announcer on the radio just said, touting up America and its products, "King Solomon in all his glory did not have even a toothbrush!" It is a Du Pont projects program. He says, "And the age of wonders here has just begun!" And what show is being done by the Du Ponts? Why, the life of Jane Addams! A dramatization in which Helen Hayes is playing Jane Addams being peddled by the Du Ponts! It does not happen by accident!!

Miss Hayes has picked up intonations and mannerisms from her good friend, Ruth Gordon. Miss Hayes is an intelligent, not imaginative, actress, not an artist.

The people of the world are in for a disagreeable surprise, a tragic revelation. They do not seem to know, unless they are Marxists or sit in high places of government or business, that the present war is the first one in history which will not end by one or more decisive battles, will not end by lands grabbed or surrendered, nor by treaties signed. This is a continuous war which only revolution will end. 1919 is as far away as the sixteenth century as far as precedence is concerned. Fundamental institutions must fall into the dust and mud before this war stops: nationalism, capitalism, exploitations of foreign markets—all of the God-given rights of the ruling classes. In the United States this is scarcely suspected by even those in the highest seats of government. They scarcely realize that the frantic crawl of Hitler and his maggots betokens the presence of a dead body somewhere above the sod. We are in for continuous war until that time when the ordinary men of the world rise up and slay left and right their present leaders. There is no doubt of this: tomorrow morning must come!

———•———

Wednesday, May 22, 1940

May is drawing to a close with much rain, the air muggy and uncomfortable to the feel of the body, as today is. Late at night now, the wind is blowing the strong rain against the windows, giving me a sense of snug comfort because I am shut in and away from it. The city is quiet and sleepful, drawn into itself like a snail in its shell: tomorrow will be a clearer time.

I went over to Lee Strasberg's for a pair of hours. Cheryl Crawford was there, cordial but deftly probing. She is apparently a very emotional woman who is always pulling away from her own emotion, and this gives her conduct a sort of flat affability. She seemed very composed and untroubled, even attractive.

I was interested in a point brought up by Lee after Cheryl left. He says it would be a good idea to take ten thousand dollars and give a tenth part of it to ten talented playwrights, at the same time giving them a play idea to work on, as a movie producer assigns a story idea to a scriptwriter. With an organization like the Group Theatre behind this plan, he thought, plus a director and a guiding playwright, some good results should come from such a plan if it were well organized before starting. I agreed and suggested that we discuss the idea again as soon as possible.

This is the first idea related to the Group Theatre life which has made me lift my eyes at the mention of the theatre in several months, since the closing, the unhappy closing, of *Night Music*. The Group Theatre cannot exist as a one-director theatre nor as a one-playwright theatre. I am anti-one!

My eyes pain me: too much smoking.

———•———

Thursday, May 23, 1940

I've been thinking of it for days, but I decided I would really strike out for a trip to Philadelphia. Which is why I called Boris Aronson, asking him if he cared to go with me. He readily accepted, said he had been working and listening to the war news at the same time, was nervous, restless, very unhappy. We planned to leave sometime before midnight.

Boris arrived late, being Boris, looking like Boris, restless, quietly despondent, his face creased, slightly bewildered, as if he had just gotten out of bed, the way he always looks, soft, protesting, flavored with a pinch of disgust against everything that exists.

We soon were riding across Jersey in the excellent Cadillac, a true friend. Boris was worried about the war—it was all we talked about except for lapses during which we tuned in the radio for war news. So soon we were bouncing along Roosevelt Boulevard in Philadelphia. We parked the car next to the Drake Hotel, took a comfortable room there, and were soon asleep in our twin beds at past four in the morning, a large breakfast stuffed into our respective bellies.

I forgot and mention it now because of the good feeling it aroused in me. A special delivery letter arrived from Fay Wray, just before we left New York. She was worried about me, she wrote, wanted to know how I felt, said I was very dear to her.

Friday, May 24, 1940

Boris was up and out before I awoke, but he joined me for a breakfast of roast beef! He wanted to see a young fellow who had been his assistant but was now living in Philadelphia, making models of trains, boats, and airplanes for a living. We drove up there, on the way passing 1721 Sixty-eighth Avenue where my family had lived for so long. I told Boris that my mother had often said how happy it would make her to see her only son drive up to the door in his own car. Well, here was the car and the drive and the door, but no mother. It reminded me that this year I had forgotten the date, May 8th, of the death of my mother now dead five years. Dear mother, I remember you almost every other day.

Driving downtown we stopped in at the home of the Fabians. We drank coffee there, chatted on the outer porch, although grandmother, mother, and daughter put on sweaters and hats to sit in the damp air. It was true, as Boris pointed out, the grandmother was like the child of the family, timorous, careful, almost shy. Such women live protected careful lives—they cannot face even a strong north wind. And the conversation while we sat there, constant admonishments to be careful, to eat more, the tonsils must be taken out, the kidneys, the cancers, and the cautions. Finally I blew up the whole thing with laughter, telling the child to be careful of not breaking her arm while putting on her sweater.

Next we rode down to Aunt Esther's house. There it was fine; Boris and I breathed more freely. He was very struck with my Uncle Rossman, whose original character sticks out all over him, often to the distress of his more "civilized" daughter who said, "My father's always telling everybody everything about us." The tone of that household is a much happier one since they get weekly checks from me. For the first time in many years they were almost gay, my aunt and uncle jibing at each other, laughing, indulging in mock recriminations. At the table Uncle sang a couple of Hebrew chants to show that he would have made a fine cantor but for his lack of proper pronunciation of the words.

At the Academy of Music TAC was playing a benefit. What is it about left-wing organizations and their affiliates and the people who work in them? There is usually as little life in them as in a reactionary American group. They are mechanical, without depth, impoverished of spirit and humanity, raw, bleak of character, despite all the correct ideas in the world. I am sure no social advance will come out of these bleak people; Marxism in this country seems to be in the hands of a lot of bulletheads.

We had promised to join a crowd at a café across the way, but one look at two crowded tables made us turn away. What Boris and I wanted was to sit and chat with a human being or two, a woman, a feminine woman or two. Only now do I realize that there is almost as much pleasure in being with a real woman as there is in sleeping with her.

Back in the hotel room we looked over the war news, all bad for the allies. Boris kept assuring me that I did not know the German people—they are all beasts and will do whatever they start out to do. Finally, completely wearied out and disgruntled, Boris turned over and fell asleep. I was turning over in my mind two problems. One of them came to mind because I read in the paper that Archibald Mac-Leish said in a speech that the younger generation had no moral values, that writers like himself, debunking the last twenty years, had been responsible for it. This shocked me, the answers to that sort of twaddle being very simple and quick ones.

And I was thinking about women. To Fay Wray I wrote a long note because I was yearning for her. What I admire in Fay is that she has remained a woman, no matter what has happened to her. In modern America there are few women. Instead females are hard, driving, nervous, not a restful spot in them. (They do not know how to flirt, Boris said.) Joan Crawford has always typified to me the modern American woman and for my taste I know of no woman so ugly and desexed as Joan. They are Sears, Roebuck women, pushed into a certain mold, made to order, tailored, neat, and oh so hard! Perhaps what destroys a woman (as Luise so often said) is having to make her own way in the world, for destroyed they are in modern life. The men, too, help in this destruction for they do not stand as men to their women. More and more I see the powerful place a man takes in a woman's life—it is almost everything! Thinking about this problem I made many notes a few months ago, particulary about F. Fr. [Frances Farmer]. From this point of view the modern woman has never been put into an American play. It must be done soon.

———•———

Saturday, May 25, 1940

Boris was out of the room, wandering around town, when I got out of bed. But again he joined me for breakfast, again roast beef! This time he had news—a musical comedy was in town. [Vera] Zorina one of the stars. There, I said, is one of the real women we yearned for last night. Yes, said Boris, let us go to the matinee. I protested no shave, not yet quite awake, no bath—we compromised on seeing the evening performance for which we secured the last available tickets. What interested me about going to the show was visiting Zorina backstage—Boris knew her better than I—and taking her out. Particularly, as I told Boris, since Winchell had printed an item that she and her husband [George Balanchine] had separated or were going to do so.

The musical show was not very good in my opinion, but on all sides I heard strong expressions of approval and Boris, who sees many musicals, assured me that this would be a smash hit when it opened in New York the next week. Well, it did have the excitement, color, and theatrical glamour, the energy and life that even the worst musicals have. I watched Zorina with strong desire. Boris said her husband might be backstage since it said on the program that he had arranged the ballet numbers in the show.

Backstage we trudged after the show. The husband was there— Balanchine, a nervous, thin Russian, "hopped" up, excitable, curt, something vicious and brutal about his face, albeit creative. He and Boris went into a long Russian conversation while I sat on the other side of a circular padded seat, one of the show props pushed to the side while the stage crew quickly dismantled the show, packing it into freight cars. I watched them work, amazed at their activity and expertness, although it was easy to pick out the shirkers. I found myself nervous and depressed. What, I asked myself, am I doing here? I have read in a cheap gossip column that this man on the other side of this seat is having a quarrel with his wife. Immediately I have a mental resolve to try to get her to sleep with me. I will woo her first by my reputation and one casual meeting before in an elevator. A thousand men who have read the gossip are now thinking what I am doing. What kind of values are these? What sort of desperation brings you here with these thoughts in your goddam head?!

Suddenly Balanchine jumped up. He had sighted his wife through the door opening on the alley. He hurried, said farewell to Boris, and ran after her. I asked Boris if that had been Zorina. He said yes, we lighted cigarettes, and after a moment walked out into the thin drizzle, I feeling soberly depressed but brutally energetic. The husband had told Boris that he was having trouble with his wife. What sort of trouble? Just trouble. I asked all sorts of questions, for they had chatted ten minutes. Boris didn't want to answer; he explained that the husband was the sort of man who merely intimated things, did not speak them out. Boris said he had once seen the husband having affairs simultaneously with three girls. He had asked him how he hoped to have a good marriage with a girl like Zorina. Balanchine had answered, "Don't you think she has done some things in her life?" Boris asked me how I could believe that about a girl who looked like Zorina. I said I could, that there was something very unbalanced (in quotes) about her face, the eyes too far apart, etc., etc.

On Broad Street there was a new nightclub sign which said George

Jessel was playing there. I suggested that we go up and see him. He greeted us warmly when he arrived. Both Boris and I liked him, for he is a real faker, not a fake faker. His good friends are men like Jimmy Walker and Al Jolson, all intricate networks of ego like Georgie himself; be a big shot, make money while you can, keep your position, appear at benefits, let the world know how good you are to your relatives while you groan humorously about the burden they have become, be a credit to the Jewish race, develop a philosophical turn of speech, etc., etc. He is a pierrot, albeit soiled, a cigar stuck in his mouth at a tilted angle, or enjoying a steak sandwich at four in the morning, or called off to a corner, and he has perhaps "knocked off" a girl. He is sentimental, wanting respect, a user of words like "elite" and "apropos of," this mixed with all the expressions of baseball, vaudeville and other show business, racehorse business, big finance, sexology, songwriting, and the editorial page of the *Daily News*. He is going, he said, to soon write his autobiography, *It Shouldn't Happen to a Dog.* For this purpose, he said, he is airplaning to California in the morning "to join his child bride."

What you like about Georgie is that he is still a poor boy, clinging with gravity to his Jewishness because he is homesick, not for its moral values. He went out on the floor—after a poor show in which two enthusiastically received midgets were the main feature of the bill— and told stories, deftly turned stories against himself and others, sang songs he had written over a period of twenty years, called his mythical mother on the telephone, introduced me to the audience as "what I undoubtedly conceive to be the greatest playwright in America," and altogether traded on the sentiment of this being his last performance of a two-week engagement.

After this we had some more drinks in the bar, meeting many of the Philadelphia bums who were there. A master of ceremonies from another club sat making wry bad jokes such as "making a movie for Repulsive Pictures." We ate our steak sandwiches restlessly and went home, wading through the show girls, of whom the emcee had said, "This place has the tallest whores in Philadelphia," simple bovine girls, blondes or made into blondes by their own hands. One of them had come up to our table and been introduced to us by the bitter emcee as his fiancée. We treated her respectfully, carefully acknowledging the introduction, but when she left the emcee said, "I put her on my cock and just twirl her around."

Sunday, May 26, 1940

In the case of Boris and myself, when you are nervous every insult is doubled; we went across the street to look at some paintings of a newly discovered American "primitive," Horace Pippin, a Negro. We were told that [Dr. A. C.] Barnes, the eccentric art-collecting millionaire, had bought the best of these Pippins. This brought up the question of a possible visit to see the Barnes collection. Special permission is necessary for this viewing of the finest collection of modern art in the world. A whole legend has grown up around this Barnes creature. Supposedly he is very crusty and crabby, antisocial, unwilling to show his collection except in very special cases. So with the greatest of trepidation his phone number was handed over to us, I to call his collection secretary to ask if we might drive over to see the paintings.

I write all this because the situation revealed me to myself in an interesting phase of the secret life one leads. The PROSPECT of REFUSAL made me so uneasy that it was only with difficulty that I could approach the telephone. I realized then that opening myself to refusal was something that I rarely permit in my life. It often accounts for the fact that I so seldom leave the house, so seldom permit myself to arrive in situations where painful refusal is possible. Pain and fear are the paralyzing agencies here, and how subtly the mechanism is set up in the self! One does not want to begin work, does not want to enter negotiations or situations in which one may be seen to be inadequate: so daring goes, inventiveness and calling on reserves are lost. Be careful of what drives you inward, of what keeps you "at home," of all the things which curtail extension of the self and experience. Open yourself to refusal from even the most humble elements and personalities around you. Playing safe is death!

The visit to the Barnes collection was refused. What did I do? Joked about it, passed it over lightly, made believe it was not important. None present knew for a moment that I would have punched in the face of Dr. Barnes if he had been there. So goes the wilderness of the self.

All of a sudden Boris and I decided to head back to New York. We decided to stop off at Luther and Sylvia's farm for dinner. The green countryside looked brilliant in the gray light of the day, vividly fresh, pregnant even, but certainly nubile.

Luther and Sylvia had been half expecting me, even holding off with dinner till past eight to prove it. To a lonely man their talent for friendship is very warming, all other considerations aside. I read Thomas Mann's essay on Goethe, all the time Gurdus raising a minor noisy hell with the radio fixing.

Several ideas from the Mann essay followed me as we drove home at midnight in the damn fog and drizzle, creeping only for fear of going off the road. Mann writes of what success is to Goethe, of the artist's secret life, etc. At home I put the book on my night table, resolving to finish the essay soon, perhaps even writing an essay myself on what happens to the artist who becomes a success in America. This idea has been with me a long time—the self-opening interests me more than an audience who may read it.

Boris I left off at Forty-second Street, having driven him to the subway station. He was grateful for the trip, for despite my self-immersion I could see how much good it had done him. More good than I received from it.

Roosevelt made a speech by radio tonight; we heard it at the farm. He is a master politician. A third term is his if he wants it. He spoke of preparedness, of the state of the world, generalities, diffuse because of political reasons, a speech which was significant only because of the warm human tone in it, fatherly and friendly. He refuted, particularly, enemies of his administration who have been claiming that it has wasted previously allotted sums designated for armaments.

I needed a woman who will help me become more an artist, whose life is devoted to that task. No other woman. Good night.

———————•———————

Monday, May 27, 1940

It is no longer Monday—Tuesday, four in the morning. What a morning, what a gray morning in the world. What a horrible morning, unless one believes it is the beginning of a new and better world.

When I got out of bed it was three o'clock in the afternoon. I played the radio, ate some food, thought whether or not to go out for a walk. But soon it was too late for walking, eight o'clock, nine, ten—the hours slipped by as one. I was reading all the old *Nations* and *New Republics*;

I made some notes, scratched my head, drank cold soda out of the icebox.

I must have been acutely lonely, for a dozen times I looked out of the window at the lighted windows across the way. I thought, shall I turn the phone on? Will someone call? Do I want to talk if someone calls? Instead I went back to the magazines.

I learned, fishing for war news on the radio, that Reynaud, the French premier, was scheduled to make a speech in Paris very soon. After several vain attempts the announcer, at 3:25, said, "Apparently atmospheric conditions over Europe are very poor." There was no doubt, from any point of view, poetic or practical, that he was right.

Suddenly the announcer said Reynaud was talking in Paris. It was 8:30 in the morning there, 3:30 here. Sure enough, a French voice came in, zooming up and down, gliding, shattering—a very poor distance reception. I tuned into another station and it was better, although the reception howling did not cease. It sounded hellish, as if the battle were being fought in the receiving horns.

In a few minutes—Reynaud's speech, they said, took four-and-a-half minutes—there was a translation. But first the French broadcast station played the "Marseillaise." This was very stirring, more than all the newspaper reports of the war I've read so far. Everything was grave and dramatic—French politicians do not make early morning radio speeches for the joke of it. Translated, the substance of the Reynaud talk was that they are all thinking of their soldiers, every man, woman, and child must hold solidly—"We must expect certain limitations on our future life." Immediately John Gunther appeared at the microphone, there to interpret the speech. He said it meant something was up, but he evidently was stalling, not knowing what it meant because it was so brief. I could just see Gunther leaving the Stork Club at three in the morning to get to the studio. What a thing, I thought, sitting here myself, eating chocolate mints, thin, not too sweet, appreciating candy keenly!

While Gunther stalled I went to the window and saw it was raining in a fog, a hell of a night. Back at the radio, unimportant items: the German drive is being conducted with unprecedented fury; they are pushing the British into the sea; they are trying to get wounded across the channel—all sorts of boats, big and little—but the Germans are giving no quarter, bombing hospital ships and any others they sight. Some wounded British soldiers were picked up trying to swim across the channel.

Gunther's voice runs along lightly, nervously, a helpful and lifting lilt in it. He is trying not to be sensational, but says the Allies are under a "dreadful stress." I want to vomit as I listen, but there is a real fascination of the horrible in the steady flow of news dispatches coming in. Apparently the dispatches are being pushed into Gunther's hand as he is talking, for he repeats old news while, as he says, he is looking over the new. He explains the situation, that the Germans have a million Allied troops encircled in a trap. It is incredible—on a small piece of earth several million men are fighting like wolves. Both London and Paris report that the German dead are piled up in heaps— MEN! I am sitting here, drinking milk, coffee, eating candy, drinking Coca-Colas; it is raining; my pajamas and robe clothe me; two electric lamps are burning; all around me are sleeping citizens who will soon get up to go to work—over there are MILLIONS OF MEN KILLING EACH OTHER with every possible weapon, murdered dead, living ones drowning in the channel, groans and screams, a roar such as no battle before ever made. No, I do not understand it—it cannot be felt or comprehended. I can't understand it, that's all. The fog at the window is understandable to me, or the pile of discarded magazines on the floor, but not the war over there. No, people do not understand abstracts. We do not understand even the invasion of another country like Belgium or Holland. You say Brussels has been taken, Louvain and its library fired and destroyed. It is only words, an abstract. When you say, "Your country is next," it is less an abstraction, but even then my finger cut will be more real to me. But if I hear one refugee weep, see one child hurt, dead, then it is real and I understand the millions. Am I sure of this? No, for only this apartment is real to me now.

Gunther: suddenly his voice jumps up. "This IS news!" he says, so it is. It explains Reynaud's speech. The Belgian force has just capitulated by order of King Leopold. It is an A.P. dispatch. Gunther himself is shocked by this news. He wonders aloud where King Leopold is, perhaps on the battlefield. Now another dispatch is read. The King ordered a surrender against the unanimous advice of his ministers; they are on their chairs in London and he is on the battlefield—he sees the slaughter and they are probably being cajoled and threatened by the frantic English. For this means that all of the channel ports on the French and Belgian coasts are now open to the Germans; it means fearful attack on England; it means hell let loose in every shape, by every means of expulsion and impulsion that man can leash to gasoline and gunpowder.

You can almost see Gunther shaking his head as he walks away from the microphone. The stiffly correct and pompous announcer makes his sign-off notification, an organ plays "The Star-Spangled Banner," and the air is silent but for the low, powerful humming of the radio set.

My mouth is dry from tension and smoking; yet it is not real. I think I'll write this down. When I bend down to get some paper out of the drawer I feel a deep movement in the loneliness in myself. A thought comes to me, "Ought to get together quickly. Get together, build a life with another, make a home. It is the only way you will shut out the agony of this world."

It is just as foggy out as before, impossible to see the clock at Fourteenth Street. My head aches faintly, distantly. The carbon paper in my hands is real. I can't make that war as real. MILLIONS OF MEN, MILLIONS, millions!

———————•———————

Tuesday, May 28, 1940

I have a role to play in America today. I am irresponsible in relation to it. It is possible for me to flood the country with fresh progressive ideas, ideas to lead the people to a richer and fuller life.

Yes, I admit irresponsibility towards this idea, but I must say this in extenuation—the task needs tremendous organization. Who will help me? What assistant can I win over by loyalty to the meaning of my work, or by plain hire at good wage? Then after this there is the advice of Van Gogh: "The artist must approach his work without artistic prepossession, like a cobbler!" Vapors and moods be damned, delicate filaments of sensitivity be damned! To work! The time is ripe; the world is hopeless in many sections, but you are not hopeless. You are strong, as healthy as a pig! To work, pig, to work! Blow the clover out of your nose! To work!

Today I discovered an article on the theatre by Julius Bab in the *Encyclopedia of Social Sciences*. It is first-rate, each theatre historically located and explained socially. The Group Theatre was started on the basis of what is in this article, although I never heard Bab get any credit for his ideas. It is a real excitement, one of the best pleasures of life, to every so often find work such as Bab's.

I am alone today, having asked Sir Secretary to stay at home, an indulgence I will ask from him more and more.

The French and British are raging against what they call the betrayal of King Leopold. They have dug up facts of his family relationship to German and Italian royal houses, these proving that he was pro-Nazi all the time. The truth is that he and his men grew tired of pulling the allied chestnuts out of the fire. Belgian soldiers have been living on biscuits for four days, according to dispatches.

Thursday, May 30, 1940

Last night Bette came down here and we went to Lindy's for dinner. We saw two newsreels, neither of them more informative or revealing than the newspapers. What we saw were propaganda shots, refugees composed of children and women and the aged, and hospitals wrecked by Nazi bombs.

Then I drove Bette home and stopped off by the Stork Club. Later, with Lyons, I went to the Monte Carlo Club and the El Morocco. What places in which to seek surcease! I went, finally, to bed at dawn in an agony of feeling.

But the evening had a crown. Here Bette and I listened to the Yvette Guilbert records. It was the first time in weeks that I was delighted to the very soul. This old woman could win me even to the war. She sings these ditties and I do not understand a word of them, but she is a whole nation and a whole culture; at once, together, simultaneously, she is wise, old, cynical, naïve, witty, mocking, shrewd, patriotic, weary, charitable, scolding, admiring, whorish, deeply motherly, ripe, capable, wordly, provincial, girlish, and quick. Her singing, herself, she is so delightful, so delicious that this rediscovery of her was a happy event for me.

Today, Thursday. It dismayed me to find how nervous and uneasy I was made all afternoon by the prospect of having dinner with Mrs. Roosevelt. I knew there would be other people there, but it did not mitigate my uneasiness. In fact I was so nervous that several times I thought I'd send a telegram pleading illness. This is no different from not going to a grammar-school graduation party because a girl, a certain girl, was there. Finally I dressed carefully and went there, to a place called the Cosmopolitan Club. I took some vermouth first but my mouth was parched. Mrs. Roosevelt was standing in the reception room on the fourth floor. I walked forward and introduced myself in such a low voice that she had to ask me to repeat the name. We shook hands and I walked to one side so she might continue to meet the others who were rapidly arriving. There I was able to get over my amazement at her size—she is over six feet tall, I think. She moved around the room, introducing people, chatting here and there a few sentences—she has the hostess form down to an art and science combined. When the room was full, cocktails served, we went into dinner. Martha Dodd and her husband were there, MacKinlay Kantor, Elizabeth Hawes and her husband, Joe Losey, one of the older Harrimans, and twenty others. I sat near the head of the table, two away from Mrs. Roosevelt. Conversation making was easier than I thought, albeit painful—I'm not practiced in these things. After an excellent dinner Mrs. Roosevelt made a little speech. A contribution, too, was hinted at. Many questions were asked and all well answered.

Trouble comes when one retains a static policy in relation to a fluid life.

It is not "a lost generation"! Nonsense! It is a wounded generation. Wounded, we are all wounded little birds.

I am looking for a simple, modest secret life which had better be found soon!

The successful artist finds he is two persons—the Public Man and Himself. For a healthy life and progress in work a wide gap must be kept between the two. When the gap closes, when the artist sees himself as the Public Man, he is through, finished, wiped off the slate of creation! It is the chief danger and threat to your development as an artist. You can live and work only in the humbler of these two lives, only occasionally putting a foot in the other world. More is dangerous. Humpty-Dumpty sat on a wall! You cannot live the symbol, boychik!

Clemenceau's character, I think, has much in common with what you hear in the singing of Yvette Guilbert.

Friday, May 31, 1940

The New York Times is a blistering rash of war news, war hysterias, war plans, screams for democracy. It seems from their pages that tomorrow the Nazis will be here with a mechanized invasion of our forty-eight states. But look inside the financial page. There it tells that the Germans are quietly making payments of interest to American banks on almost fifty millions of loans. There one learns that Italy, urgently requested on the front page by Roosevelt not to enter the war, has just shipped four millions in gold here. And the *Times* financial expert tells the moneymen not to worry—Roosevelt has given assurances that he will not close the market, will not make artificial prices, etc., etc. Meaning that the usual channels of profits and gambling in war woe are open to all, as usual, at the old stand.

This conservative newspaper is really frightening. Aside from several puny items about auto accidents and the opera house the entire paper is devoted to war stories and what groups are doing here to meet emergencies. In the meantime June 1 has been ushered in by a morning (I am writing this at seven in the morning) enveloped heavily in a white fog. Nothing is normal, not even the weather. The paper says that we have had almost seven inches of rain in May, a record only once before reached in this city.

There is a certain moment at which all of America can be touched off into the most astounding explosion. The moment was two weeks ago. In this short time it is highly possible that all of the social gains of the past seven years have been destroyed. It remains to be seen, but in the meantime it is an amazing demonstration of the hysteria which lies fallow in the American people, perhaps the fury of repressions. Every piece of daily and weekly reading material is one festered load of propaganda now. Even the British retreat across the channel has become a crusade of democracy. The soldiers did not break their ranks—they moved backward gallantly, pure sterling silver in their souls, etc., etc. Not one word is mentioned in all the papers about the palpable treachery which made their position so untenable, so murderous—not one word about the extraordinary series of "blunders" (!) which permitted the Germans to invade the Allies' countries. No word of the complicity of those who sit in English and French high places, may their souls burn in hell!

Then, too, Miss Shirley Temple has recently retired from the world's cinema screen at the ripe old age of eleven. The world is going to hell as fast as it can go!

These are educative years for a young man, no matter where he sits in the places of the world, if they do not kill him!

I spent the evening with Boris, eating a fine dinner at his house, talking about the American middle class, looking at some of his paintings and stage models on projected slides. When we went to Lindy's for coffee, there we met O. [Oscar] Levant. Boris went home, I to O.'s house, meeting his pregnant wife and listening to some recordings of three pieces of his music. Disorderly, lazy, turgid work. He played some fragments of Beethoven sonatas on an excellent piano, playing rather well, but merely fragments. O. is in all things and ways a man of fragments, a minor singer of the sentence. This is why a relationship is an uneasy one with him. An unhappy rambunctious boy, a startled clumsy Jewish faun from Pittsburgh.

———•———

Saturday, June 1, 1940
&
Sunday, June 2, 1940

Bette came here for dinner. The last time she was here she confessed that her name was not Grayson, that she had lied to me and for months had been trying to straighten it out but did not know how to begin. I did not ask her any questions. She merely did what all young girls in the theatre do, gave herself an interesting background—educated in Ireland, born in the West of romantically assorted parents. Her mother died on a ship when she was a little girl and they were traveling to France. Perhaps some or all of this is true with her.* I did not want to inquire because I am not in love with her.

---

*Bette Grayson Odets, the daughter of Milton and Janet Lipper, a wealthy New York stock brokerage family. Bette grew up in New York and her mother did indeed die on board a ship en route to France when she was seven. Her mother was a talented amateur painter who spent much time in France painting. After her death, the family, including Milton's second wife, Frances (with whom Bette did not get along), and Bette's French nurse, moved to Beverly Hills.

Bette and I slept together beautifully. She is like a ripe melon. Afterwards I could not sleep although a fog-covered dawn was up at the windows. I thought of an idea for an antiwar *Lefty* which can use the same form. Will see, will see, will . . . see.

Up late on Sunday, scarcely looking at the Sunday papers. What is in them, in any section—news, books, drama—piffle! Pure unadulterated bunk!

I am just beginning to know myself. There are certain dangers involved in meeting and knowing one's self. The discovery comes through the spirit and through the appetites, separately and in amalgam. I have them both, husband and wife, dearie!

The American men who make their women pursue *them*. Is it any wonder that they cease to be women?

I tell you, a secret simple modest life! Air and sunshine, a little room, a walk in the park, a concert twice a month. A man in the masses, muscles in his arms, reading in the public library, alone unknown, eating in the Automat. Give me liberty or give me death!

———•———

Monday, June 3, 1940

In the late afternoon I was out of bed and gloomy, but as the afternoon wore out into the evening it was better. Sid Benson came up, made an appointment for dinner tomorrow when he will bring Ordoqui, the Cuban, here. He told some news of the Communist Convention held this past weekend, and left.

Such a lovely June evening had come that I was charmed into a quiet passive state, thinking ahead of a stroll down Fourteenth Street and Second Avenue, a preface to a cool supper. Before doing this I spent a few minutes at Morris Carnovsky's apartment. He wanted some advice about Hollywood agents, feeling that Lyons was not trying to get him

---

She lived there until age eighteen, when she "ran away" from home to New York and lived with her sister Janet.

When Bette died in 1954 (her son was seven, as she had been when her mother died), Odets moved their children, Walt and Nora, from New York to Beverly Hills, unknowingly renting the same house she had grown up in (her father having previously sold it).

some work—he is in a bad financial way. They both gave me the sense of allowing everything to slip, hopeful but inactive, living on small sure pleasures like fairly good food, a cat who had just had five kittens, little pranks, and visits to and from old friends. In the meantime they are hopeful about the future of Group life and Phoebe brings everything into line according to Communist doctrine. "I do not care in which European country the revolution comes first," she told me, and that is that!

In my little walk, so pleasurable because so rare (my right foot is almost crippled by a flattened arch), I enjoyed the shop windows. At Ratner's, the owner's daughter told me that little Max, the former cashier, so harmless and apparently unimaginative, had recently disappeared, leaving behind a message that he was going to commit suicide and must not be looked for. He gambled, she told me, a man making only twenty-two dollars a week—it must have been that the "shylocks" (small loan racketeers) were after him. Many secret gamblers like that.

And a good enough walk back to the house then. I thought that some of these side streets were as strange to me as the side streets of Havana, as interesting, as full of life, as varied. Then I invited Morris and Phoebe and their dinner guest up here. Modern music, since we played Berlioz, Prokofiev, Milhaud, Ibert, and Shostakovich, is interesting, not very varied. It is lyric, witty, nervous, seldom of very serious intention: One is content to keep one's head above water, it seems.

Later I proposed another walk with Morris. We walked across the square, admiring very keenly the night stillness which stood among the leafy trees there. Homeless men were sleeping on the benches; we lowered our voices.

And now a healthy morning is at the windows, near six. There are many notes for the short antiwar play on the desk. It seems to me a good idea to take the notes, plenty of fresh paper, and the typewriter away to some retreat for a few days.

The morning is misty but the sun is coming over a Fourteenth Street building like a fat red orange, or, if you like, a hot nickle. Now it is already clear of the building, before this line is completed.

———————•———————

Alfredo Valente/courtesy Walt Odets

Portrait of Odets taken in 1935 after he had burst on the scene
with *Waiting for Lefty* and *Awake and Sing!*

Maurice/courtesy Walt Odets

Bette Grayson, who married Odets
in 1943, in a photograph taken about
1942.

Artist's rendering of One Fifth Avenue, the building in which Odets lived until the summer of 1940.

Elia Kazan, Jane Wyatt, and Morris Carnovsky in a publicity still for *Night Music*, from a newspaper article in the *New York Times* a week before the play opened in New York.

Producer Jed Harris provides a dramatic moment for columnist Leonard Lyons (seated, center) while impressario Billy Rose (seated, left) and Odets look on.

At one of Odets's favorite night spots, the Stork Club: (left to right) Stork Club owner Sherman Billingsley, columnist Walter Winchell, Myrna Loy, Loretta Young, John Garfield, Janet Gaynor, and Quentin Reynolds.

Luise Rainer and Odets at the Stork Club, 1938.

Fay Wray and Odets at the Stork Club.

Both Odets and Luise Rainer were devoted to Beethoven's music, and this 1937 photograph perhaps shows the phonograph Odets speaks of in his journal.

Frances Farmer, as she appeared in Ernest Hemingway's *The Fifth Column* in 1940.

Phototeque

The Group Theatre in 1938: (rear row) Art Smith, Walter Fried, Sanford Meisner, Ruth Nelson, Lee J. Cobb, Lief Erickson, Roman Bohnen, Morris Carnovsky, Lee Strasberg, Kermit Bloomgarden; (middle row) Luther Adler, Phoebe Brand, Eleanor Lynn, Harold Clurman, Frances Farmer, Robert Lewis, Elia Kazan; (front) Irwin Shaw.

Hanns Eisler

courtesy New York Public Library Theatre Collection

Stella Adler, Luther Adler's sister, who married Harold Clurman in 1942.

Sylvia Sydney, who was married to Luther Adler during the period covered by the journal, in a 1941 publicity still from Warner Bros.

Bette Grayson, after her divorce from Odets, in a scene with John Garfield from a revival of *Golden Boy* in 1952.

Odets, as he may have looked at home on an ordinary day.

Odets, in a casual shot, probably about 1942.

Tuesday, June 4, 1940

Nothing.

Is that possible? No, I admired the weather, read a few pages of letters of Rilke (and determined to read more, carefully, quietly). And I wrote a brief note to Fay Wray, and, after dinner, I met Lucy Gerhman and admired the woman that she is.

But the constant hypnotic reading of the newspapers throws me off the shadowy base on which I stand. And it is not better to read the liberal weeklies either, *The Nation, The New Masses,* and *The New Republic.*

I was stubborn and contentious. Contentious got me in trouble, made people dislike me. I began to tread softly; the requisite stubbornness is going. Oh, don't worry, boy. YOU ARE STUBBORN! Don't flatter your soul! You are the mule with human visage!

But you are indecisive and that is agonizing!

———————•———————

Wednesday, June 5, 1940

A short time ago they bombed Madrid; today they bombed Paris. They are all criminals, those who permitted the bombing of Madrid then, those who bomb Paris now. In the meantime, frantic and hysterical, myself a little, the Americans view the brutal drives of the Nazis with horrified admiration: they are so businesslike!

I haven't come to any decision about the short antiwar play which began to take shape in my mind a few days ago. Here I am, indecisive because I do not know truly what I feel and believe. I cannot follow the Communist line, so simple and mechanical, on this issue. It seems to me that they are wrong, that defense of this country is important, defense of the best-working democracy in the world today. And, on top of that, no matter what they say, it is beginning to be my belief that despite the imperialistic background the Allies are nevertheless waging an antifascist war, if only out of desperation. What does a Jew do or feel in this situation? I don't know, for I never think of problems from a Jewish point of view. I view life from an American progressive or radical pair of eyes and heart.

However, I do not trust my feelings right now. To espouse an unpopular cause means giving up much of a comfortable easy life, inner peace, attracts insult and injury to the proud self. *My deep need to be accepted*, with me since boyhood, unsatisfied by even an enormous success, is a need I don't trust. It makes much trouble in my life, and generates talent, I must add.

I was happy when Hanns Eisler telephoned and invited him along for dinner. He is very cool about the war, seems well informed; perhaps because he has been through one, not to mention revolutions and numerous difficult times. He is living on his farm, minding his business, steadily doing his work. It seems to me to be the way an artist should work: a better day will come and the headless hunter will not find it.

Hanns had to leave at ten, but Lee Strasberg and Paula came to take his place. They had wanted to go to a nightclub along the Hudson, but it was not difficult to convince them that it was too hot to move off the cool quiet terrace where we sat for two hours. We talked about the theatre problems. When Lee does not agree with what one says he observes a silence, without comment. The war, he says, somehow does not disturb him. He is going ahead with his work, thought, investigation, production problems; says this is a very fruitful problem for him, fruitful period, I mean. But he adds that most writers he meets are too disturbed to write.

All together, we drove Bette up to her house and then I drove them back to their street and went home. Then I was sorry that I had taken Bette home. For an hour I chatted with a cabdriver in front of the house. We sat in the quiet night air and discussed world problems. He is unusually intelligent, forced to recognize himself as a Jew in what he assures me is a very anti-Semitic world, particularly manifest in Italian cabbies for whom he has an undying hatred. He adds that it is their special characteristic to gang up on you, never attacking you single-handed. He works a twelve-hour shift and assured me that he is often able to bring home twenty-five or thirty dollars a week. If he could not buy milk for his two kids, he says, he would not want to live. Nor would he want to live in a world where anti-Semitism is the rule. What moved me about him was his cynical alert manner, a little speech defect which caught him every other minute, and his supreme lack of self-consciousness or awareness: his to work and sweat, not more. His bright Semitic eyes gave his face a beautiful dignity.

———————•———————

Thursday, June 6, 1940

Liberty connotes an opposition, a connection, a rooting in an environment. For this reason there is no liberty without responsibility, without connection with others. A man alone, irresponsible to time, place, and humanity, has no more liberty than a prisoner in a cell.

A batch of curious mail and telephone messages greeted me when I came out of the bedroom this afternoon. A letter from Helen Deutsch in California where she is writing a movie. Troubled, a little dippy, bitter, taking out a general discontent on me.

I was moved to sympathy, not resentment. For she doesn't know what is wrong with her—she is trying, like so many American women today, to live by masculine standards, through masculine behavior. She would throw up everything for a good marriage—money, fame, career, independence, and all. No woman wants "independence" in the sense that the word is used in this country today.

And from Kay Morrison, once Luther Adler's wife, a phone call which I answered. Now she is in a very bad way. When Luther left her she came to my door. Several times I slept with her. She begged to be permitted to stay, saying she would be the cook or the servant. That was impossible and I told her so. In the intervening years she found and lived with or married a nice fellow who writes for the *Times*. Six months ago she had a baby. Since then she has been in a broken-down state, hysterical, unbalanced. On the phone she said that she has been in hospitals for months: "The psychiatric one was the most interesting!" What did she want? For me to come to see her. When? Saturday night, when the maid would be out and "we can be alone together." Then she caught herself, adding, "That is not the inducement!" Sick girl, sick women, all unbalanced.

On top of this my sense of Bette—young, fresh, just entering *the arena*. My sense of these things is what makes me so careful and guarded with her; yet I've not had the courage to tell her that our relationship cannot be a permanent one. Even she said last week that she wasn't sure she wanted to be an actress, as Frances Farmer said it six months ago, as Luise has said it before . . . all of them instinctively fearful of the competitive world which kills their inner life. Horrible. Often I tell people that it is the middle class that will profit most from a revolution that brings a new and more human way of life, but most people don't understand that. Every woman, if she but realized it, would work for a socialist society and way of life. Of this I am certain, positive! Such a play, on this theme, could be called *The Arena*!

So I thought of Luise. Without help Luise will be nothing, without a man. But that man I could never be, not to give and not to be given. The part needed a great juggler, something I will never be. Bad casting that was. Here is the truth: she would have ruined me or made a great man of me. A potent demanding personality, never in repose, fluid, without concentration. And I look for repose and discipline. She shattered me, delighted me, disturbed and enraged me, fired and fussed me: she was too much for one young American man to handle.

My intuition marches far ahead of my knowledge. This is why I think I'm beginning to understand the war and postwar generation. My sense of life is gearing into this hell which has broken loose in Europe and is foaming over to our shores.

———•———

Friday, June 7, 1940

Surely this is the finest time of the year in the East, these soft June nights, tender, grave, quiet. They would calm down a wild beast, even the Blatant Beast, Hitler.

The Little One came here tonight, past seven, bright-eyed, like a hummingbird, like Debussy music, as I later told her in bed and so she gave an extra squirm of delight. But before this we sat in the cool deepening dusk, drank a bottle of chilled *vin rosé*, and gradually both became so relaxed that she crawled into my lap where I soon had her undressed naked, the room being so dark by now that it was scarcely necessary to draw the curtains. I had not changed from my pajamas, having risen late in the afternoon, so it was nothing for me to soon be as naked as she was. What was strange was that until she sat on my lap I did not know that her mother had died just two weeks ago. She told me how broken her father was, and in this minute I became her father, tears in my eyes, rocking her back and forth like a baby. She needed someone, said she had often wanted to call me but had been afraid. I told her to call me any time she felt lonely. We kissed with our mouths, sat back, chatted, were silent, deeply relaxed, so unusually relaxed that we both commented on it several times. Then I carried her into the bedroom where I told her how I was going to do what I was going to do to her. She opened like a flower, all over, and we had three or four arcadian hours together, the deepest sort of comradeship. She told me she loved me, but seeing my silence, said for me not to worry about it. "I know you are a lone wolf," she said; but only a half hour later, "Oh, can't you say you love me!" she said. I said I did; "I love you," I said.

She had to meet some friends at Far Rockaway where they were going to spend the weekend together. She asked me to drive her out there and I said I was happy to do it. She is very womanly for a little girl, a woman in miniature, although she is twenty-three. I saw that she resented my suggestion that I invite a friend for the drive out. "Don't be afraid to be a woman," I said. "Resent aloud." She admitted, as I had seen, that she wanted to spend the hour alone with me. And so we had this fine ride out to the beach, twice getting lost, but finally reaching her friends who were waiting for her in front of a dark hotel. Then I was soon off alone, headed back to the city, driving with relaxed hands, a mute mind, and a fresh relaxed body. The man who says that this sort of sexual contact emasculates a man, he is a fool, a snob of human values. All of this verified again and again for me the deep tonic qualities of the hours in bed with her. This, I thought, as I pulled onto the Fifty-ninth Street Bridge, is direct contact with the road, with the wheels, with the air and the night. There is a type of person, it occurred to me, who had this direct contact with all things and people, all situations. He is a primitive, his behavior "uncorrupted," a Van Gogh, everything contacted directly. He lacks form, lacks convention. He lives deeply but very painfully, often. For forms are necessary or one goes mad or develops into an unbalanced being. How to keep the direct contact and yet find a form in which to move! There, friends, there is the problem of a life worth living!

———•———

Saturday, June 8, 1940

Haydn is decorative, meaning the music is a convention, a cold form, in the sense that no level of emotional experience is expressed, no psychological experience, nothing personal or autobiographical. Of course this does not necessarily mean that the music is spurious.

I told Harold Clurman a long time ago that one of my main problems is to simultaneously present the dynamic linear movement of a *Lefty* with the psychological texture and depth of a *Paradise Lost*. I told him that no playwright, excepting Shakespeare, has ever done this satisfactorily, and Shakespeare was able to do this because the theatre convention of his time permitted him to stop the plot line or linear movement so that the character might deliver a long speech expressive of his psychological state. (Ibsen's characters I find dry, often only types, even if his own types.) Notice that the psychological life of Shakespeare's characters is not expressed in their deeds, in their plot moves, but in the soliloquies, their asides, and long speeches: the convention permitted such apportioning.

All this is written because it is also one of the main problems of Harold as a director and I must remember to tell him so. The production of *Night Music* was spotty; so were *Rocket* and *Paradise*. None of these scripts is spotty in the writing, at least not as I laid them out and would direct them. Well, why were the productions spotty? Because the director of them stressed character depth where I had written situation and forward plot movement. In these cases the director's problem was exactly what I have written above as my own writing problem.

Sid Benson walked in here at six. He gave me a pamphlet reprinting a speech Lenin made in 1917. But it exactly fits the war situation today. Then Geebee came in. At ten we rode uptown, we three, ate a light supper at Schrafft's, saw a newsreel and two films, or part of them. One with Heifetz fiddling, his deadpan face white and serious. The other an old film, the first F. Tone made when he went to the coast in 1932. Very instructive. We move so fast in this country that the film, the acting style, the lighting and settings, the clothes—all are already old-fashioned. Franchot was not bored then, not blasé, but fresh and impulsive.

After we'd dropped Sid at this house, Geebee and I returned here. We listened to Chopin, then to bed and bed and bed—take off the third bed! Now I'm here writing these words at almost seven in the morning, Geebee asleep behind the closed door. Myself too, soon.

———————•———————

Tuesday, June 11, 1940

I'm up at Green Mansions Camp, having arrived here early this morning with Sid Benson for a partner in the all-night ride through dark and rain. With me are many of my files, some books, plenty of paper and a new typewriter ribbon, and an intention or desire on my part to write the short antiwar play. Our president has come out for the Allies and immediate aid to them in no uncertain terms. I think he is trying to act as cement to keep England and France together, for France may sign a separate peace. Then Italy declared war against the Allies on Sunday night. *Il Duce* made a filthy bombastic speech, talking of destiny and friendship, all prime crap. In the meantime Lewis Mumford has joined a group of liberals and wealthy men who favor the participation of the U.S., men and materials, immediately! Peacetime conscription, too, is favored in many quarters and may become a law of the land almost immediately. Liberalism is truly and officially dead now for all to see. Liberals are the cushions and springs of capitalism, easing the bumps. They are a cleanup crew sent into action before the bigwigs begin their dastardly work. I find it impossible to see any difference between this war and the last one. Not even a capitalist can save a man who insists periodically upon cutting his throat from ear to ear. For this is a war to save capitalism. Who can pretend, and be he honest, that England and France are fighting for democracy when they have given a half-dozen democratic countries to Hitler in the past three years? A race for trade, simply that, will cost millions of lives, billions of dollars, and the ruination of the old world, a world already dead but writhing with malice and hate. For a new world is ahead, as tomorrow is certainly ahead. Only this thought can give true men true purpose, reason for fight, hope, for love. The only other alternative is suicide. In between, if you will think about it, there is nothing to fear but the prison cell into which you may soon be placed. The censure, the unpopularity, the blows against you, all are child's play in the face of the socialism which will make a garden of the world. Believe me, a garden!

Sunday night a letter came from W. F. [Fay Wray]. She loves me; she is all womanhood, all tenderness. I yearn but do not yield, not being able to trust myself to give her a happy life, for one thing.

———————•———————

Thursday, June 13, 1940

Last night I was able to begin the antiwar play, two scenes, slight, but a real beginning. Tonight I will continue my work with feeling for it. For Paris is occupied today by the Germans and all I can think of are the pitiful people, the people always duped, always suffering. Tools in the hands of unscrupulous leaders like Laval, Blum, Reynaud, and Co. Over here those whose voices command the radios and newspapers— the barrage is incessant now—do not distinguish between the people and their false leaders. Forgotten are the betrayals of all the small democracies of Europe by the so-called two big democracies. Forgotten is Munich, unmentioned that the Germans opened, fought, and won this war with tanks made by Skoda in Czechoslovakia, and that these were the tanks which mowed down the English Tommies and French peasants and workers. That the English and French governors did not even prepare adequately enough to protect their soldiers, that is not mentioned. No one can say how many hundreds of thousands, yes, hundreds of thousands, are dead, bleeding, and torn apart tonight, everything scrap and garbage, human garbage, bags of crushed flesh, refugees, babies, children, women, streaming eyes, screaming hearts, choked throats, maniacs of the moneymen. May they be slaughtered with choice delights of torture, those wicked men of money bags, those financiers and traders, they who made Hitler the beast he is before they betrayed their people to his maniacal brutal strength! May they lose their hands, their eyes, and tongues and become a word of hate, a remembered vile reptile hacked and slaughtered and left in the dust of the road or hung from the highest tree! May those merchants be backed into the sea, in England, in France, in Germany, forever remembered, never forgotten, for the crop of hell-heaving wars they have sworn in their greed and lust!

And here it begins. Ears do not deceive me—politicos, mangy merchants, professors, war majors, all are coldly, with calculation (for their propaganda is too cleverly purveyed to be unconscious), planning to put the United States in this war. They know the Germans will assault our world markets, that we will have to meet their competition in South America, that they will try to lower wages, that they will not be able to regiment, and so lower costs in a democracy, industry.

Communists have this on their side: things always come out as they predict them. Theirs is the only eye which is able to penetrate this fog of contradictions and gassy lies, these vain false shibboleths that the radio spouts all day. They have merciless logic on their side; any intelligent and honest man must admit this.

Today I rowed a little on the lake; it was a happy hour in the sun, a wind spanking away the clouds of the past few days. Tomorrow the sun will be up high in a cloudless sky. But now to work.

———•———

Friday, June 14, 1940

Six years ago I was like the group of young actors and actresses who are working here. These young people were so impressed with me that it was almost painful to work with them, although they were very well mannered. I wonder to myself how this came about, what about me deserves this respect. It is often painful, but one comes to almost expect it, learning to face it. But it cuts one off from other people.

The point I meant to make: that being "famous" cuts one off from all normal intercourse. People meet you in two ways—either they are defiant and rude, aggressive and hard and scornful (so righting their own selves), or they shrink away and refuse to expose their genuine selves to you. Invariably they end up by being amazed that you are a normal human being.

Hitler's armies are all over Paris today. The cant about the Allies fighting for the liberty of the world continues. Yesterday the League of American Writers issued an antiwar statement.

I saw in two papers today that Harold Clurman is back from the coast. Why he has come back I don't know, but if it is because Stella is in New York, there is no longer a Group Theatre and I sever producing connections with him. Stella through Harold can no longer continue to impair the creative life of the actors and myself; she has done so for many years, no matter what explanatory extenuations Harold finds.

The trip up here has been very good for me. It made me see clearly the meaning of the present war and made more firm my tone of approach to the issue which is facing the whole world today. One has no right to ask more from a trip of four or five days to a camp.

I have not thought about poor Geebee since being here. This I regret, but the fact is the fact.

—————•—————

Saturday, June 15, 1940

Many new guests coming up here. Probably I am the first sight pointed out to them. All day I am thoughtless. They stare at me and I stare at them.

Bad news from Europe for the Allies. The only line with which I can feel any sympathy is that of the Soviet Union.

In the late afternoon I attended another rehearsal of the farce [being performed by a group at the camp]. This work carried on after dinner for a third session. By this time the lower-than-mediocrity of the script was so annoying to me that I became almost speechless before it as the actors kept running through. At three in the morning we broke up, having fixed some of its worst spots.

So a drink of brown rum and to bed. The nights are cold here. I am very alone in a sleeping grassy world. Many newlywed couples come up here during June. Surely they are not asleep in the night. It is sweet to see them around the camp, pretending that they are not connected because they don't want to suggest by any remark or gesture that they spend hour on hour in copulation. They disavow each other as much as possible.

I have the Hollywood feeling, the Cuba feeling, loose, sprawling, unconnected, a fat fish at the bottom of a heavy murky sea.

—————•—————

Monday, June 17, 1940

The writers do not and will not say what has happened to them. They all wither away here before they are forty—they have been attacked by some mysterious malady which kills them slowly, as a lethal gas would kill; and yet they are silent—from fear, for hope that life may return to them?

We are back in New York, Sid and I, arriving here at six this morning.

Here there were interesting letters from Marion Post and Faysie. I left a note for Herman, telling him to go away and leave me here alone until I call him. So getting out of bed Monday afternoon I found myself alone, no maid, no others walking in and out, in a word alone!

Since then I have been doing some research, making notes and planning future scenes on the antiwar play. And eating, three meals, and listening to war news on the radio. France has asked for a separate peace. It's far away from me—I don't feel it, if I must be honest, because I have no experience of it.

I am very lonely. I keep looking in other people's windows. Patience, time flies!

———•———

Tuesday, June 18, 1940

This living from the jowls and testicles is murderous for me. It engulfs me, a man with an essentially religious purpose and use in life, a sort of sunken cathedral of a person. I know what it is—it's a desire and search for peace, so usual in the young artists of the time. The early youth was lived so fiercely, so it seems; life was so harsh, the personality keyed so high, that now the personality looks for peace and rest. Which is to leave out the murderous world in which we are all living. All right, then you find peace, peace! And what is that but a refusal of everything that you are, of everything that you must continue to be. So the self yawns, snarls, grows petty and irritable. Now you have yourself, you have "liberty," you have peace, you are alone . . . and you are under the sea! Up, Odets, up!

Last night I found a long letter from my dead mother. I cried twice as I read it—what did you think I would do? A lot of people would be surprised (as the little boy said) if they knew how often during a single day and night my eyes flood with tears which seem unreasonable. Up, up from the depths—a torpedo, up, up!

I am out of bed and the hours vanish. Shall I call her, call him? And the hours are gone and the nighttime is here and midnight is on the way again, and after that all the morning hours until I sleep again.

I've been working on notes and outlining further scenes for the antiwar play. I am out of balance; the personality won't come together. All the parts are before me, like a clock taken apart, but there is no will to put the machinery together and wind it up for the steady ticking and forward movement of the hands which is necessary for work.

Ticktock, my friend! Trust yourself!

What a luxury it seems to be here alone, no daily secretary, no maid, no one but my naked or dressed self, exactly as I choose. This is the anarchy of a child.

An editor speaks of Rilke's characteristic "unease of living." Well, that is the whole thing.

———•———

Wednesday, June 19, 1940

Again a four-in-the-afternoon resurrection from the bed. Sid Benson waked in a little later, in time to share my coffee. We chatted for a few moments about the antiwar play which he knows about.

Geebee came here past seven, a cold in her nose and her eyes looking distressed. We drank wine and chatted about the war and the Group Theatre. After which we made love in the bedroom, on the bed. At eleven at night we drove uptown, ate cold lobster salad and iced coffee, and went to one of the cheap movies on Forty-second Street where we saw Gracie Fields in an absurd piece of British propaganda and Gabin and Simone Simon in a good French film called, as I remember, *The Beast.** How genuine they are able to make the

**La Bête Humaine.*

relationship between a man and a woman. Renoir directed this film, which showed, another point, what Hollywood can do to a real young woman like Simon. In a Hollywood film she is a tart, hard, unreal, unfeminine; but here she was a breathing woman, young, lovely, palpitant all over, always interesting. Hollywood, like Midas, kills whatever it touches. They did the same thing with Luise: a splendid shell is left and the inner life is drained away. Pitiful!

The picture was stimulating enough to make me think of doing a Hollywood film again, or at least trying. It made me think of *Night Music* as a film which I'll soon have to journey out to the coast to write. Three attempts at other films don't give me much hope.

Geebee said she had met Harold Clurman today and asked him how the coast was. "Boring," he said. "And how is Gadget out there?" she asked. "Bored!"

Thursday, June 20, 1940

What's in the wastebasket beside my bed? For some idea of what I've been doing these past few solitary days: two discarded book catalogues, an old electric plug, the core of a roll of toilet paper, an empty beer can, the shells of two hard-boiled eggs which I ate in bed last night, the wrapper from a cake of soap, an empty toilet water bottle, two cotton swabs used, a dozen cigarette butts, a discarded *Time* magazine. Pregnant days!

Lying in bed, reading, thinking, it was past noon before I went to sleep. At almost eight I awoke, loaded with the glimmers of many fragmentary dreams (almost notes for dreams). Then to listen for war news, to eat some supper—a half-dozen eggs—and read the newspapers. I fell into bed again and slept till five in the morning. Now it's Friday noontime.

One thing makes me feel good: I am completely clear on the war issue.

The morning mail drives me mad—six requests for money!

Saturday, June 22, 1940

That lonely smell is in the house again, the smell of white soap, drying flowers, and placid dust combined.

Waldo Frank has a few good ideas, many very bad, in relation to his writing on what he calls the troubled waters of today. His chief defects are two: that he has an ego badly out of control; and that he seems to have no sense of the need for a period of militant communism in which it is impossible for attention to be paid to deep human values. He does not or cannot see that fire you must fight with fire and that there must be destruction before one can think of spiritual values. Before the art there is the life, before the values the man—that he cannot see. He does not see that we are fighting for our lives, naked, pressed. Waldo thinks himself the new humanist, but he understands the type only with his head (and only half), never with his emotions. He is really a very old-fashioned man, stubborn from his ego . . . not from his growth. Gorky could show him the way, not André Gide. Waldo's kind of "human dignity" is what all the aristocratic Englishmen, for instance, have had for centuries. Pah!

Last night with Sid Benson ate at Lindy's, there meeting and talking for an hour with that sordid little clown, Billy Rose, who pretends aloud that he cannot understand, lying, as he said, in Eleanor's room, what he did to deserve all of this, the money and the luxury and the lady's breasts, I suppose. By which he means to say that he has done pretty well for a little Jew boy from nowhere. He has an idea for an air show in which planes take formations like chorus girls and a love duet is sung from girl to boy through loudspeakers. He has much admiration for organizers and organizations, using the phrase "organizing ability" very often. He sees himself as some little Napoleon, and not so little at that. In the meantime, I am told, that the Broadway Napoleon, Walter Winchell, is being profiled in *The New Yorker* magazine through six issues! Surely it is the year of the gnat!

Then we saw the first anti-Nazi film, made by Metro, *The Mortal Storm* with James Stewart and Margaret Sullavan, who is going to play in the movie version (!) of *Night Music*. From such a theme—the breakdown of a non-Aryan family in Germany—not one distinguished moment, but not one! A modern version of *East Lynne*, modern only because of the technical means used in the filming.

Shyness or some other dominant trait in a person makes for a complete style of body movement.

Tonight, Saturday, Bette came here, the Kozlenkos (Lee looking very seductive, for some inner reason I could not fathom), and Boris Aronson later. We all went up to Lindy's for a big dinner, roast duck or roast beef, both whopping meals there. After a ride, taking them all home finally, I told Bette I would take her home as I wanted to go home and work. She was very depressed, cried a little, openly when the car stopped in front of her door. She wanted, I knew, some sign from me that she was important in my life. I could not lie, I could not pain her then by telling her that her tacit fears were all true: speechless. Then she apologized for making this faint scene—she makes so little trouble (which is the trouble, by the way, for she does not stimulate)—and said good night. I rode home feeling very sorry for her but unable to do anything about it except terminate our gentle relationship, so promising to her, so unmeaningful to me.

Here red peonies in a white vase, dying, dripping dead petals to the floor.

Sunday, June 23, 1940

Up at seven in the evening, slept out, no longer tired, ready to face life again with a grimace. For a half hour I lay in bed thinking that this one or that one is not the girl, hoping that Luise is making more out of her life on the West Coast than I am doing here in the East. Then boiling brown coffee, cigarettes, an egg, a piece of Swiss cheese—and war news! Ah, war news. France has completely capitulated, fascists in charge of her government. Apparently Churchill has made a strong statement against the French surrender. No, it is not all over; it is the beginning! Hear me on this, it is the bloody beginning of the new world! Otherwise there is nothing left to live for!

Called Harold Clurman. He wasn't in, as he was not when I called him yesterday. Then, on an impulse, called John O'Hara and made an appointment to meet for dinner tomorrow night. I told him that we should talk about the problem of success for the young artist in America, that, as I belive, we have much in common, being of the same generation, involved in the same muck during the past years. He said he had much to say about that, so a meeting tomorrow.

Poetry, Coleridge says, is emotion and order, as much of both as possible.

The true ending of the story of Aladdin has never been told. His mother, a shrewd peasant woman, after watching him for a long time said to herself, "My son has all this fabulous wealth, castles, horses, armies, the wife of his heart. HE HAS NOTHING now!" On a midnight she took the magic lamp and rubbed it. The obedient slave appeared and asked her wish. "Destroy yourself," she said, "for you have already destroyed my son who no longer draws in a sweet breath or is able to spend a restful hour. Give him back his life by destroying everything he now owns. Take away his property, give him an open heart, an open mind, give him liberty!" The obedient slave snarled, for this old woman had guessed his secret, that he was not the slave—those whom he seemed to obey were HIS slaves!

In the German character there must be some element of fearful uncertainty and insecurity to make it give up so completely to discipline and a total machine.

Riding up to the camp last week, a strange thing. At three in the dark morning, on a road miles from human habitation, a woman steps out on the road and signals for us to stop. She is dressed in a heavy coat, underneath it a longer white dress or gown; a little white dog stands beside her, as appealing, as mysterious. We do not stop because we are too startled at this sudden apparition, because it may be dangerous—a female plant for some scheme, etc. But this apparition is all we talk about for the next half hour. A week later we start back for New York, planning to return by the same road. I say, "How strange if that same woman is standing there tonight."

———•———

For Sunday night, June 23, 1940

The phone rang near nine—Harold at last—and I said I'd be up to his hotel after a shower. Done soon enough; Aaron Copland and his friend, Victor, were there, Aaron giggling about the way I greeted Harold, thumping him heartily on the back. Then we sat and chatted for two hours, mostly about the state of the world.

Harold said little about the West Coast—his disgust was evident—little about anything else; in fact his manner was noncommittal for a long time, as if he were having difficulty readjusting to me. Fay Wray he said he had seen twice and she was "really a very sweet girl"—responsive, I think he added. He told me a few trifling stories about the movie industry (can one tell other kinds?) and then we adjourned to Lindy's for coffee and cake which wound up with sandwiches, coffee and cake, more coffee and more cake.

Harold said, with good reasons on his side, that he was against the Communist line in relation to the part of the U.S. in the war. Yes, he says, the main enemy is Hitler—he is the one to finish off first. To lump the Allies with him, both sides imperialists, is wrong even though it is correct. Furnish the lesser imperialists with guns with which to vanquish Hitler. When this is done the masses, guns in their hands, can turn on their enemies at home. Any other course he thinks utopian, foolish, since you will spend the war period uselessly in jail. No, he insists, help the war and as you are doing so be instrumental in guiding it, insisting always on the fullest civil rights, etc. He has a real point here, plus defense of the U.S. I asked him if he could put his position into a simple phrase or slogan, but by this time the cannibals were at the table and all serious conversation was impossible.

Monday, June 24, 1940

A long letter from Ouida Campbell, the Cleo of North Carolina. How mature and considerate she is for nineteen. I had sent her the Rilke book of letters to a young poet; she discussed the letters with high intelligence, pointing her finger right on the point of Rilke's isolation and his specialized quality which comes from that.

Paul Strand's long-delayed album of prints of his photos arrived, the Mexican set. They are works of great talent, care, and order, each of them looking exactly like his own face, sombre, dark, serious, intent, a trifle worried. I don't know how it is that a good painter always paints his own face into a portrait, but so it always seems to me. This mirroring of the self is often a subtle one but it is present in all important artists to a marked degree. So it is with Paul's photos, proud works, hard, something relentless about them, always carefully held in hand by the man behind them.

A wasted unhappy evening of the sort in which the boredom can become so acute that suddenly you are saying witty flashing cutting things. This unfruitful evening was spent for the most part with John O'Hara. He came here for dinner since it was our plan, as discussed yesterday on the phone, to try to mutually come to some understanding of the problems which face young writers in America today. He had several drinks, another at the dinner table at "68," on top of that some soup, and a bottle of Chianti which we split. Thinks he is worldly (is really very rude) and a ripened personality. (Of course John is only a Katzenjammer kid with two prongs to his fork, women and booze, neither genuinely relished, I fear.)

What chance was there then of a conversation which might pull him out of the muck of his small success, might begin to make him sense what it is to be an artist, helpful to both of us? By this time a slack string myself, we drove to his house where he proceeded to genially boss his respectful wife around, she no more able to really live with him than one can really live in a rowboat—you are a tenant there but you don't live there!

Talk about Roosevelt. What anguish to listen to people who do not make even one consecutive sentence come alive in you, only words: "Yes. No. Sure. Perhaps. Agreed. Why? Oh." I understand that Chekhov had the knack of getting right to the heart of what a man really knew, to the interesting matter that even the most humble artisan has in his possession. How can I learn that? Later I tried for a moment with the wife, John gone to the toilet "to receive a call from the coast," as he put it. I asked her, "Where do you come from? Pennsylvania too?" "No," she said, "from New York." And that was the end of that. It was no better when we moved on to the Stork Club at John's suggestion, although he had serious doubts about the wife coming along. I said it was ridiculous, and after a solemn moment of blinking at the wall he agreed, saying, "Put on your shoes then and come along, Belle."

Mumble jumble from him at the nightclub. People sitting, chatting, drinking, dancing, nonsense. Some feeble sallies from John, more coffee, more Scotch, looking up, looking down, smiling wanly— I was glad when Lyons walked in and signaled for me to join him. He was with Winchell, who was having supper with his girl.

Walter is all excited about a group of fascists, Coughlinite boys who were on trial for conspiracy against the government and have just been freed. He said priests intervened on their behalf, etc., etc., and now he, against them in all his columns, is in danger of being bumped off, only the gun in his pocket to protect him. I advised him to keep out of dark places, appeared worried for his natty sake, suggested that problems were not as simple as he was making them, that fascism and its rise is understandable only by understanding the conditions and conflicts behind it. You have to be a trained fifty-yard-dash runner to get in a word when Winchell takes the floor, which is from noon to midnight and midnight to noon.

As Winchell left a strange human organization named Jimmy Durante came along. I had never met him before; a really pleasurable event. He had taken his whole family to see G. [*Golden*] *Boy*, knew all about me. I said he would be fine in a straight play, but what was interesting to me was his sweet nature, which expressed itself in giving you a hug, leaning way across the table. Every time he said something which he knew to be ridiculous, he indicated this by a humorously hopeless shake of the head. He is a real old Italian *commedia dell' arte* player, as fresh as a fish peddler, although he has fallen into a certain routine of doing and saying what is expected of him. Any new person met is the king for this jester, energy, sweat, and the sweetness of nature.

Unfruitful night, fruitless day. But does one ever know which experience is the productive one and which the sterile? Anyway, since last night I have been thinking about that little *trio* play.* I think it will be easy to open the door of that little beehive and let out the swarm.

———•———

Tuesday, June 25, 1940

I have a desire of the heart which I am always confusing, making the need of a woman a thing of sex and so soiling one of the best impulses in me, and so soiling whatever woman I meet. Morals don't bother me, but immorality does.

Geebee called me. I didn't want to be alone with her—it is the week of the locusts in our relationship and I am uneasy and evasive because I

*Mentioned briefly earlier, this play will become *Clash by Night*.

see and know she wants some definite word. All I can say is a negative saying. We went to see *Harvest*.

Home I came to write on the trio play. And yet this goddam acute loneliness makes me leave the telephone on, hoping that by accident someone may call. And then the phone rang!—the Little One, the hummingbird, drunk, she said. I asked her to come right over, slugged two brandies in my belly, undressed, and then paced the apartment with a beating heart—this setting of the stage is so exciting in itself. She came here in record time, whereupon we fell upon each other and slept and awoke and chatted and massacred each other again and again and then she fell asleep and I prowled around the house, unable to sleep until past ten in the morning, she stained and scented beside me with all the exercises of the night.

Way in the late afternoon she left, tiptoeing out, almost apologetic, hoping there was something between us and yet knowing there was nothing. This is a brutal way of living, an unsplendid way, if I want to be kind to myself! It agonizes me and pleases simultaneously!

A nice note came from W. F., who is much in my mind.

I want to conquer and be subdued at once; that's the crazy drive in me! There are contradictory pulls—one to live with tightened discipline, sharp, hard, and cold; the other to go hotly and passionately to hell as fast and as fully as possible.

The more agonizing I feel the pressure of my unbalanced riotous life, the more unhappy it makes me, the more often people say, "How well you are looking these days." It draws a sallow smile from my tired face.

———•———

Wednesday, June 26, 1940

Harold Clurman came here at seven in the evening, we to go to dinner and discuss the Group Theatre and what must be done if it is to survive. The old ground, the old clumps of sod turned up again, nothing new from either of us, although he did most of the talking. He brought back from the coast a proposition from [Oscar] Serlin that I dramatize into a play the Nijinsky biography and material which Serlin has bought from Mrs. Nijinsky. This interests me very much and I said so. We are to see Serlin next week, Harold as a sort of director of the project, although Serlin is not interested in the proposed play as a Group production.

Gide is the artist and explorer of the wound, as Rilke is, both very special. They are like two shell-shocked men who have been so sensitized by the battle of modern life that every tremor of the air disturbs them. They are the poets of the dropping of a leaf. Always I find them interesting, but in an uneasy way, as one might be at lifting the skirts of a nun. Is this true?

MacCartney sent a cable from London, wants me to guarantee the visit of an artist friend to lecture here. Will do so tomorrow. Mac says that things are tight there but the spirit is excellent. They are waiting, of course, for the Beast to begin his attack on the British Isles. It looks bad. The Soviet Union, in the meantime, has taken Bessarabia from Rumania, which has gone fascist. I think that Russia positively must come into an organization of England, the remains of the French (where the French fascist bastards are now setting up a fascist government), and the United States. Japan is moving towards French possessions. The world stinketh! Oh, malarial stink! Putrefaction! Cancerous rotting galled stink!

———————•———————

Thursday, June 27, 1940

Now you have another responsibility, not to take everything that is offered to you—women, adulation, money, easy and good times. Did you never realize this before? Take nothing! Go back to your narrow life before it is too late!

I am told Luise is in town. It anguishes me for a half hour and then it is gone. Pangs me, I should say, for anguish is a great word and my feelings are not great. She sets my bowels on fire, not my heart. I long to have her in bed—we made wonderful music together.

Geebee called today. So did her sister, to whom I did not speak. It made me uneasy since I thought perhaps the sister wanted to play the role of an irate parent. Perhaps, I thought, the kid has a slightly swollen belly and is ashamed to talk about it. It made me very uneasy, I must say.

———————•———————

Friday, June 28, 1940

I am a painted man on a painted sea. Sea? No, swamp.

———◆———

Tuesday, July 2, 1940

Even this journal doesn't write itself. But I see notes for the missing days here on a pad. Scrawls, scribbles, while I am fighting for my life in these two rooms now grown hateful because so much of my unrestful and uneasy months have been spent in them.

NOTE: "Who is that?" "Shh, shh . . . Odets . . . writer . . . Cliff . . . Theatre. . . ." I no longer feel foolish, at least not fifty percent of the time, when hearing that behind my back or to one side. So be it, great man.

NOTE: (last Thursday) letter from Heath, London agent. Little Theatre wants to do *Rocket* and *Night Music*, Unity wanting to do *Awake [and Sing]*. They seem to be playing theatre like mad in all that blackout darkness and tension. Gave them a year's option of whatever they want to do.

Mr. Wendell Willkie, prominent because he fought the New Deal on behalf of huge utility companies, was nominated by the Republicans as their Presidential candidate. If you saw his rivals in the newsreel you would understand why he got the nomination, having a personality and appearance much like Roosevelt's. The others looked exactly like a handful of sweet potatoes, unshaped, lumpy, expressionless, so mild.

NOTE: (Friday) Geebee here. I propose get drunk, get drunk, what the hell. I see she doesn't dare demand her status. Suddenly on my lap (hello, you chair, you undressing chair), and bang in the bed, and bang in the belly. Late leisurely supper at Lindy's. Say we will meet tomorrow night again since it is her last night in town, she going up to Saratoga for eight weeks of summer stock.

NOTE: (Saturday) Geebee here with Harold Clurman and Sid Benson for dinner which we had over at Café Royale, one of the few places in New York with culture, meaning here a home. A newsreel showing Hoover and other Republicans at their convention, paper hats, toy whistles, a bunch of booby kids, rambunctious, completely benighted, blithering, and hopeless, but making a president of the greatest country in the world. William Allen White said once that if you gave him a few billion dollars he could put even a Chinaman in the White House. Correct!

NOTE: First clear article explaining how French fascists sold out their country to the Germans in Sunday *Times*. Pitiful, the war of dollars!

Thinking of Luise. A matchbook cover with a print of a reclining nude lady, left on the table, nude lady looking like Luise. Slipped it into my pocket and brought it home, where I put it in the pocket of my dressing gown. Looked at it twenty times in two nights. Luise is not on my mind; she is in my system, an invisible marauder feeding off the host. Six months or a year more of married life and she would have had me forever, which she didn't know, which I fought off like a man fighting for his life, which was what I was doing, the life of a writer, a modern minor artist.

NOTE: (Sunday) *hectic* Berlioz, so rechristened by me.

Sid Benson here at six in the afternoon and lugging me out of a bed that I am not too anxious to get out of. For what? Dress and ride uptown to eat good food at the Stork Club. Then to Sylvia and Luther Adler back from a week of stock at Amherst. He asks for recommendation for another play to do in Atlantic City. Say I'll write them one in three weeks. Half joking, but only half, for I'm loaded to the gills with creative tension.

NOTE: (Monday) Wrote exactly half of act 1. Feeling good but work rough, but all there in outline and direction. Satisfactory, very, for a first draft.

It suddenly occurs to me that I am trying to put off the inevitable: learning to write. The plays before were mostly easy, came easily, not much work. Now it is necessary to learn to write. Which explains much of my uneasiness of the past year. For is that an easy thing to admit to one's self? That you don't know how to write? Admitted then! And to work on the trio play!

———————•———————

Sunday, July 7, 1940

I am at Luther and Sylvia's farm, having been here since the evening of the third, driving out from the city after an evening spent with Oscar Serlin and Harold Clurman. I have agreed to write the play on Nijinsky, Serlin holding the rights to all the material, production time somewhere around the fall of 1942. In the meantime Al Lewin on the West Coast has sent me a script of his new film, *Flotsam*, from a novel by Remarque, and some puerile suggestions for the movie *Night Music* which I shall do my best to ignore. The Hollywood isolation from all reality has never been so well demonstrated as in these suggestions sent by Al. No man of intelligence, which Al certainly is, a reader of Keats and Shelley, could possibly suggest these ideas unless he were half-drowned to death in the banalities and clichés of California. The danger is not to be swamped by them oneself when one is out there.

Working hours, sleeping hours, those for walking and talking, everything is shamefully mixed. I am like a rooster scratching around in an enclosure, as aimless, as variable, as unconcentrated, finally as cocky. I sent a small wristwatch to Geebee, a sort of farewell gift. Also wrote a note to my father on the West Coast.

Late at night I went up to the Stork Club, too indifferent to work, to eat some of their good food. There I met Burgess Meredith, Franchot Tone, and John O'Hara, and a brother-in-law together at one table. Meredith was leaving for a Western ranch vacation the next day, so they were celebrating together by getting drunk and more morose each minute. They were in moods of careful (or cautious) self-abnegation, admitting carefully that their lives were useless, that, as Franchot put it while discussing Maxie Baer, the fighter, "the thing is to look good even while you're going down." Franchot, whom I like, still a very unusual acting talent in the theatre, always brings out in me a certain caginess and overconsideration, a real and acute discomfort.

After the Serlin meeting, dining together in a Rumanian restaurant on the East Side, I drove out to this farm in rain and fog. Luther and Sylvia were still up at two in the morning. I settled into their house like a honeybee among apple blossoms and went to bed at about four in the morning.

———•———

Monday, July 8, 1940

Yesterday I read Lewin's script, *Flotsam*. It is so bad that I could make few serious notes, finally finding myself speechless before its lack of human perceptions and its "movieness." They will make a smooth high-class product probably, respectable and expensive. There was one eloquent scene: "Exterior, evening. The sheep are in the fold." I don't know what to write back to Lewin.

Today, Monday, after an afternoon sunbath, very hot and penetrating, arousing good feelings all over me, Luther and I drove back to New York where I hope to continue working on the trio play, cool, comfortable, and alone in my apartment. We had an interesting conversation on Luther's childhood while driving in. It was very much like my own, one of rejection and a sense of inadequacy, and it explains his tendency to look for accommodation from others.

There was a stack of mail which I read with pleasure—a note from Geebee but none from Fay Wray, which momentarily disgruntled me. Sleep overpowered me, come heavy sleep, and I did not wake up till ten hours later, at seven in the morning of Tuesday, which is when I am writing these words. How fine this "normal" rising seems, feels. The day is coming up and I with it. Hurrah!

———•———

Sunday, July 7, 1940 (continued)

Sylvia has all of the standard books here on the lives of Nijinsky, Diaghilev, and the rest of the unsavory talented crew. Have already read four of the books and made many notes. I feel nothing about the material and don't want to get too involved with it until a first draft of the trio play is finished and I am, at least, on my way to the coast to do the *Night Music* movie.

I forgot to say that Luise called in town a few days ago. Herman spoke to her, she saying that she wanted me to call. I don't think I will. She is still very exciting to me and, frankly, the prospect of a visit with her makes me uneasy, not that any woman living has the strength to make me do something I don't want to do. My feeling for women tends towards Fay Wray, whom I often think of with real tenderness. We could make a life for ourselves, in the country, this way. I want children.

Stella Adler showed up out here yesterday afternoon. Won't change, but something is happening to her, to one side of her nature. For the first time I noticed that she is growing hard and vulgar, truly. She is driving the car I gave Harold Clurman for a present last year. For a moment I resented that, but it is his car, his love, his affair, his sad, I am afraid, life. His love for her does not seem to let up. She pangs him and pangs him with repeated stabs of her female knife—she is a whole cutlery shop of such weapons for him. Bleeding and stuck all over, he asks for more and more.

———•———

Tuesday, July 9, 1940

The trio play is going to be interesting. Brutal too, I think. It writes itself easily too, always a good sign with me, no notes beside me. It is going to be a hot little play.

At eleven I rode uptown to meet Harold Clurman at Lindy's, Kermit B. [Bloomgarden] with him, both fresh from seeing the Sherwood play; not impressed. Talk. Nonsense. Mr. Rose outspoken in his opinions of world affairs. Billy is *ne plus ultra*, a sordid raccoon. Again he repeated that he lies in bed and wonders what he did to deserve all this.

Weary, home to bed, seeing that the papers have printed the announcement that I am to do the Nijinsky play.

Wednesday, July 10, 1940

Roosevelt announces that we positively will not send soldiers abroad. An Italian woman in the Bronx killed her six children by gas; she feared she was going insane!

First human letter ever received from my father received here today. No preaching, no pretense, merely giving me careful detailed instructions about how to drive a car along the mountainous, hot, and desert roads if I drive out to California. The first letter of his in over thirty years that ever touched me.

Billy Rose said yesterday, not liking a certain congressman, "Make an appointment for me to spit in his eye from nine to five!"

Thursday, July 11, 1940

In a capitalist society criminals, artists, and revolutionists are brothers under the skin. For similar reasons they are all men of opposition.

Many Group Theatre dissatisfactions still in my mind and feelings. Harold's plans are to go right ahead with a season with the use of a script or two, doing nothing to resolve the difficulties which face all of the actors and the Group itself as an organization which must have some reasonable promise of continuity of life in order to attract new talent to it. It is now necessary for me to become very particular with him, outlining what is needed and how to get it: a general manager, a plan for creating a pool of scripts, the return of Lee Strasberg, organization of audiences, and money with which to work and guarantee some financial security to the actors.

The day was so hot that I kept an electric fan running without stop. The Little One came along, cool and freshly powdered. We listened to music for an hour, I suddenly and unreasonably fatigued for some psychological reason I could not fathom, probably because I felt I should be working instead of sporting with a lassie. (I had been making critical notes on Lewin's script before she came.) Then she said, sitting on my lap, "Don't, don't," as I began to undress her. "You will be sorry." She was not sorry and I was not sorry, although I knew she meant she was "ill." We "made love" on top of the bed and finally fell asleep; and I woke up at dawn, chilled and empty, and slept for another few hours, and she awoke, dressed, drank coffee with me, and left.

Someday I want to develop this point and use it in a play: the sharp and dramatic cleavage between appearance and reality in American life; how one lives in conformist patterns here; and the weird fruit of this inner disunion and dislocation.

———•———

Friday, July 12, 1940

A note from Geebee. No note from Fay Wray, which I would like to have because the thought (if not the possession) of her is so dear to me.

In the following I am using the words *adjustment* and *activity* in their Stanislavsky acting method sense.

The truth is that most people do not live by actions or *intentions*. They do not "intend" their conduct. They are not active; they are passive; they live mostly by *adjustments*, the meaning of that word being clear and simple. They walk into a situation, they meet with friends, function in life only passively. They are friendly, envious, inimical, sympathetic, tired, eager, etc., all of these being merely adjustments; or they are respectful, disrespectful, inferior, superior— all only adjustments. Generally speaking, the only times Americans are "active" are when they want to get something from you or when they are defending themselves from giving something. (THERE ARE NATIONAL ACTIVITIES in this sense!) While this lack of activity is seen in the American, it is particularly true of people like the Mexicans and Russians who live by feeling (or adjustment), seldom by activity or intention, since they do not have the utilitarian philosophy which the Americans have. Of course it is true that a simple adjustment often makes an activity: an adjustment of superiority, for instance, can soon develop into, again for instance, an activity of "to boss," "to teach," etc.

However, all people do have a main few activities which come out of their backgrounds and conditioning, i.e., the kind of persons they are. (These are what make character!) A supposed inadequacy on the part of a person, for instance, makes a strong activity of defense, covering up, convincing the other that one is not inadequate, etc., etc.

Today I dictated and sent Al Lewin five pages of notes on his script. The script is undramatic, the characters merely heroic impulses, types, conventional, the whole thing the usual Hollywood mechanism.

Hanns Eisler came here for dinner, behind him, unconnected, Sid Benson, as neat and brushed as a pussycat. The pushing and almost brawling energy of Hanns, his marching tramping ego, gave me a very painful and real headache. His fine talent has this dangerous side, ego hunger. He will permit no piece of music to be played without giving it a hefty shoving around.

Here is what is so wearying about Hanns. My ego is strong too, but I generally manage to call a truce when I am with friends I like. Not so with Hanns—he is a stumpy little gazelle who runs all over the landscape, a chamois of surprising nimbleness. I do not fight his activity but resist it inwardly with such force that every nerve in my body tingles into complete somnolence. It is impossible for me to be with him for more than an hour with any pleasure, but since I like him so much I say nothing about it.

The last time Hanns was here he asked me to write some small words for a set of five songs which he would quickly write. He brought up the subject again tonight, at the dinner table. I suggested five brief excerpts from this journal. He was very struck with this slight idea, saying he would call the songs *Five Excerpts from a Writer's Journal (Clifford Odets)*. I read him some excerpts and he picked two, one about people singing a certain song in Europe—"wind, wind, take me away with you"—and an excerpt about the solitude of a bachelor's life.

Saturday, July 13, 1940

Not Luise, but my life with Luise is more than half responsible for this terrible and brutal stupor in which I have been simmering for the past year. I looked for peace and found it in complete torpor, where I am now, sluggish among the alligators, lost in the Everglades, a swampy swimmer waddling through the swamps.

Now will you rise up? The hurricane is over. You need the world, are needed by the world. Do your work. Start simply, with the smallest realities if necessary—the reality of typewriter ribbon, of paring the nails so that the fingers may hit the typewriter keys more truly. Do your work, writer.

The cold noon changed to a mellow summer day and I stretched on the bed and read Van Gogh letters for an hour—they are very useful for an understanding of Nijinsky. Above all he wanted "a group," not to be alone, not to be cut off from society, not to be forced into isolation and opposition.

Benson came up. I showered and dressed and we walked up and down Fourteenth Street jammed with Saturday crowds. We bought some summer shoes and continued our walk down Second Avenue. We ate a cool supper at Ratner's—cold *tchav* soup with sour cream, cold fish, a very flower of a dish consisting of fresh huckleberries boiled inside a dough jacket and then soused in more sour cream, iced coffee, and an excellent Havana cigar. Do I mention this too carefully? It was the only reality and pleasure of the day for me.

On an impulse we jumped into a cab and told the startled dozing driver to get us to the World's Fair in a hurry, to the Aquacade to be exact. Landed in Eleanor Holm's dressing room in back of the pool. It was interesting back there—scores of young boys and girls, summer, swimming, a whole tent town, shacks, budding romances, night, fire-work displays on the fair lagoon next door, music from portable radios, some boys and girls playing Ping-Pong, playing jokes, languid long-legged girls, naked bodies bronzed by the sun. When Eleanor passed us in through the gate we saw a show that was real and attractive only because of the young human bodies using themselves in swimming and diving. It is really the summer that puts on the show, and I could not help remarking that the huge audience was more of a show than what took place on the stage.

We went backstage again and picked up Eleanor and joined Billy Rose who was up in the office counting the money—enormous profits. He told me that some weeks last year the net was over a hundred thousand dollars!

We walked over to Billy's car and on all sides there were salutes and deferential bows for the king and queen of the Aquacade. A Negro chauffeur drove us back to town. Billy chatted quietly, calmly, the lord of all he surveys.

And so the Automat, then the Paramount, then a walk through Broadway crowds to Lindy's, then cake and coffee and more bows and salutes from the Deferential. Then political discussion, talk on economics, Billy unconsciously comparing himself to U.S. Steel, Ford Motors, and others while talking about government restriction of big business. He is bitterly antiunion, anti anything which interferes with what he calls special skill, the proud property of men born only once every twenty or thirty years, meaning himself. His morality is that of the master, boasting modestly that he gives work to sixteen hundred men and women every week—the country needs him, the people need him, and they must make it easy and pleasant for his organizing genius to function, or else—! He is very deft and covert with his boasts, yet Billy always manages to let you know what enormous income taxes he is paying, how gifted he is, how altogether attractive he is. He is not bad, merely ambitious. I don't dislike him.

———————•———————

Sunday, July 14, 1940

Sunday, Bastille Day in France. They celebrated with tears.

Out of bed at five. The long Sunday afternoons of the New York summer are beautiful: the placidity, the hushed quiet, the sun falling softly, the people strolling calmly through the untrafficked streets . . . like a Japanese print.

I scratched my head, clipped my fingernails and hitched up my pajamas, and went to work on the trio play. Mr. Churchill of England spoke on the radio and I listened and smoked more cigarettes and wrote more pages and wanted to rush out of the house and not come back. I walked into the bedroom and looked at it—it looked back at me without a quiver.

I labored on till past two in the morning, read more papers for an hour, carefully put the finished pages and notes away, washed my face and hands with cold water, settled myself in bed with an interesting article on Dostoyevsky and Gorky (in this month's *International Literature*), and fell asleep.

———•———

Monday, July 15, 1940

I was out of bed so early today that for a few hours I had the illusion of being a normal citizen. The illusion did not last long, for when I went out into the street—determined to get and savor the day and summer sunlight—I did not know where to turn or where to go, who to see, what to do. I walked around the block twice, laughing at myself, finally going to the garage where I made several phone calls. No one was home. I got in the open car and drove four blocks back to my house, uneasy, depressed, uncertain.

Worked till nine on the trio play. Sid Benson came along. We drove uptown, saw a newsreel and ten minutes of *The General Died at Dawn*, which I wrote for Paramount four years ago, and ended up in Lindy's for coffee and cake, sitting there with Billy and Eleanor and Irving Berlin and some songwriters.

———•———

Tuesday, July 16, 1940

Nothing but that Fay Wray sent me a letter and a gift for my coming birthday. It moves me very much that she thinks of me, reaches out to me. Otherwise becalmed, dead, like the weather, heavy, costive, muggy, indifferent.

In the early evening I worked for a pair of hours on the trio play.

Then Len Lyons took me on his rounds of the clubs, finally landing us at the Stork Club where W. Winchell sat in a mellow mood but complaining of the fact that his life was threatened by Christian Front boys, that his phone was tapped, that altogether he was a pretty important fellow anyway you looked at it. He said that he had received an item that I was giving expensive jewelry to Bette Grayson; I assured him not.

Earlier Lyons introduced me to the famous Johnny Broderick, detective in the Broadway district. A very interesting type, assuring us profusely of his love for the Jews, sounding off about the political situation, saying Roosevelt would never be elected again because all the Catholics were against him. A hard-punching detective with a great reputation for slugging and beating up people. As he talked he kept pushing us slightly, grabbing us by the arms, half turning us, drawing us to him, so that the three of us must have looked a little rolling and seasick, as if we were going with the deck of a moving ship.

At dawn I wrote for another hour, undressed, and went to bed, feeling sluggish and drugged, insentient—stupefied, in short.

———•———

Wednesday, July 17, 1940

Out of bed by two in the afternoon, another pregnantly heavy day out of which, unfortunately, nothing is born. At least many interesting books here, secondhand ones I ordered yesterday. A history of the Jews, a book on Japanese prints, Rostand plays, and many others. Oh for a home, to be at home and peace somewhere, settled down, reading good books, working well, clear, bright, regular!

Here I am now, past three in the morning of July 18th, my birthday, witless, torpid, swimming for my life (you won't die, buddy!) in a clammy sea of confused pains and desires.

Fay Wray wrote in her letter, "Think of me when the dawn of your birthday comes." Well, I am thinking of her. Before I was thinking of Geebee, thinking always of some clear-eyed woman who will take me out of the wilderness of my self, my tangled unhappy self.

———•———

Thursday, July 18, 1940

Today thirty-four years old. I never expected to reach it, as the romantic always expects to die young, feeling always some doom hanging over him, some oppressive shadow.

The usual small group of friends sent greetings or a gift, my father, sisters, Aunt and Uncle Rossman, some flowers from Herman and menage, a camera no less from Bill and Lee Kozlenko who came here in the late afternoon to deliver it in person, almost making me exclaim, "But you can't afford such expensive gifts!" Silence was more friendly.

How well Lee looked, as if she were in love, her eyes soft and shining, her figure slimming down, her whole self relaxed by the warmth and the pleasure and proprietorship of giving a gift.

The three of us went to Ratner's, after playing many German songs, where we ate all sorts of cool foods and ridiculous pastry—like *kreplach* filled with cheese and huckleberries. Then, top down, we rode through the hot city. We skirted past a place where two cars had driven off the road and fallen to the street many feet below. Dozens of cars were packed there, their owners staring down as if at trained seals in a pool below. We, needless to say, did not stop, but rode by carefully and steadily with that creepy feeling all over us. I don't think people look at such a sight out of primitive lust for bloody sights. Much rather it is because such a scene quickens their lives, giving them the illusion, but real, of living deeply, sharply, and fully, everything in them alert and shocked to attentive quickness.

Then we rode back to their house and listened to the Democrats on the radio. Roosevelt expressed his choice of a running mate and he was nominated: Henry A. Wallace, which certainly constitutes the most liberal team that ever ran for these two high offices in my brief life. At two in the morning I came home through the hot torpid city in the open car—a small gem of a ride.

I never approach my house late at night that I don't think and hope that some amazing adventure will be waiting there for me: some interesting letters or telegrams, perhaps a beautiful mysterious woman waiting; and even when I open my own door I half expect that she will be sitting and waiting, perhaps on the bed. Mostly this mysterious woman is someone I am unconsciously yearning for, Luise or Fay Wray.

In the afternoon I worked on the trio play for two hours. Geebee sent a birthday telegram, longing for me. I looked into Briffault's *Europa* and found it very interesting, particularly since it explains the Nijinsky period. Berenson's books on the Italian painters came, very interesting by reputation.

When I left their house I thought of Lee Kozlenko again, looked into her face furtively: she is in love, with that swimming softness I saw just a year ago in Frances Farmer's face, extraordinary sight, rare feeling in this closed-up world. It frightened me, so beautiful, so tender. It is the thing that all Leonardo faces have, every one of them—that confusion of the senses and thoughts which run so together that they seem to exhaust the woman and open her to the utmost for the taking thrust of the man (or swan in one picure, the idea of the swan exciting me very much).

Friday, July 19, 1940

Decided to go out to Luther and Sylvia's farm for the weekend. It took me more than two hours because of delay on the roads. A car had broken down in the Holland Tunnel; two long lines of beastlike autos slowly moving forward added to almost a feeling of terror. The sense of the overwhelming mechanical beast was immense until I concentrated on examining the inner structure of the tunnel itself. Even then I shot out of there like a bat out of hell once the signal for moving ahead was given.

And so the farm, other guests there before me, a Mr. Lopert and his wife—he is a Russian Jew with a Continental background—a movie producer. His wife was harmless but annoying, a bleached blonde, a little of everything—she gave me goo-goo eyes. Later, when she gave foolish opinions, she would preface them with, "May I be scientific?"

How hot, how hot on the terrace behind the house. The three men played pinochle to almost six. Only Lopert and I were left and we sat on the cool terrace for twenty minutes of the rising dawn, one solo star shining till the sun was almost up.

Then to try to sleep in the hotter bedroom and feeling vague discontent through the whole late afternoon and evening. This time I thought longingly of Geebee and her strong young body and firm breasts and her quiet cool temper and her being in love with me. All evening I had been wishing she were with me, finally saying to myself again and again, with disgust, "What can you expect? You cannot even make peace with yourself enough to have that fine young girl. You make peace with nothing, nothing—your mind is always pushing, never accepting the values of the others—no peace, no peace!"

———•———

Saturday, July 20, 1940

Herr Hitler made a speech yesterday, reprinted in full in this morning's *Times*. The gentle Herr advises England to surrender or he will blast the islands off the face of the earth. The sweet Herr complains, is querulous, as if with a toothache—the British will not let him accomplish his life's work, the making of a new social order with incomparable benefits for all!

No break in the heat. I went out and examined and admired the vegetable garden they have here. The earth is so yielding, so innocent and ample in its giving, so patient and willing to serve if you will but turn a spade once.

Arthur Krim arrived before dinner, wan and pale with the city heat. Arthur is my lawyer, the Group's lawyer, Lopert's lawyer, Luise's lawyer, Serlin's lawyer, the lawyer of Sylvia and Luther—in fact he is everyone's lawyer! He is young, idealistic, a good student's mind in his head, a prize pupil with some feeling of the mother's boy about him. His judgments are cool and reasoned.

We played more pinochle. Gambling is very relaxing for nervous tense men. The heat is unbearable except that one bears it. Heat, it must be said, has this virtue—you must give yourself up to it, not fight it. A year of all tight winter would be unbearable and shorten the lives of everyone living. The tension and tightness of it, the binding of the self and holding close of the self is very destructive. The winter is narrow, the summer ample.

Where does a new play come from? What explains this rush of feeling, these hundreds of sensory impressions that cluster around one slight idea and build it up into a whole artwork? Why do I pick the trio play to work on now? What is it in the personality which suddenly spotlights one idea above all others so that it is the play on which one must work?

At one time I was unable to tell where a play was coming from *while* it was coming. My work was instinctive, intuitive, scarcely using the conscious mind as a tool of construction. Intuition and feeling are still the prime movers in my writing, but now the conscious mind marches along with them, shoulder to shoulder. For instance: suddenly, after a winter of several false starts on other work, I decide to "assault" the trio play idea and make a play of it. In this play a man moves into the house of a good friend (although no friendships are profound in the world of the play) and takes away the unsatisfied wife of the friend. That is what I would like to do but will never do. I have need of a woman who can make a home for me, can give me children. This is a burning issue of the day in my own life. There are two married women who are attractive to me on all important counts; both of them are the wives of good friends of mine, one of them being unhappy with her husband. In real life I do not flirt with these women, do not indicate in any possible way my thoughts concerning them. But constantly I fantasize them in all relationships, sexual, homemaking, traveling together over the country, etc., etc. Then, too, in fantasy, it excites me to deal with the outraged personality of the husband when I have taken his wife away from him. Both of us are aroused, perhaps he is abject, as he will be in the play until the final scene where he murders the thief. Many feelings are aroused in me by this imagined situation which arises out of real and strong necessities in my life—lust, cruelty, the matching of wits, the play of superiority, etc. On the other side will be feelings of tenderness, shame, defiance, pity—those things which come from a good heart as hearts go in the world today. All of these feelings, be sure, will find their way into the play. As will the feelings of frustration, loneliness, the torpor of a man wearied by the constant attempts of allocating himself in relation to some sort of attachment and connection with the things he needs.

And this is why Flaubert could say, "Madame Bovary? I am Madame Bovary!" And in my own way, I could say, "I am Cleo Singer!" This, too, explains in part my deep attachment for Harold Clurman. He is the only one who knows, the only one who CARES that I am Cleo Singer and the other characters of my plays.

Too, talking of atmosphere, the climate of the trio play will be exactly that of the weather here and now—muggy, foreboding, the never-bursting-open sky. It is weather in which anything can happen.

All courses of conduct are possible, men and women may suddenly weep, reverse their entire lives under this sky—hatreds, exquisite tendernesses, love, sudden murderous wrath, relaxed amiabilities, all may happen in this climate. Out of a long chain of seeming dull trivia is born a shattering explosion, that is the line of the new play.

Sunday, July 21, 1940

Since last night a cow on the adjacent farm has been bellowing as periodically as a foghorn on a ship picking its way through fog. Yesterday they took its calf away and this regular expressionless bellow is its cry. A stricken but stupid mother standing in a world of grass, mourning by instinct between chews of the grass. It is a characterization to carry over into human life, unfortunately.

When the play on Van Gogh is to be written, remember that the rhythm of Van Gogh's speech is immediately discernible in the rhythm of his brushstrokes.

It is my feeling that if Ibsen were alive in Europe today he would be profascist or a fascist, in fact.

Before dinner, after several hours more of pinochle on the hot terrace (during which I bid and made a grand hand of five hundred, spades double!), we drank a small bottle of chilled vodka after putting on our shirts which had been off all afternoon—four naked men playing pinochle, a scene for a French painter. I remark here about the interesting chatter and banter, so special and characteristic, which takes place while four or more men are playing cards. It is always witless, extremely loose, a mere gabble of banter above a strong line of concentrated attention on the plays of the game itself. (Servants, too, chatter in the same way while they are working in the kitchen.)

At the dinner table, a heated discussion of Harold Clurman and the Group Theatre. Arthur Krim and I found ourselves on one side in opposition to the others. I was amazed by the excessive heat displayed by the others, and Sylvia particularly showed herself in an interesting light. Leaving aside a wife's jealousy for her husband's work (which she did not mention), she is vehement against Harold and the Group because she had supposed (surely first suggested by Luther) that if she played with the Group in one play she would immediately recapture all of her lost and withered talent, automatically being compensated for the lost Hollywood years and the death of the spirit from which she suffered because of them. She even cried, her eyes filling with tears, but, being strictly feminine, it was impossible to set her straight.

Luther, confused, as usual, a very woman of a man in his mental processes, slightly befuddled and enraged by the vodka, flared out against the idea that he had stayed with the Group because of the genius of one, Harold Clurman. We went into the living room and the talk continued. I explained as cooly as possible—these are enemies, whether they mean to be or not—what the Group Theatre meant to its various members, its importance in the American theatre historically, its intention, the kind of man Clurman was, what I thought were his talents and his failings—but all in the context of a whole organization and its intentions. The others kept making the mistake of taking items out of the context and supposing that these items were the whole thing. This argument and discussion, believe it or not, went on for almost four hours! Luther was finally won over to our side because the idealistic side of his nature had finally been touched. Luther, for my part, I did not coddle. I told him he could be a big nuisance to a director, that he had to be handled like a prima donna very often, and that he would now have the task of facing and resolving a main contradiction in his life—take the Broadway Theatre or take the Group Theatre and what it stood for. Despite its faults and failings. "My God," I kept thinking, "these people are so unfriendly to the Group Theatre that they alone almost assure me that the Theatre must continue despite everything!" For the more I listened to them the more I knew that everything I had said was correct and fertile, they stupid and sterile, caught like amber-held bugs in the ossification of their own prejudices and "practicalities."

I suddenly understood a great deal about average people through this fight, understood something about the "idealists" of the Ibsen plays. These people will kill an idealist, by which I mean a man who brings the truth. You are an enemy in these homes, and if you are a Prince Mishkin of truth (as Clurman is in his own way), you are an idiotic enemy at which to poke gibes and scorn. This makes me think of a play, using a weak person like Luther, another like Harold or myself. The Apollonian man is Luther, of the world, secure in his repose, etc. Into this scene comes the man of truth, awkward, timid, inept, even with an almost idiotic side. But he is the bringer of truth, the man from whom progress grows. He creates or destroys, there is no middle ground or compromise with him. Sylvia, as she does in real life, cries to this man, "Let me sleep!" Luther finds him ridiculous and yet is strangely moved beyond his known self by this man: drama!

How these people scream out for repose! With what savagery they demand to be confirmed in their prejudices instead of their possibilities! To Luther it is necessary to say, "Beware of the lullaby singers, beware!"

Arthur Krim made a very excellent impression on me. I had not suspected such idealism from him, such simple and almost naïve faith in the progressive impulses of American life. Apparently, too, he was impressed by what I said during the discussion, for he said so.

About three in the morning they all decided to go up to bed in order to rise early and ride back to the city. I suggested it would be better for them to ride into town and sleep there. They thought the idea good and packed and left in a half hour. It was so warm, everyone so tired, that I was glad to see them go and have one side of the house for myself. I went upstairs and threw my naked self on the white-sheeted bed and after some sexual thoughts—the oppressive heat seems to well up to one focus—fell asleep and slept badly till the next afternoon. The constant inhalation of nicotine through cigarettes jaundices the personality and forbids sound sleep.

———•———

Monday, July 22, 1940

Luther is building a swimming pool below the terrace. The working men, the banging tractor which is digging out shale and clay—the machine is called a bulldozer, I believe—bang their way into my consciousness and wake me up. I am listless with the heat, dull, apathetic, immediately reaching for a cigarette, not sure that I am awake or asleep. Coffee, more cigarettes, the newspapers. Then the eminent appeasing Lord Halifax on the radio to answer Hitler's speech. No peace, says the Lord, and with the help of God the English will carry the day. If all the English are like Lord Halifax it is to be feared that the Germans have already won the war!

After the other guests left Luther and frau and I stretched out on the front lawn and looked up at the sky for a half hour of starry consideration. At one time stars, the sky, trees, birds, all were very important to my world—I had a real rapport with such things. In these last seven years they have become almost meaningless to me. Lying there reminded me of a line, "What is this world, if full of care we have no time to stand and stare?" While I have not done so for more than a year, it is right to stare at the sky and at trees; it is wrong to lose the desire to stare at the silent powerful things of nature. American life tends to make us too rationalistic, too anxious to spend our time "usefully"— the mooning goes out of life for most of us, and with it the meaning. Old stuff, kiddo.

A line of D. H. Lawrence quoted by Aldous Huxley (who is not the deep thinker that so many people think and say he is, not by far!) moves me very much: "I am for one heterosexual love, monogamous and indissoluble. And I am for Respectability. And above all for Silence." I don't know what he means by the word Silence, unless it means keep silent about the relationship once you have made it—do not worry, tease, and nag it to death. But how complete and right the meaning is for a healthy life. But then how grimly Lawrence utters it.

The other day, my brief birthday quickly gone, I was very depressed with the realization that not one of the Group Theatre members had remembered it or sent a word about it.

CHARACTERIZATION IS THE ART OF TAKING OUT OF CONTEXT AND PUTTING THE REMOVED ELEMENTS INTO A NEW CONTEXT. Simply put, that is the whole thing about writing or acting a character!

I often think to myself about what a person will say when he leaves me after a meeting. Arthur Krim, for instance. "Why," I hear him say, "he's a brilliant chap!" This twingles my vanity; I often say such things to myself, covering all situations and meetings so.

The mysterious pleasures of the poet, a man who gives the fullest import to and receives an impacting impression from what others consider the "unessentials" of life. But likewise the mysterious terrors of the poet!

In the evening Luther and I gave Sylvia a lesson in the art of playing pinochle. I was surprised at my patience in the face of the fact that I wanted urgently to get to work on the play. I wondered if I would be so patient in the teaching of a game with my own wife. I thought I would if I loved her dearly. Patience in the teaching of all things, I mean. Where I would be impatient, alas, fretting and fuming, would be in the times when she wanted to teach me! Truly alas!!!

Fresh ideas came to me for the play. I rewrote some pages, changing character adjustments and background experiences which condition severely the character relationships in the play.

———•———

Tuesday, July 23, 1940

The enormous heat, without letup. In the evening, the day uneventful, we rode over to Princeton to see Miss Betty Field play in Lynn Riggs's *Green Grow the Lilacs*. After the show we went back to see this young and now highly successful actress.

What can I say about this type of new American girl? Raised on vitamins, awakened not at all, so shrewd, so able to take care of herself, such a good young fellow . . . and all of it on such a limited scale, going from A to F and F you know for what! Not that the heart is bad there, or that the personality is not idealistic, but everything a slumbering child, untroubled, unworried—in a word, unawakened! And this child is so typical in America today. We are producing the weirdest people who ever dented the crust of the earth.

Back at the house, all connection somehow lost with Sylvia and Luther, I decided to ride back to New York at one in the morning. Packed quickly. Shook hands and thanked the hosts, and a tight little ride through the muggy night, the top of the car down. A relief to be home, windows to open, mail to open, a cool bed to sleep on, alone, myself, my room, cold water pouring out of the taps, no tiptoeing necessary!

———•———

Wednesday, July 24, 1940

Sid Benson came here in the later afternoon. We stopped in at a haberdashery shop and bought some things. The clerk was one of those snappy salesmen, quite annoying: "I guess you are not interested in the best." And fingering my shirt with scorn when I said I did not like the shirt he was selling Sid. Finally I saw that he had gypped me—

charged me six dollars for a heavy summer shirt worth perhaps half. I walked out of the shop smarting, saying nothing, but hours later, while falling asleep, even then I could not get out of my mind the fact that I had been swindled. That is a thing which always makes me so mad that I can think of nothing else.

———————•———————

Thursday, July 25, 1940

Geebee sent me an excellent gift, five small volumes of English translations of German plays, published in 1811, most of them by Kotzebue, two by Schiller, others by Lessing, Goethe, and others.

How many men and women have been murdered simply by a contradiction in their natures? Murder does not need guns.

What explains the trouble with certain characters, Bobby Lewis, for instance, is their lack of flexibility. On the other hand, too much flexibility is the corrupting item in other personalities.

Of all things today, Waldo Frank here with young ladies, two sisters, Miss Nancy Green and Miss Martha Green, called Marty. They came here at dusk, the older with an interesting contradiction in her nature which does not allow her to sit in repose; the younger seeming the older and more mature because of what soon seemed to me to be an excessive repose—sleepfulness.

We talked, we passed on to a cool drink and chatting on the cooler terrace. The girls spoke in such well-bred and modulated voices that in the open air I could not hear what they were saying and I didn't care. Then we drove up to Lindy's for dinner. All that interested me about the two hours we sat there was when, by a sudden stroke, I turned the conversation to myself and the problems of my life—and only about half of that was interesting to me. It boiled down to the statement that there was no reality for me but mine own, as intelligent as I was, as aware of other people; and into this dragged Mozart, Beethoven, and Schumann, and everyone else in the zodiac.

They are people who observe more normal hours than mine, so by midnight they were all tuckered out. At that moment Jack Adler came along and told several charming and witty Jewish stories, a welcome relief from our by-then cloying togetherness. I suggested that I would stay here with Jack.

What particularly interested me about Jack this evening were several stories of his eighty-year-old mother, all of them like brief Chekhov stories, very touching and sterling in their character consistency. She runs away from home to act in out-of-the-way places, fearfully withholding her address for fear her children will demand her return. She takes dancing lessons, the rhumba and conga, because she is bored, introducing Jack as her nephew because she doesn't want to be considered aged. She is a mysterious old lady, of peasant shrewdness, once a great actress and one of many love affairs; now she is made up of rags and patches, of great dignity and stubbornness, her ways mysterious and recondite, not easily emotionalized, and very very weary.

Jack spoke very feelingly of his mother, saying that this was perhaps her last summer or two to enjoy her yearly trip to Saratoga Springs for two weeks, only there is no money for the trip—Jack is broke and none of the other brothers who have money will give it—Luther, a Dr. Heiner, and others. This makes Jack boil. He is shameless with the names he calls the other brothers, saying he is only waiting for the time when the old lady is buried. Then, he says, if he but sees a tear from them, or if they are merely wearing black clothing, he will go berserk and beat them all to pulp and scream about this old lady in a hot city in her last year and how not one of her affluent sons thought that it might have been her last summer. A scene I would like to see.

Jack and I came home and talked till seven in the morning, particularly of his strange Adler family. He despises them all, down to his weird nephew. His memory is prodigious and he mimics them all with equal talent. What moved me to a moment of real tears was when he suddenly and dramatically announced that all of the children who so revere the memory of their great acting father, Jacob P. Adler, had never finished paying for the old man's grave; today weeds grow on it as high as a man's shoulder. That made me cry; Jack too. After a few minutes we resumed our conversation, but it was daylight by then and he went home and I went to a hot uneasy bed.

Friday, July 26, 1940

Hanns Eisler paid a visit here in the late afternoon, the heat truly unbearable—suffocation is unbearable. Soon a powerful and beneficent rain came but the earth was not cooled off, not the city. We talked of many things, mostly myself, of my need of a woman and the kind she should be—all quite shameless out of painful necessity. Hanns then made a suggestion, saying, "Making some money is very important now. Three or four very bad years are ahead of everyone. I am talking as a man who has been many times a refugee, in wars and hard changes. Be not generous for now; be very cool; work not too hard; take care of everything now and keep your papers clean and in order."

Then this dear gifted stumpy little man left and I am here now, midnight less than a turn of the clock away. "Dear gifted stumpy little man" is far from an adequate description of Hanns Eisler. For he also has some of the monster in him which every artist should have if he is to survive in the world today. Monster has to do with essential toughness of fiber, ego which protects the more tender parts, energy, and resourcefulness; and more than anything else monster has to do with a line which, once laid down, one never swerves from, as if one were driving one of these war-built tanks through life. Hanns has all that too. Long live Hanns.

But I did not stay home as I had planned to do. Instead, after three or four pages of work, I rode up to Lindy's and furtively examined every man and woman who walked in the door after me . . . curious women walk into that place—life's degenerates in all sizes and shapes. Then along came Lionel Stander, sometime actor. His wife is sick in a hospital. He is an unsavory fellow, gross beyond comparison, ugly, and yet with a curious stubborn idealistic steak in his nature which is, however, fast being put to sleep by self-indulgence. He claimed he had a perfect relationship with his wife, that sexual infidelity was not important in their lives and that he would permit her the same if she liked other men. In the name of his Marxist values, but only in their name, I told him, I reject everything he says and does.

Rode home in the dawn and tortured myself on the bed for another hour before falling asleep in the blinding staggering heat of the new day.

Saturday, July 27, 1940

What wonderful books there are in this house! This history of the world here, of our country and its villains and heroes. Many nights I cannot resist the temptation of opening three or four of the books and reading a chapter or two in each. Extended reading is quite beyond me just now.

Very important: If you want to write something which is beyond doubt or criticism (fearful sensitive self!), you will so seriously cripple your impulse and productivity that you will no longer be a playwright!

In my loneliness here last week I remembered a secretary I had had at the Paramount Studio three years ago this summer. This young lady was helpful: in the afternoon she took my dictation at the studio; in the evening she came to my rooms in California slacks, a silk shirt and a red ribbon twisted in her chestnut hair. We slept together painfully and passionately—I think she was sorry for me, in part.

Early one morning Luise came there, hoping to make a reconciliation by a few passionate hours together in bed. She asked me, after a stammering half hour of polite sitting together in the parlor, "Aren't you going to ask me to sleep here?" Before I could answer she had thrown off her white shirt and slacks and was the *maja desnuda* in the bed. No man and woman ever screamed and groaned more in a bed than we did that early morning—it was savage; in all fairness the neighbors across a narrow airshaft might have called the fire department.

I mention these things here only to remember them. Last week, I started to say, I wrote a note to the secretary. Yesterday there was an answer. She is living with the same girlfriend—they are writing plays together—and she is delighted that I remember her. R.I.P.

Worked on the play in the late afternoon, several good ideas coming for scene 3. Then I stretched the naked toneless self on the bed and dozed in and out of the heat for an hour, dreaming in snatches, all frustrating items—not able to make a television set work, trying to kiss some fat lady on the shoulder and not being permitted to do so. Then I worked for two more hours and ate canned figs out of the puffing icebox.

At midnight I telphoned Sid Benson who, too, was ripe for adventure. I suggested a trip to Coney Island but it was too late. Instead we rode up to Lindy's, ate, discussed the results of the recent Cuban elections, considered the various unfriendly acts of various friends who never ask how you are or where you are, etc., etc.

Then we joined Billy Rose and Eleanor. Billy said he had bought some new paintings, so we drove over to his house to see them. And there they were on his florid walls, a very fine Titian, a Rubens, a small Holbein, and, best of all to my taste, a very small Renoir filled with fragrance and Gallic charm, this last piece on Eleanor's dresser! Eleanor, Billy said, told him, when he said he was going to put a Renoir in her bedroom, "Don't you go banging any nails in my wall!" However, her taste is truer than his, for she says, "I don't care what name is on the paintings, honey. I want to see them and then I know if I like them." Billy, on the other hand, keeps beating you to the punch, suddenly saying, "Typical *nouveau riche* stuff. What do I know about these things after all?" These statements are supposed to show you that he is superior to what he is doing. Artistic joy in America.

The ivy-covered back of his house faces the East River. He has a rare view there, as unusual as any in the city. But, says he, the birds bother him in the morning, sparrows and crackles, perhaps starlings. So they are thinking about cutting down the thirty-year-old ivy because the birds nest in it.

———•———

Sunday, July 28, 1940

What pose, what attitude do I take? Everyone takes one. With me I think it is a pose of modesty. Pah!

What is metabolism? I think it is the rate at which one's food is changed to energy and the other mysterious things which keep the body running. I have a hunch that it has a great deal to do with my personality, my torpors and impulses. A mysterious fruitful word. Gland, testicle, kidney, spleen, a thousand words like these cover mysterious functions of the body, as unthought of as the electric switch which one uses twenty times a night.

While you were getting prepared to be born your mother established the pattern of your life—unhappiness! But this, these nights and mornings, perhaps this is true happiness and you do not know it. Look how you are rooted in the city, it in you. It may never be better than this, never MORE than this: can you face it?

Some work on the trio play, in snatches. A letter to Fay Wray and one to my father. How different the styles of both letters, the style stemming from the adjustment one has to different persons, a secret of writing. Organ stops, each one automatically pulled out by one's adjustment to the person one is addressing.

———————•———————

Monday, July 29, 1940

A Russian saying: "Work is not a bear. It will not escape into the woods."

Work on the play is moving along. I write fragments until an idea comes—no one used unpredicted impulses better—then I speed ahead and soon am greeted by three or four new pages of a scene the idea of which could come only while writing. So do the fish move through water—the meander and then the sudden spurt. Two good spurts tonight.

This woman called me at ten-thirty. I am seated naked at my desk, wearing only a pair of trunks. She wants to come here now. I know what it will mean. She is married to a man I know very well, but this trip will have a meaning. I say come right along and hang up the phone. I run into the bathroom, very excited, intuitively knowing what she is going to tell me, and hurriedly wash my face and comb my hair. I pace back and forth for a half hour till she rings the bell. We are both nervous and I knock the shade off the lamp. We sit out on the terrace. Talk about the weather and the view of the city. Then she tells me that she has loved me for years and now must tell it to me in order to straighten herself out inwardly. She is unhappy with her husband. We discuss him for a half hour. (I am very reluctant to mention her name here.) The first plunge of excitement is gone now and I am able to think coolly about her and her problems. She offers to leave, knowing I am working, but I hold her back. We sit on the terrace for another half hour. She is quiet, soft, very tender, but there are bold impulses which always surprise us when we meet them in a timid person. I see she is waiting for some word from me, but I temporize by telling her that it would be easy for me to speak or act irresponsibly here as she is very attractive too, as she is. We use a great many words, all sorts of clever psychological insights from both of us, but the only thing is the emotional tension between us. Finally she moves to go and I permit it. Once within the room (knowing nothing will happen now) our two mouths wheel and turn on each other. She suddenly has wrenched out of her, "Oh, but you do not know how many years I have thought of this moment!" And such an avid mouth and I am erect in every part (but nothing will happen). She tosses, spasms in her loins—sweet sweating temptation!!! Nothing. Then I say go in the bathroom and straighten yourself out and go home. Once she closes the bathroom door behind her I pace around the two rooms and hope she will take off all her clothes (against my words) and jump in the bed and pull the sheet over her very hungry body and wait two seconds for me to jump in after her. No, she is too timid for that, but when she joins me in the hall I mention what I thought; she almost swoons again. I say she wants this, as I do, but she wants other things more, the things of her married life, a certain peace of mind and ability to look her husband in the eye. She agrees, sorrowfully, and slowly goes, reluctantly, home to the husband. I lie down in the dark bedroom and masturbate violently. No moral.

———•———

Tuesday, July 30, 1940

The battle that is raging on within me is one between the outer and inner worlds. One part of me is hungry to go where there are people and gay life. The other part is looking for a quiet spot within. The monk and the lewd winking courtier, these are the fighters which are exhausting me with their struggles. Is it possible to have both, two victors? No.

Intimacy of relationship is what I adore and need most in life. Yet it is what I have had least of. With Luise I had such intimacy. And yet it is what defeated our marriage in the end, for she would allow no larger forms, cutting everything down to "me and thou," locked in each other's arms or in a room.

Incessantly, incessantly! Locked in this small square of prison, the flesh flaming but the mind cold as steel. But incessantly!

Drove up to the Stork Club for some of their good food after a short period of work on the play. El Ernesto Hemingway is in town, usually at this club I am told, but tonight he was not there. Just as well, for he would have bought me a drink and I would have extended myself enough to show him that I like him and that would have been that. "He is a right guy," or "He is not a right guy"—that seems to be Hem's evaluation of men. Then took my usual nightly ride up the Hudson River, turning back under the Washington Bridge, roaring down to Nineteenth Street, taking all the turns with pushed-down pedal, ramming down the ramp into the dark and turning up Fourteenth Street and taking the rhythm of the lights to the garage door.

A cool dawn, fresh, a laving breeze to wash the muddiness out of the air for the first time in weeks. Great day of New York! Sleeping city soon to be awake, roaring city arrogant beyond the planets, good night.

———•———

Wednesday, July 31, 1940

Swift year, all swift years. August already here with all the ripe fruits of summer to buy and eat. Plums, red and green, yellow peaches, small seedless grapes, nectarines.

Every once in a while, intuition leaping ahead of the mind, I write a line I do not yet understand myself. In *Night Music*, "Don't be afraid—get intimate with yourself!" Which is what I am busy doing now, as painfully as it can be done. No doubt I have a real genius for pain, sometimes for agony.

Take these past two weeks, the heat, the inner turmoil, the scarcely understanding what has been happening to me.

Suddenly I thought (a fresh letter from her here) Fay Wray must help me. Quick, get married, make a life with another person, an admirable woman like that. Quick, a wire to her, quick, quick, she must come to your rescue. I rolled over in the bed and groaned aloud. Wait, wait, I thought, see if you think the same way when you wake up in five or six hours. No, no, quick, quick! I crawled out of bed again, drank coffee, reread Fay's letter, sniffed at the paper for some odor of her, savored the full womanly handwriting. Then the secretary came in, after him the maid. I compromised by sending Fay a wire in which was suggested a trip east for her, a sort of vacation if she could make it. Nothing more. I thought it would be fine if something could come out of such a trip, but I had not the decision to state or promise more.

And I fell asleep and woke up and fell asleep again. Near nine at night I opened my eyes, as if out of a fever fought through, the room cool and dark, the world dark and cool, gentle, the heat gone, myself feeling convalescent. Out on the balcony I saw that the stars were showing for the first time in many days, a cool breeze was blowing—in everything the fever had broken. I was weak but recovered—some struggle was over. (Once, after an intent reading of *Crime and Punishment* in two installments in Atlantic City, I felt just this way, a fierce struggle behind me, the self weak and triumphant.)

Triumphant self, what have you conquered? What is the victory to record here? It is impossible to say in words.

Near ten o'clock I had prepared myself to sit down and write when the operator downstairs announced that Harold Clurman was coming up. He had just returned from Cape Cod, looked well and stout. He was the last person in the world I wanted to see then; I wondered, for the first half hour, how I would find anything to say to him. Finally I told him with the utmost simplicity that I was disgusted with him, with the Group people, and that right now (although I might change my mind later) I did not care if I never saw one of them again, excepting himself as a friend, not as a theatre director. It did not matter to me, I went on, when they would need a play or when I would have one finished. My whole idea was not to worry about the future, I said, and not to be responsible in any way to a group of actors whom I did not respect as men or artists. What I was looking for, I continued, was to find the truth of myself and a simple modest secret life in which I could make small steps forward into a new clarity and synthesis.

Harold's answer to this was that he was in complete sympathy with everything I was saying and feeling. He himself had been working towards the same end. He hoped, he said, that everyone in the Group would find his or her own TRUE CENTER, for only in that way would a Group Theatre evolve which could be useful to itself and its people and the theatre in general. I said that not everyone was strong enough for that, that some of them might be made but some of them would be killed in the struggle, that it was an ugly and brutal business to look on the naked self, to find what he called the true center of the self. Yes, he agreed, but they would be killed the other way too, only it would be a slower death.

By this time, the desk between us, smoking and drinking beer, it was almost two in the morning. He said he was going to find a hotel room for the night, tomorrow moving into Irwin Shaw's summer-vacated apartment; I said I was going to go to sleep again. When he left I tossed in bed for a half hour, then got up and ate heavily and read Rilke's *Journal of My Other Self* for an hour.

Across the shaft, one flight down, a woman looked into my windows the way I sometimes look into hers, furtively, with shame, in spite of herself. She was looking into my kitchen window where I had left the light burning; in the meantime I was observing her from behind my bedroom window curtain. So it is in life, looking for each other, but for the most part never meeting. I do not know that woman's name, will never know it, even though I may admire her taste in kitchen utensils and lingerie; and she will never know who that queer man is who keeps his lights burning all night, an adventurer of the morning watch.

* * *

Thursday, August 1, 1940

In the morning mail a letter from the nameless woman of the other night, the unhappily married one. If I thought that incident an incredible one, if it seemed to me that it had never really happened, this letter is proof enough that there was such a scene. She says she has destroyed a real friendship in one fell swoop, that she will no more imagine every small thing I do or say is a personal sign to her (meaning I reciprocate her passion); that I must not break my friendship with her husband for what she has said or done, that he will never know of her visit or what transpired between us. The letter was so faint an echo (although real enough for her) of the excitement and tension of the actual scene that I did not think about it twice. She gives me credit, perhaps, for a finesse of feeling I do not have, forgetting, too, that she has flattered my vanity and that in itself must inevitably call for at least one more scene between us, her husband included one time, another time between us alone.

Often, before the other night, I thought of sleeping with this woman, of possibly outraging her husband, of what the French call a *ménage à trois*—his children, my children, a jolly gathering indeed!

But when she offered herself the other night, goodbye to all that, the thought of it—the fantasy had become a near-reality and was no longer interesting.

A wire from F.W. She cannot come east, probably because she is soon to start another film. She writes with such love that I am certain she would be here on the next plane if I said I needed her, that she must come. But I cannot demand, for I am uncertain in myself, as much as I need her. In such things, where other people's lives are concerned, I cannot be irresponsible, although I always yearn to be so.

———•———

Friday, August 2, 1940

A long letter from Fay Wray, a loving letter I shall say, but this arrived in the morning before I went to sleep.

Sid Benson arrived and I washed and went out with him, this being the first day in many that I felt the street under my shoe. At Lindy's we ate and met the pale and lonely Billy Rose. He said that he had entertained Harold Clurman, Elia Kazan, and Boris Aronson with a private view of his paintings the night before. I asked him which they had admired most. "Oh," he said, casually, "one you haven't seen yet. A new one." This was said so quietly that I almost passed it by, but I asked what the new one was. An El Greco! Yes, an El Greco, a mere *bagatelle*!

Then I suggested that we ride down to my house where I would lend Billy some art books he had expressed a desire to see and he would be able to hear the phonograph. Zing! Down to the house. I worked up a sweat dragging out art books and reproductions for his perusal, amazed myself at how many of them I own. He said that most likely from now on he would have plenty of spare time on his hands (although he is thinking of going to the coast and making a movie of Aquacade with D. [Darryl] Zanuck, the climax being a sinister sequence in which a fifteen-foot shark escapes into the pool while Eleanor is doing her swimming number and is killed by a trained seal who turns the trick, as he assured me seals do with sharks, by swimming around and around the shark and ripping its belly open at each revolution period), and he wanted to explore modest paths into the arts. Which I certainly cannot hold against him. What I do hold against him is the disparaging way, slyly enough, in which he talks about his wife, saying from time to time, "Thank God I married a happy brainless little girl. Primitive, you know—she wants those red beads. No neurotic heavyweight, just a happy girl with not too much mind." He is tender enough about her in his feeling, but it irks him to think that you think he thinks she is some mighty brain; he wants to show that he has his eyes open about those things even closest to him, that he is not one to be taken in.

The morning well advanced, past seven, we drove up to his house to see the El Greco, Sid falling asleep between us but determined to see it too. There is was in his bedroom (Eleanor can't stand the sight of it because it is religiously harrowing), heavily framed and glassed. There is was in the little man's bedroom, he insisting that it excited him and he would keep it against anyone's advice. It is a Saint Francis, the hands pierced, the whole design whirled around and tapered up to a little lighted vent of sky. A real El Greco in every inch. There it was in his bedroom—I can't get over it! No, I can't!

For myself, going down in his private elevator, I suggested a bedroom in which were hung five nudes, one by Renoir, by Manet, Goya, and two others. Said Billy, "I will take one nude Paulette Goddard in the bed instead." That has its points too.

———————•———————

Saturday, August 3, 1940

Make no mistake about it, you can get very mean when you live the way I do, unhappily, unfulfilled, stopped in your tracks.

Fortunately, I am not a drinking man.

I awake in the dark, turn over, wonder what time it is: no, it must be day, no, night—it is dark. Turn on the light and look at the clock. Why? Will you get up if you see it is such and such an hour? Let us guess— what time is it? Past eight? Oh, later, for the dark is too solid. Ten then.

Come, I thought, get out of bed. Go into the kitchen and eat. Oh, eat, what for! Instead I suddenly thought of Morris Carnovsky and wondered how he was, what he was doing. They said, someone said, he was having trouble with Phoebe. I rang his phone bell and he answered, startled, about to go to bed, this at three in the morning. "How are you, Morris?" "Fine, fine, thanks." "All right, let us meet soon." For some inexplicable reason I had had a vision of him cutting his throat.

A few words about Morris Carnovsky, man and actor. Timidity, a love of "gentility" (which probably grew out of a background of squalor, painful for a sensitive boy), made him grow into a small and restricted form, something above all safe and dependable. This form was evidenced by his friends, by the female attachments he made, all persons of "refinement," never rude or vulgar, aware of his sensibilities as he was of theirs. The credo of this little clique built itself around "good taste," its values somehow derived from Dickens's *Christmas Carol*, "God bless us every one." Is this unkind? Yes, but so was their disregard for all of the laws and duties of life.

The first law of life is be thyself, baby! I never heard of a terrier that wanted to be a bulldog—it remained for humans to breed them together. The value of an emerald, said Marcus Aurelius, is that it is always an emerald. Morris began to find this out when he began to be an artist during the first few years of acting in Group Theatre productions. He began to rake up his past, for there was need to work with his truest impulses and characteristics. So he began to change, slowly, with much struggle mixed with fear. The former small form of his life he had used up to its limits and now he was cracking it open (little of this conscious), going to a new and larger form. He began to resent his "dignity," his cello-toned voice, knowing them to be wishful attitudes rather than natural developments of the self—and knowing that whatever was false in his personality was hindering his growth as an artist.

For years he had been trying to keep his life orderly and clean (simplified), in form no matter if the form fitted or not; now he found he was unable to control his impulses, could not deny "queer" and contradictory manifestations of himself which were beginning to assert themselves despite his conscious plans. He became infatuated with another girl during the late summer of 1934. This dismayed him, but he stubbornly asserted that that was the truth of his feelings. However, perhaps because he could not stand scandal, certainly because his wife, Phoebe (yet not quite his wife, for although he had been living with her for five years he had never been able to divorce a woman to whom he had been married before, sensibilities being involved)—

Phoebe wept on her pillow. This leaping out into empyrean heights with another girl was never consummated. Out of fear he had dropped back into his old safe and comfortable form of life.

A few years later, while playing in *Rocket to the Moon*, the same thing happened. He had felt he was being stifled, that he was confused and half living. The character he was playing had bold similarities to his own character. So, like the character in the play, he fell in love with the girl he was playing opposite. Phoebe was outraged. Long asleep in the feather bed of daily amenities, she awoke long enough to let out one squeak and ran to her parents' home where she decided, between the weeping and the smarting of the outraged self, that she would leave Morris and begin a long trip south. The new *inamorata*, young but intuitive from the nerves, rather shrewd, decided that Morris was not strong enough to see it through, that he was much like the vacillating unhappy Dr. Stark he was acting in the play. Correct. Phoebe soon returned from an ocean trip to the Virgin Isles (!) and found waiting a remorseful frightened Morris, stammering and completely penitent. Phoebe then proceeded to break down in his arms and cemented their cracked relationship by having a long siege of illness which developed into pneumonia and a trip to the hospital. What gorgeous cement! What chains to tie them together again!

Phoebe does not interest me very much, so I will not mention here how she was further outraged—she who had played so many leading parts in the Group!—by gradually being relegated to the role of small-part player, truthfully because she had not grown sufficiently or interestingly enough in ten years to deserve better parts. Her tedious story ends with her last year refusing a small part in *Night Music*, saying that she would leave the Group and go out and make a name for herself, establishing herself as an important actress outside the Group. Again outraged, she brought herself a new mess of clothes, her eyes grew more brilliant, her determination giving her an interesting rhythm and impulse for the first time in years. Unfortunately, tediously, as I say, a year has passed since then and she has not worked once, not even getting herself a week of jobbing in a summer stock.

At this point I learn that she and Morris have split up again. There is a saving stubborn streak in him. He is struggling now, happiness impossible until he resolves his inner and outer contradictions. He wants to understand himself, wants to develop as a man and artist—he needs help.

When he stops playing for people's SYMPATHY and ADMIRATION he is at the beginning of wisdom for himself. He is a valuable man, a useful citizen in any republic. But he must learn that all men of ideal and aspiration grow flustered and depressed when they find other contradictory qualities in themselves. A dog may bury a bone, find it later—but the man who buries his irksome displeasing qualities may find that he has buried his whole life, never more to be found. Yet, finally dead, truly buried, earth stamped on the grave, it is those very disagreeable qualities which will stand up out of *their* grave and shout to the world. In the end they alone will be remembered!

There is a quality in this journal which amuses me. It is contained in the phrase just written, "which amuses me." That is the quality of pretending to be superior to the material herein, of being above it. The same quality follows into daily life—one attempts to be superior to anything that happens. Just the worst dirty nonsense! I am not superior to what I write here, not above it, totally *unable* TO HANDLE IT. The sad truth: I am below it all.

You can't fool me, boy. I sleep with you and know you well.

Friends, unfortunately, seem to be those who confirm us in our prejudices. Unfortunately, that makes them enemies!

Talk of psychological slips. I sent Fay Wray a long and tender letter, albeit careful, and as I was addressing the envelope my hand slipped and wrote this: "Miss Fay Wray?"!

Here is another interesting psychological item. Believe me when I say that for two weeks I have wanted to mention the newly proposed conscription play here. Every day I forget to mention this important item. Now it is up for vote and will undoubtedly pass, the first compulsory conscription plan this country has ever had. The thought of it during the past weeks has been so troublesome to me, so horrifying, that I've been unable to remember to mention it. Can it be that now, plans shifted to include only men from twenty-one to thirty-one (so excluding me), that only now I am able to mention it because it excludes me? Yes, it can be.

———•———

Saturday, August 3, 1940 (continued)
and
Sunday, August 4, 1940

No day or night goes by in which I do not think of my dead mother. As long as I endure she has a perdurable monument in the convolutions of my brain.

Into the early morning I diffled around the house, determined to ride out to Luther's farm as soon as the roads were light. They were asleep, the servants just stirring, the nurse in the kitchen making the baby's bottles for the day. Slowly the household came to life. First Sylvia appeared and gave me a hug. Next Luther appeared and did the same. In the afternoon I slept until dinnertime. Then I slept some more while listening to Colonel Charles Lindbergh on the radio delivering a speech in which he urged cooperation with Hitler on America. There, the meeting chairmanned by Mr. Avery Brundage, are the beginnings of a real American Fascist Party. Of this there is no doubt, none whatsoever! Fortunately Lindbergh's personality lacks richness and depth. There is something sulky and vinegary about him.

The Communists, strange as it seems, find themselves on the same side with Lindbergh. Changing the party line has put them to bed with some strange fellows and will continue to do so. Too, it has wrought havoc among liberal supporters of their values, for it is not difficult to see that the changes in party line benefit the Soviet Union, not the United States. I am clearly of this opinion. They are not an American party because they do not work with the objective conditions of American life.

At one in the morning we drove home to the city . . .

———————•———————

Monday, August 5, 1940

Gladiolas are far from my favorite flowers, but they can be very beautiful, as they are here now, mauve blossoms and green swords of stalk in a tall white vase. But gladiolas, somehow, always look like kept women to me. (Probably the plural is gladioli.)

LOVE is something the efficacy of which is believed in by all good Americans. It is a cure for all aches and pains, for toothache, looseness of the bowels, timidity, and all profound depressions of the spirit. If only Americans (and I yield to no one my Americanism!) could believe in companionship, as the Europeans do. In that simple believing, half of our national superficiality would vanish. This is the truth.

I have not worked on the [trio] play for several days but am not worried about it. Notes for the characters keep coming and I jot them down, a sure sign that the inner feeling is concerned with the play, a good sign.

A letter from Fay Wray in the morning mail. She says she can't come east because she has to give her baby's nurse a long-promised vacation. She says she waits for me, that each airplane she sees in the sky makes her long to be with me. She says, she says, but she does not DO! And we are three thousand miles apart.

Geebee is playing stock at Saratoga where the racing season is in full sway. What a time I had there with Luise three summers ago, us palpitant with quarrels, finally patching it up in a small dingy hotel room in Lake George (the night so long!) by the pressure of body to body and mouth to mouth. But now Geebee up there and I should go there at least to see her act (all other considerable things aside), but can't bring myself to it. Anyway, she says she will be able to come into town next week for a few days between bills. So she writes.

Hanns Eisler, wife, and technical assistant are going to California to do some work on a Rockefeller Foundation Project. In the afternoon I went up to a private projection room and saw some of Hanns's work, a musical score fitted to a series of nature shots. His plan is to fit music to every variety of stock shot, so making a sort of "Art of the Fugue" of musical accompaniment. The music I heard was purposely objective, intelligent, very workmanlike and unemotional. I like it, appreciated it for what it was, but did not find myself moved by it.

Then in walked Oscar Levant, the Crown Prince. We went downstairs for coffee and cake. They talked for an hour of Schoenberg, whom they all love and revere. Schoenberg may be the greatest influence in music since Wagner, probably so, but it was a boring hour for me. With Oscar around it is impossible to get a word in edgewise, lengthwise, or upside down, but one does not dislike him for it. Oscar is honest out of the fear that you will discover him dishonest; he is ugly, like a bloated toad, but it seems to me that he functions from a good heart despite his melancholic bluster. But so disorderly! In California he once said to me, opening up for a narrow flash, "Don't tell anyone I said so, but my trouble is that I have a very small penis. Don't tell that to anyone now!" Life seems to be a series of retreats through the marshes for him!

Now I am wise enough to read the papers as little as possible, scarcely even turning on the radio for news. There is nothing they can tell us—why indulge in the sloppy commerce of rumor and gossip? But the *Times* the other morning has as ironic and tragic an item as has been seen in many years: "New Curbs Placed On Jews In Reich"! NEW curbs! Something they had forgotten to do before. Jews are forbidden to paint red crosses on their hospitals; they are permitted to shop only between the hours of four and five; they may not carry out of the country more than two suits, one pair of overalls, one sweater, and one overcoat! A complete list of what women may take is also furnished. Curfew for Jews in most German cities is nine o'clock.

Rarely do I feel my Jewishness as a separate quality of the personality, but when I read such an article there is a sudden inner flare-up and I think, "You ought to sign your name from now on, 'Clifford Odets, Jew.'" But that is untrue, sensational, exclusionizing, even though it appeals to something in the spirit. More painful (I think) to write, yet so much more correct, so ample and free, is "Clifford Odets, American."

Before ten in the evening I went to bed, resolved to regulate my hours. Good boy! As we used to say in the Bronx, "You'll be a man before your mother will!"

———•———

Tuesday, August 6, 1940

Up early again, at seven, to enjoy a full breakfast and look hopefully ahead to the rest of the day.

By the early afternoon, I thought of going out and beginning to look for an apartment into which I can move on my return from Hollywood. Yesterday Lewin sent a letter in which he hinted that it was time for me to come out and do the movie script of *Night Music*.

After several tries I found [an apartment] over on Beekman Place, as beautiful as one could wish. Four rooms, duplex and, unfortunately, expensive. They want three thousand dollars a year but the agent is trying to get it for me for twenty-six hundred. Riding around the city in broad daylight, for a change talking to Herman, my secretary, as to a human being (and noticing that his hair is growing quite gray—which gave me a pang), thinking about moving to new quarters, looking into the faces of hundreds of hot good-natured people walking the streets— all of this made me suddenly feel as free and blithe as a bird. I found myself clucking comfortably (bird?), sweating with the pleasure of the broiling city, buying books, buying pastry, buying fresh flowers—all spreefully, as if I'd been drinking champagne.

You're a naïve fellow; often there is nothing wrong with you that walking in the daytime streets won't cure. Yet there is a good deal to my hermit's way of life, for if you want to keep freshly romantic and ardent about people (and I do!), don't go too often among them. This keeps you sensitive to them, freshly perceptive. Believe me, this way I can walk in the street and pin a man with one straight glance and see him whole, immediately, on the spot.

"Oh," she said, "I want to feel! I want to feel!!" As if she had been dead for years, this married woman of the other night. The thought of that scene keeps running in and out of my mind.

This morning, thinking of my mother, I called my aunt in Philadelphia. Immediately she asks, "What's the matter, Clifford, you're up so early?"

More about metabolism. It takes place within the tissue cells, says the encyclopedia. It is a ceaseless activity ending only with death and consists of two activities or phases. These are building up—anabolism; and breaking down—catabolism. There is a constant interplay between these two phases, sometimes rapid, sometimes slow, WITH

A STRAINING TOWARDS AN EQUILIBRIUM which is never reached while life goes on!

That sounds extraordinary and poetic to me, philosophic and psychologic, as if the greatest mind could do no more than repeat the pattern of the humble cell.

Too, I read there, a man is sixty percent water!

In the United States during the past six months a mere fifteen thousand people were killed in auto accidents. Did I ever mention that we are competitive people even when driving cars? And that there is a silent but true war constantly going on between drivers and pedestrians?

By the way, it is with poison that one destroys poison.

BOLDNESS: That is the important and necessary quality in this country, first, last, and always—boldness! We have here, too, a whole class of professional "whacks," irresponsible, glib, writers of columns, radio speakers, and counselors, so bold and so ignorant. The type must be put in a play, be he dietician, political commentator, or whatnot.

A man writes that people who keep diaries are often self-disparaging in them in order to later get credit for being better than they were. (*Et tu, Brutè?*)

———————•———————

Thursday, August 8, 1940

Every night you can hear the cricket on the terrace, twenty-two floors above the street. I hear him now, lone singer, insane, clipping the hot summer night. What else can he be singing but *memento mori*? Maybe not insane, certainly insensate.

I am still keeping the good hours, all satisfaction and a yard wide. By the time my secretary arrives, around ten, I have been up three hours. But one thing at a time—if I am regulating hours I can do nothing else, least of all write a play. But more important, the theme is taking shape in my mind, intensely personal but generally significant feeling behind it.

The theme, I will say here, has to do with a new morality, with a return to voluntarily imposed morals, to voluntarily imposed and assumed forms in a world in which there are no forms, hardly even for Catholics. When this came into my mind—all in a jump—it surprised me. Yet it is the logical outcome of the months of feeling and thought covered by this journal.

The stunning discovery of the essentially shoddy nature of most things and many, many people! I said stunning!!

Of friends, too, I could write a bitter breviary.

That Leo Kapps downstairs, the redheaded desk boy, has disappeared. It is the same case as the cashier at Ratner's—he borrowed from "shylocks" who began to threaten him.

Most people are just like dogs, unconcentrated, impulsive, whimsical, thoughtless, now in repose, next jumping up at a sound and barking like hell, then rolling over on their backs, scratching or trotting at will, indifferent to everything but the feeling of the moment, utterly looney, completely satisfied with themselves on all counts, sharpest momentary interest quickly followed by an all-pervading dumbness—a life of the moment, in short! (And not to forget that shouldering up to each other, the eyes intent but downcast, the body tense, etc., etc., etc.)

Diffidence, the modern attitude, which comes from fear or [sic— perhaps "of"?] repudiation. A form of withdrawal that, when you think about it, accounts for a generation of bad lovers. (This is a subtle remark.)

Am I alone in this? Many times, day or night but mostly night, I will hear my name uttered, once, but with the characteristic voice of some certain person.

Yesterday, for instance, it happened. I was lying on the bed just past noon and I heard my name, "Clifff-ard, . . . " like a cry of anguish, an appeal for help, a final reaching out. I recognized the tone of the voice but was unable to place it. My backbone began to tingle. "Whose voice, whose voice?" I asked myself but could not answer.

For a long time I have had here Burckhardt's history of the Renaissance in Italy. The other day I opened it for the first time and was very entertained by the many photos and excellent text. Here is what he says of the women of the upper classes: "Their function was to influence distinguished men and to moderate male impulse and caprice." Most of the "distinguished men" were Al Capones, it must be said.

In the early afternoon I gathered up myself and the gift and rode out to Luther and Sylvia's farm and wished her well for her thirtieth birthday. She was very pleased with the pewter gift.

Sylvia was watching the baby (the nurse on vacation) and planting strawberry plants in rows. Luther was bustling around, checking bills, watching the men (I with him for a time) thresh and pack the ripe oats in one operation. Not only that, but the straw is baled at the same time, chaff flying all over. Men work like that—five of them here—planting, reaping, packing, carting, and we do not see it. Right in the fields, right in the sun, and we in the city are ignorant of everything but the greedy eating!

After dinner we talked about the Group again and again. I felt myself impatient, restless, my gorge rising at each mention, and tried to stop it. I am in no mood for it, being resentful and wrathful about everything about it. It costs me some effort to even write these few lines. But I must add that perhaps a solution to the discovery of the new form (if it goes on) is to be found in the movie organization called United Artists.

Their baby is charming. So are Sylvia's breasts when I see them, when she bends to play with the baby or plant more little strawberry plants. So are the odorous green plants heavy with ripening tomatoes. So are the four dogs drawing close to the house as evening comes and the country world grows still.

Friday, August 9, 1940

"Did you hear that damn dog barking all night?" No. "Must you go?" Yes. So good-bye, and this time put the top of the car up, the sun powerful, the ride back to the city a chore, yet much pleasure from the varieties of rhythm of driving necessary in the afternoon traffic. The moment one so much as approaches the city, the rhythm of all the cars becomes very distinctive—one sits up nervously, watchfully. Here everything runs together, as if through a funnel, which is just what it is. Once you have driven through the funnel you are in the bottle called Manhattan.

Signed the contracts for the new apartment.

What you must completely stamp out of yourself is THIS FEAR OF NOT WRITING A PLAY, a fear of lying fallow for a year or two, even more—not that this is an ideal!

Some painful contradictions in the self, discouraging, depressing, probably never to be resolved: I am modest and very vain, humble and proud, ascetic and sensual, a poet trying to be a shrewd businessman, the heart good but the ego always insistently strong. And yet they are not contradictions, instead being two sides of the same coin in each case.

In the evening, tired, I began to think of some of the Group actors, getting madder by the minute. For some reason I picked up a copy of my *Paradise Lost* and quickly read the last act. Why lie?—it moved me very much, twice bringing tears to my eyes. Mostly I was moved by the wearied overpatience of the wife, perhaps because she sees everything clearly from the beginning—her realism is terrible in a certain way. "Operate," she says. "Cut off my arm and I will watch while you are doing it. I will keep my eye right on it."

I will never be ashamed of that play. It will last if any dramatic literature in our country does. To think that its worth is understood or felt by only a few dozen people!

Moving back and forth the whole evening, from room to room, the windows all thrown open, the broad summer night slowly munching the heart away. It's not easy to be alone and go to sleep in this wide summer night. How can I give an idea with these words, how can I say—? How can I explain the naked self, the fevered self on top of the bed? Concentrate of heart, of liver, of mind, of spleen, concentrate of lust, of spirit, of everything noble and everything mean! It ain't easy to sleep.

Sent F. W. a carbon copy of yesterday's journal entry.

Went to bed.

Saturday, August 10, 1940

Up past noon, immediately to finish the Noguchi book; saddened. My first sense, what a good play this book will make; a better movie. But only one living man to act Noguchi—Charlie Chaplin! Here one uses the word GREAT without exaggeration. What shall I do? Try to get the rights? Try to interest Chaplin in the project when I go out to Hollywood in a week or two? Nijinsky does not interest me beside this idea.

If one has friends, a friend or two, a wife, a lover, a brother or sister, he should know them as Eckstein knows Noguchi (although he has not quite said the last words). With tenderness for the mistakes, the errors, and faults of the other. With sympathy always, with love, in detail, with care and complete responsibility for the other, without interference, above all always with love. That is the only way one can ever hope to broaden out his life, this intimate and deep knowing of others; it is the only way one can escape from the prison cell which is himself. (No, it is not the only way, but it is the finest way!) It is sometimes possible to know an artist that way—I think I know Beethoven that way, perhaps Mozart, but no others. For the artist is dead, he submits himself in his work, and the work you can take, approach, examine, savor only when you are ready or needful of doing so. With a living person this living intimacy, this TWO INTO ONE, is almost impossible.

No one in the whole wide world knows me this way, which is why I am so lonely always, why there is a deep (or deeper than other things) senselessness to the work and thoughts and feelings of the self: a deep NOT-CARING and an underground bent for self-destruction.

Ibsen, seeing Duse play one of his plays, said, "She believes Hedda to be a neurotic, but she is absolutely wrong." All right, let us grant it, but then it is Hedda's society (and the form it imposed upon her) which is neurotic!

I was thinking of Noguchi going to Africa, working on yellow fever, being on a white smelly tropical steamer, handling animals, walking across snakes, everything foreign and strange and dangerous. I was lying on my bed thinking about this, about LIVING DANGEROUSLY. Then I thought that phrase is all nonsense, that one can live so dangerously in one quiet room, using the head and heart, that even the pockets stuffed with dynamite makes a far lesser problem. It is possible to get drunk on reality, the clearer the drunker, so to speak. Submit yourself to yourself, admit yourself to yourself, and you are living as dangerously as one could wish! No doubts about this.

Noise, like dirt, says E.B., is sound out of place.

Catholics, the Japanese, whoever has form has become very attractive to me. I think of this always.

Beany, [Margaret] Barker called in the afternoon, reminding me of our meeting in the street last week. Do I want to come to dinner tonight? No? Well, she won't call me again, coyly—I must call her if I care. She is the vehement one (of the red-lidded eyes and awkward body) whom I loved, in turn, with such futile vehemence in the early Group Theatre days.

What has happened to her since then, poor Margaret! She feels everything, understands nothing. She has grown unattractive, hysterical, stringy, more ashamed, more disorderly, a naked electric wire writhing in the dark.

After this called H. Clurman; said he'd be over around six, we'd have dinner together, that he'd just finished a long letter to me. (He called me.) Showered, powdered with tender baby talc, sniffled, thinking constantly of Geebee who is returning tomorrow evening from Saratoga Springs. (And did not stop thinking of her, in and out—a delicious secret—for the rest of the evening.)

When Harold came down here we sat for a time, discussing our reactions to B. Rose and his art collection, a way of extending his power, widening his range, although, as Harold wittily said, "Rich Americans think they can buy a way of life," to which he added, "They say you can see from the huge art collections in America that now we are a cultured nation—exactly as if one were to say, 'We are a very fertile couple—we have adopted forty-six children!' "

We drove uptown; ended up in Lindy's for iced coffee and iced watermelon and a cigar each.

O. Levant and his wife walked in ("A charming little mother," said Harold, not knowing who she was) and we joined them. His wife was heavy but relaxed, later a little disturbed when the baby began to move in her belly. What does a pregnant mother eat?—dry huckleberries and a bottle of sarsaparilla. However, it is Oscar who acts like the pregnant one, badgering the waiter because he doesn't know what to order—does stewed fruit go with calomel? Can he drink coffee? And all the time embarrassed because he is forced to demand attention and yet knows that it is irking to everyone around him.

At home again, in the still of the summer night, only thoughts of Geebee, of her youth and full warm flesh, so very happily takeable, so giving. Open, my beloved, my beautiful undefiled, my dove! In the kitchen, placed a quart of champagne to put on the ice eighteen hours from then, when she will be here, the two of us naked, together, for once not throbbing alone—oh, together!

Drank a pint of champagne myself and fell asleep soon enough.

———•———

Sunday, August 11, 1940

Again and again the only verity I can turn to is this journal, thumbing the pages backwards, hoping, wondering, waiting to turn outwards once more. On a day, a night, in some future week or month it will happen. One never dies of this.

Geebee came here, late, mistaken in her train times, so that her arrival past ten in the evening was almost anticlimactic, but only almost. Anyway, the whole day spiraled up to her arrival at the door and my pressing her in my arms, half dressed, hungry for her, trying to restrain myself for a decent half hour of conversation before we undressed. It was not more than a half hour, that chilled bottle of wine between us—for a long time we sat naked in the cool dark, smoking, making soft noises, kissing, drinking the wine, reaching out to and touching each other with hands, legs, elbows, knees, mouths, and breasts. Everything was fragrant and hot—we gushed more than buttermilk—swift flowing goodness. Past midnight we fell asleep, woke up again at four, pressed bodies together again, fell asleep in the dawn after a cold drink for her, a cup of soup for me, having been unable to eat all day and night because of waiting for her.

There is a tendency in this journal, friend (more than a tendency—a fact!), of smoothly writing only what is known and rational to you, writing what you can handle and be superior to. Keep out of that dangerous groove if you can.

Would this be a good title for the trip play? *Notes for a Dream.*

A virginal girl says to an ardent man, "Please . . . don't hurt me." It is almost in this way that I say in thoughts, "Please, I beg you—do not disappoint me." To all people to whom it is possible to give myself. (And some say the same to me too.)

You never saw a day like this afternoon, so clear and calm, the city so quiet and orderly, everything making me feel so glad. Then step into the room and hear on the radio that the English and Germans are locked in a death struggle, fleets of planes striving to tear each other down. Here I can't believe it, in this gladdening day. Surely I am not alone in the war over there having not the slightest reality for me?

Each new artwork is a giving up, a moving out into uncharted waters, the port always uncertain. Yes, there is past experience, but helpful only in the sense of *experienced reaction* to the new elements to be met. Do not be afraid to move ahead: fearlessness is necessary.

———•———

Friday, August 16, 1940

The clock has been almost all around the week since the last entry here, last Sunday. From notes here is what has happened since then.

MONDAY, 8/12: in the evening young Bette Grayson came here for dinner. Found the letter from Harold Clurman, the one he had said he would soon send. Very long, little in it that has not been written about myself and my work in this journal a half-dozen times. What was important was that he wrote it, that he was concerned enough in my work and future to write five typewritten sheets. His help has a contradiction in it—the wave that helps propel you forward, under it an undertow that draws you back. Of this dialectic contradiction in his nature and its effect on people he seems to have no awareness. This is a very subtle matter, more subtle than I can imagine, I think.

I could answer, "Yes, true," to his letter, but is his letter the thing? Is it the thing fairly and roundly seen? Never mind for now.

TUESDAY, 8/13: today did not leave the house. The new schedule of early up and early down has been shot away and lost in the foggy weather. The evening was spent in reading Gorky's play, *Children of the Sun*. Talented, not more. Gorky's stuff is not digested and recrystallized the way [Chekhov's] is. It seems to me (not at all certain now) that Gorky is a made writer while Chekhov was an artist unable to do or be anything else. I have here now the Gorky *Klim Samgin* cycle, three novels covering a period of forty years, and will know Gorky better after reading them.

Now the sad time approaching, the days already growing shorter, the nights longer, less juicy—quick the year runs to autumn.

WEDNESDAY, 8/14: an ugly little dream of being taken with some friends to a concentration camp by French Fascists in field blue uniforms. Their faces were impassive, stern, only smiling to each other. A very clear picture of myself trying to be ingratiating, sick at heart, covertly so that the others would not see I was trying to ingratiate myself. Taken to the basement of a school, old-fashioned plumbing around.

Searched for and readily enough found a one-room apartment near the new apartment to use as an office and telephone and mail depot. I want privacy in my new home.

Went to Oscar Levant's house from which we were to go out to dinner and later see the World's Fair. With us Bette and Mr. Irving Kolodin, music critic, and his wife. In Kolodin and wife a complete modesty which makes you want to extend yourself for them. From Oscar the same nonsense.

What with the heat, the weariness, the being together for six hours, I was glad to say good-bye to them and drive home with Bette. We bedded down to a good sleep after listening to a set of eight nocturnes of the Polish Nightingale.

At the Aquacade there is an actor of vaudeville, Frank Libuse, who does an act with a woman whom he abuses. The Marx Brothers use a similar woman for similar reason. This type interests me because she is a type to be found all over—a woman who clings to her regal dignity while unfeeling clowns are beating and kicking her all over the lot.

THURSDAY, 8/15: Bette and I are drinking morning coffee at noon when the phone rings from below and informs me that my Aunt Esther is waiting in the lobby. Bette away in a good-natured flash, up comes the aunt—she doesn't want me to go to the coast (I am going a week from today) without saying good-bye.

Today there was more in the newspapers about the investigation (a stupid red smear) on the West Coast, my name linked with others, movie actors and actresses, etc., supposed to have contributed heavily to the coffers of the Communist Party. This annoyed me very much because it is so pointless, etc.

Up to bed, washing, a little tight with the Scotch, I thought, "When you felt this way you used to say to the face in the mirror, 'You—mysterious clod.' Now you don't. Wonderful. Wonderful, the way you stand here, tight, an accomplished fact, all this whizzing in the head."

In Europe the blitzkrieg is on—thousands of planes battling each other, the American newspapers cra-a-zy with excitement. In the American people? Restlessness, avidity for any scraps of information (true or not), anxiety, uneasiness, and, sadly, superficiality. Never again in our time will there be an ease of living, for none of us, mates!

FRIDAY, 8/16: up wearied, sucked out with fragments of dreams unremembered.

Nothing from Fay Wray here, no word for a week. How mistaken of her not to water the bush!

Called Boris Aronson and asked him to look at the new apartment and help me with decoration ideas. Done. He admired the apartment, made very sensible suggestions (tomorrow will visit it again with a friend), said he was very envious since it is just the sort of place he is looking for.

Boris is in love. It is comical, how he expresses it, but very nice. "I am in a lot of trouble," he starts, "with a woman. This woman is driving me crazy. It is wonderful—I feel alive all over. She finds my weak spot and hurts me. I am very soft (sooft). If I were a regular man I would give her up immediately, but right away!" To which he appends, as he does after every statement, "Cliff, you can't imagine!" Or, "It is remarkable, just remarkable!"

Saturday, August 17, 1940

Week by week life grows more and more superficial in this country. Oh, I have much to say about this, much! Just let me be a little more rested in myself and you will get pages and pages of notes on this subject.

All day much rain, the afternoon here alone, gray and chilly, damp. I thought that it was a day to be in bed with a woman—a comfortable normal woman with love between you, WITH COMMON USAGE between you! To get in bed with a woman just as you might say, "Darling, make pot roast for dinner tonight."

Instead, the appetite capricious and delicate, like that of a pregnant lady, went to the kitchen and had a bowl of little turtle soup with a glass of vermouth stirred into it.

This is a day to be a Chinese, to examine crickets, eat noodles, have a woman, drink fragrant tea, shoot off a few firecrackers, read a poem or two.

In the evening took Bette to Boris's house for dinner. His girl was there, seeming sulky because she was uneasy. She seems ambitious, driving, to Boris is rude. But a good dinner with wine, conversation for hours, looking at many of Boris's paintings, many of them of real quality, without doubt the works of a real artist. Boris anxiously looked for approval, is anxious about his progress as an artist. He complains about the world, that it is impossible to be an artist today, that everything is too big and distracting. Finally, to tail off the evening (after an hour of hot expressiveness from me), Boris put it this way: "I want to make life smaller, meaning more intimate, more personal, and more real."

After a long ride in the humid air, the sky so dark (as if it has been relating itself somehow to the war during the past weeks), Bette and I landed here, looked at newspapers, took cool showers, spoke lightly in the heavy morning. I found myself pacing back and forth, nervous, restless, so tired that I did not want to lie down in the bed beside her. Finally did so and quickly fell asleep, my own sighs fading away in my own ears.

—Yield.
—No!
—But, for instance, to this paper on which you are writing.
—No!
—Not even yield to this sheet of paper?
—I said no!
—What is it you will not yield of yourself?
—I don't know.

———————•———————

Monday, August 19, 1940

About the Group, that is what I want to say a few words about. I think it is going to go on this season as it has been operating during the past few years, no matter what the actors think or say. I am all for that— several productions of scripts, two of which have already been acquired; perhaps one of my own in January or February. But it is during this time (as I briefly told Harold last night) that all plans (starting with the most idealistic conception of a theatre) must be started and worked out for the new Group Theatre, it to start functioning a year from now. Everything must be gone into, even the impossible, and then scaled down to the realism of modern life. The principle, I say, is that we will no longer have a theatre (a home, a place to work, "an ideologically cemented collective," if you please) if we permit Broadway conditions to shape us. I insist that we must make the circumstances as much as possible—force the Broadway theatre to adapt itself to US! I am not afraid of boldness, daring, courage, romanticism in the good sense. Nothing frightens me! Fearlessness is absolutely necessary instead of this opportunistic living from script to script. In short, what do we want? WE WILL MAKE IT! Otherwise (for me, for one), the movies for us! I will not live and work in a Broadway theatre which dictates conditions which I despise! In this case I am for us doing all the dictation!

After some slight talk with Harold Clurman last night, the above is part of a note I wrote to Lee Strasberg today. Harold does not talk on the subject, only around and behind it.

My eyes are two pools of nicotine.

An unhappy little note from Fay Wray. Will I make her happy soon? I cannot tell.

Bought all of Strindberg's plays in five volumes, old secondhand ones, out of print.

————•————

Tuesday, August 20, 1940

Unfinished scraps of business before I get on the train Thursday. Doesn't seem that there is time to sleep—I'm getting tense and nervous.

Harold mentioned the other night that Luise was seeing a good deal of Pete de Donato. My face got tight but I hid it. Later I didn't mind, thinking, "Jealousy comes only when you think the other man superior to you." Jealousy, my word, jealousy! All I have to do is think of the agony we had together and the jealousy goes. True? Not quite.

I'm going to sleep and the hell with everything!

Tonight saw Gadget for the first time since he has returned from the coast. I could not throw my arms around him, did not feel friendly, sat quietly and listened to Boris inveigh against world conditions, his grasp of the international situation wobbly indeedra! Harold there too, sitting there as if he were sponsoring me, mothering me.

Yellow roses here, mongrelized by short stems. Uninteresting. French soap—bought two boxes of it—much more interesting.

Well, sleep, boob, sleep.

Last night I read over two diaries I kept as a youth—1924 and 1926. Pitiful. Also 1928 in typewritten sheets, all about what I did with a lady named Powers. All that I did NOT do, I mean. Brutal with her because of shyness and ineptitude. My God, what kind of boy was I? Stoopid! Be fair now. No, stoopid, middle class, but poetic. Fair enough.

Sleep. One old entry very touching—Mother came to my bed and kissed me good night, something she rarely did. I miss my mother always.

———•———

Wednesday, August 21, 1940

If it isn't one thing it's another—now the weather, chilly, as if November had fallen down upon us. So uncomfortable, lonely, retreated into the self, as autumn weather always makes me do and feel. Autumn is always dying for me; I dislike it. I am waiting to get on the train, impatient now to be off, not wanting to go but quite willing to be on the train, snug in the small compartment, en route, en route always being a good feeling.

Yesterday, outside of Mexico City, Trotsky was assaulted and stabbed. Today he died, a friend and confidante the assailant. This depressed me and yet was the right way for him to die, for surely he lived by the sword. He was one of the few characters living who could be said to be on a tragic plane of life and suffering. In his life there is an epic play.

———•———

Thursday, August 22, 1940

Bette had stayed and it made me nervous to have her there in the morning. She wanted a long sentimental good-bye, but I did not feel it that way and could not give it. Then packing, packing, and packing, calmly and neatly enough. Only to get on the train, that is all—just get on the train and be locked away and routined by the railroad schedule!

For farewell, Benson and Herman there (Harold dropping up for the last minutes), played several Mozart pieces—the C-major piano concerto and the G-minor quintet, the top of his talent. I thought: "Well, you've heard this music deeply, felt it, understood it. It doesn't matter now if the train turns over, you get hurt, killed—you have this music right behind you."

Oscar Levant and his wife (momentarily expecting to pop a baby) are at the railroad station when we arrive there. And then happily soon on the train, the great Twentieth Century Limited to Chicago, a proud run of sixteen hours, always on time. I am still poetic about trains, poetic meaning as if you are riding on them and seeing them for the first time. I am happy (although it can be a great nuisance) that very little is casual with me ever—always some adventure in things and situations which most people have long since taken for granted.

When you are on a train it is useless to fight it, to be annoyed by it or any part of the trip. Oscar does not stop complaining. He does all of this with a certain kind of good humor, putting on a grim visage which he can not sustain for long. He is ashamed of genuine admiration and the expression of it, of enthusiasm or overt feeling about anything.

I began to read the famous Ostrovsky play, *The Storm*. Heavens!

Steam on, proud train. In all the cars the children, dogs, and parents sleep. Only Oscar tosses in his compartment all night, I doing the same in the next one. Too much coffee, too many cigarettes, too unexercised in all the parts. Steam on, proud swift train!

My sister Florence, at the party, looked very sad, depressed. I didn't know what to say to her. "Be of good cheer," I said in parting.

Pretense, dispose of all pretense. Why not? It is the law of a good life. Why should there be pretense about even one little thing in your life?

Before going to bed I looked at a very popular little American magazine called *Reader's Digest*. No magazine extant shows better the

American craze for self-improvement and betterment. All you have to do is take down the bottle from the shelf and take so many spoonfuls thrice a day. Total garbage! They say, for instance, that many people talk of Thoreau but that few have read his *Walden*. They then proceed to condense it to six pages! You take it like a vitamin capsule!!

———•———

Friday, August 23, 1940

We are just pulling out of Kansas City, near eleven at night.

Oscar is worried. He doesn't say so, but he is worried about what I am writing about him in here. "Do you mention me? What do you say about me? Never mind, I don't care, I don't want to know."

Adventure. I always hope there will be some adventure on a train. There never is. This morning, changing for the Santa Fe Chief, I saw that all night a young woman had been sleeping in the compartment behind me, a woman heavy in the legs and breasts but with a very delicate face. In the morning she looked at me in a very frank marked way. You see, I thought, you missed that adventure!

This afternoon, on the Chief, I heard a woman's hot voice in the next compartment. A man was trying to hush her down. Adventure, I thought! She was bitterly accusing him of having had some traffic with another woman, training with her across state lines. She said the girl was an innocent girl and that she would have the man arrested unless he continued riding with her to Los Angeles. Apparently he wanted to get off the train. By evening the man had vanished; the woman was a little drunk and took all her luggage off at K.C., but not before she had the entire train searched. She looked very unhappy and vacant, but very bold too. All the passengers smiled and smirked behind their hands.

In Chicago there is a four-hour wait while one changes from train to train. Oscar was for looking around the town and trying to find musical comedy people who are here with the Al Jolson show. Well, we did finally land in Jolson's hotel suite. Got him out of bed, neither of us knowing him very well. I was surprised at his delicate legs and ankles and feet (he had recently broken a bone in one of the feet) when he got out of bed in a long pajama top, but his nervous frayed ego did not surprise me. Nor did his desperate unconnected unhappiness. He said that our visit had been the first pleasant interlude in weeks, and he was believable—we weren't in competition with him, nor did we want something from him. He spoke of his wife as "that c——," but without harshness. It seems that she has gone ahead with plans for divorcing him and it rankles him, every injured cell protesting in offhand oblique ways. He said he was for Roosevelt in the next election but immediately told us two anti-Roosevelt jokes he has in his new show, not at all seeming to connect one significance with the other. He is waiting, he said, to place his bet on the election. Which candidate? It depends on which one looks like the winner, he said. Also he had given up a girl he has been going out with in the show: "I don't like her friends and besides I don't wanna get tangled up no more!" Life's delicate little child! The lot of them, Jolson, Ed Wynn, Bert Lahr, and the rest of them.

———————•———————

Saturday, August 24, 1940

Today en route. A combination breakfast and lunch at noon. Woozy, the way I always am on a train, passive, splashed out and soft, a whizzing going on in my head for the whole trip.

Yes, a soiled Saturday but no matter. For most of the afternoon Oscar and I played casino. He talked about the theatre, about my last play and its ending. He found it dull, he said, meaningless, etc., etc. I told him with some heat that if he pretended to admire my plays as much as he said he did he must at least see them more than once before he presumed to talk about them. I told him that the superficiality and lack of respect for people and their work and study sickened me now and would continue to do so till the day I died. By this time he had flushed and unflushed, stammered and stuttered. When I said that I DEMANDED attention and respect from a friend, he did not know what to say. In short, I was asking him to be an artist, which, unfortunately, he is not.

Well, why superficiality and opportunism here? In great part because nothing is seen or examined in context. Nothing is seen in relationship, nothing is located or situated. Dirt, for instance, is matter out of place. But it is good and valuable in a garden. But if you do not situate it (or put it in a context), what is it? And this act of situating is the only way that one can identify anything! No one knows anyone else, no one touches anyone else: it is all mysterious, abstracted, and blank, so very blank!!!

Yes, admitted! I am arrogant, arrogant out of hunger and need for connection with the people and life around me, hungry for understanding and depth of relationship in all things. I am starved for men and women of conviction instead of the OPINIONMONGERS I meet on all sides. More and more I am finding myself forced into a cold (shall I say contemptuous? do I dare?) contemptuous relationship of mere appraisal of the men and women I meet.

How sad that we are a people of opinions and not of CONVICTIONS! How sad that we have no forms here. No, there are forms—a gentle good Sunday school life of limited imagination and hungers. That life gives a sort of form—but is it not a form of death?

Oh, how uninterested I am in opinions! Give me convictions, give me men to brawl with and fight—hissing and hatred—yet I will respect them for their convictions and they will respect me for mine. Let us have here the joy and zest of positive living instead of this negative lying fallow in all seasons and years.

———————•———————

Sunday, August 25, 1940

I have never approached California by train (this is the fifth or sixth time) without finding myself extremely uneasy and nervous, almost as if engaged in some illicit traffic, some secret underground business.

The first time I think I was nervous because it seemed to me that Hollywood was a sinful place where my talent would be engulfed. (I did not trust my character, am only learning that trust now.) Too, I was worried about what many people would say about me—that I had "sold out," etc., etc.; all drivel, but enough to truly worry me. Then, too, I had been hearing for years that California was a very reactionary state, policed by vigilantes. With the reputation of being "America's Number One Revolutionary Boy" (as *The New Yorker* magazine put it) behind me, I was really frightened by the prospect of being tarred and feathered. (It has been done in these United States!) Then there was the difficult task of meeting many new people, facing gossip writers and rude stares (which I stare right back). On top of this came a fear that maybe I couldn't write a movie after all. And above all, most likely, I was out of my milieu. Enough to scare the wits out of a much bolder man than myself!

After this, Hollywood a known quality, my nervousness was chiefly due to and conditioned by my relationship with Luise Rainer. One time I was escaping from her—good! Another time I was approaching her after months of yearning for her—good! Always much of the nervousness was caused by not knowing what I was riding into. Didn't the climate make me lose my mind? Would I ever write another play? Why are the movie people so hostile to me? (For once I was on a producers' blacklist for supposedly having caused them unionization trouble among the writers.) Always I was trying with nervous and apprehensive effort to keep a balance—which means being clear and concentrated enough to write a play. It always worried me to think that Luise would kick this delicate balance to pieces—and she usually did.

As the train stopped at San Bernadino this morning I was reminded of the time I met Luise there when SHE was returning from New York. We had quarreled at Brentwood, perhaps two weeks after our marriage. Immediately packed, she jumped on the train and was off to New York. (Since I had chased her out of her own house, as she put it.) Furthermore, said she, if she were a man she would visit every whorehouse in New York while there. Vain boast, excused by her extreme anger. In a few days, loving wires, growing warmer and warmer, were passing between us. She stayed in New York about ten days and a bad sore throat attacked her. If I had only known (as I know now) what damned nonsense all this was. Anyway, I hired a big car (official-looking and from her studio, where they hated me more than they hated her) and met her at San Bernadino, which is two hours out of Los Angeles. How sick, I thought, meeting her, how sick this relationship of ours is.

How often she deftly enraged me (I seemed always, by instinct perhaps, to save up the accumulated wrath for a weekend when I pulled out all the stops!) by telling me that she had married the wrong kind of man. Often I thought, by the way, that she was right but did not dare to say so.

"Do not run around in your naked feet," I used to keep saying to Luise. "You will catch a cold and maybe pick up splinters and things. Please put on slippers." Simultaneously this angered and pleased her.

On the one hand it made her feel that I was bossing her the way her father (merciless bourgeois!) had done for the unhappy years of her girlhood; on the other hand, such admonishments meant that I was thinking of her, attending her, fathering her in the good sense. Again, I did not trust my character, for soon I kept quiet since everything I did or said had two sides, two reactions from her. Ah, if she had only been a simple girl! Or if I had been a more mature man! (Frequently the dog broke wind too.)

Out the windows of the train the eucalyptus trees, favorite trees, fine trees, characterful trees. Very pleasant to see them again, like saying how do you do to old friends.

Al Lewin met me at the station, smiling, looking scrubbed, looking a little remote (or feeling so) because of his defective hearing. I confessed to him my nervousness and felt better for the confession. A brief good-bye took place with Oscar (met by Lea Gershwin) and we were on our way in Al's car. I was about to blurt out that he had nothing to worry about concerning me and my relationship to so-called radical activities on the West Coast. This is a disgusting sort of toadying on my part which this time shocked me. I immediately resolved not to do this with him, not now, not later. Goddamit, what a thing!

We drove to the Beverly Wilshire Hotel, where I intend to stay for a few days before settling down elsewhere. The clerk gave me a poor five-dollar-a-day room and, seeing my signature, asked me how Mrs. Odets was. "Fine," I said. Then we drove to Al's new home in Santa Monica, the beach, the ocean, infinity staring at him through his back windows. I looked pensively at the roads and turns of corners, all of them so often covered by Luise and me in the car which she drove so recklessly (or shall I say temperamentally?). Saddened me. Why say more? And yet some new feeling of confidence, as if one had lost a battle on these grounds but would know from that defeat how to win the next. (With Hollywood I have lost every battle and every campaign!)

The new Lewin house was designed but not furnished by [Richard] Neutra. It is jammed with paintings, books, and other artworks, almost, it seemed to me, as if one did not really like art but was trying to overcome this dislike by an abundance of the product. Yet the paintings all show real taste, most of them by unknown artists nevertheless really talented. Several are by Angna Enters, the dancer, a friend of the Lewins. She is obviously a gifted woman.

At lunch I was annoyed for a time with the "head man" quality of Lewin's conduct, something common to all movie producers. It is a habit with him to say the final word on all subjects, politics, economics, art, literature, whatever is brought up for discussion. Perhaps I am annoyed because perhaps the same habit is in me. Perhaps. It doesn't matter now. Later, during discussion of scenes and characters, it will become genuinely annoying and will have to be faced WITHOUT TOADYING!

I enjoyed very much a few minutes of gazing at the Pacific Ocean and thought that in these last few days I had spanned the distance between this water and the Atlantic—an accomplished fact physically, but in inner terms it will take weeks before I know it. This makes me say that a place is what one is. Am I understood? Probably not. Anyway, the air was very good here and the afternoon passed quickly.

Met the musical director of MGM, who laughed at everything one said—his way of toadying, a habit acquired from long years of work in a movie studio; and an actor, another laugher. From these one may learn the ethics of slavery, well-paid slavery.

The night fell quickly—there does not seem to be any period of dusk here—and the air grew cool and remote suddenly. The neon lights came on; it was the empty evening—I had a heartbroken feeling for a long time. I thought that I am used to this by now, this empty feeling of loneliness. Now, I thought, is the time to call Fay Wray. Filial duty (what I have of it) dictated a phone call to my father, who is living now in Los Angeles. No, I could not get him on the telephone. Nor, when it came to it, could I get Fay. She was gone, flown the coop, off to some gala picture opening in Colorado! I turned away from the phone as petulant and hurt as a child.

Anyway (for God's sake, shorten this story), I felt better after a long hot shower and a simple supper of ham and melon and coffee. By midnight I was used to being alone, resigned and sleepy. I slept. Sweet child!

———————•———————

Monday, August 26, 1940

Up gladly and early. Cabbed out to Universal Studios where Loew-Lewin does its work. Shook hands with Loew and Lewin. Walked over to the stage where they are shooting scenes from *Flotsam.**

*This film, released by United Artists in 1940 as *So Ends Our Night*, was based on Erich Maria Remarque's novel.

Shook hands with Freddy March, he of the somber softness, knowing he is soft, knowing he is a failure, which is what I like about him. [Von] Stroheim was working in the scene too, but he I don't know and did not meet, although he kept giving me the eye as if I were a woman.

Lunch in the commissary. Then back to Lewin's office. We spoke about the picture for an hour, mostly an effort on my part to clear the way for the work to come.

On the way back to the hotel—having made an appointment with my father for dinner—I stopped off to see Fay Wray's girlchild of four. She remembered me from last year and we spent a very pleasant half hour together. Her name is Susan; she is blue-eyed, clear-eyed, and unworried by anything. She is a good child, swift of impulse, chattering and wonderstruck. Sitting there, the mother far away, how I sensed the life of the mother.

Father and his wife here. My connection with them (although I was happy to see him) is a certain form of voluble amiability. He is looking very gray in the thatch but his face looks firm of tone, the color good. They are both in love with California.

No impressions. I think the damned climate is going to put me to sleep again. It usually addles my brains, but this time I may do better since there are no worries or pains but the work to be done on the script. Now to reread *Night Music* for the first time since its Broadway failure.

———•———

Tuesday, August 27, 1940

This morning, my father assisting, started out to find a permanent home. Soon enough found, on Franklin Avenue in Hollywood—the Chateau Élysée. I always thought that a place with such a name must be a place for the miseries. Not at all!—an excellent hotel, spacious and airy rooms, even luxurious, set in a whole block of green grounds. So here I am, settled, unpacked, and very happy about it all. In the late afternoon (long after my father, that business hound, had left off his talking about business, his old boasts about what an unusual fellow he was and is, and had gone home) I walked across the street to one of the spacious California-style food markets and stocked up with very good edibles—best of all, melons as big as your head that sell for only a few cents over a dime! Happiness in the house!

At the studio saw the young boy (now playing the lead in *Flotsam*) who they propose to place in the leading part of *Night Music*. Young and affable, a boy, idealistic, all of that making him look at me with great candid respect, an unusual way for anyone to look at you out here. Think his name is Ford.* It is an easily won bet that in a few years he will get just like the other movie people, bored, sprawling, careless, an overly relaxed fallen angel—they are all affable boys out here, almost tramps.

I don't live life with my eyes very much but this California light is very disturbing to me—thin and intense, quite cool out of the direct sun, something vaguely uncomforting about it.

I keep thinking if only my mother were here with me. What joy for her.

Called up Julie (now John) Garfield. Over he came in a hurry, thinking that he should not be feeling juniorish to me and yet feeling that way. We talked a long time, he mostly uneasy because of a waning connection with his wife and a prurience that makes him, so he said, want to sleep with every woman he looks at. What could Poppa do? I talked to him like Poppa! Of course without moralizing but trying to show him that a certain difficult way of life is a fruitful way. He said that it didn't matter here what you did or who you were—it was only a matter of different brands of canned tuna fish, screen actors, films and all. Correct! Several times, to make certain points about form and disciplined living, it was necessary to read excerpts from this journal. He thoroughly enjoyed himself, said that he had not spent such a night in two years; there is no one here to talk to.

I went to sleep gladly when he left, almost two in the morning—ah, California air!

Nose-bobbing is a major industry out here, by the way. It is now as easy here to change your looks as to have a wart or a tonsil removed. Even Julie's wife had her Jewishness removed. (Really, the aerial perspective is so disturbing here.)

*Odets is correct, the actor is Glenn Ford.

———•———

Thursday, August 29, 1940

Fay Wray is back from her trip and I've just called her and will cross the street and see her in two hours. I know that I have forgotten how very beautiful she is, how womanly and gracious.

The abounding health of everyone here! In the meantime you are falling asleep! Last night came ten o'clock and I was ready to call it a day, the eyelids refusing to work on their hinges. I know the trick now—don't fight it; let it make your hours and habits.

Thought for hours about the movie problems of *Night Music*, read over all the old notes and scripts. The way they start working on a movie here is to construct a plot line, effective and prickly, based on nothing, related to nothing. The prime impulse is to be effective, no matter what about. (I suppose it is the same in their private lives too.)

This is all yesterday that I am writing about. Did not leave the house (twice ate out of the icebox) except to cross the street for an hour's visit with Fay's child. She was bursting with energy and I read her two stories from her book. Suddenly, as children do, she began to fade away; it was the time when she goes to sleep—this glimmering blue gem suddenly lost its sparkle, fell silent, became a piece of colorless glass. When I left, a few minutes later, it was necessary to pick her limp body up off the floor and put her in her nurse's arms.

Today, Thursday, the same calm weather. Last night the fragrance of the garden below, above everything the sweet scent of night-blooming jasmine. Give nature a few inches of top soil here and she works lavish wonders. I think I will buy some more melons, if no one minds.

I am reminded that the Hollywood producer or director usually puts the writer (moi!) in the same relationship as his wife. This outraged me, I remember distinctly, with Milestone. Most of these men treat their wives as something half human, walls or cushioned sofas to lean against. Pah!

Last night, too, I looked at the script I began to write for Milestone before we went to the writing of what later became *Blockade*. Its working title is *Love in the West* and it is possibly an excellent play and movie. I underline the title because I don't want to forget it.

The man makes of his wife something mechanical here, a mechanism. It is exactly what he does in a story conference, with the characters of a movie he is building. The characters are titled with names, boy and girl, but they are not human beings; instead they are dead bodies which can be slung around and moved to and fro to further the plot progression. Real life, in other words, is subordinated to device, cliché, and plot movement—to the supermechanism! This disrespect for human qualities, this lack of genuine life values the average (I do not say all) movie person carries right into his personal life. (Which comes first I am not prepared to say at the moment.) I can hear many a Hollywood writer saying, "Let us leave this place—let us become men again!"

Today came a letter from Rokotov from Moscow, editor of *International Lit*. They are going to translate and print *Golden Boy*. He says it is my most profound play. A very interesting comment from Russia, for here it is regarded as one of my lesser works, myself considering it the same way. There its thematic value is immediately seized upon; here we say it is an exciting melodrama, but is it as exciting as the next one, etc.

Sent a note to Sylvia and Luther, remarking to them of the trip west with Oscar Levant that "I had all of the disadvantages of traveling with a woman with none of the advantages."

The result of the meeting with Fay was that I felt very content. She so complements my own personality that I begin to feel very important, charming, and gifted when with her. She is so adaptable, adjustable, and flexible that whichever way you turn there she is, and all of this done naturally and simply, not with trickery or disgrace. She is a real man's woman, as the saying goes. She'd previously made a dinner appointment elsewhere, so the best we could do was to spend the evening together. I told her when she was here—as it actually was— that it was so difficult to make love in the wide-open shameless California daylight, and so many windows here!

So I had dinner with Julie and his wife, Robbe, she so much like a gleaming little blackberry. We went to a place called Chasen's, where all the movie people were hard at work on expensive dinners. Very difficult for me to walk through them, made me nervous and uneasy. I feel unfriendliness from them, feel it for them, and yet (is it strange?) one wants their approval and approbation (which is the dangerous thing!). Already Julie and wife are a drowsy young pair, conscience being a fatiguing element there too. We chatted fitfully and aimlessly over a long dinner, very expensive, splendiferous, and without the slightest trace of character! The small bottle of good French wine seemed unrelated to anything else on the table.

This unimportant story must be briefed down to the fact that I ended up at Ira Gershwin's house where we played poker till three in the morning, I out almost a hundred and fifty dollars then. Julie drove me home, his wife half asleep, and that was the end of the day.

———————•———————

Friday, August 30, 1940

To get out of bed after five or six hours sleep is not easy here. That I had to do this morning in order to go to [Walter] Wanger's studio with Hanns and see John Ford's latest picture, *The Long Voyage Home*, made by D. [Dudley] Nichols from the short O'Neill sea plays; excellent job.

Back at home I went ahead with my investigation of the movie possibilities of *Night Music*. The trick is to try to throw the play out of one's mind—not easy; unfortunately I am able to look only compassionately at the play script and the people in it. Anyway, I am getting somewhere in a small way.

Fay came over in the late afternoon. We talked, held hands, made love, the blinds drawn, the bed taken down out of the wall—an invention of the devil. So went the balance of the afternoon, the early evening up into the night. She was depressed, from uncertainty, I suppose. I cannot make her life more certain since mine is so uncertain in its own way. She looks at me and seems to say, "Give me the word, give me the word!" My silence on this point saddened her a little, or so it seemed to me.

After she left, past eleven, I went back to the movie, but the night air was heavy upon me and the drowsy self had soon to drag itself to bed.

———————•———————

Saturday, August 31, 1940

And waking with a dream that Geebee was pregnant, patient, and calm, the two of us walking to the front of a large apartment house, my heart pounding uneasily, not knowing what to do.

I had a bookshop send over a book called *Four-Star Scripts*. It contains four first-class movie scripts, particularly the script of *It Happened One Night*, a very successful picture. I wanted to examine it for technique but felt ashamed and hid the book in the desk when I went to join Milestone for luncheon over in Beverly Hills. We talked of Jed Harris, with whom he had had a working combination until a month ago. He adores Jed but is outraged by his inability to sink his ego enough to work with anyone.

He wants a picture story for Ronald Colman and I suggested the *Love in the West* idea. Yes, he was all for that story, had never forgotten it, but the hitch was that he would have to wait for it since I am now busy with Lewin. For myself perhaps, I'll do two pictures in a row—the money situation is going to get tight in this country and the funds from two pictures might see me a long way into the future. I played around in my mind with the idea of perhaps not doing a play this season and staying out here for one or two pictures more.

Milly had been very friendly with John Steinbeck; we talked of him for a time, interesting to me because I want to drive up to Steinbeck's ranch and meet him as soon as possible. We are very different from each other and yet have more in common, I think, than any two writers in the country today.

Milly invited me to stay at his home. He said, too, that there was a very funny play in a false Dies* visiting Hollywood to investigate un-American activities in the movie colony—this to be written to the formula of Gogol's *Inspector General*.

Nothing, I told Milly, opens itself to that satire method more than our country today. I've been turning over satire/farce ideas in my mind for years, the Gogol way seeming to me most adaptable for the American scene. Someday soon it will come about—a first-class (I hope) satiric farce will roll out of this very typewriter. Soon.

---

*Martin Dies, Representative from Texas, won approval to create the Committee to Investigate Un-American Activities (later the House Un-American Activities Committee) in 1938, and was its first chairman.

Sunday, September 1, 1940

I am going to learn something from working on this movie script. That makes me very happy. For one thing must be said, the devils must be given their due—these Hollywood writers know the art (or let me say business) of construction, and practice it as the world has not known it before. It is something to admire.

For instance, the case of Riskin's *It Happened One Night*, which I've just finished carefully reading, although too much care is not necessary as it is all so patent and simple. How effective, though! A series of small beads of scenes, all good-natured, simple, and "human" (American human), is strung on a long line of plot. Each scene serves the purpose of advancing the story and winning the audience. Never of deepening or enriching the characters. What is excellent here (oh, if it could only be done with characters really alive and ample!) is that as you read or watch and listen YOU CAN ONLY THINK & FEEL THE WAY THE WRITER WANTS YOU TO. In short, you are shrewdly manipulated every second the picture is in play. Nothing to lead you astray, in other words. You are on a railroad track, the wheels rolling, and never once does the train derail or stop: from terminal to terminal with not so much as a blocked signal in the way.

Shrewd and inhuman. I will learn from the shrewdness and furnish my own humanity, whatever that is. This is a season of learning for me. Overjoyed at the prospect!

(The virtue and vice of this sort of script is its mechanics. The same is true even of Ibsen, of course on a much higher level of perception and experience.)

Leonard Lyons called—he is here with his wife on vacation. Would I come to a cocktail party that Dorothy Parker was giving for him? Decided to go. Should I ask Fay to come along? As I shaved I resented the fact that I had to call her, that it seemed necessary to explain my moves to someone else. Turned the whole thing over in my mind— called her and asked her if she would come along.

Cocktail party: Dorothy Parker, looking fresh of face, puckered up humorously, telling everyone how well they looked, being a hostess, really good of heart. Georgie Jessel with his much-publicized young bride, a rather brash vulgar girl. Georgie hugged me with pleasure. He said of his wife, "People ask me how it feels to be married to a child. It's wonderful. I mean no [dis]respect, but I wake up in the morning and she's got a doll in one hand and my l—— in the other! Wonderful! No disrespect!"

Melvyn Douglas was there, a leading man with political aspirations, speaking of world affairs very glibly withal with some information. Robert Benchley, shaped like a medicine ball, earnest with Scotch and water, politically minded too. The same for Don Ogden Stewart, looking less fatuous than ever, perhaps helped by his recent marriage to the widow of L. [Lincoln] Steffens. They cornered me in the bedroom and tried to discover "where I stood." I had no secrets and promptly told them I was for Roosevelt and beat the damn Nazis into the soil and more soil on their heads! That seemed to please them both, as if they had a monopoly on common sense.

Everyone liked Fay, who sat there discreetly with a drink. I drank steadily, shaking hands with Artie Shaw, the bandleader, whom Len assured me was a very clever crazy guy; Harry Kurnitz; Norman Foster and his juicy wife, a sister of Loretta Young; and others and others, I forget which others. Boys, boys, not a man in a room-load of them. This prompted me to say to Fay that I must be half woman because wherever I go I look for a man and don't find him. It is part of the painful superficiality of our country.

Fay and I drank more Scotch than we supposed. The proof was that we came back here (Dotty saying good-bye by saying, "Please come again [and meaning it] and bring that beautiful thing with you!") and in a long night, once eating food in the mute kitchen, sporadically flared up in the bed like bursts of fireworks, fell asleep, flared up again, parting only at four in the morning. In short, a bed brawl in the California style.

———•———

Monday, September 2, 1940

A holiday, Labor Day, the streets more quiet than usual.

ITEM: in this climate my beard grows almost twice as fast as elsewhere.

ITEM: there is a group here called "Society for Sanity in Art."

ITEM: an actor gets an interview in the newspaper in which he says that he has induced himself and ten friends not to ride their cars on

Sunday. He says that he has learned that every tenth car here kills a person on Sundays, that if they all stay home they will have saved a human life!

Rode out to Santa Monica to Al Lewin's house. After lunch a conference there, he pleased with most of the story ideas presented to him. I find myself working so hard to make myself heard, so extending myself that the extension becomes an empty form and half the time what I am saying is nonsense.

In the evening Fay and I to Polly Paige's house where Hanns and Lou are guests. Heard many amusing stories from Hanns, who warms up like a furnace when he is the center of attraction. His stories about the peasants of the Ukraine were very touching.

All night I watched Fay, hovered near her, wondered and probed myself about her, thought that it is best to let things take their natural course. Don't be optimistic or romantic—do your work, live your life—see what happens. Above all, trust yourself, your character.

———•———

Tuesday, September 3, 1940

By today, being here a week, I have earned twenty-five hundred dollars. Superbo! Work is speeding up on the movie. I am at a fairly good outline now, worked at it diligently until my father came here in the afternoon.

My father! So much business talk from him—why things did not work out before, how well they are going to work out in the future. Alibis, true or false, are a recent form with him—in the past few years nothing has come right under his hands. He says it is because he is getting old and they don't want gray-haired men; he thanks "the good Lord" that he has me. He keeps stressing his various economies—cheaper shoes, living simply, hasn't bought a new suit for years, etc., etc. He shows me numerous copies of sales letters he has written, goes over all the ads he inserted in various newspapers for jobs.

Now, it seems, the illnesses are coming. The first shy peep since I know him is to tell me that his blood pressure is low, that last year's attack of phlebitis has left its mark on his foot and he is not able to exercise as much as before. Then he said, "And in the meantime I need some money," quickly adding, "This won't last long." Then I tried to make light of the whole thing and he embraced me and tears came to his eyes. I advised a sound thorough medical examination and, calling a Dr. Marx here, felt like his father instead of his son. As I talked on the phone I wondered if he felt any of that, for I saw that I was giving him a comfort, something I was not and have gotten from him.

And yet a vain man, proud as a peacock, literally. Let him go on waving his tail feathers—it is no loss to me.

By appointment Leland Hayward, the agent, sent his car and driver for me to take me to see his wife, Margaret Sullavan, at their house. First we picked him up at his office. I don't know him well. He made agent's talk about playwrights getting better sales terms from the movies.

I was interested in seeing her generally and particularly, the latter because she is going to play in the *Night Music* movie. She has real charm, apologized for being dressed up—they were going to go out for dinner later—she was not really like this. Sprinkled with gold dust a little—after all, a movie actress. An interesting impulse and refusal of the impulse in her; inwardly still uncertain of herself, that giving much of the charm. (I had no difficulty adjusting to her.) She is womanly, after all the mother of two small girls whom I saw later before their bedtime. She is "regular," has an impulse to say small barbed things but immediately withdraws them. She has a real horror of putting on "airs," refuses to take them from anyone else. My hotel, she said, was a place where she always stayed in between her marriages. Then looking at her husband and smiling, "Of course I haven't been there for a long time." She demands the right to be reckless in small things. Each time her husband would make an agent's remark, typically careful, reserved, or noncommittal, she would plunge ahead to say the truth of what she felt. For instance, about the Lewin script she is working in now—didn't like it, was disappointed. Her husband, on the other hand, said that he thought Lewin was a good man as a producer. I don't mean by this that her husband is a bad fellow—I don't know him that well and he is reserved—but after all he is an agent with a typical activity in life.

They had to be off to dinner (I thought it unfair of them to have invited me there for an hour) so we spent only a few more minutes downstairs. Evidently she felt uncomfortable about having to dismiss me; I made it easy by saying I was going and of course she said they were in no hurry. She is very intuitive, still restless underneath, although she says a happy marriage and children has put her here to stay if necessary and she will not mind. My sense was that she was afraid somewhat of the outer world, of being put up in a high place to be slapped by the outrageous slings of fortune.

When we walked to the door, her husband half-dressed in dinner clothes, I felt very depressed and she knew it, although I hadn't shown my face. She said for me to come again. I said I would. She said it again, insistently, herself feeling depressed for some reason. Again I said I would come again, neglecting to say, "When you invite me." A third time she said this as I was climbing into their car to be driven home by their chauffeur. We said good night twice and I drove away, the air chilly, the night so suddenly dark, so depressing. I wanted to burst into tears and didn't speak to the driver all the way home, although we had chatted about everything going out there, about Roosevelt versus Willkie, English fascists, and whatnot.

Home, I bought some more melons, a pound of ground steak for dinner, feeling all the time like some eccentric recluse, which is what depressed me. And yet, to tell the truth, I don't know who is really eccentric—a successful man like Hayward, business, family, and all— or myself, unsatisfied in many fundamental respects, alone, always yearning like an unrequited schoolgirl during her first love affair. And that, by the way, is the kind of girl Margaret Sullavan is too.

Tomorrow I must meet with Lewin for a story conference, so will go ahead for the rest of the night on the movie outline.

Wednesday, September 4, 1940

Why write in here if there is nothing to write? For today there is nothing to write, except that when I came back from the studio, past five in the afternoon, Fay came over here looking as beautiful as any woman you want to see by land or sea! We talked briefly of the political situation in the world, finally coming to the fact that there was not one thing that you could be for today, not with certainty that what you were for you would be for tomorrow too. Nothing moves so fast in life today as a political situation.

Most of the day I spent at Lewin's studio, a dull place peopled by dull people. Lewin was so busy with the picture in progress—a snip here, snap there—that I could not converse with him for more than an unbroken half hour at a time. Of course that is very annoying.

In the evening took Hanns and wife to dinner, Fay and I. Good food, something! Then a poor movie, MGM's finest, *Pride and Prejudice*. Pasta fazoola! Now home, past midnight, disgruntled. Think I will eat another melon and consider the bed. A dull life among the aborigines, mates!

The average actress tries to give all of herself in a performance and so ends with giving nothing. If she would give two or three carefully chosen elements of her own character it would be interesting and singular.

But did not go straight to bed. Instead wrote a note to Geebee, then a letter after it, thinking the note too brief and it already in the mail. This makes me smile, but I can't help it—here I think of her and how girlish and beautiful she looks, there I think of Fay and how womanly and beautiful she seems. Boy, boy, what do you want?

A very interesting music, if you but listen, is the sound of heavy traffic which you cannot see.

All my boyhood and youth I thought of the word *nobility* and what it meant. Nobility of heart and soul, of mind, were big items in my thinking and feeling life. Who fits that word today? What minds even think it? None I know. It seems a remote romantic attribute. But INSOLENT! Who is not today?

———————

Thursday, September 5, 1940

Well, I see that you will have to turn more and more to this journal for solace while you are out here. And yet there must be some way to make people talk of what they know best—the writer can talk about his writing problems, the cameraman about his problems, the marketman about his melons. How do you get them started? Try tomorrow.

In the early afternoon I went to the studio for a conference with Lewin. No use: we can't get an unbroken hour together. Right now I don't mind this, but in another week I will walk out and go home and wait till he calls me. Today I suggested that we meet at night, so tomorrow I'll have dinner at his house with the hope of spending five hours together after.

I was introduced to a Paramount writer who happened to be on our lot. He had just finished a script, he said, and was waiting for his producer's okay. He said this reminded him of the schoolteacher who was being examined for a job by the rural schoolboard. Testing his knowledge, the chairman of the board asked him if the world was round or flat. He answered, wanting the job, "I can teach it either way, gentlemen!" All the work is to make the characters as likable as possible through the most conventional means.

The people around the studios seem at first to deserve congratulations for their constant affability. You soon learn that you were wrong—instead their asses should be kicked, high and low. It is the affability of a fellow lying in the sun, his belly full of good food.

Later I joined Milestone and wife at Chasen's restaurant. Seated at the table with the Milestones and party, I admired most Miss Betty Field, who sat across the way. I admired her with desire, if I may say so, thought about calling her on the telephone. She is hot in coolness, so to speak, attractive, even though I wrote here about her shallow girlhood once. There is an interesting quality about her—I can't place it yet—a sort of suspended animation, as if she were caught in her senses, overpowered by them, like a person listening to a persuasive voice that you don't hear as you sit beside her. Well, nothing will come of this.

Milly said two things that interested me. Eleanor Holm, the backstroke swimming champ, he said, once stated that she was the only woman who ever made good in Hollywood by being on her back in an honorable way.

Von Stroheim, when he used to direct, made use of opposites in a very theatrical way. If a wedding, for instance, was taking place, a funeral was passing outside. A man raped a woman at the base of a church altar; and a boy and girl made love sitting on a sewer.

So the day and night.

————— • —————

Friday, September 6, 1940

According to today's newspaper (or Hearstpaper, which is not really a newspaper), four men committed suicide. One of them left a note with a postscript which the paper termed enigmatic. The P.S. said, "Money is the only friend you have."

Too, four men, according to an AP dispatch, were beheaded in Germany today for treason. Let me remember these unsung heroes here: Kaiser, Worm, Zink, and Busson, fifty, thirty-one, thirty, and forty-eight, Josef, Rudolph, Karl, and Wilhelm. Live long, unseen friends!

In the meantime, today England is huddled under the worst air bombardment of the war. At Dover it took over ten minutes to count the planes passing a given point.

Under the influence of friend Stendhal (he so scornful throughout his writing of the bourgeoisie) I must admit that the quality in my own character most irking to me is my BOURGEOIS CAUTION.

Secrecy is another middle-class quality in my makeup. Yet this secrecy, sometimes reserve, is a very good thing for the artist. I remember that some painter, Degas or Manet, said that the creation of every artwork should have about it something of the secrecy of a crime, such intentness and privacy. Yes, true of a creation, and just as true of the creation of an inner personal life, a thing these pages stand for.

Well, after all, I am the playwright of the middle class, that can't be denied. But there is middle class and middle class, Beethoven and Brahms, for example. No, idiot, I did not say I was a Beethoven or a Brahms. (And there you see the caution at work!)

Called [Erich Maria] Remarque, the German writer, thinking he might be an interesting man to meet. He answered the telephone but refused to admit that he was Remarque, insistently demanding to know who was calling. As doggedly I refused to tell him unless I knew to whom I was speaking. Finally, with grim disgust, he admitted his identity; a moment later he apologized: "Excuse me, they are always trying to sell you wine and things on the telephone, or to have long conversations with you." He said he was finishing the rewriting of a novel and would be happy if I came there for a drink early next week.

The other day, seeing her pass by in the Universal commissary,

Lewin referred to Marlene Dietrich's "alumni association." Remarque seems to be a disconsolate member of it.

It is a mistake to elevate to the dignity of a principle whatever you find to be good for yourself. Middle class too, laddie! The middle class is always intolerant, will not live and let live.

Very feelingful was the experience of driving past Westwood Village, that little white mushroom of a place where Luise and I had lived together. I saw us in that little warm white bedroom together, attitudes of love felt, smelled, tasted—had! It was no wonder that I stared at the two women in a curious way when we reached Al's house. His wife finally said, "Don't stare at me as if I am saying something profound." I explained what I had been thinking; they laughed; I smiled; it was done.

Al and I worked well for several hours. The ladies returned from a poor movie (suffice it to say movie!), and I drove home.

———————•———————

Saturday, September 7, 1940

First I want to quote a few lines from a book on German literature by a man named Felix Bertaux. He says of T. Mann the following: " . . . he invariably takes life at a point where it seems to degenerate, to struggle against destruction, to seek a discipline." I mention this because it is so clearly expressed, true or not, and because it is possibly the theme of my next play, part of the theme of my present living days.

If one waits and trusts the whole self, everything comes together in the end. Here I am talking about the problem of the American man, living in America today, becoming an artist. (No, one is not born an artist. One is born with talent or with genius, but one makes himself an artist.) Nothing is more difficult than this process of becoming an artist.

The young writer here seldom understands his own nature. It is like some magic cow that chews and chews whatever is in sight. It drinks water, absorbs sun and air—it is a female organism. And then it gives milk, or milk is taken from it. The cow does not understand what made the milk; the artist seldom understands what made the artwork. But a certain passivity is germane to creation (call it creative repose, perhaps).

Now let us sketchily look at the American man, particularly when he has made a quick and popular success with a first work or two. Firstly, he resents being milked. He wants respect and power, wants to "be as good as," not realizing that competition is the breath of death (the artist is never in competition!). He begins to look for immediate awards and rewards, strains for recognition and fame beyond the next man. He wants to appear complete and upright in the eyes of his fellow Americans, never NEVER ridiculous or at a loss. He looks always for status, demands guarantees of who he is and exactly where he is going. He develops a protective complex THAT ENDS BY COMPLETELY CLOSING HIM UP (or say the lactic glands dry up)! And that is the end, for if there is no giving nature, there is no artist! Where there is no OPENNESS, there is no artist! (Exactly the same, let it be said, is true of the woman in our modern society.)

Young artist, you must permit yourself to be milked, jeered at, rained and snowed on. YOU MUST KEEP OPEN AT ALL COSTS, bearing ridicule, accepting all the pains and "incompletions." Yours is always the power of birth, of giving, of being open for the take—you are not the taker in this sense of the word.

So, as I started to say, everything comes together. All of the weeks of entries in this journal stream to this page. And this page explains, too, why I have been so moved during the past months by the problems of women in the world today. For whatever is the problem of a woman is the problem of the artist today.

Furthermore, now I can see what I fought in Luise so desperately, albeit instinctively. I fought her attempt, not deliberate on her part, to close me up and so destroy me as an artist. Or shall I say I fought her attempt to keep me open *only for herself*, which amounts to the same thing! If she had wisely permitted me to stay open for all and everything, I would have been all open for her: we should still be married, happily too.

I am sending a copy of this entry to Harold Clurman as answer to his letter of a few weeks ago. Many of these things he said in the letter, but I said them first, many times in this journal, again and again. (It seems important to me to have said them first!)

Really, how much more important to me is this journal than the completion of a play or even two!

———•———

Sunday, September 8, 1940

The freshness of being here is dying away. The days and nights become the same. By tomorrow I will have earned five thousand dollars since being here.

Thought several times about Betty Field. Found, too, that she is living in this very hotel. Ridiculous of me to have called her agent and asked where she lived, asking him to call me back here. I squirm when I think of the romantic things I think of a girl I don't even know.

————•————

Monday, September 9, 1940

When I asked about Miss Field today, the elevator boy told me that she has moved. Moved? Well, no, but she had gone out on location—working on a picture for Paramount. Here I will say what my dream was of her. It seems to me that she is much like Cleo in *Rocket*. Suppose, I thought, mused—dreamed—suppose you married a girl like that, determined to develop in her every one of her latent possibilities. Cleo I think of as the hope of America. I will write the further adventures of Cleo again and again, and this young and maturing person will play the part. This will be a unique and valuable relationship, one in which both of us will grow—a valuable working and living relationship in which we cannot help growing richer, deeper in values.

So goes the dream. The fact is laughable. The elevator boy told me, too, that the day before I'd rode up in the elevator with Miss Field but hadn't recognized her!

In the evening I enjoyed a ride out to Santa Monica where I had dinner with the Lewins and later worked rather abortively with Al on the movie. He said, at dinner, that there were great stories waiting to be written about Hollywood characters of the past. People seemed smaller today, less living, less inspired, tamed, without magnitude. I observed that the same was true all over the country. I could only liken the change to aviators who once flew wild, by instinct almost, without instruments. In their battles with the elements they developed and quickened all of their senses. They grew inventive, alive in all parts and COPED with strange and difficult circumstances.

Today, with the development of commercialized aviation (and so standardization, sure concomitant of commerce), the aviator uses nothing but his eyes. Nothing need quicken or awaken him—HIS NEED TO COPE IS NECESSARILY REDUCED TO THE MINIMUM!

All of this, I feel, IN ALL WALKS OF LIFE, is cutting down the modern man and woman to a certain size and form.

———————•———————

Tuesday, September 10, 1940

It is beginning again, waking up in a stupor each morning, unable to shake it off for hours. In these cases the daylight outside makes me even more timid and awkward than ever. Sometimes I do not leave my room for hours, often not till evening has come.

I spent an hour with Lewin at the studio. The progress of the work is, to me, unsatisfying, although Lewin thinks we are moving rapidly. Today they sent me my first salary check, three weeks' salary (by contract) at once. Taxes deducted in advance by the sovereign state of California, the amount is over seven thousand dollars. Immediately to the bank, a hundred in cash in my pocket. Truthfully, I feel this money is two-thirds unearned. But this is the movie business and I am still one of the fastest writers who ever hit the Hollywood trail. And yet, foolishly, I can't resist a small squirm of shame as I take the money. Ha! Just let them try to give me less!!

I said in a joke, meeting Hanns and Lou, with Fay [Kendall] for dinner: "Well, let us go out and spend the hundred dollars in my pocket on a good dinner." Hanns took me seriously, immediately protesting with a very sober mien: No! "I do not allow it," he said quickly, startling me with this intensity.

Perhaps this was why he told me, a few minutes later, about the good men in concentration camps in the south of France, most of them wanted by the Nazis. He said that relief was being sent to the men with famous names, but that these "unknowns" were in for hell at the hands of the Nazis unless aid was sent, aid in the form of money with which to ship them to Mexico where the government will permit entrance. But what is one to do? Each man needs over three hundred dollars for passage. (Later I'll send money for one.)

After the dinner we tried to find a movie to see. Tried, that's all, for all the theatres are engarlanded in garbage. Finally we found the much-discussed *The Ramparts We Watch* and saw it. It's a documentary film made by the editors of *Life* and *Time* magazines, deals with how a small town in America was aroused to entering the last war against Germany. Admitting that the film makes good and necessary propaganda against today's Nazis, nevertheless it was a depressing film to me, for it explains our entrance into the last war in terms of the very phrases and emotional pulls of 1915–17, as if since then no one has learned the truth about what made the last war for us! A web, a web, they are weaving the web again! What will happen? Where will we be in a year or two or three? It cannot be answered, cannot be seen.

At home, two in the morning, I read Stendhal for an hour, liked this idea: "It is necessary to put fresh events between ourselves and our grief, even if we do it by breaking an arm." Sic!

———•———

Wednesday, September 11, 1940

Put yourself to the test with whatever you are afraid of. Learn the truth of yourself in all ways. After you have learned the truth, learn to accept it. (How easy to write this, even up to this parenthesis!)

John Barrymore, our first actor, fast going to pieces, has just opened here in a movie satirizing the last few years of his life as roué and drunkard [*The Great Profile*]. Last night Hanns Eisler said, "We must see this remarkable film. The first time I know for a dying actor to spit in his own grave."

The climate has this effect on me: the sex impulses are dormant and I urinate steadily, three times an hour.

I decided to visit Remarque. It was a very pleasant meeting; for him too, I hope. In one room, where we sat, were four Cézannes, an unusual Utrillo, and a small but first-class Daumier. I admired the paintings very much but said I knew more about the qualities in music;

he said he had gone from being a music student to a great lover of paintings.

From the first, excepting a few minutes but not more, we were very easy with each other. He aroused confidence in me, something another person rarely does. He was masculine, strong and yet tender, with a quiet humor which played only around his lips. He has a German solidity but to this is added a slight touch of elegance, something sensitive and sniffing, although he does not point this quality at you. He was shy about his English, which naturally hampered his expressiveness; said he spoke German and French very fluently.

Right now he is finishing a rewrite of a novel which has already appeared in *Collier's* magazine. In fact it is the story *Flotsam*, which Lewin is now making into a picture. He said he found this arduous work, a grind, but he was sticking to it so that it might be published before the picture appeared.

I saw or felt that I was trying to pour too much into one hour, ideas of form and technique, ideas of American life contrasted to European, etc., etc. Instead we turned to a discussion of European actresses. This was done by mentioning Luise, whom he had seen once or twice—he knew we had been married. He sighed, groaned humorously, said, "Do not tell me—I do not ask you—tell me about her only when you like to do it." He said his father had been a very sensible helpful man in his life, and that he had said, "Never fall in love with an actress." His father was right, he had discovered, he said. He said these actresses were so typical that he was sure he would be describing mine if he described his own, meaning Marlene Dietrich. He said such women fell in love with men with minds, loved and admired and built them up for that, but really the only sort of artists they really understood were actors. He laughed as he said, "Then they hit you hard on the head and you fall, you are stunned—you don't know where you are. But next they are saying, 'Why do you have such a long face? That man over there, look how charming he is to me.'"

Near eight o'clock I left. A kind of sober mask fell on both of us, as if we had been a little ashamed of our garrulity. It seemed to me as if we were two men who had been yearning for weeks to talk to someone. Anyway, I was heartily glad to have made the visit. We promised to meet again soon.

For the rest of the night, after an omelette supper on my own kitchen table, I worked for several hours on the story line of the movie.

I could not go to bed, was restless—read half of a Molière play and finally climbed into the bed past 4:00 A.M.

A letter came from Geebee. Well?

I spoke to Fay on the phone. Well?

Who are you, Beautiful Unknown? Well?

———•———

Thursday, September 12, 1940

A letter from Harold Clurman in the morning. The Group needs funds with which to run the office. He suggests asking Milestone for a loan. Also, he is sending out a script of Irwin Shaw's new play [*Retreat to Pleasure*], thinks I might arrange for movie backing for it.

The tone of this journal annoyed me when I looked back glancingly at some of the past entries. My God, boy, don't you like anything!? Well, in extenuation, much of the seeming intolerance comes from the activity of taking an attitude about everything. But, of course, this need of taking an attitude is almost as unpleasant as the intolerance! Swine! (And yet look how easily you let yourself off.)

Lewin came here for dinner and work. The dinner we had elsewhere; returned here at nine. I am strained with him. I am always on the verge of telling Lewin that I think that what he is saying is nonsense; peace were better—you are not an artist here! I disagree with him on the end of the story but will soon agree. You are a businessman here: do your business! But keep clear to him that it IS business, not art! A movie producer walking around a lot with his claque is just like a pasha in his harem. Or like a rooster in the barnyard with adoring clucking hens around him.

———•———

Friday, September 13, 1940

Lewin in the morning. I felt ashamed, like a virgin, to let him see me in a half-stupefied condition, but I received his suggestions for concluding the story, said they seemed all right to me at the time—which they did—said I'd type them up in story outline and bring them to the studio in the late afternoon.

At the studio I gave Lewin the outline, which he thought near completion. He has given it to his partner, Loew, and tomorrow we'll have a conference about it. Then I walked on to the *Flotsam* set and spent a half hour with M. Sullavan, who was very shy and nervous with me. I said I'd be happy to come to her house again if invited; she said I must invite myself; I said that was painful; it ended by my taking her phone number.

She is going to have another and third baby. She so informed Lewin today. He and partner are worried, or distressed. It means the picturization of *Night Music* will have to be delayed. Apparently my contract with them reads that it must be done by a certain time or all the rights revert back to me; I said for them not to worry. I thought Miss Sullavan very attractive.

Too, at night, after having dinner with Fay, we went to a movie and it appeared that along with a few million other American men, I find Miss Ann Sheridan, movie player, very attractive. Sure 'nuff, honey!

How can I confess this? I do not want to admit it to myself, no less write it down here. How can I marry her? Every day I am getting uneasier. How can I give her the stabilizing word when it is not true in me first?

I am going to read Stendhal, MY FRIEND, for a half hour and go to bed again. From now on I shall refer, be warned, to these days as "melon days." But soon the taste for melons will sicken with surfeit and I shall call them simply "nothing days"!

Saturday, September 14, 1940

A literary morning! At the studio at past eleven in the morning to hear what Dave Loew had to say about the story line of *Night Music*. He had little to say, that not being his forte. The little saying done, we all retired to the commissary for lunch. Lewin asked me if I was interested in giving a contribution to a committee set up by William Allen White called the Committee for Defending America by Helping England Now. I said that I was not sure that such a committee interested me, later in the afternoon explaining that I thought Hitler should be punished for his crimes but so should certain British imperialists, the group headed by the appeasing Chamberlain; Lewin agreed with a sad smile but added that we could not make too fine a division at the moment.

Freddie March joined us at the lunch table and accepted one of the contribution blanks, saying that he was not sure he would fill it out as he had already given an ambulance to France and contributed heavily to the Red Cross. Freddie tells sort of heavy doughy jokes, and now proceeded to tell a couple which were as heavy as the luncheons he eats, as if he had been digging ditches all morning.

Seeing the products of the previous day's shooting, looking at parts of *Time* magazine—finally I get tired of waiting for Lewin and head back for his office. In his office he has an informative but undistinguished book on the lives of great composers. The essay on Beethoven adds to my general gloom—gloom for the offended ego, gloom about Fay, and gloom about the long line of one's life, which is what the Beethoven essay makes me begin to think about. What I am thinking about is that without my impelling faith and belief in the high future of mankind, I am nothing! The unyielding quality of Beethoven's life makes me think that I am so yielding, growing cynical and weary, that I am so easily seduced (not all true)—the flame may easily turn to cinder is what I think.

For all your talk (you with the thinning hair I am talking about), there is a real acute resistance in you against learning that which does not come easily. Are you aware of this? Specifically?

So here I am, young artist, trying to construct a life against the possible day of being called to give a year of the life for military service. Am I worried or nervous? I am both, although I think my eyes, my bad right foot, and my support of relatives will put me in the deferred class.

How do I feel about national conscription in peacetime? I must be honest and say I don't know. Not abused, it could be a fine thing for the youth of the country. Youth here (don't quote me just now) needs a discipline imposed from above, a form imposed from above, as no other youth of the world is needful.

I know the good thing to say and often say it. But that does not mean I know the good thing to do. So one keeps the self in a good light.

At dinnertime I called Julie Garfield. The moment I heard his wife's voice on the phone I knew they had been quarreling. With some persuasion they agreed to join me [for dinner] and called here for me. We went to Chasen's, which swarmed with movie people. Charlie Chaplin, for instance, walked by with Mr. Justice Frank Murphy; in the booth next to us sat Dotty Parker and her group. For a half hour, our dinner gone down the hatch, we were joined by Miss Elaine Barrie, not at all a bad girl, now nervous, talking a blue streak, uncomfortable and tense, headed for a nervous breakdown. She knew all my plays, even quoting some of the lines and teasing me out of discomfort for being silent and judicial, which I was not, instead being very sympathetic and sorry for her. It touched me that she looked at me as if I should be able to settle some of the problems of her hectic young life by a few choice words.

Julie and Robbe came up here for a few minutes before we parted past three in the morning. I talked of my play plans and of the difficulty of keeping one's head in this marsh of success and glamour. They left and I turned to the bed well satisfied with myself, even glowing. Why? I had been a success during the evening!

———————•———————

Sunday, September 15, 1940

In the evening Fay and I went to the house of the Paiges where, with Hanns and Lou, they gave a small dinner. Many people joined us later, among them James M. Cain and wife and pressingly nubile young daughter; Shepard Traube and wife; [E. E.] Paramore, writer and wife; Julie and Robbe, who dined with us too; and a few others.

Hanns, flushed with a good dinner and wine, played a long group of Schubert songs as I have never heard them played or sung, even though his singing was fierce. Instead of reverie there was almost revenge, a quality I have never heard before in Schubert. Was I bewitched? Hardly, for I saw that Hanns was adding some of his own temperament and talent to the performances. But I could see that so much of Schubert is never expressed by the professional concert singers.

The evening wore on; people drank, smoked, played backgammon, or talked. Cain interested me—he looks and talks like a confident mule-team driver, very American, full of "common sense," every small thing just as important to him as the large, slow, and heavy, even a little ponderous. Not at all a bad man, but not at all an artist—nothing like the high-class pulp he writes.

The Paiges, for some inexplicable reason, had a photograph of André Malraux and myself taken during a visit at the Paramount studio some four years ago. Here it is, during the first year of my marriage with Luise, myself thin and worried, a mute testimonial of a nervous year of early development.

———————•———————

Monday, September 16, 1940

Today, in the march of time, a footnote. In other words, a melon day! But I had a healthful hour of sun on the roof from noon to one. In the middle a female voice asked timidly if the booth was occupied. When I came out, dressed to the gills, there was sitting Helen Westley, calm, relaxed (although she quickly pulled up the strap of her bathing suit), grinning, and saying, "Oh, so it was you in there!" A curious dame, that one. Her quality is something like, "No matter what happens I live my life"—just a statement of fact, never challenging.

My father visited me next. Again he is wrapped up in one of his grand projects. He is getting out a small booklet which tells business-men what is wrong with business. It ends with him offering his service as a combination merchandising and advertising man. I feel certain nothing will come of it, but in the meantime he wanted my advice, the grammar corrected, a word of encouragement, and a dash of admira-tion. I think I gave him all of it, although I am no hand at encouraging nonsense. A painful situation any way you look at it, unfortunately bound to be more painful for him in the end.

Then I called Fay out of a sense of duty, not more, to be honest. I told her I'd have to work. Instead, an hour later, I called Julie and asked him if he cared to go to a movie. He did and we went, seeing Milestone's new picture, a light comedy with spots of real charm.

On the way to the theatre a man, when we tooted our horn, asking him to move over so we could round the corner, this man turned and swore at us so violently, calling us such filthy names, that even Julie, rougher and tougher than me, was shocked. I mention it because this sort of filthy abuse, this violence, this wrath lies so close under the surface in American life. Julie and I moved on to the theatre in shocked sober silence, uncomfortable, saying nothing to each other about the incident.

Another American note: after the movie we had coffee in the Brown Derby. A woman came over and asked Julie for his autograph, presenting the reverse side of her auto driver's license for the signature. Then she turned the card and showed him her name. "Did you ever see a name like that? Read it—it makes a whole sentence," she said. Julie read the name aloud: "Anna Mae Laywell." "I like you," she said, "See all of your pictures." Getting no response, she left.

To consciously fix limitations of the self (accepting the boundaries of the self) is an act of locating the self (situating). Few Americans will do this, preferring instead to live in hopes of another or "better" self. Thus the self never grows, never functions or realizes itself.

———————•———————

Tuesday, September 17, 1940

I spent an hour at the studio and am now ready to work alone, reporting to Lewin only once a week with finished material. Up, heart!

In the evening Fay and I went to the house of Dolores del Rio in Bel Air. We were to have dinner with her and Orson Welles, her light of love. She is a typically Mexican woman, charming, feminine, chatting lightly, and feeling about anything that catches her eyes. We drove to a restaurant where Welles joined us later, tired with work. He was very gracious and articulate, as usual, in fact articulate enough to be very glib. I did not mind this. He is a sort of biological sport, stemming out of Lord Byron through Oscar Wilde, I should say. But he has a peculiarly American audacity. Of other people he said just what he thought of them, with scorn and derision; with us he was deferential, once referring to me as "in the foremost ranks of the talents of the world"!

I liked best when he suddenly said of himself, "I have a touch of rhinestones in my blood," meaning he is part-charlatan.

This dinner, as I later told Fay, depressed me because I want to do and be all the things he is being and doing. A prime trouble with me is wanting to be all men; wanting, too, as Welles is trying to do, to beat the game. I want to be a poor poet and a powerful businessman, a sensational young man and a modest artist with a secret life. I understand every impulse in the American man because I naturally have the impulses myself.

I found that I disagreed with everything Welles said and like him in spite of that. He is a very octopus of ego, but for all of that there is a good side to him, a sense, for instance, of humble people. A communion of intelligence is possible with him; finally, too, he also is in opposition to the values around him, even though they may finally swallow him up.

———————•———————

Sunday, September 22, 1940

Entries for the last four days are missing because I have been busy with the movie script and because one whole night was spent in a poker game. Here are the missing days as I make them out from scribbled notes on the desk.

WEDNESDAY: Geebee has written me a distressed note. She has read an item in Winchell's column, to wit: "New York is talking about Fay Wray's breathless romance with Clifford Odets." She begs for the truth of the matter, apologizing twice for seeming foolish. Now I must write and tell her there is no breathless romance with the lady in question, but neither is there one with her. How can one dismiss without seeming to dismiss, without hurting a sweet and idealistic girl?

I often grow disgruntled and depressed out of a combination of fear, cowardice (evasion of what seems to me to be duty) and simple inability to handle practical details. This makes a really UNMANLY attitude towards many problems and some persons. As with Fay tonight—I did not want to call her or see her (oh, breathless romance!), began to find myself very disgruntled. Finally I said to myself, "Call her. Tell her exactly what is on your mind. Be clear, simple, candid, instead of whimpering here in the loneliness of one room, evening falling outside!"

ITEM: the rock-bottom trouble with the movies is their ideal of complete ACCESSIBILITY.

ITEM: the fear and evasion of responsibility and duty towards the woman, this beginning to often preclude the possibility of pleasurable love connection makes the self autoerotic too.

ITEM: this basic fear of exposure, of not exposing one's self to life.

THURSDAY: The first of the gray expressionless days here, a high fog above. There is a whole season here of such days. Too, mourning doves on the lawn here with their soft coos.

Late last night I discovered that my movie contract orders me to finish a first draft of the movie in six weeks—beyond that I am not paid, except for time devoted to revisions. This angered me because it is such a stupid contract, made by an agent who calmly collects ten percent of my income, no less!

Those neurotic back pains came back in flashes, waiting for me to make up my mind about giving in to them. They were aggravated or started perhaps by the excessive amount of typing I'd been doing.

In the evening, when I'd gone to a poker game, the pains came back strongly. There is a good characterization in what happens to me in a poker game. Losing, I get good-humored (perhaps afraid of being bad-natured!) and witty, cracking jokes at my own expense, sighing in a certain comical way, growing rueful, very giddy and alert simultaneously. You may see the whole life cycle of a man in one card game—his attitude in the face of disappointment and defeat, victory, etc.

FRIDAY: up in the early evening. Spoke to Fay on the phone. Went over and spent a half hour with her and child.

SATURDAY: notes, answers to mine, came from Theodore Dreiser and Albert Basserman. A letter from my cousin, Frank Lubner, who is a Navy recruiting officer in Oklahoma City. He says he has been thinking about me in relation to the draft and wants to help me by finding something easy for me in case I am called. I will answer and thank him, for I am finding myself very worried about the possibilities of being conscripted. More worried than I want to write here.

Fay and I to dinner, feeling very relaxed with her, nothing begrudging in my conduct. At home (Fay across the street in her home) I wrote notes to Geebee and Ouida Campbell, from whom I'd received a letter. To Geebee I broke the bad news, as softly as possible, regretfully.

An indifferent week, as you can see.

———————•———————

Thursday, September 26, 1940

All the days run together here—one cannot be told from the other. In the meantime I am working on the script of the movie, fifty pages of it finished, more than one-fifth of the script.

Leading trends: I am very worried about the drafting bill, worried about being conscripted. In Europe the war is going on fiercely, planets hurling themselves at each other—millions of tense, straining men at and upon each other in an embrace of death (no, no poetic figuration!). Now Japan is making trouble, now French colonials prodded on by German agents. The United States may soon be in the war up to the hilt.

I am thinking about staying here and doing another picture after this one. I scarcely know why; at least one makes money here and that is some guarantee of a future.

No element of success, not one, has given me any pleasure. I tell you this because I am thinking it. My self-esteem swims low, where the frogs and algae are.

Two days ago I awoke from a horrible dream. My father was having an affair in a big hotel with a woman other than my mother. Relatives called me away from my work to make me comb the hotel and find my father. I was burning with anger but could not find him. Finally I rode away in a car; he drove after me in a bus, jumping out of it to taunt and tease me with a comedian of a companion. This dream horrified me. A few hours later my father actually called me on the phone; I was unable to speak to him with civility.

In the afternoon I said one of the few spontaneously witty things I've ever said. At the lunch table at the studio: "So far as women are concerned, I am interested in volume and quick turnover." Even if it is not exactly true!

I think Fay, my present love, proves that I am not ready for marriage and never will be. I am unable to give up and there is not help for it. Last night Fay was here. In all ways she is admirable, worthy of a man's love, of a good marriage. I doubt if I shall ever meet a woman more suited to me. Shall I be romantic? Then I will say that I do not love her.

Last night she comes here at seven. Our avowed intention is to go out for dinner. She looks serious, treads lightly, looks soulful. I jest; I scorn; I scold myself. She tells me she "feels funny." I understand immediately that she means she is going to have a baby, although she is not certain. She has missed a period. I say I will be properly concerned when I know that what she says is a fact, not a feeling. She says she never misses a period unless, on second thought, she has been in the mountains, and she has been in the mountains recently. I tell her frankly that I don't know what a man is expected to say at such a time. To say he is concerned is her answer. I assure her that she should know I am concerned, of course a silly remark. Of course I am being cautious; I know I don't love her. Perhaps she sees a future together; I do not. Then I see that she wants to get in bed. I undress her and myself after her; naked, we rub together; after two hours of intense lovemaking (and she smelling like Luise!) we fall asleep in the cool room. At midnight we wake up, surprised that we slept so long. We go out for some supper. I feel sick, in a cold sweat, and say so, smiling to myself to think how I have taken the stage away from her with this nicotine sickness, which is what it is. I take her to her door (really sick but trying to make little of it); tomorrow she is going to the doctor for a pregnancy test. At home I try to go right to bed, am exhausted—but it is an hour before I can fall asleep, having to be up early for an appointment at the studio with Lewin and the movie script, an interloper in my life. Oh, piss on your life!

The afternoon of yesterday was better. By previous appointment went to see Theodore Dreiser, who has been living here, I learned, in a Hollywood court for the past two years—he has been sick and the climate is good for his health. He is living with a women, perhaps his wife, of about forty. He is around seventy. The woman looks like a character in Toulouse-Lautrec without the evil. The man I respect, and my opinions opposed to his are unimportant in the face of the respect he arouses in me. He is the only American writer I have met who arouses this respect in me; Hemingway is a boy alongside of him, and Sinclair Lewis a sort of zany who missed the boat. This man has dignity and stature, the last so unusual that all may be forgiven in the face of it.

We talked about the movies and their stupidities. He looks at you with old blue and sort of blind eyes, his head heavy and big, Germanic, if anything. He is another one of those men who arouse confidence in me. His views on affairs in the world and America are as progressive as a colt's. He seems to speak from a deep wisdom—I loved him, perhaps more the IDEA of him; which, I don't know. Anyway, it is not something to probe now. I left, making an appointment for dinner next week. To respect and admire someone living—whee!

Today I tried to smoke less, was unable to do so. This sickened and disgusted me.

Two days ago Fay's child had a birthday, is four. Six children attended. I walked in there to watch them. Children are very saddening—they tremble so, on the brink of tragedy. Even the most joyous child I want to sweep up to my chest and cry over.

Anyway, good night. I have a bad cold and a little fever. I have eaten my melon, said no prayers (to what, to what, to what does one pray????); now go to sleep, unhappy man.

At least I have learned to wait. Have you?

I think so.

————•————

Friday, September 27, 1940

Thomas Wolfe's new and last book [*You Can't Go Home Again*] just came out. I will mention it here, remembering the time I rode south to his funeral and almost got killed myself outside of Lynchburg, Va.

The movie producer will say, "The boy wouldn't act that way." I'll answer, "This boy would act that way, that is the kind of character he is.

But for you there is only one sort of boy—movie hero; one sort of girl—movie heroine!"

The *Eroica* Symphony is an awesome and terrible piece of work even to modern ears. What then must it have been like when it was first produced and played for a sleepy flower-scented world! In one stroke it made all music before it old-fashioned, for which do NOT read worthless.

Tonight I listened to Beethoven's fourth piano concerto. This time the sheer theatrical effectiveness overwelmed me. The characters of the orchestra never for a moment stop their exuberant conversation. The themes are passed out among them for the most extended and dramatic dialogue—not for a second do they let up. By now I am convinced that the way to listen to a concerto is not as a total piece; better grab the tail of that comet of a solo instrument, hang on, and fly through in the comet's wake.

I went ahead on the script, the writing beginning to deepen. In the evening there came here the secretary I used to have at Paramount, Irene H. She looked so young and attractive—so melonlike, as I told her, that I could not speak about the work I wanted her to do. The work is to type out this journal so that I may have an extra copy in case this one gets lost.

Irene sat here for hours. We kissed. I told her that I remembered her to have the most beautiful breasts in the world, etc., etc. Then I had the sense that she was another Cleo in our American life. We spoke of this for an hour, I explaining what I meant by the Cleo type. She agreed with me, by this time all of the good side of her nature coming to the surface (she had been so brash and bold when she first walked in). All in all it was an evening well spent, I never so happy as when cast in a teaching or explanatory role.

To be an artist here is tantamount to being a woman giving birth to a child while swimming around in an aquarium. Can it be done?

————•————

Sunday, September 29, 1940

On location in the mountains within a hundred miles of here, making a picture for Paramount, is a young lady who unwittingly figures often in my thinking of the past few weeks. This would be (as the *Times* puts it) Miss Betty Field, young American actress. I've previously written here what my thoughts are about her.

If you think this way you must tell Fay, if only from friendship, that you see no possibility of a permanent future between you. This is fair and honest, must soon be done, particularly since you are so decided on the point in your own mind.

There are beautiful yellow roses here. Yesterday I sent some to Fay, and Theodore Dreiser too. Yellow or white roses seem to me the finest of all.

Last night, sick and stuffy, tired of the house and this depressing cold, I called Julie and joined him at the house of Garson Kanin, where a mock farewell party was going on for a writer who has been unable to sleep for fear of being conscripted. Kanin will go far in this world. His gentleness and consideration are very winning. I told him that, my having heard that he and Luise were going out together some months ago, had given me an idea for a movie story about a writer and an actress. Whereupon he told me an amazing scene in which Sam Goldwyn was faced by Leland Hayward who, as agent, was bringing Henry Fonda to be interviewed by William Wyler, the director. The discussion of a leading lady for the proposed picture centered around Margaret Sullavan, who has been married to Fonda, Wyler, and now to Hayward. Wyler claimed she was cold, it seemed; Fonda pooh-poohed this idea, and Hayward, an agent, had to play both sides against the middle. Apparently the situation grew quite hot and was headed for a real explosion, but the men suddenly realized the absurdity of the situation and burst into laughter instead.

Time magazine reports that the board of directors of the Bank of England met last week in one of the bank vaults during an air raid and declared a six percent dividend!

Hanns and Lou Eisler went to Mexicali, across the border, last week, to reenter the U.S., this farcical procedure necessary in order to gain an extension to stay. Now I hear they are stuck there, the U.S. (through its various consuls and subconsuls) not sure if it will permit them reentry. A refugee's life is no fit subject for a musical comedy! We are trying to help them in the meantime.

No, I must change my mind about an item I wrote on Beethoven the other day. The heart CANNOT be too proud!

Yesterday, too, there was a note from Geebee. She gives up, says my note of a week ago has made her unhappy, has not slain her. Says she, all of twenty-one, "Believe me, things like this I don't take too hard anymore. . . ." And thanks for the happy moments, she writes, although she adds later on that she, like others too, is looking for security and is just as "mixed-up" as the others. *Sic transit*, but I am so sorry to make her unhappy, she just entering the Arena.

Every time I see Franchot Tone around town, something stirs in me. He is one of that fraternity equally at home here or in the East, drinking, sleeping around, trying to suck the marrow out of a bony friend or two who has no marrow, making a movie, looking for a play— he is too good for this sort of life; that is what touches me about him.

Having a cold, towel around my shoulders, I think: this is the way your mother moved around the house, so slowly, gently melancholic, savoring small things, unconcentrated, weak because, partly, of an extreme self-suggestibility which you yourself have inherited from her.

So the mother, the dear dead mother, peers from behind the face of her living son.

Now, in the late afternoon, there was a cocktail party given by Dotty Parker for, as the telegrammed invitations read, the Countess Ilya Tolstoy. Riding there in Julie's car, Fay told us that the Countess Tolstoy was none other than the former Bea Stewart, wife of Donald Ogden! A painful discarded not-young not-old shoe with a few good kicks left in her toe, some unhappy way of life having given her a persistence and vindictive determination all covered by a tired affability. It was now too late to turn back—we were on the way—and besides I wanted to go where there were a lot of people, a wish fulfilled to the hilt.

In one silent empty room there was enough food—whole turkeys and hams—for a regiment. Among those present were (remember, this is a playwright's journal!): Judith Anderson, looking as if she had just gotten out of bed, having slept on a crocheted pillow slip; the former Mrs. Jock Whitney yclept Liz, insolent, looking at everyone as if he or she were a horse, a red medal appearing on each handsome cheek when she is approaching the drunk stage; F. Scott Fitzgerald, pale, unhealthy, as if the tension of life had been wrenched out of him, making me feel sorry, particularly since an introduction between us went off on a bad foot and I did not mean it to; and many gabbling hens and gay cocks drinking up as quickly as they could be poured.

It was a curiously mixed gathering, even the Piggess, Elsa Maxwell, popping in for a few minutes. Curious because Reds and Whites, to use a convenient phrase, rubbed elbows with each other. Dotty explained this later by saying that the Countess had given her a list of the people to be invited.

Fay talked with Fitzgerald; I found myself pushed up against one end of the bar with Groucho Marx, [Rouben] Mamoulian and his peek-a-boo girl, Julie later joining us. Groucho was in fine form, cracked wise without stop (always as if he is afraid to stop talking, perhaps because of his palpably crossed eyes?), hit or miss, often miss. During a period of this stellar grouping, Mamoulian and I both denying that we looked like each other (as everyone says), Groucho said, "Cliff is a fanatic." Whatever I answered led to a talk on the writing of comedy, that Groucho would be wonderful in some Molière plays, that Groucho was soon going to cut himself off from the other brothers, that we must all have dinner at his house this coming Saturday and discuss the matter. Done.

Then in traipsed Joan Blondell and husband, Dick Powell, getting oldish around the gills. Miss Blondell, mother of two, is still an eyeful who filled the eyes of many of the gentry present, her green dress cut down to the navel and there pinned on with spit or glue. During this time Mr. Pat O'Brien did an impersonation of Bert Williams. Then Milestone joined us after a few words with Sam Goldwyn. I remember Mr. Goldwyn to have a very infectious laughter, but here he seemed to me a shrewd merchant who acts a sort of absentminded (but important) friendliness, a sort of helpless quality which masks the habits of a man who knows what he is doing every minute of the day. He spoke as if he had a great idea, spoke of the seven million people of New York, asking me if that was not a great theme. I assured him that it was, that it interested me mightily; he flattered me to the extent of saying that he had been thinking of hiring me to write it. The waves of drinkers and eaters then passed over and around Mr. Goldwyn and I did not see him again and probably never will.

Louis Berman is a special friend to the special out here, to those of "the progressive movements." Briefly, he is a Jewish and radical waiter who suddenly said to me, as I stepped on Miss Kay Francis and Laraine Day (not that they knew it) to cross the room: "Well, Nero is fiddling. . . ." This led to a prolonged conversation in which he admitted that the first time I came out here he had sorrowfully announced to himself, "The way of all flesh, I said about you." He spoke feelingly of the change of attitude of many radicals and liberals, referred to the press as "the poison-pen prostitutes from who[m] poison emanates." Tray in hand, he seemed sweet, quixotic, and ridiculous; but at this moment it seems to me that I would not trade him for two pitchers and an outfielder of the sort present at the party. He talks from a center of love, pity, and conviction, humble but real pleasures; can as much be said for anyone else who was there?

So, at the bitter end, Dotty Parker cornered me near the door and flatteringly said, "You are the first person I have talked to in three hours who doesn't make me want to vomit." I was too polite to say that I didn't believe her, but I didn't. Here is how this genuinely sweet and lost lady approaches everyone—"I have sinned," she seems to be saying, this accompanied by an activity of THROWING HERSELF ON YOUR MERCY AND GOODNESS, during which she snipes with a remark at the person she has just left. Then, leaving you, as if she resented you making her murmur *peccavi*, she snipes at you to the next person. Very curious practice, no malice behind it: instead an overgenerous heart and painful self-consciousness and the tremulousness of a leaf.

Tuesday, October 1, 1940

In New York I am moving from the old to the new apartment. I wish myself well in the new place since no one else will think to wish me well. Poor you!

The stitching of the wound.

Wouldn't you say it seemed simple if I said to you that two of the main problems of the artist are to remain virgin and impervious to certain worldly blandishments?

I wrote a long letter to Archibald MacLeish in Washington today, asking him if he could say a good word on Hanns Eisler's behalf, and telling him, too, where I stood politically at the moment. Each day I believe more deeply this—that if anything is permissible to save the Soviet Union (and it is!), then anything is permissible to save the United States, faults and all. What must be saved here are the gains of

the last eight years and the best part of what Roosevelt stands for—
liberalism with all of its vacillations and withdrawals when the going
gets hot.

We had dinner with T. Dreiser and wife, Julie and I, Fay unable to
go because she is working on a picture now and must be up at five in
the morning. When Dreiser was warmed up, a bottle of Pommard
drunk between us, he began to expound a theory of life that strangely
enough sounded very fascistic. This was very puzzling to us, but finally
I understood him to mean the following: you are born with certain
chemical elements in you which you can never change or condition—
he insisted again and again that any social conditioning was a product
of other chemical compounds which could not be changed. What you
are you have to be, he insisted. This made man very primal, I said.
Dreiser's answer was that he is. Yet, he said, there are people of good
heart and they must be good no matter what they do or say. It is they
who fight the evil. In short, there is no free will, he ended.

Julie was very puzzled and distressed by these views, but I pointed
out to him that one didn't sit with Dreiser because of his thinking
capacity or because of his intellectual theories. It comes to me more
and more that you must know what you want from different people. It
is very possible that a woman who is very wonderful in bed makes very
bad coffee, but it is not coffee that you look to her for! Do I make my
point?

On the way out we met Milestone and stopped at his table for a half
hour. (Dreiser and wife went home; I said I'd drive home with Julie.) M.
was very disgruntled because he was being UNaccommodated by me
since I had not called him up in order to discuss with him the manufacture of the Hollywood movie. John Steinbeck came in and sat with us for
ten minutes, shy, uneasy, off-balance. I was glad to meet him and asked
him for his phone number since he seemed so uneasy here, as any self-
respecting person would. After this Chaplin walked in, soft, feminine,
saying "Sit down—you make me feel feminine," when Steinbeck stood
up to shake hands. It was strange to see him move his arms and hands,
handle his eyeglasses, lift his mouth as Chaplin does on the screen. I
know one thing: seldom meet an artist that you respect (whose work you
admire) in real life—always a disappointing thing.

Later I thought it was strange that when I met Chaplin I didn't think
of Noguchi, the idea of him playing Noguchi having been so exciting to
me in the East. Well, you don't think of living things out here.

I met Helen Westley in the hall when going to dinner. Said she:
"Stay, stay. Make money and put it in the savings banks."

Writing of my own is like vomit to me—impossible to go back to it with pleasure, difficult to rework it.

The point I meant to make before is that the American man expects a woman to have everything and give him everything. Oh, baby, does he get disappointed!

———•———

Wednesday, October 2, 1940

The abnormal fixation on the orgasm as an end in itself—ah, that costs!

The frankest dialogue I have ever had with a girl took place here late at night. I asked a girl to spend the night with me, seeing that she was as fevered as I was after some infield work. She refused to stay, fending me off with stiffened arms; then she would drop the arms and close her eyes and I would do likewise. Still and all she refused to undress and stay (or stay and undress). Why? We sat down on the settee and spoke over every reason. You are afraid of a baby? No! I have a cold and you don't want to catch it. Silly! There are too many lights in the room, or too few; I am too strange to you; you are afraid of what I will think of you tomorrow; it embarrasses you to think of standing here while I take that bed out of the wall; you are ill; you are afraid you will fall asleep and not go home; you don't like me; you are afraid you may grow "fond" of me, or I of you? No, none of those things! Then I thought it was splinters of all those reasons, pieces of them. Later it struck me that the reason she hadn't stayed was because even as I pursued her from behind my spreading chestnut tree of a mouth, I still unconsciously kept about me a semiamused air, as if it were not at all important whether or not she stayed. She sensed rather than saw this, and rightly did not stay. But in the meantime, sitting on the settee, I said, seeing it happen: "How can you not stay? Look what you are doing—your two legs are murmuring to each other, your thighs are nuzzling each other, right there where I should be, right there where you are so hot and moist! Stay, stay, please stay!"

Postscript: she did not stay!!

I was overjoyed, before going to bed, to get a peculiar and unique sensation from casually picking up a volume of my plays (something I seldom do) and getting a solid sense of a growing body of work from

looking through them. I remember and yet do not remember (do not
FEEL) having written them. *Rocket* surprised me, part of the second
act, almost in every line, as if someone else had written it, several of
the lines bringing tears to my eyes. When the final word is said, to
whom do these lines mean more?

When I read this stuff (and a few scenes of *Golden Boy*) which jumps
off the page, I say one thing: "Boldness—full speed ahead—and more
boldness!" A half hour like this gives me a spurt of self-confidence and
self-esteem such as I have not enjoyed in a year.

I see, too, that much of the acting of the various roles by Group
actors was overexpressive, and wrangled and tugged and worried out
of shape many of the scenes in the plays.

There is a small framed picture here—my mother, my older sister,
and myself at the age of six. I always turn the picture face down when I
do something my mother would not have liked.

———————•———————

Thursday, October 3, 1940

Up befogged and quickly off to the studio with a batch of the fudge.
There Lewin, as we talked about how I was to be paid for the work,
painted such rosy pictures of the profits I am going to make from the
movie—I hold ten percent of the producer's gross as my share—that
my head began to swim.

Then I went onto the set of *Flotsam* to read a small part for the
director, a part I intended to play in the picture. Sullavan guyed me
about this; I grew tired of waiting and left after six, determined not to
play the part, not having read for the busy director who was busy for
hours adding spittle to talcum powder, all of it later to total up to a dull
movie.

Most interesting to me at Kanin's house (Julie and Robbe Garfield
there too) were his mother and Joseph Schildkraut, a curious creature,
unfulfilled, unhappy, with the acquired manners of a diplomat, he who
was famous in the New York theatre fifteen years ago for being impossi-
bly temperamental. I thought to myself that I liked him best the old
way, although I never knew him then, he then being one of the
theatre's great while I was a boy wanting to be an actor.

I did not call Fay before I went to the dinner, as I had promised to do, there being reasons for it. There is no possibility of a flowering between us and I shall leave unmentioned every other reason but one, flatly put: I do not love her. At the same time she thinks she is pregnant and has simultaneouly started on a picture. Next week she is going to the doctor: abortion, for which I shall gladly take the responsibility. Oh, if I only loved her, if, if, if!!

It seems to me that a boy like Julie, already having had his full of Hollywood, would be ready now to come back to a Group Theatre in New York. This is true of others too—Bromberg, perhaps Lee Cobb, and one or two others. We spoke of this here, Julie having driven me home. Yearning, as I wrote somewhere about Chekhov plays, is a condition of life, not death; and all these people have a yearning away from the movies.

At three o'clock in the morning I felt a faint earthquake tremor. My heart pounded and a humming sounded in my ears. It did not last more than a few seconds but I sat poised, waiting for more to come; nothing.

This whole journal is a preparation for forgetting myself. Will it come about?

———•———

Friday, October 4, 1940

Nothing.

Dictated for three hours in the afternoon, beginning to reach the middle of the movie, but only coasting along, not more.

Julie called and came over in the evening after I had returned from dinner with Fay, an uneasy dinner memorable because of the quality of the rare roast beef.

Miss [Irene] Hempfling was working here—she has been coming here for several evenings to type copies of this journal. Julie breezed in past ten and sat here for several hours. Jed Harris wants him to jump his movie contract and come to New York to play a farce. Julie is all for it, but it won't come about because it is risky from all sides, and I should be very surprised if Jed retains interest in his script long enough to get it on. Jed is a one-bite man, after that throwing the apple away.

When Julie had left, I trifled with and touched Miss Hempfling's flesh scented with the best perfumes most lavishly used; next she had gone home, leaving me unsatisfied and still heated with the quality of that brainless flesh.

I learn Miss Betty Field is returning here tomorrow night. Well?

So to SATURDAY MORNING. Sylvia had to work at Warners and could not go to meet Luther arriving on an early train. But I rented a big car and driver and drove the baby and nurse out to Pasadena where we soon met Luther stepping off the [Santa Fe] Chief.

I slept till five or six in the early evening, washed, called Fay, and went upstairs to Luther's where Fay met me. We drank some vodka and rode to Chasen's for dinner. After that we went to see *Pastor Hall*, an anti-Nazi film sponsored by James Roosevelt, his mother speaking a foreword. It was mostly a dull picture but when we left I realized it was the best picture I'd seen since *Grapes of Wrath*. It was about something, serious, with intention, spading up the soil of indifference which is apt to pack down on anyone's heart these days—who can digest the chain of horrible events happening in the world today?

Yet, when I came back here, what interested me most was the answer of the desk clerk when I asked him if Miss Field had checked in: yes, in room 217. I will have my happiness if I must grab it by the throat; I must take my life in my hands and bend it to my puzzled will!

———•———

Sunday, October 6, 1940

Today is really Wednesday, the ninth, and only now am I going back to the beginning of the week, making entries from notes scribbled on pads.

Sunday I found myself troubled by my unmanly conduct in relation to Fay, all of our meetings becoming fumbling, nervous, strained, the eyes roaming away from each other. She is too intelligent not to be troubled by this behavior on my part; besides, she is emotionally involved. The lack of manliness comes from not saying what is on my mind; it comes from a refusal on my part to look her straight in the eyes. It develops a certain gingerliness: everything is fuddled up.

It is all my fault, the fault of an impulsive nature. Some mornings I wake up unhappy—the rest of the day is clouded by the oppression of a relationship I do not want to assume. The more I talk it out with myself (which is what this writing is), the clearer I become. I am only waiting till Fay is finished with her picture (another week) to tell her everything in the kindest possible manner. If I loved her I should be a very happy man now.

I called Betty Field today and we appointed Wednesday night to meet for dinner.

Too, a note from F. Scott Fitzgerald in answer to me. We must meet on a Sunday afternoon. A gay poof of a note, it seemed to me—an appearance, not a reality.

------•------

Monday, October 7, 1940

Luther Adler told me a strange story. While out for an auto drive one Sunday afternoon, his father decided to see a doctor he knew. The car drove to the door and the father asked Luther to run up the steps and ring the bell to see if the doctor was in. Luther rang the bell and a young woman answered by opening the door. Luther looked at her, she looked back at him, both silent. Suddenly he began to gently push her backward, she yielding, moving backward step by step until they had moved down a long dark hall at the end of which was a room. In this room, on a bed there, they had a violent but brief union. Luther put on his pants and walked out. Answering his father he said, "No, the doctor was not in," and they rode away. He never knew who the girl was, never found out; nor did she know him.

Writing well, as I did tonight, means writing that generates out of a whole center, a whole feeling or mood, from a dominant sense that the writer has of life or some part of life. Each of Chekhov's stories is such a piece of writing, for instance—from any one of his stories you may know what the writer feels about the people around him, how he sees them, the sort of man he himself is, no matter what incident or plot he finds himself trifling with.

Luther came down here and we talked of his plans, my plans, and the Group Theatre's plans. He feels that there is no longer a Group Theatre; I said it would have to be made, that Harold, holding down the home base, was holding the place where it was to be made, that it was valuable for him to be there. Luther said that the main thing with him now is to keep busy by having plans and executing them, a good instinct it seemed to me. Particularly he has a French play made from one of Colette's novels, *Duo*. He wants me to adapt this for him and Sylvia to do it on Broadway this season. He said we can produce it jointly or he himself will do it. He had some other ideas too, but none of them as concrete and practical. One of them, for instance, concerned the writing and making of a cheap picture in New York, [Ilya] Lopert wanting to use some of the best refugee French actors in it.

He said, too, that I mustn't go around raising hopes in women's hearts and then dropping them with a bump. I asked him what a man does when he is looking for love and a happy home somewhere with some woman whom he hopes to find. He counseled, of all things, restraint. I thought to myself that this is a case of the kettle calling the pot black.

———————•———————

Tuesday, October 8, 1940

Up late and immediately to the studio because Al Lewin wanted to talk to me about the last two batches of the candy pie. When I got there, after waiting an hour for him while they ironed out some wrinkle on the set, he said he thought the last writing static and not cinematic, although good for the stage. I agreed with him immediately, to his surprise, having been dissatisfied with them before he ever saw them. Promised to do better and rewrite them when I have completed a whole first draft three or four days hence.

Sylvia called from upstairs. Said she, "Luther is feeling spiritually impoverished. Please come up and keep him company." "What!" said I. "Already? And out here only less than a week?" Up I went in the late afternoon and stayed for dinner and a reading of the last half of *Duo*, which I'd not yet read. Fay was home late from work, could not join us for dinner but came up later, and two comfortable hours were spent around a coffee table even though the air was warm and stuffy with cold germs and remedies since Sylvia and Luther both have colds.

Curiously, perversely, Fay sitting there charmingly, the both of them persisted in telling stories about babies and births for the best part of a half hour. From there we went on to older children and children's camps; I told the story about how a typhoid epidemic hit a boy's camp where I was a counselor in 1929. IT MIGHT MAKE AN INTERESTING AND ORIGINAL MOVIE, by the way. Conversation then drifted to my father and lower-middle-class life in big cities. IT WILL CERTAINLY MAKE AN INTERESTING AND ORIGINAL PLAY, by the way!!

I went to bed, after working well again, with sweet warm and generous thoughts of Luise. I am sure she would not have thanked me for them, and rightfully so, since they have no continuity and flatter only myself.

———— • ————

Wednesday, October 9, 1940

When all is said and done, this seems to me to be what I think about the political situation in the world today. It is true, as the Communists say, that the present war is a fight for world markets between rival imperialists. But it is not true, as they continue, that one imperialist is as bad as another. One merely asks one's self, "Would you rather live under Nazism or under a United States and British government headed by Roosevelt and Churchill?" The answer to that is obvious. Then they counter with a statement about a third sort of govern-ment—socialism. But the answer to that is that anyone who works *directly* for socialism today is obsessed with a fixation on an end obtainable only through fighting fascism to the death.

Reprint from a column here:

Clifford Odets and John Steinbeck met for the first time at Chasen's. They were both pleased to know the other.

—What are you doing here? asked Steinbeck.

—I'm writing the scenario of my play, *Night Music*, answered Odets.

—Steinbeck said, Why don't you leave that for the people who know how?

—I need the money, said Odets.

Another quotation, from Marcus Aurelius:

"What more dost thou want when thou hast done a man a service? Art thou not content that thou hast done something CONFORMABLE TO THY NATURE, and dost thou seek to be paid for it, just as if the eye demanded a recompense for seeing, or the feet for walking?" (Stress mine.)

I like that phrase, conformable to thy nature, for everything about life is in it. Personal fulfillment and individual dynamic come from it. One truly lives only when one lives conformably to one's nature. I don't know many men and women who do, not even the poorest of natures: bourgeois life, easy to prove, is against it.

In most men and women a living dynamic is lacking. Mine is in giving—it is only in that act that my personality comes alive on all fronts. A mother's too, for instance, is in giving, and in so doing she becomes more a mother, more herself, not less.

Betty Field came here for dinner. I did not want gossiping columnists to write about us, thought it would be more comfortable here. She said she was not tired but she seemed so to me. We could not (although we were not uncomfortable with each other) relate ourselves to each other. I don't know, that's all. She seems guarded, repressed, afraid of blooming. Or she may be literally anemic, I can't say. After dinner we rode to the movie theatre and saw the new Hitchcock picture, *Foreign Correspondent*.

———•———

Thursday, October 10, 1940

Clemenceau, I read in Lyons's column (which he is sending me), said, "Marshal Pétain will live to a great old age—he has no heart, no soul, no insides." Clemenceau was right—Pétain has lived to head a fascist France!

Our quarrel with Japan seems to be that she is able strategically to cut off our supply of tin and rubber which we get from Dutch and French colonies in the Orient. This makes it possible for a few million men, white, yellow, and black, to say in the near future: "I was killed for some tin, for some ingots of rubber." Think of that when you play with a rubber band, when you throw away your chewing gum wrapper!

Since we are on the subject of animals, it struck me the other day that Hitler must die of contradictions soon, say sometime in the next few years. Shall I predict?—then two years and nine months from now.

Contradictions: his internal stability (which is only an appearance, not a reality!) can be retained only by going to war. In short, his economic, political, and social welfare can be maintained only by war. Then this frantic animal (for such he is, all propaganda contrary!) goes to war and captures other countries; necessarily he must immediately exploit these countries and their peoples, which means use of those consumer and capital goods on hand, none of which are replaceable for *the duration of the war*. The people at home become restless and must be policed constantly; certainly the same is true for the captured populations—not one tenet of the Hitler philosophy wins their loyalty, as was often the case with the Napoleonic invasions. In the meantime a fresh war begins (now with England), a stupid mouth which swallows millions of human lives. This is a war in which no enemy is beaten by one victory or even a series of victories (see Napoleon!). The necessary supplies begin to drain away; uneasiness at home builds up; in all opposition camps, the hearts of men hold flint and steel. Hitler finds he is in the position of the boy with his finger in the leak in the dike: his army is the finger, while behind the dike are the resources and men of an outraged world. At the same time it is almost impossible for him to exploit his prizes; instead he must cope with disease, starvation, and rebellion, which his invasions have brought in their wake.

Just now he has made another coup, has taken the oil fields of Rumania. These will furnish gasoline and oil for his motors, but that is all. All in all, I am confident, Mr. Hitler is a skyrocket whose fuse has already been lighted. He is a one-chance rocket. Soon he must fall and come to earth, fulfilling the nature of the rocket by spluttering to death in the dark. This does not mean he will not do great damage before he dies, probably by his own hand.

I have a cousin, a son of my mother's sister, named Frank Lubner. At the age of seventeen or eighteen he ran away from home and joined the Navy, which over a period of twenty years made a man of him. At the end of twenty years, not yet forty, he was retired with a good monthly pension. We were never friendly but he kept in touch with my mother and aunt. Once or twice he tried contacting me, once coming to see me in New York. I saw a dark, lonely, moody man with a surface amiability, but who looked as if he had the devil's own temper. The meeting was not much of a success. He thought, as I remember, that I was too cold, too remote, which may have been true as it was difficult to entertain a total stranger, a man whom I could not meet on some common ground.

Frank has a great deal of pride too, so I did not see or hear of him for a long time. Recently he asked my aunt to have me autograph one of my books for him. This led to a letter or two being exchanged. The Navy has called him back—he is now doing recruiting duty in Oklahoma City. Two weeks ago I had two letters from him in which he said he was very concerned for my welfare in relation to the draft. He was trying, he said, to find some way in which I might legally evade service. Last week I answered his letters and thanked him for his thoughtfulness, saying that I had been moved by his efforts. This has resulted in a third letter from him—the flower has opened. He is scornful of any government which would take me for service when I might be useful elsewhere. He tells me how he treasures my books and an autograph; he is all for me, in any possible way, and he wants me to write again, but only when I find time.

I mention all this because I was so struck by the tone of his letter, by his curious but very real and sincere nature, by the touches and flashes of cynicism and humor which are in every other line of the letter. It would be interesting to meet him again and I shall try to arrange it. We have a stronger relationship than that of cousins—we are the two homeless boys of a whole family; we are the only two who spit on the values of our lower-middle-class background; we are two renegades who become as visitors from another world every time we step into an aunt's or cousin's house. Frank does not realize what we have in common. Perhaps I shall tell him about it in a letter. It is in the nature of a discovery for me too!

The reason, dear successful man, one of the reasons success is often a curtailment instead of an extension of your powers is because success often means fewer responses to the articles and beings of your environment (coy note!).

I conceive the following to be true of a certain type of modern man: he moves towards his food and away from his waste products. That happens, too, to be a half-scientific description of a one-celled animal!

Fay had a husband who drank considerably. At a certain stage of inebriation he would have her drive the car. He would cry faster, faster, and she would go to sixty. Faster, faster! She would go up to seventy on the dark roads which lead down to the ocean. Faster, faster, lying there drunk, once an aviator instructor, and she would take the car up to eighty, racing through the night, unhappy woman. It would seem that he wanted to kill them both together; and probably she was half of the same mind. Later, last year, he destroyed himself alone: hanging in a closet.

————•————

Friday, October 11, 1940

A doctor writes, "Civilization is the extension and mitigation of our environment. . . ." He should add, ". . . for the private profit of the capitalists primarily, the benefits accruing to humans generally being a byproduct of secondary or tertiary importance." The capitalist, by the good doctor's definition, is not a civilized man: old news. He is a recessive sport, throwback to the time when one man hit another on the head because he wanted the other man's roasted potato.

The capitalist brought his rapacity with him, but we have taught him contempt and arrogance. He sees himself retard civilization, refuse the bounty of all nature to most men—for this he reaps the respect of the community and loaded bank vaults. Why should he not be contemptuous when, after years of amused and cynical self-contemplation (although even a stupid man may grow sick of himself!), he sees the pickpocket arrested for a ten-dollar theft?

The day will come here! You know what day!

Yesterday I went to Lewin and told him I was nearing the end of the script but that the proposed ending did not seem theatrically strong enough. So I dictated most of the afternoon, came back here at night, and worked on till almost seven this morning. Hosannas! The first draft is finished.

Today, at his office, Lewin thought I should give them more time without salary, time enough to polish up this draft. Contractually they must pay me off now, my job finished; next, for revisions, they must put me on a weekly salary. We tugged at this problem for an hour and agreed that we would settle it on the morrow. From this scent I conclude the following: do not do business with friends, for you cannot press them or measure your work by the letter of the contract. For this reason, if for no other, it is better to work for a large corporation—a certain anonymity of boss-ship keeps you tough and firm.

Lewin is a man who quotes *Macbeth* at me; he will often discuss the

King Arthur legends with a great regard and knowledge; a few days ago
he discussed the Druidic remains at Stonehenge with the background
of an archaeologist. Today, in his office, this curious little man said the
following: "Don't kill me, but I want to suggest another title for the
movie instead of *Night Music*."

—Shoot, said I.

—You won't kill me?

—What is it?

— . . . *The Mating Call*.

I looked at him, thought he was joking. Not at all. "It will be great," he
said. I quickly changed the subject. No, *he* changed it, saying, "Don't
react now. Just think about it. Let's go to lunch."

Lewin would be quite disturbed if he knew that I thought him a
dead man. He is a dead man, twice as dead as his partner, Dave Loew,
who may never have heard of Macbeth for all I know, certainly not
Stonehenge. But for their purposes, for the purposes of making
money, they may both be very much alive for all I know or care.

At dinner with Fay I was very elated, the body of the work behind
me. I told her stories about the many professional comedians in New
York: Wynn, Lahr, Jolson, Jessel, Holtz, all monsters of ego, sick and
unhappy. I threw in little Jack Pearl for good luck.

Saturday, October 12, 1940

I told them at the movie office that I would give them till next Friday
for revisions without further salary. I will omit, in all unfairness, that
they supposed this free period to be their right. A stupid mix-up,
costing me five thousand dollars. However, they promise such fabulous returns for me from the finished picture that perhaps I had better
silence my snarling mouth!

Fay finished her picture two days ago. She visited the doctor again
and today he told her she was going to have a baby. We both knew this
would have to be discussed, from there moving on to a clarification of
our entire friendship. Tacitly we agreed not to discuss it at dinner,
which we ate at Chasen's. We drove around for an hour, then came
back here.

Fay is a true woman. She made me more a man, continues to do so.

When the tears rolled down her face, splashing on my shirt (polka dots, she said), I could only keep my arms around her for the longest time, silent, having said just enough to let her know we could not go on with her constantly hoping that our friendship would develop into marriage, which is what she needs. Of course the borning baby could not go on either.

She proposed that we get in bed, not with words but with gestures, with moving her mouth, twitching in her loins. We stayed in bed for two hours, I finally half pretending a drowsiness. She dressed and I sat on the settee in a robe. We drank cold milk and were very calm and quiet. She talked with real dignity and feeling about her relationship to me. I discovered that she has real distinction of character—not merely character, real subtlety. Before, in bed, she had had the wildness and beauty of defeat; now she was calm and impartial enough to see both her point of view and my own, although perhaps I might have been more emotionally stirred by her if she had been less impartial, as I so often was with Luise whom I cursed to myself as I loved her.

I think the main thing which has kept me cool to this very admirable young woman is knowing that another man gave her life (brought her out of her girlhood); that he left in her face the marks of his fever or the fever he aroused in her; and perhaps that she bore his child. Of course I didn't tell her this but continued to babble nonsense and be beguiled by it myself. Yet I wonder if there is not some truth in the remark that a stabilized family life (which she could make with one hand tied behind her back) would kill three-quarters of my talent.

She noticed, as often before, that unconsciously I winced or frowned when she told me that she loved me. This, when I thought about it, was because she was presenting me with her rock-bottom reality and I could not enter or partake of it—not now, never. It was not my reality but hers (so warmly, womanly), and I am no boy for entering into or living by another's reality—not, God help me, even in such a tender moment. I know many men can lie about these things, or be casual about them; I can't, and it shows on my face.

She went home at past two and I tried to sleep, but everything had conspired to so key me up that it was dawn and past six before I fell asleep.

I don't think all the above words give any impression of what happened.

———•———

Sunday, October 13, 1940

Re: eucalyptus trees—the room, windows open, is full of their astringent medicinal scent. These trees seem to give off their scent only at certain times, perhaps the fall or when their buttons are ripe—I don't know.

Yesterday there was another AP dispatch in the newspapers. The Third Reich beheaded four more Heroes of the People for "high treason"; they are named Karl Hoffman, Erich Schulz, Willi Tosch, and Herman Chill. Long remember, boys!

There was a brief unhappy note from Geebee two days ago—would I write? Today I sent her a wire, telling her to be of good cheer and that I'd write soon. I read yesterday, too, that Oscar Levant's wife, June, had her baby. Sent them a wire today, "Love to cards, spades, and a little casino."

Fay is unhappy across the street. Spoke to her on the telephone, asking her to join Luther, Sylvia, and me here for dinner. They will all be arriving any minute. Telephoned my father too, asking him to come here to dinner tomorrow night and bring with him the old Bronx neighbors, the Henry Wagners.

Oscar having a baby—he must be confounded!

Business of the early evening: dinner for five at the Beachcomber's. A good dinner, good drinks, excellent and authentic atmosphere. Milestone came through in a large party. This spoiled my dinner by half, for I felt stupid being there with a pack of movie people. Too, Fay wanted to worm herself into my consciousness and kept rubbing and handling my knee till I could have jumped up through the roof; for almost two hours she did not take her hand off my knee. I will admit she had a perfect right to do that, but I can not stand "undying devotion" and the "I adore you, darling" look and attitude. These make me uncomfortable and bore me and end by closing me up completely.

It was the same thing when we arrived home here. Luther and Sylvia went right up to their apartment, since she must be up for an early studio call and he had fatigued himself with rum drinks. I wanted to go to work—clear these damn entries off the table, get to a clear view of the corrections needed on the movie script; but Fay wanted me to hold her, wanted to feel a sort of last togetherness. You would think I might have been gracious about it for another half hour or more. I could not—kill me, I could not be! I did not want her in my consciousness. We sat on the settee for ten minutes and I took her home, refusing to let her press herself into me, which is what (with all the justification in the world) she wanted to do.

Business of the later evening: work!

———•———

Monday, October 14, 1940

Up late, discontent, not working well because of a distracted mind. It is necessary to say again that the artist is at a loss when the outer intensity is more dense than the inner. It is for this reason that he often tries to throw off the burden of outer connections, despite the necessity of them and the pleasure too.

My father and his wife came here for dinner. With them were Henry Wagner and Hattie, his wife, both of them old Bronx neighbors of the earliest period of my life. As a child of eight I put a glass splinter in my finger and fainted; it was "Uncle Henry" who carried me upstairs.

At dinner downstairs we talked of political conditions, of who would be the next president, of what makes wars, I finally slowing down because I was feeling a little bumptious from an effort to be a good host. They went near ten and I was then free for a whole night of work.

———•———

Tuesday, October 15, 1940

From the papers today it was possible to learn that the Germans claimed to have dropped two million pounds of bombs on London last night.

Ready to continue with this cursed movie. Instead, went walking with Sylvia and Luther; saw a newsreel. Then we came back here and a long talk developed, mostly about self-indulgence, about Luise, about theatre plans. Sylvia was moved again by what she considers her loss of talent. I told them that we would all go back to New York and do a play together under Group sponsorship. They are to play it, I to write it, perhaps Lee Strasberg to direct it. The play is the trio play.

So to bed thinking of registering tomorrow for the draft.

It occurs to me that there is no more virtue in honesty than there is in, say, irrelevance, which is what honesty often is. But it depends on the context in which honesty is placed. Honesty of self is the only honesty worth mentioning. Of course it is another matter if one says, "Honesty is the best policy." That is a middle-class saying, which is really saying that honesty pays dividends—that is why it is good.

These months are mainly concerned with finding out what the world is about—the nature of it REALLY!

The Beethoven Seventh. You have to be virgin of heart and spirit to write it. Beethoven did not lose the innocence. You have to lose it in the world to survive—you lose the innocence. Yet, curiously, all Americans are innocent. Just think how the Europeans cut Woodrow Wilson to pieces.

I could not put Fay out of my mind. I understand her feelings but reject them in self-defense, don't want them pressing me.

------●------

Wednesday, October 16, 1940

My father came here before noon. He wants me to help him meet influential people here. He talks this way: "Your dad is not a dumbbell. Your dad was not raised in a stable," etc., etc. This means I am not to be ashamed of him, that he knows how to deport himself among the talented and mighty. It never occurs to him that perhaps I will be ashamed for myself, for my role in such introductions.

I don't know what to do with this man. I was on my way to the draft board and walked him to his car. He dramatizes what he is saying by pausing, by pretending to fish for words, by breaking up his glibness. I said I would see what I could to, although I assured him that I knew only some writers and actors.

The registration board was meeting in a little private home, an American flag hung in front of the porch. Two men rocked on the porch and we exchanged greetings. Inside, three middle-aged women were gossiping—not unpleasant women. A dressmaker took down my answers to the form questions. How did I spell Philadelphia, she asked. Then I said I was employed at Universal Studios. Was Universal spelled with a *c* or an *s*, she asked. I was overpolite, treated everything gingerly. I signed the blank she had filled out; in turn she signed and filled out a small card which all registants must carry on their person. Now is the time for all good men . . .

On the good side Beethoven gives one strength and love, always innocence, blessed innocence. Do you ever get tired of having to walk around in the world with a gun hidden in your coat? I do. Everyone carries a gun in the world, it seems to me.

———•———

Thursday, October 17, 1940

At the studio in the late afternoon I suggested to Lewin that we do a movie on Beethoven, something we have mentioned before. He said he was willing to go ahead with plans for such a project if I would work without salary, taking twenty-five percent of the net profits and a drawing account of seven hundred and fifty dollars a week. I told him I thought that would be satisfactory. [Paul] Muni is the actor for the part, the whole project dependent upon his acceptance.

Spoke to Fay on the phone. Did not have the heart to ask her if she had been to the abortionist: "Were you there? Did you go?" I could not ask. Instead I asked her how she felt and she answered cheerfully that she was fine.

Twice she said to me, "My hobby is being loved," by which she meant being desired, being wanted, being adored by a man she respected. Only she meant, "Being loved as *I* see love, not as you see it." And yet a dear woman, so dear, so deserving and needful of love; so important forever in my life!!

It is possible, too, to dishonor others with gifts. It all depends on the impulse behind the gifts.

Best of everything of the week was to go into a big bookshop and send Hanns and Lou some good books. They are still imprisoned in Mexicali, read two or three books a day.

It is necessary to have not the slightest fear of what fools think of you; it is their respect that you must eschew!

————————•————————

Friday, October 18, 1940

Up late to find it the hottest day of the year here; freak weather. I didn't go out but the hot air walked in through the windows, although it was cool here. I called my secretary, the English girl, and had her come here where I dictated part of the script corrections.

Luther came in later, just as I was finishing the work. He is bored with this place, wants to start working soon, is restless. We discussed a contract Sylvia is about to sign with Warners, one that it seems may keep her out here for the best part of the year. That, it seems to me, is not good for her, not good for their marriage, which has been going so well up till now. Perhaps I am wrong about the contract.

I am very happy with the Stendhal book. Stendhal is "my" man.

He says he knew a German who threw himself out of the window to show his vivacity!

To be loved at first sight, he says, a man should have at the same time something to respect and something to pity in his face.

He says, against Freud: "Self-contempt is one of the principal causes of suicide; one kills one's self in order to satisfy one's honor." "To possess strength of character one must have felt the influence of others on one's self; so that these others are necessary to one." This must be why he says elsewhere that one may develop anything in solitude but character.

In giving and in being discontented with myself and others, plus a dusting of not wanting to appear ridiculous—these are what move me to activity and life in the larger sense. Ambition or career-making are no dynamics of mine; neither is envy, but the competitive urge, long ago masked, does enliven me. From overt competition I withdrew a long time ago—a painful sport for me. This is why I must always do my learning in private, away from others to whom I may seem ridiculous. It is not easy for me to accept being bested in jousts; so no jousting!

Sent Louis Veda a hundred bucks.

————————•————————

Saturday, October 19, 1940

The artist here is expected to be a sort of performing bear when away from his work. If, at parties and other gatherings, he does not waltz around on his legs, he is considered a dull man. I am very content to be considered a dull man; reports of such opinion of me are always arriving here.

At the studio, in Lewin's office, the weather hot and dry (ninety-seven degrees), spoke to Lewin and Loew of the Beethoven project again. I spoke fluently of Beethoven and some of his main problems in relation to his times and personal life. Lewin listened in a sort of flushed silence—it is difficult for him to take a conversation on a topic about which he is little informed. I should worry!

At home to wash and dress quickly and pick up Fay and Dorothy Arzner to ride them to the house of Henry Blanke and frau for an informal dinner.

Ernst Lubitsch and wife were there when we arrived, she talking about horses and how to ride them in shows. He is a witty man, keen, appetites sharp; he was unable to keep his eyes off Fay, whom he likes and obviously would like to have. This seemed to amuse his wife, who seemed often on the point of making sharp remarks but did not.

The rather undelectable Kay Francis showed up with a young male friend; Eddie Robinson came in with wife who is busy and thrilled to the core with working in the Roosevelt campaign, her whole manner of facing the world learned from her husband, mannerisms and all, except that she doesn't smoke cigars. We expressed a desire to see his collection of French paintings and were invited for any time. Fritz Lang looked in, drank some rye and water, and disappeared. One of Reinhardt's sons was there; with him, Salka Viertel and one of her sons.

The dinner was excellent and plentiful, served out of doors under tall weeping willow and eucalyptus trees. Many jokes were told at the table; everything was easy and informal. Later they played Ping-Pong, a sort of tournament in which Fay was very good. Since she did not press me, since she was free and easy (and so handsome), going about her business of enjoying a party, not clinging to me with an excess of feeling—because of all of that I was able to stand off and admire her and appreciate again all of her fine qualities.

With Lubitsch I turned the conversation to American actors, later to war. The quality of his mind did not attract me; his personality always did. I was able to say, suddenly feeling mad, "I am still old-fashioned—I still believe that capitalists make the wars!" Robinson agreed with me, to my surprise, for he fuddled me up before with a chat on fifth columnists and how he hoped to write a radio sketch against them. He does a weekly broadcast and kept insisting that he wants me to write one of the playlets. He talked of moral values all night. I can only say that his heart is in the right place, if his mind is not. Very soft from success is Robinson.

———————•———————

Sunday, October 20, 1940

Mrs. Grey [a secretary in Lewin's office], the English wife and mother, seemed so alone here, so needing of friendship, that I offered to take her to the Garfields' pool on a Sunday with her two children. So I had to be up very early, very tired, but the bargain made.

Children always touch me very much, perhaps because they are always trembling on the brink of catastrophe. I love to be with them and watch them, particularly if they have real personal character; when I tire of them, I move away. These two closed up like anemones when other visitors came to enjoy the pool, particularly the loud and brash Bromberg children, Conrad and Marcia, both of whom have not the slightest interest for me; they are without charm and childishness, although the boy has an even, good nature and the girl a sort of mother wit.

Luther and Sylvia, Fay and myself, we ate good food at a Hungarian restaurant and washed it down with two bottles of wine. After that we went to see the movie Kanin directed (adapted by Bob Ardrey from Sidney Howard's play), *They Knew What They Wanted*. Again and again it missed the point of human relationships—the essential loneliness of such people, etc.—but it was worth seeing. It was well directed as Hollywood films go, but I could see no signs of Kanin's own personality in it. [Charles] Laughton, very gifted, needs a good spanking for his self-indulgent mannerisms and patent laziness. Carole Lombard had one good scene, the rest ordinary, despite high advance praise;

either she has forgotten her own early life or does not know how to go to it.

Back here we chatted for a half hour. Left alone, I worked till almost seven in the morning and finished the movie script.

———————•———————

Monday, October 21, 1940

The first thing I wanted to do was deliver the finished script to the studio. Did so as soon as I got out of bed at three in the afternoon. They have finished their other picture, *Flotsam*, just today.

Chatted with Lewin about future plans. He wants me to come out here for six weeks more of work on our film, just before they get ready for production. In the meantime they will use the just-finished treatment as bait for a good director and as good a cast as can be found.

Had dinner upstairs with Luther and Sylvia, after this going for a walk down Hollywood Boulevard. They told me of a scene that happened in Ciro's nightclub here the other night. A. [Anatole] Litvak, director, and P. [Paulette] Goddard, actress, were drunk there together. They have been sleeping together, in public, for weeks. Drunk at Ciro's, sitting at a ringside table, he took out her breasts and kissed them passionately. They were stopped by the help but later continued the same thing on the dance floor. For this the management banished them to the outer sanctum of the bar. There A. Litvak suddenly disappeared, finally was discovered under the bouffant skirt of Miss Goddard on his knees, kissing the "eagerly sought triangular spot" with the blissful unawareness of a baby at a bottle.*

For my part, I told Sylvia, I would rather be like Litvak than lead a life of wooden caution.

A warm feeling came to me when I began to think about the trio play this evening. I hope to come to it again with real excitement. Part of the theme of this play is about how the men of our country irresponsibly wait for the voice and strong arm of authority to bring them to life,

---

*Many versions of this story have circulated in Hollywood over the years. Perhaps the calmest and most accurate is recorded in Jean Negulesco's *Things I Did . . . and Things I Think I Did* (New York: Simon and Schuster, 1984).

etc. So comes fascism to a whole race of people. Danger ahead—I see it all over, even in myself. Nothing stands for authority and I wait for its voice! There is something in men in the world over today that welcomes dictatorship; the children are seeking for the father to arrange their lives for them!

I heard the other day (perhaps read) of a man who was afraid he was going to commit suicide. Several times the impulse to do so was so strong that he became frightened. Finally he purchased a fine expensive watch telling himself, "Just before you kill yourself throw this watch to the pavement and shatter it to bits." This prevented him from following out the suicidal impulse.

Is he man or is he mouth? Man or hands? Man or appetites?

A character, in writing or acting, is a specialist who specializes in a few discernible characteristics.

Wednesday, October 23, 1940

Friends, I have had a good experience tonight, seeing Jimmy Cagney's new picture, *City for Conquest*. God help me, it moved me to the point of wanting to burst out into tears several times. (Fay and Julie Garfield, who returned from New York today, enjoyed it the same way.) For a long time, seeing the obvious hokum of most of the picture, I could not understand why I was so moved. I wondered if I still believed all the bunk about the poor boy reaching the top, the usual success story. No, it was not that. What it was was that Jimmy made real the ASPIRATION of the leading character—the people in the picture aspired to development, to wealth and unfolding of their talents.

This makes me say again that as one moves from impoverished obscurity to opulent success, one is trading not death for life but certain true values for other often more tawdry values, all popular superstitions to the contrary aside. Poverty has its beauties, its rich human values, and it seems for the most part to be the only soil in which aspiration flourishes. That is a bad comment on our civilization, but racking my memory does not make me remember one successful man who truly keeps his aspiration; very few American artists too.

Aspiration which is simultaneously personal and impersonal (which shares its loveliness with others) is a very beautiful and moving stuff!

Fay looks very beautiful. We say nothing about our relationship, but see each other. I do not see one bad quality in her unless it be an excess of giving of the self from time to time. I spoke to Luther of her this afternoon: he recommended a marriage like his, the recommendation not being without sense!

A word about some white chrysanthemums here. They are seven inches across, as beautiful as any flowers I've ever seen. They are a feast for the eyes—white, silent, gravid with life, graceful as swimming swans—great beauties. I find myself looking at them for five minutes at a time; they make violent impulses come into my hands.

HANNS AND LOU EISLER ARE BACK TODAY!

Thursday, October 24, 1940

Yesterday Roosevelt made his first campaign speech. A devastating speech which must have thrown the Republicans into a panic. I heard that a prominent Republican said, "We ought to pay Roosevelt a million dollars to make a speech for us."

Last night, after seeing his picture, I sent Cagney a note. There must be more notes of admiration in modern life when admiration is deserved! I told Jimmy this picture proved that he had a fine heart.

In the early evening I crossed the street and spent fifteen minutes with Fay's child. I was amazed at her strength—her muscles are firmer than mine and she is only four. This comes about because her nurse is a mountain woman from Virginia; all day they tramp the California hills together. The child will grow up to be an acrobat or a bareback rider in a circus!

Fay and I rode up the Hollywood hills, up Outpost Drive, and joined Hanns and Lou Eisler, who have returned from Mexico and are living again at the Paiges' house. It was a warm reunion, all of us touched by their return: our friendship has moved up to a higher level now. We all chattered happily, glad that their entry problems are over; the government has admitted them permanently to this country and they are ready to take out first citizenship papers.

On this good feeling we had as good a dinner at the Little Hungary restaurant which, it must be said, serves the best food in Hollywood. After this we went back to the Paige house and Hanns and Lou told us of their adventures in Mexicali. Hanns has a good dramatic instinct; he laid out everything for me as if he were a playwright, hoping that some day I would use the material to write a play on refugees who sit in a Mexican hotel, waiting to enter this country, while just across the street—a hop, skip, and jump—glows an electric sign which reads "United States"! Both Hanns and Lou described the various types and characters they met, the officials on both sides of the border, the refugees of seven different nationalities, the hotel owner, a Hungarian waiter with pull, the various sorts of border outlaws and gamblers, the vice-consuls, one of whom crosses the border into Mexico every day to buy meat for his family because it is cheaper there than on the American side!

———————•———————

Friday, October 25, 1940

Miss Conway, who was my typist on the movie script, is typing copies of this journal for me. After typing the first fifty pages she sent me the following note: "I appreciate your confidence in me."

The draft for one year of military training has brought all young men between the ages of twenty-one and thirty-five together. They look at each other in a different way, feel related, are less restricted with each other. This delights my soul. Yesterday one of the switchboard boys suddenly produced my draft number for me, saying he had picked it up for me at the draft board while looking for his own number. This feeling of togetherness is very important in the lives of living men; it is a feeling that a capitalist state never gives, except in times of emergency, as when men band together to fight a flood or, say, a forest fire or in times of war, which explains the real attractiveness of war for men—joining together to fight a common enemy! On the other hand, as is not understood by people who have been raised in a competitive society, the very meaning of socialism implies this togetherness at all times—a constructive togetherness, never, never possible under capitalism! The essence of capitalism is competition, and it is a competitive urge that tears men apart from each other, making them enemies till the day they die: you fear and so hate the man who may take your job away from you, your profits, your house, your farm. Yes, an atmosphere of the spirit! Blather about moral values! Where is the maniac who expects love to flower under the roar of Niagara?!

They are throwing eggs in this election campaign. Willkie has scraped them off himself and his wife a dozen times. Many people are shocked by this, by the lack of respect for a Presidential candidate. Frankly, this shocked me too until I realized again what Willkie is. He is the representative of big business—he has worked for years for corporations who have not scrupled to loot the public resources of the nation; they are high-grade thieves.

Today they had the first big rain here, a seasonal thing, the nominal beginning of the rainy season. It was interesting to see what the rain did to people—relaxed and abstracted them, made them quiet and thoughtful.

Went up to Luther's for dinner. Sylvia, Fay, and Howard DaSilva. We heard John L. Lewis on the radio. He came out against Roosevelt, beseeched votes for Willkie.

The day and night were like March in the East. It seems that in wet weather the eucalyptus trees give off their characteristic scent. We ate a good dinner, eating with it a fine cake that Fay had baked! After that we played rummy and blackjack for quarters. THE RADIO WAS PLAYING AND WHAT WITH THE WARMTH AND HOMEY ATMOSPHERE I THOUGHT OF ALL THOSE TERRIBLE YEARS IN PHILADELPHIA, those horrible nights when I yearned myself out of that home but thought I would never escape it, yearning, yearning, "How will I ever get out of here?!" How can I have forgotten all those years?

At the end of the evening Fay and I went down to my apartment and had a curious hour together on the couch, both tired, she a little desperate, I unfeeling but tender with her because of the great love she bears me.

———•———

Sunday, November 3, 1940

This is being written in New York City, two days after arriving from California by train. I shall write below previous happenings as I noted them. Going backwards:

SATURDAY, 10/26: my father came here and I settled with him to give him two hundred and fifty dollars a month and pay his insurance premiums of almost a thousand dollars a year. I was very annoyed by the insurance part since, as I told him, he has no money and yet insists upon putting it in the bank in the form of insurance.

Fay and I went to Julie's house for a good dinner, had a fine time there, talking of acting problems, quiet and relaxed. Fay wanted to leave early so that we might be alone; I could see she was annoyed. I left Julie with a motto, he having brought up the matter first: "A slack string has no tone." Anyone with any character is always worried in Hollywood by the slack feeling of the self.

SUNDAY, 10/27: again Fay wanted to be alone with me but I could not bear the idea of it for some reason. She was piqued, but silently. For my part I was beginning to get panicky about the imminent train trip, the packing, and the last-minute details. I begged a sleeping pill from Luther, took it, and went to sleep like a willful child.

MONDAY 10/28: reported to the draft board here, told them I was leaving for New York and to transfer my number there. They did not seem very efficient, took the change of address on a scrap of copy paper.

Said good-bye at the studio, asking my father along because he wanted to meet some movie executives. Then I paid a florist bill of almost seventy dollars and for only three weeks at that!

Julie and Robbe had arranged a farewell dinner at their house for all of us. After listening to Roosevelt make a campaign speech on the radio, we went there and ate the dinner, chatted idly, laughed, listened to music, and left early. With Fay, Sylvia, and Luther stopped in at my room and we drank a half a bottle of vodka, all of us depressed (for different reasons, subtle ones in each case), feeling low and wanting to feel high.

Fay and I were alone soon, finishing the vodka by ourselves. She stayed till six in the morning, creeping away only with the morning light, both of us so tired that I had fallen asleep twice before she left. I have only one thing to say: this beautiful womanly woman adores me and I am unworthy of her adoration, leaving all quibbling aside!

TUESDAY, 10/29: panic and sweat, packing, last-minute details, nervousness, worrying about making the train. Sylvia had to go to work at her studio, so only Fay, Luther, and I drove to Pasadena to get the train. We were there with a half hour to spare, our baggage safely in the hands of a sturdy porter. Be alone, Luther implied, withdrawing to one side. (He has been acting very much the matchmaker during the past weeks, swearing that he never met so beautiful a person as Fay before!) The two of us strolled up and down the station, I feeling haggard and restless. And Fay? All I can repeat is the word adoration. And finally getting on the train after pressing this woman close. And seeing her through the window as the train began to pull away, her little gifts to us in my hands, a bottle of champagne and a little cake she had baked, even a deck of playing cards. How this woman looked!! In love, beseeching, anxious, her very muscles saying, "Will I ever see him again? Throughout the trip Luther kept referring back to this moment of farewell until I said with a mixture of disgust and good nature, "Do you think the sight of her standing there on the platform meant more to you than it did to me? For God's sake, shut up!"

WEDNESDAY, 10/30: a dull day, although Luther and I found we could play very exciting games of casino with the cards, being evenly matched, often winning a game by one spade or one card. We sent wires back to the girls, saying that we were boring each other. The only thing that interested me was a boy standing alone in a yard. He was wearing a football helmet, an orange jersey, blue pants, and football shoes. In his hand he twirled a football, playing by himself, a boy of twelve or fourteen. A symbol of something in this country, I thought.

A special dinner at night. Fresh brook trout which they pick up at La Junta in the afternoon. I felt a dullness which Luther did not awaken, not even when he spoke vehemently (why so vehement, boy?) against Clurman and the sad remains of the Group Theatre. He works out everything for his own good and/or comfort and pretends to be doing the opposite. This becomes very trying. Too, he pretends a great competence about everything, but as I see it he is really extremely incompetent.

I told him I did not care for his marriage ideals; they demanded too much convenience from marriage, convenience being something he is always looking for. It suddenly and importantly occurred to me that

HAPPINESS IS NO END IN ITSELF, that the phrase "the pursuit of happiness" is utter nonsense, that a fixation on such an end is not only dangerous but precludes any possibility of happiness. Americans, I beg you to listen and learn! Finally (oh, young man!), a fixation on any end is as dangerous as death itself!

We spoke of the play I am about to begin working on again, the trio play. Luther is against giving it to the Group; I reserved my opinion but told him to understand clearly that I expected him and Sylvia to stand by to play the leading parts in it, work to start in about six weeks.

THURSDAY, 10/31: dead October! Luther connives about small things; he means one thing and says another.

He has decided to stay over in Chicago for twenty-four hours; I am anxious to get to New York and refuse his offer to stay over with him. In truth, he has been a little wearying on the trip, a compound of boy and man which has not yet congealed one way or the other, this all larded over with a great air of authority which often covers a real uncertainty and/or timidity.

In New York City the first number picked in the draft lottery was owned by a despised Oriental, a Mr. Yuen Chong Han, a Chinese. Others among the first chosen ones included more Jewish and foreign names than so-called American names, many Italian and Poles among them. Will this be remembered in the difficult and dangerous days to come? I doubt it.

FRIDAY, 11/1: the train has been delayed by fog, is fifty minutes late. The Twentieth Century express slips by us, we limping in behind it. Herman is waiting for me at the station. We throw the luggage in a cab and ride to the new apartment on Beekman Place. It looks strange and uncomfortable, the decoration seeming awkward and foolish in some cases. Too tired, too tired. I loll on the bed—the bedroom is good for sleeping, dark, warm, silent. Then I get up at seven and telephone Geebee. I want to be near someone, close, feel alone. She comes over at eight after I bathe and shave. We drink a quart of champagne and undress and get in bed. The quality of her flesh is simple and rich. We share each other for a long time and it does not matter to either of us that we are not in love—this friendship is nourishing in itself. We fall asleep late in the morning and let it go at that. That is the slogan of the week: "Let it go at that!"

SATURDAY, 11/2: the new apartment is in my way, difficult to adjust to. Nothing about it pleases me—the bedroom is good and dark, excellent for sleeping. In each of the four rooms there is a fireplace. Everything looks expensive and tasteless, has nothing to do with me.

Sid Benson and I talked politics for hours, he trying to convince me that the Communist line here was correct; I could not agree. There are dark and disagreeable days ahead, I am afraid—repression of civil liberties in the name of national defense, etc., etc.; in fact they have already begun. The country is in a tailspin. Perhaps some sort of order will come after the elections on Tuesday. Order? Did I say order? Fascism too is a sort of order! There is a smell of cold steel in the air, of superpatriotics!

I listened to the opus 28 piano sonata, to two late Mozart piano sonatas, then went to bed dumbly.

SUNDAY, 11/3: so now Sunday, a fine day outside, but by evening I tired of being here alone and so rode across town (in the good Cadillac!) and ate a sort of supper at Lindy's. Soon in came Leonard Lyons, who introduced me to some people working in the Roosevelt political campaigns. Oh, bootless night! Oh, dull heart and empty whizzing head. Lionel Stander stopped me as I was walking into Lindy's. "You are a first-class man," he said. "What are you doing with these nit-wits?"

Oh, bootless night! I came home and finished Gerhardt Haupt-mann's play, *Drayman Henschel*, reading it because I had somewhere picked up an idea that it dealt with the same theme as my trio play. No. I am a better playwright than the young Hauptmann who wrote this play. Nothing to learn there.

Dinner: Bill and Lee Kozlenko came here, admiring and disadmir-ing the apartment. We rode across town to Lindy's and ate a heavy dinner. More discussion of politics. I am beginning to feel like Luise: "Why must we discuss politics? I do not care to know something about it!" On top of this, in came Lyons and wife, Irving Berlin and wife (I thought her very charming, liked her face), back from a Roosevelt preelection night rally at Carnegie Hall. They had with them a porta-ble radio which they put on the table, and through it we all listened to last-minute pro-R. speeches by Wallace, Hull, finally FDR himself, a quiet calm country-squire speech from his Hyde Park home, ending with a prayer for the welfare of the country.

Accomplished today the purchase of a desk table and a new type-writer ribbon.

I saw Moss Hart for a moment, he entering Lindy's as we were leaving at midnight. He looked like I feel, unhappy lad!

Later: I come back here at ten minutes to six in the morning to report happiness. I sent off a long letter to Fay, saying that I wished I might make her happier in our relationship by making it more definite for her. The moment I mailed the letter, with characteristic indecision (there's the painful rub!) it seemed to have been the wrong thing to say; I thought then that I could not give that admirable girl up. Too, in the letter I wrote: "I am half flint, half gingerbread, for which read mush!"

But the happiness consisted in going upstairs and playing in this order three Beethoven piano sonatas, opuses 90, 78, 111—enough in them to go from high to low comedy, from pathos to tragedy of a great spirit. How refreshed I am now, how pleasantly tired.

I was looking out the window while playing the bagatelles, finishing up with the *Caprice* Rondo in G. The river traffic is amazing, the boats going by in the dark, tugging or pushing or dragging immense barges loaded with freight trains. The tugboats breathe in a low hoarse way, ever so busy, concentrated on their tasks, seeming not to look left or right but only ahead with a certain touch of glumness added. It does not take them long to disappear down the river.

How fine I feel this fresh morning.

———•———

Tuesday, November 5, 1940

Today I learned that Herman, my secretary, was operated on last night for acute appendicitis. I spoke to his wife and brother-in-law, who reported that he is doing well.

It is constantly amazing to me the way people run to types. As I sat eating dinner in a beer saloon on Fifty-sixth Street (frequented by the "smart people" around the town because of its good steaks), I saw a Bessie Breuer, a B. Cerf, and a George Raft. To see a type and immediately know all of its typical behavior patterns and activities gives one a real sense of power. It seems to me that the types are very pronounced in this country, that technical and industrial progress are deeply related to that fact.

At eleven at night Geebee came here by invitation. We listened to the election returns rolling in via radio. It was seen early in the evening that Roosevelt would be reelected. In the meantime, sitting on the settee, we drank a quart of champagne, listened (in a manner of speaking) to a Mozart violin concerto, and undressed to the sweeter music we were making between ourselves. Love by firelight, love by election returns. Roosevelt the next president, we moved downstairs and showered together (lovers' delight!) and finally found a weary bed where we were immediately resuscitated and, so to speak, galvanized into the most exquisite activity. I managed, wonder of wonders, to make Geebee a little loose, and she enjoyed this extra relaxation and lack of reticence as much as I did.

Generally speaking, I like a little looseness in a woman, as between a husband and wife. But of course never in public. It is something that a woman must save only for the private view of her man. This hidden looseness, this secret abandon, seems to me to constitute one of the few virtues of the English woman (J. Adler assures me that all English women are nymphomaniacs).

Suppose I write this here, what Napoleon said of himself. Said he, "Will, character, application, and audacity are the qualities which made me." I am waiting for a concern of chemists to manufacture and put out those various qualities like a vitamin capsule! I will settle for a hundred capsules of will, the others naturally following from it.

———————•———————

Wednesday, November 6, 1940

In the middle afternoon I walked down Third Avenue and bought a fluorescent lamp for my writing table. This uses the new long tube type of bulb in which some sort of vapor is ignited to give a light twice as powerful as the old-type, electric bulb.

At home I read the day's news in a pair of newspapers; was particularly interested in the editorial expression of the reactionary *New York Sun* as it related to the reelection of Roosevelt. Good! There is no bunk about them, no putting on a mask of good fellowship—they are mad and don't mean to hide it. It is always good to know where you stand with such Tory rascals who stand for the editorial policy of such a paper.

And finally, past midnight, to turn to an examination of the hundreds of notes for the trio play. Too many notes spoil the broth. Now comes the difficult period of gearing myself into the material and characters and their milieu.

At five in the morning I ended in bed with a reading of Strindberg's *There Are Crimes and Crimes* half behind me. I finished it in bed and went on to reread most of *Miss Julie*, which I found more interesting in every way—a pert vivid play even now. The other one is a good example of what was bothering Europe at the beginning of this century. The symbolism (if it can be called that) of this play is as interesting as a clothespin. Will that happen to my plays too?

Anyway, I have put the five volumes of Strindberg on the floor beside my bed and will go through all of them. At present I feel that Strindberg is historically interesting, not much more. I shall be happy to be proved wrong.

———————•———————

Thursday, November 7, 1940

My Aunt Esther sent me a set of dishes. Now I can get married!

At two I eased my uneasy seat into the Cadillac and rode up to the Bronx to look at Herman and see how he was feeling. He was in relatively good spirits but wan and needing a shave, like the other three men with whom he shared a room in one of those small private hospitals so dearly beloved of the lower middle class. I told his wife, Rae, I'd take a public ward any old day in preference to this dingy, smelly institution whose only reason for existence is that it keeps up the social status of its patients.

Are you aware of how famous people in this country are afraid of being "personalities"? There are more false modesties in this country to the square foot than there are earthworms! For yourself, by no means unimportant, it is necessary to remember this: DON'T BE AFRAID TO BE A PERSONALITY, even though it will displease many! In other words, do not go underground because you are a celebrity!

The artist, to put it simply, is a man or woman who uses himself in all senses of the word usage.

Our people are very honest; we have less evil impulse in us than any other people in the world. This is true, too, of idealism as a raw impulse. But we are not a very deep people, so what does the honesty and the idealism avail?

[Boris Aronson and I] had an excellent steak and tap beer at the Fifty-sixth Street saloon. The men and women that keep passing in and out of a place like that have never been written seriously or deeply into American literature. Men like Hemingway and Faulkner (myself in another way) deal with a kind of people who are in the vast minority in this country, even though they often express certain TENDENCIES of our national life. Steinbeck? I don't know, to tell the truth, but it seems to me that his characters are not typical Americans either. By typical Americans I mean the sort of people the Lynds wrote about in *Middletown*, them and their children who emigrate to big towns like New York, who live alone, who eat with one another, read *Esquire* and *The New Yorker*, who beat one another on the heads, who begin to sag at forty, honest, never evil, essentially mediocre, hanging on to respectability, trying to be fashionable, trying to be "in the know" and "in the swim," not moral and not immoral, aspiring dimly, proud to be "regular," little fishes in the brook!

They need a real poet! I am sorry for them; they always touch me.

Now Boris and his love affair. It makes him moody. The girl does not love him, he admits, and yet she keeps reaching out to him because (as I said) she may be lonely. I told Boris to be careful, not to find he has married some woman because he was lonely, because she happened to be the only woman who came around to see him. (Has it not happened before in history?) As I say this I am thinking of Fay, that perhaps I have at last found a woman. This makes me feel warm as we sit there at dinner.

Fay, it occurs to me, does not really express herself in words, either written or spoken. Of course she is sharply intelligent but does not attempt to do much with words. She is capable of real nobility and self-sacrifice, although everything she has done with and for me up until now has been in line with her own needs and desires.

Boris is trying to prove to me that he is a superficial man. (I insist that he is not.) He says he is interested in forms and shapes, not in depths of character. He says he fell in love at first with this present girl because she was wearing a hat with a certain line across her face. If she dressed badly, he says, he could grow to hate her in a few times. Anyway, he is unhappy and puts his hand across his face again. He wants to leave New York. I say it is best for him to stay here but go out, see people, get to know a lot of women, for many of them would find him attractive if he but showed himself in public.

He suggests that we go up to Harlem, to a Negro café, and hear two excellent pianists. We step in the Cadillac and are up on 116th in ten minutes. The pianists are superb, playing with real feeling and bite. One of them is a Sunday school type, blind, wearing black glasses below a shaved head. The other laughs and glitters while his somber eyes never change their expression once. The blind one is modest and softly lyrical, except when he is spurred on by the lad at the other piano who is a show-off and prickles all over as soon as he sees two white men are watching him. Boris says the latter smokes marijuana and perhaps it is true. Directly in front of him on the black closed piano top is a small white ashtray holding a lighted cigarette; next to this, on a small pad, is a thin barglass half full of water, a jigger of white gin beside it, evil flowers!

The exquisite articulation of these two pianists is exceptional: each note is a word of understandable language. Sometimes they play along, each relieving the other. The blind one paraphrases bits of Chopin or Beethoven, once Scarlatti, before he starts his jazz numbers. Boris and I are drinking highballs; then two "fairies" come in and sit directly in front of us. They loudly order, of all things in New York's 1940, Pernods, drinking them in tall glasses with ice and water. They pretend to be very cultured, but one of them suddenly asks the blind man if he can play *The Socerer's Apprentice* on the piano. We get up and leave. A slick colored fellow runs in and says Franklin D. Roosevelt, Jr. is on his way here. Who is he with? Why, with his wife! At present he is at a nearby place dancing the lindy hop all over the place, but he will certainly be here—never misses this place.

Today (this juxtaposition meaning nothing) Franklin D. Roosevelt, the old man, has returned triumphantly to Washington from his Hyde Park home. Ickes has offered to resign, saying that he feels everyone in an appointed post should do likewise for the President's new term.

A Great Monster behind me—I often feel its breath on my neck. Always almost catching me but not yet caught: our Civilization! Great Beast!

Will it sound strange if I say I am comforted by my watch? I take time to handle it, finger it, listening to its delicate ticking, fondle it—in short, I am comforted by this fine instrument.

The apartment is beginning to shape itself to my person. Let there be happiness and work here! Or is it enough to say work? You are one of the laziest men I know, you, with all your talent!!!

———•———

Friday, November 8, 1940

Incredibly, I have been back in New York only a week. At least a month seems to have passed since I stepped off the train.

It occurs to me that Trotsky, undoubtedly a great man, lived by the *neurose* and died by the *neurose!*

I am snuggling into this house now, enjoying it. It will be a real living place before long. Would be a pity to start wrongly, with bad habits, for the place where you do bad things becomes a bad place.

On an impulse called Lee Strasberg in the late evening and rode up to his house, a new place on East Ninetieth Street, getting there past ten. We chatted about my recent Hollywood experiences, drinking tea in the kitchen. From there, Paula gone to bed, we moved into the front room and I told him about the trio play (a new synopsis laid out tonight). Of course I told him about it after saying that I expected him to direct it if he liked the idea, Sylvia and Luther to play the leads, the Group Theatre to present and produce the play but only if we all get together, Lee and Harold particularly, to talk over plans for a new Group organization.

Lee was pleased with what I told him of the play; I outlined both thesis and story line, sketching in scenes as I went from beginning to end. Agreement or not (although I don't often disagree with him), Lee Strasberg is one of the few men whose opinions I respect about most everything, particularly the theatre. Now he is ready to go to work as soon as I hand over a new draft of the play to him. As for me, I am beginning to feel the play and this coming week should see real work on it.

At home past two in the morning, I began to read and finished Strindberg's *The Dance of Death*, part 1. A strange play, theatrically very effective, superbly written, but search me for what it means. It seems to have been written at a time in Strindberg's life when he was obsessed with the good and evil of which men are capable. It seems to me to be more a kind of ballet than a play, although it is all dialogue very shrewdly written. What does it mean? I don't know! There is a second play and I shall read that this coming week.

However, about this play, it has the same theme as *There Are Crimes and Crimes*, the same character allotments. That is a clue to its meaning.

Traffic, traffic, traffic on the river. The city never sleeps. Great city!

————————•————————

Sunday, November 10, 1940

Saturday and Sunday are over; now it is past six in the morning of Monday and I am about to go to bed after a reading of the second part of Strindberg's *The Dance of Death*. I see from this reading (now it occurs to me) that Eugene O'Neill was strongly influenced by Strindberg. This particular play and its two parts could be adapted to a modern meaning, antifascist. Any other way I do not understand this play, and of course Strindberg did not mean it that way.

It is interesting, by the way, that all gifted playwrights had the same path of travel in the continuity of their work. They all went from naturalism to a sort of poetic symbolism, dealing in the end with very lofty and abstract themes: Ibsen, Hauptmann, Strindberg; Maxwell Anderson in our day, O'Neill, O'Casey, etc. In the end of their careers their meanings are so lofty that they are recondite and no longer theatrical. I even think of Shakespeare ending up with *The Tempest*, with Good and Evil raging all over the place! What accounts for that similar journey in the lives of these gifted men?

Saturday night was distinguished by the charming and fleshy presence of Geebee. We listened to music, drank coffee, cordial, and brandy. And we have seldom before had such a splendid and royal time in bed till the early morning. The quality of this girl's flesh is warm and good, youthful and giving. If these hours do not make her a more confident woman in the world, nothing will. (She lacks confidence, almost is timid.)

I called Bill Kozlenko, saying we would be there with a bag of food, Geebee and I. So rode over there with a cold chicken, some sliced tongue, etc., not to forget a New York cheese named elmo, a real discovery.

We left Bill's early since I wanted to get to my work on the trio play. Geebee I left off at her hotel which is only five blocks away from here. I came back here alone and looked first at the morning papers. Chamberlain, he of the Munich kiss, died yesterday. That is no loss, for he was as evil as Hitler—only his MANNER more moderate. A filthy old vulture who had some heart left, for that is what he died of, a broken heart shrunken out of shame and lost face! Too, there has been a great earthquake in Rumania, upsetting the plans of the Nazis, who have recently helped themselves to the Rumanian oil wells and wheatfields.

I worked for four hours, starting again from scene 1. I've already begun reading Lewis Mumford's new book, *Faith for Living*.

Daylight on the river now, it throbbing with traffic. But in the dark, all night, the gulls were screaming there.

———•———

Monday, November 11, 1940

Nothing so delicate as taste, so corruptible. Beware of your taste once it begins to slip; it drags you down with it! And if that can happen with you, think of what happens in the lives of the multitudes, they with little or no defense against the onslaught of radio and journalistic slime.

An old Jewish saying: if I am not for myself, who will be for me? And if I am only for myself, what am I?

Talking of taste, for years we had a "pianola" in our home when I was a boy. This was a mechanical piano which played mechanical paper rolls cut out into so-called four-handed arrangements. The music galloped, wooden and mechanical, decorated all over with grace notes and embellishments. It was many years before I could listen to a mere pianist with two hands, alive and adding personal nuance and character to his playing; he seemed deficient in volume and energy, in music-making. And yet it was from that crazy stupid pianola that I first acquired a love of music.

All day a wind has been spanking the awning which covers the small balcony outside my study. Tomorrow the awning will be ruined beyond repair.

YOU ARE BECOMING A MONSTER OF SELF-INDULGENCE! (Specifically?)

I stopped in at a little bookshop on First Avenue and spent twenty dollars for some excellent items, among them the letters and journals of Lord Byron (ah, Byron!) published in 1830 by Harper's of New York, and a fine set of Macready's journal, not to mention two autobiographies of Balzac. More and more, as I pass it here, the period of Balzac, Flaubert, Delacroix, Stendhal, and Heine interests me, not forgetting Hugo, the rich love of my boyhood days. (*Les Misérables* was the most, *is* the most profound art experience I have ever had: I was a boy who could give himself up without the slightest reserve when I was reading alone.)

Hugo, since I have stopped here, inspired me, made me aspire; I wanted to be a good and noble man, longed to do heroic deeds with my bare hands, thirsted to be kind to people, particularly the weak and humble and oppressed. From Hugo I had my first feeling of social consciousness. He did not make me a romantic, but he heightened in me that romanticism which I already had. I loved him and love him still, that mother of my literary heart. In the face of all these famous gifts, it cannot matter that he taught me self-pity too.

At nine in the evening Harold Clurman came here by previous appointment, our first meeting since my return from California. He did not look different or talk differently from when I last saw him, almost three months ago. He has had, during the past weeks, the terrible and lamentable experience of looking for a backer for the new Irwin Shaw play, not to mention flying to the coast to find a suitable man, one who would be satisfactory for the backer. I was horrified when he told me all the ins and outs of the backing deal, when he gave me a mere glimpse of what goes on before a Broadway production opens.

Concerning my work, I told him I was writing a new play in which Sylvia and Luther were to play the leads, that I would give the play to the Group Theatre to produce only in the event of a beforehand agreement that the Group Theatre be reorganized into some semblance of the theatre we all need so badly for our inner peace.

We talked, particularly of Luther and Sylvia, he giving a very good characterization of her and the main impulses of her life. Vividly, he said she was a burnt-out ember, afraid to burn too brightly, afraid to go out, both fears stemming out of her need of making a good secure home in which she was willing to subdue everything to the needs and comfort of her husband. This, he rightfully said, made her less interesting as a woman, interested as she is above all in SAFETY, and it killed her stone dead as an artist. I did not disagree, even when he said her range on the stage would be a very limited one.

I remarked to myself in him a certain shyness, as follows: when he wants to warn me of some trend in my life that he supposes dangerous for my development, he talks instead of another, pointing out in the other the faults that he means to bring to my attention for my own sake.

At midnight he left, a little puzzled and disturbed by my attitude, which was one of constraint and a certain coolness. This came about because I saw that he knows he is incompetent to run a Group Theatre but refuses to admit it; he seldom sits down with open hands, so an honest talk is not possible. I was amazed, when I think of it, of the defensive awareness he has developed in the past few years. Either he does not talk, listening AHEAD of you all the time, making a very dangerous mistake (common to all men of such extreme talent) of thinking he knows all about you; or he is a long jump ahead of you, saying what you are saying before it is out of your mouth, this in extenuation of any laxness or fault on his part. However, these are not serious faults. If I could only see this man unconnected in my own mind from a Group Theatre, we could have an enduring fruitful friendship till the end of both of our days.

He agreed with me that this was the last chance to make a Group Theatre, even when I said that in six months or a year it would be too late, even if at that later time we had the means at our disposal.

I could not work, so walked the city at three and four in the morning. It is only left to report all well with our city by night. With what loneliness and yearning I used to tramp the streets by night; now there is a confidence and I am never poor and hungry.

———•———

Tuesday, November 12, 1940

A woman can do that to a man, make him defensively aware. With Harold Clurman it was Stella A. who for ten years told him he was incompetent and useless, telling him this, mind you, when he was most open, open to the woman he loved more deeply than any other person in the world. This woman did not care what she did to this man; that was the evil thing in her, nothing else.

I didn't go to bed till noon today, having worked for a few hours on the trio play after returning from my night-prowling walk. So I was not out of bed till eight this evening. Prowled around the house, puttered, drank some "morning" coffee, and read *The Masqueraders* by the eminent theatre practitioner, Henry Arthur Jones.

My cousin, Frank Lubner, sent me a good pencil for a gift. After it came a note asking me not to be disturbed by a gift from him, since it made him feel good to send it!

Fay, a few days ago, sent me phonograph records, duplicates of a set I gave her little girl. They are readings of Stevenson's verses for children. If you were moved by them as a child, it is impossible not to be moved by them now.

Writing in the trio play. Am in the rewrite of scene 2. Am I always this way, thinking I can't write, worried, uneasy? Yes, until the characters come alive. Oh, blessed week!

It rained all night. In the morning mail there was a long letter from Fay which ended with the line, "I believe in you." Dear God, what does she believe? I'd like to believe the same.

———————•———————

Wednesday, November 13, 1940

Let no one envy me for the dog's life I am leading!

This minute Herman's wife called to tell me that Mom Levy, [Herman's mother] died at three o'clock this morning of a heart attack. I am very moved by this old lady's death. The father of this fine family died about fifteen years ago and they never stopped talking about him. Now the mother has died and they will pass her on like a legend, how she cooked for a regiment (which her family was), how she played cards, how everyone was her friend, etc. Sweet angels attend thee, Mom.

What worries me about this painful period in my life is that it may not be a period of mellowing but of DENATURING!

And yet some intolerance is necessary to the young artist: how else can he protect his flimsy disorderly talent?

And for the bourgeois too, intolerance is an indispensable quality: how else can he keep his way of life going?

Yesterday Mr. Al Lewin sent me three copies of the mimeographed script of the movie of *Night Music*. Here, yes, is what he had typed on the deckleboard cover: "*The Mating Call*, an original screenplay by Clifford Odets." I tell you this play, this *Night Music*, with all that has happened to it and to me because of it, may yet be the early grave in which I find myself sleeping forever!

I shall not answer Mr. Lewin. Undoubtedly he is waiting for some reaction from me; I shall not react. And this is the man who expects me to continue to make movies with him, a movie on the life of Beethoven next, no less!

Whatever is difficult or painful for you to do—do it! Whatever you tend to shirk—do it! What your laziness avoids—do it! Your senses, your greedy senses will seduce you to death!! You are drowning!! Now begin the clean vigorous swim!!

Whatever you do—and I see so plainly what you are trying to do!—you will never conquer the MORAL MAN within you! You are trying to kill him, but he will not permit it; he will murder you with regret and anguish first!

Can you not make peace between those two inner men? That is the necessary thing, an amalgam of both the selves. You are alone in the world in this case: there is no one to help you; you must do this job yourself!

At last, in the trio play, a tiny burst of flame at 4:00 A.M.!

——————•——————

Friday, November 15, 1940

I dressed and went out for a walk and some dinner. Having had both I returned here and was all set for working all night with a good, clear tone inside.

I must admit that seeing a naked woman in a window across the way disturbed my concentration. When she was joined by a naked man I found myself less interested, although I should have continued watching had they not lowered the blinds.

Soon enough it was the dawn, three out of nine pages being excellent ones. I went back to the front of the house to look across at my naked couple, but only the tomb of passion looked at me through the eyes of two blinded windows.

It was a clear cold morning at first. Sea gulls floated backwards on the river. The *Comet* (of the Colonial Line) passed down the river, a boat which comes and goes from here to Boston, I take it. Then the *City of Birmingham* passed by. And then began a fainthearted snow at ten. I called Miss Dolly Haas and asked her if she'd have dinner with me some night next week. She said she was going to Canada now for a broadcast and I said I'd call again next week.

And in bed continued reading a play by Arthur Wing Pinero, *Letty*. He is much more of a writer than Jones, more of a person and man. He arranges things well but his content is without depth. These old boys are sorts of superior interior decorators, but no living human being walks through their rooms once they are finished. But Pinero, it seems to me, is the best of them, almost convincing one that his types are alive.

The self must be tight and restricted for creation; grimness is needed, not blandness. This is true for my type of man.

———————•———————

Sunday, November 17, 1940

Our newspapers and other opinion-makers are so blinded by prejudice and eyeless hatred that a misconstruction is put on every move the Soviet Union makes. First, according to them, it is Stalin who is responsible for the present war. Next, Stalin is as bad as Hitler, itching for his share of the plunder. After this they add that Stalin is forced to follow after the Nazis because of his weakness.

I will make this prediction. The Soviet Union has the strongest army, in all branches, in the world. The morale of its soldiers is the best in the world. It is strongest in equipment and materials, its sources for these things virtually unlimited. All newspapers join in stating that Stalin quakes in his boots every time Hitler issues an order. I am willing to stake any bet on it being the other way around. Hitler cannot last a year if Stalin decides to move in against him! Of this I have not the slightest doubt. (And I am willing, too, to admit that the Russian is not the soldier that the German is!)

Last night Boris Aronson and Sid Benson came here for a pot roast dinner. We drank some good American wine about which I am inordinately delighted. Boris is always despairing within. Life, he says again and again, is not intimate enough for him. He protests that he would not work on Broadway were it not for his money needs. He is horrified that everything lacks character, strongly condemns the business of the theatre, almost weeps that a man cannot exist as an artist, that he is "typed" once he has made a success in a particular field, that everything is *accidental* here, including success; all is confusion and waste.

Well, it's an old story. But we talked for two hours about these things and finally agreed that the Americans do not know life but live instead a nervous abstraction.

We rode over to Bill Kozlenko's house for an hour. John Gassner and his wife were there. Casual chatter about the theatre and plays. Then we drove back to New York, leaving the Gassners at a subway station while we drove on to Lindy's restaurant.

We sat there and drank coffee, I wondering why I was not sleepy with only five hours sleep behind me.

I thought of Luise: it fades, it fades. I try to remember how she looks, feels, and can remember nothing. Let her die within!

And I thought of the time I waste, of the hundred trifles of self-indulgence, all of it followed by an inner voice which comes like a very twitch: "But the next scene?" it asks!

Winter cold is coming now. In the late dark night the apartment gets cold because winter air comes down the four fireplaces, one in each room. But at dawn the heat begins to rise in the radiators again, the radiators coming to life with a noisy protest, a creaking which makes me think someone is walking the house. Then the starlings set up a chattering outside and the late sun begins to rise in the east across the river and soon the river is very bright and my tired eyes cannot look at it.

Monday, November 18, 1940

I read a book in bed this morning, *The Age of the Fish* by Odon von Horvath, who will write no more books because he was killed in Paris last year by a tree falling on his head. It deals with the Nazification of schoolchildren in Germany, the writer telling the story as if he were their teacher. It is done in pastel shades, using the sensitized consciousness of a Rilke and a Kafka. A good useful little story, written by a man of my generation, the generation I am coming to call the Class of Stepchildren.

It is in this book that one of the pupils complains of the teacher, "He was always telling us how things should be in this world and not how they really are." The author says, too, that ours is the generation which lives for self-gratification. This book could make a very fine experimental production for the theatre; Bobby Lewis to direct it.

Difficult to work. From midnight of last night till eight this morning, eight hours of nighttime silence, I wrote three puny pages: dismayed! Concentration wretched, that is the trouble.

At nine in the morning I dressed and rode down to Macy's to shop for household items. I purchased sterling silver cutlery! Trays, wineglasses, smokers' gadgets for a dinner table, cloths and napkins for the table, a fruit dish; best of all, a bag of half-dozen different cheeses. I forget two floor lamps of simple wrought iron.

Determined to live more regularly, I slept for only two hours in the later afternoon, first inviting Lee Strasberg and Paula to come here to dinner at seven. By the time I was up and showered and dressed, they were here, she not staying for dinner.

Lee and I talked about Russia's position in the world today, merely conjectured, for what can anyone know about Russia's inner strength? After this we moved into the living room, discussed music, played some records. Downstairs, in the study, we talked of the theatre, of writers' problems. For my part I confessed a fear of writing, said that it was so painful for me to run the gauntlet of a New York opening night (with all that it means to produce a play here!) that it was beginning to stop me from writing. Success, I told him, has been the most painful affair in my life, particularly since I grew up with a typical American conception of success and happiness, a conception which is diametrically opposed to reality. I remarked in myself A SUBTLE DRIFT TOWARDS A SEEKING FOR PERSONAL SUCCESS RATHER THAN THE SUCCESS OF THE ARTISTIC CREATION. On this his face lighted up in his typically restricted way, and from that point he spoke clearly and well, to the point, distinguishing for me between the two types of success, a talk which it was good to have from an outside person of intelligence with interest in those same problems that concern me. He pointed out that the Group Theatre used to be a place where all emphasis was on the inner artistic success; now it has gone more the way of the world around us, most judgments beginning to be predicated on the personal success basis.

I felt refreshed and strengthened by this talk. I told him, too, that I was getting too clever for my own good as a young artist, meaning that

I was dissecting and analyzing emotional states of being in this journal before the act of capturing them in plays.

Before this we discussed various styles of theatre production, problems of form and content. I put him in a cab at almost two in the morning; sleep came easily, I feeling glad to begin the new schedule of hours. May this be the beginning of a less "bohemian," of a more wholesome and "normal" life! For another year or two of the life of this last year and I can kill myself. Yes, this year has been everything, I think—all of the contradictions out of which will come a richer life and work, or a deeper death, the very winter of a shabby existence!

———•———

Tuesday, November 19, 1940

So up at nine this morning!!! Inwardly I shouted gladly at the morning on the river, the starting of the day from its beginning. After coffee I went right to the typewriter and wrote a scene in the play, concluding scene 3. Now I shall force myself to these working hours, every day giving myself some tasks to do and complete. In a certain way I have invalided myself; now recuperation into strength and goodness!!!

Glad, glad, to be glad!

I looked through Delacroix's journal; this man brings out love in me.

Fay, about whom I am not concerning myself at present, is a woman who makes me feel stronger and wiser. Luise, on the other hand, made me feel weaker and more ignorant, fine business for a young man who felt inadequate enough before! And yet, to be truthful, the latter would eventually have given me more: it called out more in the personality. Maybe it is axiomatic that there is no growth without a gnashing of teeth and groaning!

At any rate, to be sure that it is always best to go to those who call out the most in you, no matter how uncomfortable or painful it may be.

Victor Hugo: "A little work is a bore. A great deal is a distraction."

Mention of the fact that Hanns Eisler was here Wednesday last was neglected in the journal. We spent five hours together, all of them pleasant, ending up in Harlem to hear those two Negro pianists. There we remarked about the various types of Negro in our modern society, coming to this classification. The Sunday school Negro, the "Uncle Tom" type who weakly accepts his role of servant, winning the rather ghastly admiration of the whites he serves. Next, a dissolute type, sarcastic and erotic, this hidden in a sort of sniggering sophistication, the man really holding contempt and hatred for the whites whom he meets. Then there is the light Negro, often shy, holding other Negroes in contempt, assuming the manners and styles of the whites, pretending a sort of aristocracy and so elevating himself in his own eyes. After this comes what is called by the whites "the bad nigger"; he is moody and silent, bitter and hating, a killer, really a dangerous man, resentful of the world, distrusting of all white people, justifiably scorning the values which have relegated him to the kingdom of the ape. Finally there is the Negro who stands as a dignified free man (not that even he can escape his black skin); mostly he is a class-conscious radical, aware of his capabilities and possibilities. He has self-possession, pride, dignity, and objectivity: Paul Robeson is such a type.

I do not say that this is how the intelligent Negro classifies his race, but I think, from the outside, that this is how an intelligent and sympathetic white man would do it.

Hegel (in which book did I read this?) says: "The principle of magic consists in this, that the connection between the means and the effect shall not be recognized."

Beethoven must have had extreme and extraordinary self-suggestibility: to revise fifty times and keep such fluidity and spontaneity of emotion, such unity of feeling and purpose, such, finally, inevitability!

I kept to my good resolve and was in bed, like a good child with clean hands, at a reasonable hour.

———————•———————

Wednesday, November 20, 1940

And again up early, before ten. I learn from the morning paper that John L. Lewis has resigned, the bad climax of a fight between the right and left elements in the CIO. He made a great speech at the union convention—wept, the paper said.

Other news, daily bombings aside. Two famous racehorses in France were eaten for food, one of them called Clairvoyant.

Bought some new books, chiefly from Goldsmith: Whitman's letters to his mother, some of them; his *November Boughs* and *Drum Taps* in first editions; two volumes of theatrical chitchat published in 1825, giving a valuable sense of the times.

I feel like a child instead of a man.

Continued on the play but felt tired, the details of the house very distracting; but it will soon settle down to routine. Things which you own begin to distract, nag, and worry you; until you get used to them you are always busy taking care of your things.

Made a dinner appointment with D. Haas for this Friday night.

By five o'clock in the afternoon it is dark these days. Dawn comes around five-thirty or six.

I am looking through Gorky—the key to many modern problems is in his writings, particularly his journalistic articles. The characteristics of the modern hero may be found in those writings, some of them.

Went to bed, putting away Mumford's last book, turning over gladly and sleeping well.

———————•———————

Thursday, November 21, 1940

Thanksgiving Day here, a holiday, stores closed, a turkey to be roasted in the oven. AND I WAS UP AT SIX-THIRTY THIS MORNING, clear of mind—I felt it—and at seven-thirty was at the desk writing. Finished half of scene 4, dressed, and went out for a walk in the early afternoon.

How the day drags: I think it must be dinnertime but it is only one hour after noon!

Geebee will be here tonight for the turkey dinner. Also my sister Florence, Boris Aronson, and Sid Benson.

Simply put, the danger resides in this: the breaking down of former real or fancied restrictions (or forms!) and not replacing them with others.

That is what has happened in this country (perhaps in the entire world) during the past twenty-five years, a span of years I know about since I have lived them here. But where does one stop and build up a new form and what is it to be? (THIS IS THE THEME OF A PLAY!)

For there is no dynamic in life or art without form: paradoxically, the prison cell is what gives the freedom! And all men, knowingly or not, yearn for a dynamic. Democracy here during the past decade has had no dynamic but that of industrial expansion, of selling more and buying more. Paltry enough! But now even that is gone. So what is to be the new dynamic of our democracy? Fighting against fascism? (Which is not a moral matter, as they say, but a new method of selling more and buying more!)

We had the turkey for dinner, and very good too. Then we went into the other room and chatted, having as our guests Billy Rose and wife, who were passing by and dropped in for a "moment." This moment became the entire evening, Billy talking of his paintings with great aplomb, indeed of the entire art world.

Soon everyone left and I went to bed. Geebee with me in a fatigued love clasp.

———•———

Friday, November 22, 1940

The good hours continue, those which are good for *me*, I mean. In the afternoon my sister brought over a great stack of mail and magazines which has accumulated because my secretary is still recovering from his operation. We sat in the study and talked for almost two hours, the first easy session I have been able to have with my sister in many years. Most of the talk was about our father, he having sent an urgent note requesting a check with which to pay his insurance. This so sickened and disgusted me—the idea of sending him money to put in the bank—that I was wrathful about him the whole afternoon, recalling aloud much of our unpleasant past together. Finally I sent him the check and with it a cool note in which I made plain that I did not intend to continue such nonsense in the future. My father, who has not given me a happy day in twenty years!

Dinner with Dolly Haas. It was not a good meeting, even though I did not go to it with great expectations. Yet I could not help looking for Luise in her, since they are so much of the same type.

I went to bed immediately after I returned from bringing her home before midnight. She is nervous and birdlike.

———•———

Saturday, November 23, 1940

Up at eight, the morning delicious. All mornings are beautiful, particularly in this apartment which takes the varying conditions of light so well. And at nine I was at the typewriter, writing little but feeling everything beginning to stir in me.

I am trying to stop this harmful cigarette smoking with the usual lack of success, the inability to stop making me more nervous than the smoking itself. But now I am going to pipe smoking—this will break the reflex of reaching for the coffin nails at every unoccupied minute, actually minute!

In the late afternoon I looked for someone to invite to dinner but could think of no one. It was just as well, for Marion Post got in touch with me, here for a mere two days, returning tomorrow to Washington to go out in the field again and photograph the undernourished third of the nation.

Marion came here at eight, so simple, so fragrant with the decent and useful work she has been doing, so carrying with her the whole atmosphere of activity and simple truths that I was quite depressed and felt for the first time in my life like a comfortable bourgeois. We had dinner in Levy's Tavern on Third Avenue, a place where all bourgeois eat, then came back here and looked at many of the photos she has recently taken for the government in Kentucky and the Mississippi Delta sections. Look at these faces and living quarters and dare to talk of the superiority and moral values of democracy!

Tired, I asked Marion to sleep here because I knew she wanted to and because it would be good for her. She is a lovely womanly person who spends six months at a time in the various wildernesses of the Southern states where any woman who takes a drink in public is a prostitute. So into bed tumbled we and around the bed tumbled us.

———————•———————

Sunday, November 24, 1940

Marion is gone now, on her way. We chatted in bed, waking at ten. After that we embraced and loved. She showered while I threw on a robe and went up to the kitchen and brewed an excellent pot of coffee which we enjoyed with cheese and toasted muffins. Now she is on her way to Washington again, there to pick up photo supplies and push on again into the mountains of Kentucky. You have to be a woman of unique qualities to live that way, doing that work week after week without respite. I have spent mere days in some of those Southern states and been unhappy for being in them. Now there goes this young woman for months!

The day is quiet and gray, the house soft with the gray light. A wonderful place to live, truly!

One of my main faults, I thought, was that I want to make all of the rules of life. As if one were able to tell the seed how to germinate!

I am having genuine pleasure from reading a volume of three plays by Lenormand, obviously a talented writer for the theatre. In the late afternoon I finished his *The Dream Doctor* and started on *The Coward*. I remember his *The Failures* as one of the most extraordinary and horrible plays of modern life I ever read. Would like to get a copy and reread it now. Where is this Lenormand now, dead, living, writing, what? And where, too, are Romain Rolland and Gide in the war-messed Europe now?

In the early evening Geebee, Elia Kazan, and his wife came here by appointment. We chatted, admired the apartment, and trekked off to dinner at Lindy's. Irving Berlin was there, modest and sweet, off in one corner reading and eating a meal of some venison steak he himself had brought there from upstate. He insisted that we have the rest of the large steak cooked for our dinners, although he kept insisting that perhaps we might not like the taste of venison. So it was cooked in a delicious sour cream sauce and was well worth the eating, as we assured Berlin, who by then was ready to leave. Venison tastes like turtle meat, both of them a form of rough bunch veal so far as taste is concerned.

And what did we talk about? Only of the discontents of working in the American theatre, in the movies, of all such difficulties. Kazan did not enliven me, nor I him. We were all soon mute and ready to go home.

Geebee stayed with me; I love to put my head between her breasts.

———————•———————

Monday, November 25, 1940

In the morning a swift and gladful letter from Fay. No more silence, she writes. I have had time to get into my work and she means to break into my sanctum with some letters. There was a note from A. Mac-Leish too. He writes from Washington that he hates to answer my letter to him with a mere paragraph but has to do just that because he is so busy. His handwriting is hasty, nervous, and wobbly.

I am up early again today, one resolution well kept! And working on the play by nine-thirty. Late last night I discovered that a character indispensable to the play's thesis had not even been thought of! Today I caught him in one stroke, almost immediately, a sniveling cunning little local fascist. The whole play benefits from this gent—he brings scenes together and rounds out the thesis. But think, to have neglected him until this late time!

———————•———————

Tuesday, November 26, 1940

This journal is going dead on me. That's because the play is coming alive in me. You do not hear any complaints on that score!

Sylvia and Luther came here in the afternoon to talk over the production of the play. Luther wants to go into business, to be impresario, director, and actor. His interest is not really in the work of acting; it is a more worldly thing that interests him, so that I find we are talking from two different points of view every time we have a discussion.

Sylvia, for her part, is not sure she wants to play in the play. Let her make up her mind about it—the deepest problem is her young and almost wasted life! It would make me happier if she were not in the play, for she is not the most striking or gifted actress around the town.

Not to get bitter and cynical at the discovery of life—one of my main problems. What a slow maturer am I!

One of the best things I know is for a man to live in and through the succession of seasons. Winter, spring, summer, autumn—these are each right and wholesome, unique and sweet of character, right, beautiful. Go with them, man, ride with them!

———————•———————

Wednesday, November 27, 1940

The work is getting better each day now. But this is not yet a boast, for it is not good enough to show without blushing. Too, I am keeping the good early rising hours. You will soon see here a miracle of freshness! Yah, yah!! (He jeers at himself.)

Spoke to Boris Aronson on the phone at noon. He said J. B. Neumann, the art dealer, was interested in having me visit his art gallery on Madison Avenue. Done! At four I appeared there, a few minutes before Boris, who is always late. Neumann was out to please me and did—he is the sort of man who knows how to please neurotic modern women and so finds young American men an easy matter to handle, even if they are slightly (more than slightly!) off the type like myself.

And what did I do? Will you believe it?—PURCHASED A UTRILLO! A painting of charming quality, a snow scene, a street, a typical Utrillo but an excellent one from his so-called white period. I fell in love with this painting and had to buy it because I wanted it. Then I purchased another painting, a Gromaire, an artist whose name I knew only dimly. And this painting I like as much as the Utrillo. They can't be compared—the personalities are so different. Each in its own way is an excellent small real thing. The Gromaire is of a nude woman powerfully composed, very strong, exciting to me. Well, I am overjoyed! The Utrillo is in my bedroom, and before going to bed I had looked at it ten times; the Gromaire upstairs too. I rest in the contentment that these wonderful things give me.

Boris came home with me, helped me hang the two pictures, drank a glass of sherry while I was eating supper, then left to have dinner with some friends. He spoke very clearly tonight, is feeling well, working well, that being everything to him or any other artist.

Then Hanns and Lou dropped in for an hour, she seeing the house for the first time. They both had been drinking I think, and Hanns was very loud and noisy and it gave me a headache, so that I was glad to turn to the bed as soon as they had left.

Thursday, November 28, 1940

Soon these new good hours will cease to be news.

The other day I purchased two first editions of Whitman merely because Whitman (man first, poet second) gives me such a feeling. It is impossible to think of Walt without being pleasured. This morning I read that Whitman, according to Emerson, was "half song thrush, half alligator." Good, but he omits saying that each half of that creature fed the other half and one was unthinkable without the other: they comprised *all* Whitman!

And yet to still feel like an amateur writer, capable of all blunders and foolishness in writing.

In the hours of sexual hunger I often think of Luise and how we fitted each other. Male and female, delightful and refreshing always!

Today the play is really rolling. Less than ever do I lack confidence about it. I am beginning to be in the right climate for writing. Pull, pull, pull one's self up a high hill and at last the air is right for the proper breathing! Up, Odets!! (Or is it down, down, sunk into the self?)

Neumann, the art dealer, came here in the early afternoon to see how I had hung the pictures. Hung okay, said he. Then we played some Mozart. His life, at this first totaling, seems to be composed of part nursing activity, part sponsoring, yearning out of loneliness, reaching for some new sort of form, a certain cynicism that is never expressed as itself but as something more generous and commendable, a certain holding of your hand and looking you in the eye, a certain fishiness, a real love of art and the creative, a somber dissatisfaction with most of the facts of his life, a real or *fancied* curiosity about the facts of YOUR life. He seems to have that thing I detected in Stokowski and Ernst Toller (even looking very much like Toller did): a content which has long grown away from the form in which it once lived—the content which was the aspirational is now grown tired and only the form is left.

———————•———————

Friday, November 29, 1940

Wanting everything just so, this in that place, that in this place—it is a kind of minor madness. From this comes the puttering and lack of concentration. In the heart of the disorder there is a certain passion for order, as if I were a housewife! (So the female bird prepares the nest for the egg?)

The psychiatrist makes this mistake. One should say to the neurotic person, "Your self—it is material. So start using it, for it is as good as any other you will get. In fact the so-called normal will be less interesting." But in America particularly, the psychiatrist reaps a rich harvest—every American wants another personality which, once acquired, he would sterilize and render as useless as the old one.

I think I am even getting a daylight look since rising so early in the mornings. For instance, a daisy has a daylight look; the orchid has the nighttime look. Yes, there gets to be some orchidaceous look in your face if you live by night. The senses no longer respond to daylight except to protest. Repose comes into the face, a certain color and flabbiness.

The dinner date for tonight with Morris C. and Serlin is off. Lee Strasberg comes here for dinner alone instead. Before he arrives I have the pleasure of reading Rolland's essay on Berlioz in a book of essays published long ago. Rolland points out Berlioz's character weakness which finally ruined him—his inordinate desire for love and sympathy, a certain unwillingness to pay for being talented. About those elements in the character of Berlioz I think I know more than Rolland does, more about the romantic's fight with a cold heartless world and what makes a romantic.

Lee and I talked about Berlioz, then went upstairs for dinner. After this we launched into a talk on the problem of Luther and his expanding desires in their relationship to the production of my coming play. From here we moved on to a discussion of the lack of scripts in the theatre and how to work despite that lack. He wants to hire writers to dramatize novels and biographies, at present has [Ferdinand] Bruckner working on Werfel's *Forty Days of M.D.* [Musa Degh]. Next he would like to do the recent biography of Madame Curie. When he said that Luise Rainer was the perfect actor for it I promptly said I would be glad to do that adaptation job. Lee said, and rightfully so, that with a stream of such good theatre pieces steadily coming along it was possible to keep a Group Theatre going; only such a set-up could support the production of a "peak," by which he meant an art play, adding that until now my plays—"peaks"—had had to support the entire theatre instead of being supported by the theatre itself.

This talk with Lee I found very very invigorating—it is the first light in the dark of the theatre practice of the past few years that I have entered. Truly, for the first time in years I felt that something could really be worked out, simple, clear, honest work in which ideals or religion need not be mentioned.

After this we played some of Berlioz's music, Lee not having been familiar with its power and freshness and its modernity. Then we went downstairs to the study and looked over many of the books I have been purchasing during the past few weeks. Finally, near three, he left with a heavy armful of books which I was only too happy to give him for gifts. FOR LEE STRASBERG IS A WITNESS TO MY LIFE AND WORK! Shall I say the NEW witness?

———•———

Saturday, November 30, 1940

This was a day of days, the first of the long days since the production of *Night Music* that real creative life stirred in me. The only worthy scene of the play was written today, enough to assure me that I can go back and rewrite the play with quality in all its parts. Oh, the power of working well, the feeling of power that races through your veins and heart! Oh, the deep content of sitting in the creative climate! In that warmth there is no longing, no yearning, no loneliness or unhappiness. One functions and the self is forgotten, although it is the self most alive and quivering. It is joy, no other word.

So, let me hope, has a circle been completed and I am back to myself again. Yes, I thought, shaving in the early evening, you are all right; you are an artist—they have not spoiled you or taken away your power.

———•———

Sunday, December 1, 1940

A good breakfast of eggs, sausage patties, toast, and coffee. Looking out at the river, enjoying the air, the light, the self, the girl's self—in a word, RELAXATION! Sid Benson over at three. We talk of the paintings I've bought during the week. Decide, the three of us, to walk across town to see the exhibition where I bought the two American paintings. We do so, enjoying the brisk weather, chatting, joking. This is called *joie de vivre*! We look through the same paintings I saw on Thursday with Neumann. Then we move on to a similar American exhibit just three blocks away. There I find a little painting that seems talented to me. Buy it for thirty dollars.

———•———

Friday, December 6, 1940

Looking back on the week, the following items:

On Monday I had a letter from Lewin. He wants an extension of time on the production date of *Night Music*, thinks it needs much more work. My plan is to sell him everything if possible, lock, stock, and barrel; and then he can get someone else to write his movie for him. I have had too much pain and trouble from *Night Music* in all of its reincarnations!

I see from a note here how struck I was by the prose style of Thoreau on looking at some of his small essays, parts of larger articles collected in a book. Simply, a remarkable style, impossible for a man who lives indoors. More to read there.

Life must continue to be as it was during this week, all for the work, the day and the night, all hours and thought. Everything else must be incidental.

Sent a note to Lee Cobb, who is doing a movie in the West, this note in answer to a wire from him which was an answer to a Sunday wire of mine asking him to keep open for a part in the new play. He is interested and should be, if only for career reasons. Apparently he has had an unhappy relationship with his wife, for he says that "family trouble" is helping keep him away from New York.

Tuesday: worked all morning, noting that Vincent Kress, that new character, is running away with the scenes. The gent will have to be tucked in later when I am in third draft!

Wednesday morning, by previous arrangement, called for Lee Strasberg in the car and we drove out to Luther's farm together. A good trip, talking about many theatre affairs, particularly our new joint venture, the production of the new play. We determined how we would meet Luther if he should prove difficult to handle.

It was past noon before I arose out of the bed on Thursday morning. It did not matter to me if I worked or did not, I felt so confident of having the control of everything in my hands. So loafed the entire day but enjoyed very much looking over all the new books purchased during the past few weeks—about four hundred volumes, I should say. Read much in the life of Edmund Kean, for instance.

At night there came here for dinner Lee again, Morris Carnovsky, and Oscar Serlin. We met to talk over the possibilities of a new Group Theatre forming, using the best of the old, adding new elements and plans. Morris, representing the actors, could at first see only some quick action, starting next month almost. We, the others here, found we were not impatient, that, for instance, we were quite willing to wait till we had organized a number of suitable scripts, etc.

Past midnight we broke up, they leaving, I going down to my study where, by a witty previous phone call, Geebee was waiting for me. We chatted quietly, drank some brandy, undressed, and soon moved into the bedroom where we made a warm fire, one in the fireplace and one on the bed.

Now it is today. A little breakfast with Geebee, who was soon on her way when she saw I wanted to get to my desk. There I began to sort hundreds of stray notes on the play, preparing to clear my desk for the third draft which I start on tomorrow.

In the evening I yearned to go out into company but decided it would be better not to be distracted by even one person. So ate alone at the saloon on Fifty-sixth Street, stopped in at a bookshop and bought more books, and now am back in the house. It is midnight and in an hour I shall go to bed.

SELECTED BIOGRAPHIES

The following brief sketches, neither exhaustive nor extensive, include primarily those who were professionally and socially close to Odets in 1940.

LUTHER ADLER (1903–1984). Brother of Stella, Luther Adler began his career as a child actor in Yiddish theater, where his father, Jacob P. Adler, was a preeminent figure. He joined the Group Theatre in 1932 and appeared in *Awake and Sing!*, *Paradise Lost*, and *Rocket to the Moon*, but his most important role came when he played Joe Bonaparte in *Golden Boy* (a casting choice that resulted in the departure of John Garfield). He later acted in film and television. He was married to Sylvia Sidney.

STELLA ADLER (b. 1902). On the stage from the age of four, Stella Adler studied with Maria Ouspenskaya, Richard Boleslavsky, and Constantin Stanislavsky. She joined the Group Theatre in 1931, appearing in *Awake and Sing!* and *Paradise Lost*. She made her film debut in 1938, and in 1943, she became an associate producer at Metro Studios. From 1940 to 1942, she was head of the Acting Department of the New School for Social Research under Erwin Piscator. Since 1949, she has directed her own school, the Stella Adler Conservatory of Acting. She married Harold Clurman in 1942, and they were later divorced.

BORIS ARONSON (1900–1980). Born in Kiev in Russia, Aronson designed his first theatrical production in 1924 in New York. As the Group Theatre's designer, he worked on *Awake and Sing!* and *Paradise Lost* and later, *Clash by Night*. He is known for his highly stylized settings, greatly influenced by Marc Chagall, and for his use of evocative lighting against neutral backgrounds to change mood and atmosphere fluidly.

KERMIT BLOOMGARDEN (1904–1976). Brooklyn-born Bloomgarden began his career as accountant and general manager for the highly successful producer Herman Shumlin. His own producing career began in 1940 with the failure of *Heavenly Express*, but the 1945 success of *Deep Are the Roots* was followed by such plays as *Another Part of the Forest*, *Death of a Salesman*, *The Crucible*, *The Diary of Anne Frank*, *The Music Man*, *The Hot l Baltimore*, and *Equus*.

355

MORRIS CARNOVSKY (b. 1897). Born in St. Louis, Carnovsky was a member of the Theatre Guild from 1924 until he moved to the Group Theatre, where he appeared in many Group productions and all of Odets's plays with the Group. His successful film career ended when he was blacklisted in the fifties, but he continued to work in the theater with the American Shakespeare Festival in Stratford, Connecticut, where he has been widely acclaimed for his King Lear.

HAROLD CLURMAN (1901–1980). After study with Jacques Copeau and Richard Boleslavsky, Clurman's first professional theater experience was the Greenwich Village Playhouse in 1924, where he worked with Kenneth McGowan, Robert Edmond Jones, and Eugene O'Neill. In 1931, he founded the Group Theatre with Cheryl Crawford and Lee Strasberg, was its intellectual guide throughout the thirties, and directed many of its productions, including *Waiting for Lefty, Awake and Sing!, Golden Boy*, and *Rocket to the Moon*. In 1936, he became the sole manager of the Group, until it disolved in 1941. Co-producer of *All My Sons*, he later directed *The Member of the Wedding, Bus Stop*, and *Incident at Vichy*, and in 1963–4 was executive consultant to the Vivian Beaumont Theatre before it opened at Lincoln Center. Highly respected for his writing about the theater, Clurman was drama critic for *The New Republic* from 1949 to 1953, and for *The Nation* for many years thereafter. His books about the theater include *The Fervent Years*, a history of the Group Theatre, *Lies Like Truth: Theatre Essays and Reviews*, and *On Directing*.

LEE J. COBB (1911–1976). Born Leo Jacoby, Cobb joined the Group Theatre in 1935 and appeared in *Waiting for Lefty* in a small role, *Golden Boy, The Fifth Column*, and *Clash by Night*. In the forties, he began a film career, but returned to the stage in 1949 for his most famous role, Willy Loman in *Death of a Salesman*. He later appeared in a revival of *Golden Boy* in 1952. One of America's most successful and acclaimed actors in theater and film, his roles are too numerous to mention here.

HANNS EISLER (1898–1962). Born in Leipzig, Germany, Eisler studied music with Arnold Schönberg and began composing for film and stage in the late twenties. He was forced to leave Germany in 1933 after a film he was associated with was banned. After emigrating to America, Eisler composed both for Broadway and for film, often with fellow expatriates like Fritz Lang and Jean Renoir. A committed Marxist, Eisler was one of the first to testify in the 1947 hearings of the House Un-American Activities Committee. He was deported, and settled in East Germany, where he continued composing. Among his works is East Germany's national anthem.

FRANCES FARMER (1913–1970). Born in Seattle, Washington, Farmer became famous when she won a trip to the Soviet Union. She made her screen debut in 1936, and met Odets when she played in *Golden Boy* in 1937. She fell passionately in love with Odets, but he ended their affair when Luise Rainer returned from Europe in 1939. She returned to films, but subsequent problems with the studio, her family, and alcoholism led to her confinement in mental institutions, essentially ending her career.

JOHN GARFIELD (b. Julius Garfinkle, 1913–1952). Known as Julie, Garfield studied with Maria Ouspenskaya and began his professional career in 1931. He joined the Group in 1934, appearing in *Awake and Sing!*, but he left in 1937 after he was refused the lead role in *Golden Boy*, and went to Hollywood for a long and successful career. He appeared in *The Big Knife*, but was blacklisted in the early fifties, and died soon after starring in his final stage role—the lead in *Golden Boy*.

THERESA HELBURN (1887–1957). Executive director of the Theatre Guild from 1919 to 1932 and administrative director thereafter, Theresa Helburn studied drama at Yale University, acted, and wrote plays and drama criticism for *The Nation* during her long and much-honored career. Strong-willed, tenacious, and conscientious, she was one of the most important forces in the Guild's later productions, notably *The Philadelphia Story*, *Oklahoma!*, *The Iceman Cometh*, and *Picnic*.

ELIA KAZAN (b. 1909). Born in Constantinople, Kazan emigrated with his family to America, where he attended Yale Drama School. He began his theater career as an actor, and he appeared in *Waiting for Lefty*, *Paradise Lost*, *Golden Boy*, and many other Group Theatre productions. His lasting contribution to the theater is as the director of *A Streetcar Named Desire*, *The Skin of Our Teeth*, *All My Sons*, *Death of a Salesman*, *Cat on a Hot Tin Roof*, *J.B.*, and many others. He won Academy Awards for directing *Gentleman's Agreement* and *On the Waterfront*, and his other films include *A Streetcar Named Desire*, *A Tree Grows in Brooklyn*, and *East of Eden*. He was a founding member of the Actors Studio, where he remained until 1962, when he became a co-director of the Repertory Theatre at Lincoln Center. When this enterprise failed, Kazan largely retired from the theater to pursue a successful career as a novelist.

SIDNEY KINGSLEY (b. Sidney Kieschner, 1906). Playwright and director, Kingsley was introduced by the Theatre Guild in 1933 with their production of his play *Men in White*, which won the Pulitzer Prize in 1934. He began a successful directing career with his next play, *Dead End*. In 1943, he won the New York Drama Critics Circle award for his play *The Patriots*. He also adapted Arthur Koestler's *Darkness at Noon* for the stage in 1951, and served as president of The Dramatist's Guild from 1961 to 1969.

ARTHUR KRIM (b. 1910). The attorney for the Group Theatre and Odets, Krim was a partner in Phillips, Nizer, Benjamin & Krim until he became a motion picture executive. He was president of Eagle Lion Films from 1946 to 1949, was named president of United Artists in 1951 and chairman of the board of United Artists in 1969. In 1978, he co-founded Orion Pictures. He was awarded the Jean Hersholt Humanitarian Award in 1974, and the Legion of Honor from France.

OSCAR LEVANT (1906–1972). Musical prodigy, raconteur, and high-strung martinet, Oscar Levant was born in Pittsburgh, where he learned the piano and began composing, with only fair success. In 1938, he became the musical expert on the radio program *Information Please*, where he remained for six years. This led to concert tours and recordings, especially of Gershwin, a career in films, and many television talk show appearances.

ROBERT LEWIS (b. 1909). Director, producer, and actor, Bobby Lewis joined the Group in 1931. He performed in *Waiting for Lefty* and *Paradise Lost*. In 1938 he directed the touring company of *Golden Boy*, and was appointed director of the Group. With Elia Kazan and Cheryl Crawford, he founded the Actors Studio in 1947, and he has, in addition, taught and directed widely throughout the United States. At Yale Drama School, he was chairman of the acting and directing departments from 1974 to 1976. He is the author of *Method—or Madness?* and *Slings and Arrows*.

LEONARD LYONS (b. Leonard Sucher, 1906–1976). Lyons studied and practiced law until 1934, when he began one of America's most popular gossip columns, "Lyons Den," for the *New York Post*. Lyons was famous for his elaborate filing and cross-referencing system, and esteemed for his efforts at accuracy. The column was eventually serialized in more than a hundred newspapers, and continued until Lyons retired in 1974.

SANFORD MEISNER (b. 1905). Born in Budanov, Austria-Hungary, Meisner was a founding member of the Group Theatre. He appeared in *Awake and Sing!, Paradise Lost, Golden Boy*, and many other Group productions. He is best known as the teacher of many of America's most well-known actors at the Neighborhood Playhouse, where Meisner is head of the acting department.

LEWIS MILESTONE (1895–1980). Born in Chisinau (near Odessa), Russia, Milestone emigrated to the United States in 1913. During World War I, he was in Europe as an assistant director for army training films, and after the war he went to Hollywood, as a screenwriter and assistant director. In 1925, Howard Hughes hired him as a director. He won one of the first Academy Awards for directing *Two Arabian Knights* in 1928 and a second for *All Quiet on the Western Front*, which he also adapted. His last successful film was *The Front Page*.

RUTH NELSON (b. 1905). After studying with Richard Boleslavsky, Nelson first appeared on the stage in 1926, and joined the Group Theatre for its first production in 1931. She appeared in *Waiting for Lefty* and *Rocket to the Moon*, and remained with the Group until its reorganization in 1941, when she began a film career, appearing in *A Tree Grows in Brooklyn* and other films. In 1963, she joined the Guthrie Theatre, appearing in *The Three Sisters* and *The Glass Menagerie*, among others.

LUISE RAINER (b. 1910). Born in Vienna, Rainer was a member of Max Reinhardt's theatrical company in Berlin until she emigrated to the United States in 1934. She won Academy Awards for *The Great Ziegfeld* in 1936 and for *The Good Earth* in 1937, the year she married Odets. Strains between them caused her to sue for divorce in 1938, but she and Odets were reconciled briefly, until they were finally divorced in 1940. Her initial success in films was not repeated, and her career declined, although she appeared on stage in *A Kiss for Cinderella* in 1942 and later acted in both film and television.

BILLY ROSE (b. William Samuel Rosenberg, 1899–1966). After a brief attempt at songwriting, Billy Rose became one of the greatest showmen of the twentieth century. He produced his first play in 1930, and by 1939, he was in charge of the New York World's Fair and the Aquacade, as well as the Billy Rose Music Hall and various nightclubs and restaurants. In 1941, he produced Odets's *Clash by Night* (Odets's first play outside the Group) with Tallulah Bankhead.

SYLVIA SIDNEY (b. Sophia Kosow, 1910). A student at the Theatre Guild school, Sydney first appeared on stage in 1926. She subsequently joined the Group Theatre and appeared in *The Gentle People* and many other plays. She also appeared in films, including *Street Scene*, *Les Miserables*, and *Summer Wishes, Winter Dreams*, for which she was nominated for an Academy Award. She was married to Bennett Cerf, Luther Adler, and C. W. Alsop.

LEE STRASBERG (1901–1982). Strasberg studied acting with Maria Ouspenskaya and Richard Boleslavsky at the American Laboratory Theatre, and made his stage debut in 1925. He founded the Group Theatre with Clurman and Cheryl Crawford, and directed its first production, *The House of Connolly*, and many others, as well as the Theatre Guild's production of *The Fifth Column*. After the Group ceased production, he directed Odets's *Clash by Night* and *The Big Knife*. In 1948, he joined the Actors Studio, and became one of its most influential teachers of method acting. He later founded the Lee Strasberg Institutes in New York and Hollywood.

FRANCHOT TONE (1905–1968). Tone was among the original members of the Group Theatre, but simultaneously began working in Hollywood, where he appeared in *Moulin Rouge*, *Mutiny on the Bounty* (which brought him an Academy Award nomination), *Five Graves to Cairo*, *Advise and Consent*, and many others.

WALTER WINCHELL (1897–1972). One of the most influential columnists of the thirties, forties, and fifties, Winchell began his career in 1922, and his "On Broadway" column became a New York institution, especially after he began writing for the *Daily Mirror* in 1929. In the thirties, he was a supporter of the New Deal, and a dedicated opponent of both fascism and racism, although he later became more conservative politically.

FAY WRAY (b. 1907). Canadian-born actress, best known for her screen roles, especially *King Kong, The Wedding March, The Four Feathers*, and many others. She married screenwriter John Monk Saunders, with whom she had one child, a girl. Saunders committed suicide in 1940. She later married again, and retired in 1958.

CHRONOLOGY

July 18, 1906	Born to Pearl Geisinger Odets and Louis Odets in Phila-delphia. In the next ten years, the family moves several times, finally settling in New York. Sister Genevieve born 1910; Florence, 1916.
1921	Enters Morris High School, where he acts in school plays. Leaves school in 1923.
1924–1930	Acts with several small theater companies and ultimately the Theatre Guild; works as a radio disk jockey. Under-studies for Spencer Tracy in the Broadway production of *Conflict*. Begins writing.
1931	Charter member of the Group Theatre. Acts, directs, and begins writing *I Got the Blues*, which becomes *Awake and Sing!*
January 1935	*Waiting for Lefty* is an overnight sensation when per-formed at a benefit for *New Theatre* magazine.
February 1935	*Awake and Sing!* opens.
April 1935	*Three Plays* published by Covici-Friede.
December 1935	*Paradise Lost* opens.
1936	In Hollywood, meets Luise Rainer.
January 1937	Marries Rainer.
November 1937	*Golden Boy* opens.
1938	Separation and reconciliation with Rainer. *Rocket to the Moon* opens in November.
1939	Separates from Luise Rainer. *Six Plays* published by Ran-dom House.

1940	*Night Music* opens.
1941	Odets withdraws from the Group Theatre. *Clash by Night* opens in December.
1943	Marries Bette Grayson. In Hollywood, writes screenplay for *None But the Lonely Heart*.
1945	Daughter Nora born.
1947	Son Walt born. Odets named by the House Un-American Activities Committee as a Communist.
1949	*The Big Knife* opens.
1950	*The Country Girl* opens.
1951	Divorced from Bette Grayson.
1952	Questioned by the House Un-American Activities Committee.
1954	Bette Grayson Odets dies. Odets moves with his children to California. *The Flowering Peach* opens.
August 18, 1963	After eight years working in Hollywood, dies of cancer.

INDEX